Selected Readings in Business

Selected Readings in Business

Myra Shulman

ENGLISH FOR SPECIAL PURPOSES

John Swales, Editor

Ann Arbor

THE UNIVERSITY OF MICHIGAN PRESS

ISBN 0-472-08134-9
Library of Congress Catalog Card No. 90-72020
Published in the United States of America by
The University of Michigan Press
Manufactured in the United States of America

1994   1993   1992   1991   4   3   2   1

To K.

Acknowledgments

I would like to express my thanks and appreciation to the following people: John Swales, director of the English Language Institute, University of Michigan, for his thoughtful evaluation of and comments on the manuscript; Mary Erwin, my editor at the University of Michigan Press, for her sound judgment and expert guidance; Christina Milton, of the University of Michigan Press, for her knowledgeable editorial assistance; Christine Feak, of the University of Michigan's English Language Institute, for her thorough review of the manuscript; Gilbert Couts, director of the English Language Institute, American University, for granting me release time to complete the manuscript; my students and colleagues, for their helpful suggestions; Isabelle Brugere, for her excellent computer skills; my family, for their encouragement; and my husband K., for his business acumen and support.

Grateful acknowledgment is given to the following publishers for use of copyrighted material:

The Economist Newspaper Limited, for "Drugs: It Doesn't Have to Be Like This," *The Economist,* September 2, 1989, copyright © 1989; and for "Gone Fishing," *The Economist,* January 6, 1990, copyright © 1990. Reprinted with permission.

Forbes Inc., for "Hold That Body Count!" by A. Gary Shilling, *Forbes* magazine, January 22, 1990, copyright © 1990; for "The Mind-Centered System" by Michael Novak, *Forbes* magazine, February 6, 1989, copyright © 1989; for "Greed Does Not Explain It" by Michael Novak, *Forbes* magazine, April 3, 1989, copyright © 1989; and for "But in the Office, No" by Joshua Levine, *Forbes* magazine, October 16, 1989, copyright © 1989. Reprinted by permission of *Forbes* magazine.

Foundation for the School of Business at Indiana University, for "American Management as Viewed by International Professionals" by Ashok Nimgade. Reprinted from *Business Horizons,* November-December 1989. Copyright © 1989 by the Foundation for the School of Business at Indiana University. Used with permission.

Goldhirsh Group, Inc., for "Classroom Conundrum: Profits + Ethics = ?" *Business Month* magazine, February 1990, copyright © 1990; for "Taking the Grief Out of Going Global," *Business Month* magazine, February 1990, copyright © 1990; and for "Sorry, Wrong Number," *Business Month* magazine, January 1990, copyright © 1990. Reprinted with permission. The Goldhirsh Group, Inc., 38 Commercial Wharf, Boston, MA 02110.

Lefkowith Inc., for "When in Rome Sell Like the Romans," by Edwin F. Lefkowith, *Business Month,* December 1989. Copyright © 1989 Lefkowith Inc.

McGraw-Hill, Inc., for "Is Your Computer Secure?" and "A German Hackers' Club That Promotes Creative Chaos." Reprinted from August 1, 1988 issue of *Business Week* by special permission, copyright © 1988 by McGraw-Hill, Inc.

Preface

Selected Readings in Business is an advanced reading textbook for English as a second language students who are studying business as undergraduates or pursuing an MBA. It can also be used by students who are preparing for the GMAT or GRE or by companies whose nonnative employees require training in reading skills. It is based on two premises: (1) reading is an active and interactive process; and (2) reading comprehension, vocabulary, and speed increase when readers are interested in their reading material, find it relevant, and, thus, are motivated to read it. In light of these premises, I have tried to produce a book that fulfills a clearly perceptible need—for an engaging and conceptually sophisticated reader/textbook for students (both ESL and adult learners) with a business orientation. It reflects my seventeen years of experience teaching ESL and the particular methods and concepts I have developed in the classroom at The American University.

The text is designed to help students improve their reading skills through the use of current business journal articles. Emphasis is placed on vocabulary acquisition, comprehension, and on inferential, structural, and stylistic analysis. The thirteen chapters contain unaltered readings chosen from well-known business journals and written by authorities in the field. Foreign students at the higher level of proficiency are best served by reading authentic texts that equate to texts used in their academic courses.

I selected these readings according to their content, style, and level of difficulty. The content is timely and stimulating, with many of the authors writing from a global perspective. The style is readable and accessible. The articles are challenging but neither overly complex nor too long. At the end of each article is a glossary containing definitions of difficult or unfamiliar words. The glossaries are based on definitions from *Webster's New World Dictionary*, Second College Edition, copyright © 1986.

The articles, which offer a variety of styles and organizational patterns, progress in difficulty and length in order to constitute a complete semester's work. The focus of these readings is on a particular topic, not a method of organization. However, analysis of the structure and style of the articles is included in order to clarify the connection between form and content and to emphasize the importance of the logical organization of ideas and clarity of presentation.

Selected Readings in Business has the following goals:

1. to improve reading comprehension and speed;

2. to increase general vocabulary and business vocabulary;

3. to encourage critical analysis of ideas, structure, and style;

4. to motivate students to do library research;

5. to provide examples of well written standard English;

6. to strengthen logical thinking in written and oral expression; and

7. to present current business theories and new techniques.

Ultimately, this text seeks to enhance the students' analytical skills. Since reading comprehension is the necessary prerequisite to critical analysis, the immediate purpose of *Selected Readings in Business* is to improve reading comprehension by intensive as well as extensive reading. Students begin each chapter by previewing the material before moving on to reading comprehension exercises that analyze main ideas, major points, and specific details. They are asked to evaluate explicitly stated data and make inferences, with the goal of learning to read for general ideas. Vocabulary acquisition is encouraged through exercises centering on difficult words as well as commonly used idioms and expressions. Each unit also includes thought-provoking discussion questions, a research assignment that provides articles for extensive reading and serves as the basis for an oral presentation, several writing assignments, a realistic case study for group work, a business writing task, and an additional reading. The appendixes are guides to giving oral presentations, writing summaries and essays, and reporting on case studies. Examples of a summary, an essay, a synthesis, business letters, and memos are included.

Large numbers of foreign students come to the United States to study business. *Selected Readings in Business* is an up-to-date and comprehensive advanced ESL reader for those business students who have mastered the fundamentals of written and spoken English but may be unprepared for the sophisticated reading and critical analysis they will be required to do. It exposes them to high interest articles by academic experts, journalists, and business leaders who are communicating their theories about the major business issues of the day.

The text, which is learner centered, focuses on reading as an interactive process involving reader, writer, and text. Readers make predictions, process information, and answer questions not only by analyzing the text but also by drawing on their personal experience and knowledge. They are encouraged to react to the ideas in the articles, to produce responses (oral and written), and to justify those responses. Thus, *Selected Readings in Business* implements the integrated skills approach to ESL learning, as the four communication skills of reading, writing, listening, and speaking are integrated throughout the text.

Contents

To the Student: How to Read Efficiently

Reading, like any skill, can be improved by strong motivation and steady practice. Being a good reader means reading actively, efficiently, fairly quickly, and with maximum comprehension. It also means reading for the author's general ideas, not for specific words. If you come to an unfamiliar vocabulary word, try to guess the meaning from the context of the sentence and paragraph, rather than stopping to look up the word in the dictionary or the chapter's glossary.

When reading the articles in this textbook, or any other reading material, follow these three steps to be an efficient reader:

Preview
Read
Review

A. Preview
1. Skim the article for the author's name, the title, and all headings.
2. Ask yourself what the title could mean.
3. Read the first and second paragraphs, looking for the author's purpose or main idea.
4. Read the last paragraph, looking for a summary or conclusion.
5. Look over the visual aids (pictures, graphs, or charts).

B. Read
1. Read actively, with a pen or pencil in your hand.
2. Underline or highlight the main idea, major points, and important examples and supporting data.
3. Make brief comments in the margin when you agree with the author ("yes") or disagre ("no"), or have a question ("?").
4. Keep in mind what you want to learn from the article.

C. Review
1. Read the article again, but only concentrating on the words, phrases, and sentences you have underlined or highlighted.
2. Make brief notes in the margin when you react to specific ideas.
3. Write one or two sentences that express the main idea(s) of the article.
4. Write one or two sentences that express your reaction to the article.

Chapter 1

"Gone Fishing"

Chapter 1 is an explanatory chapter intended to serve as an introduction to the structure and methodology of the book. Therefore, in certain exercises, answers are provided and explained.

Preview

Previewing, which gives you an overview of the text, is mental preparation for reading. It increases both reading comprehension and speed. Efficient readers generally preview before reading a document thoroughly. Previewing can take from 30 seconds to 10 minutes, depending on the length of the reading material. In this text, previewing includes skimming, questioning, scanning, and guessing the vocabulary from the context.

Skimming. Skimming involves quickly looking over the reading material in order to gain a general impression of the content. You should glance at the author's name, title, headings, and the first and last paragraphs. If there are illustrations, cartoons, or graphic aids, briefly glance at them also.

Skim the article quickly to find the following general information.

1. Read the title and all headings and look at the illustrations.

2. Read the first and second paragraphs, looking for the author's purpose and main idea.

3. Read the last paragraph, looking for a summary or conclusion.

Questioning. Questioning encourages you to think about the subject before reading the article in order to assess what, if any, knowledge you may already have about the subject. It increases comprehension by making you anticipate or predict what the author will discuss.

Answer the following questions and discuss your answers in class.

Economist 314, no. 7636 (January 6, 1990)

1. What does "Gone Fishing" have to do with business?

2. What is the meaning of the illustration, and how does it relate to the title?

3. What will the article discuss?

Scanning. Scanning involves quickly looking over the reading material in order to find specific information. You should glance over each page, trying to find the key word or words from the question. When you locate the answer, stop scanning.

Scan the article quickly to find the following specific information.

1. In America, by the year 2000, what will the proportion of workers over 35 rise to?

2. In the EC, what is the unemployment rate?

3. In which western country do 86% of women with young children work?

4. What is the average age at which American men retire?

5. Which country has the highest participation rate of working women over age 55?

Vocabulary in Context. Guessing the meaning of new or unfamiliar words by using context clues is an important reading skill. It is not necessary to guess the precise meaning; a general idea will enable you to proceed with your reading. The context includes the meanings of the individual words in the sentences as well as the overall meaning of the sentence or paragraph.

Read the following sentences and try to guess the meaning of the italicized words by using the context. Then replace the italicized words with synonyms (words or phrases that have nearly the same or similar meanings).

1. "For a start a small *recession* in the early 1990s, should it come, will lengthen dole queues again."

2. "Statistics tell only part of the story. Anecdotal evidence of a tightening labour market *abounds*."

3. "Sadly, many such workers are unemployable—except by those few companies that are willing and able to offer *remedial* education or training."

4. "For example, a woman might *opt* for shorter holidays in return for better child-care provisions."

5. "On the Conference Board's reckoning, 62% of American companies offer early retirement plans and only 4% offer *inducements* to delay retirement."

BUSINESS

Gone fishing

NEW YORK, LONDON AND TOKYO

Soon there will not be enough skilled workers to go round. Companies everywhere need to sharpen up to attract them

1 DURING the 1980s employers never had it so good. Lengthy dole queues made it easy for businessmen and union-bashing politicians to impose their will on the same organised labour that had often humiliated them in the 1970s. In 1981 Ronald Reagan took on America's air-traffic controllers and won; in 1985 Margaret Thatcher trounced Britain's miners. In the same year Mr Carl Icahn, an American raider, was able to dismember TWA, an American airline, without a whimper from its workforce.

2 The 1990s will be different. In most of the big OECD countries the total workforce will continue to grow, but there will be a shortage of young, skilled workers. A return to the mass-union power of the 1970s looks unlikely. But the shortage of younger workers will mean that companies in America, Japan and Europe will have to find new ways to attract, develop, motivate, reward and retain employees.

3 The "demographic time bomb" may be well hidden. For a start a small recession in the early 1990s, should it come, will lengthen dole queues again. But unless the world economy goes badly wrong, the labour shortage is sure to worsen in the 1990s. Consider:

4 ● America's workforce will grow by only 15.9m (1.2% a year) in the 1990s compared with 22.2m (2.6% a year) in the 1970s and 18.3m in the 1980s (1.6%). There will be an absolute fall in the number of people aged between 16 and 24, while the proportion of American workers over 35 will rise from 39% today to 49% by 2000.

5 ● The population of the European Community will stay at around 325m (assuming no additions to its 12 member countries). But there will be many fewer young people, and many more over-65s. Ireland apart, all the EC countries will have fewer young workers. The number of under-25s in France's and Britain's labour forces will decline by around 2% a year until the turn of the century; in West Germany it will decline by 3.6% a year. East German immigrants may help, but only a bit: East Germany also has a shortage of young people.

6 ● Japan's population will grow slightly in the 1990s. But the proportion of pensioners will rise from 11% to 15% of the population. The number of under-25s in the workforce will decline by 2% each year. The Japanese practice of paying by seniority rather than merit means that an aging labour force guarantees a steady rise in labour costs. That is one reason for Japan's current investment boom: manufacturers know they have to replace workers with more machines.

7 Statistics tell only part of the story. Anecdotal evidence of a tightening labour market abounds. In Japan some employers have resorted to *kosoku*—"kidnapping" young graduates by luring them to hot-spring resorts and then forcing them to sign contracts. Job-hopping in mid-career has also caught on there, to the consternation of traditionalists at Japan's big old conglomerates, but to the joy of a new industry of headhunters. In Britain each spring Le Manoir aux Quat' Saisons, a fancy restaurant near Oxford, is booked up by management consultants also bent on kidnapping.

8 A youngish labour pool still exists in America and much of Western Europe—but not the one that most employers want. Six out of ten American 20-year-olds cannot add up their own lunch bills. Most black teenagers are unemployed in inner-city slums in America and Britain. In the EC unemployment is still hovering at around 10% of the workforce—but half of these have been unemployed for over a year. Sadly, many such workers are unemployable—except by those few companies that are willing and able to offer remedial education or training. Mrs Elizabeth Dole, America's secretary of labour, warns of a "skills gap".

9 That skills gap has become increasingly important as the big western economies have moved from dull manufacturing jobs to service ones where charm and intelligence win customers. Service industries accounted for 55% of EC jobs in 1986 (against 40% in 1963), for 68% of America's workforce (58%) and 52% of Japan's (42%).

Softly, softly, catchee granny

10 The struggle to recruit talent will take place on two fronts: first, companies will compete for the few bright young people available; second, they will try to build up alternative labour markets—essentially either bright old people or bright married women who are not at work. Neither option is cheap.

11 Most companies will still prefer to have recent graduates. Shell, an oil company, already admits that it can attract high-flying graduates only by promoting them above their less-gifted seniors. Pechiney, a French aluminium manufacturer, is creating its own pool of skilled labour for a new plant at Dunkirk by agreeing to share the costs of educating 500 workers with the French government years before the factory is com-

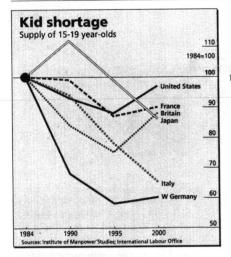

Kid shortage
Supply of 15-19 year-olds

1984=100

United States

France
Britain
Japan

Italy

W Germany

110
100
90
80
70
60
50

1984   1990   1995   2000

Sources: Institute of Manpower Studies; International Labour Office

pleted in mid-1992.

12   Other firms are paying graduates while they are at university. Messerschmitt-Bölkow-Blohm sponsors British engineering students at Brunel University, if they come to work for it in Germany after graduation. A fifth of the graduates hired each year by ICL, a British computer company, are sponsored students.

13   However, money is only part of the bait, because cash is becoming less effective as a lure. Mr David Baker, who has recently completed a survey of the British labour market for J. Walter Thompson, an advertising agency, reckons that British undergraduates are becoming less interested in financial reward and more concerned with the quality of life at work and the reputation of their employers. He predicts that the most successful recruiters will be those who have created a good impression with students before the corporate "milk round".

14   Mr Mitchell Fromstein, the chief executive of Manpower, an American employment agency, says for the first time in years, more and more corporate recruiters are, plugging the message "here-is-a-nice-company-to-work-for" to try to drum up job applicants. That means companies will need to bolster their corporate-affairs departments—to project a better image to their workers (both present and potential) as well as their customers.

15   Few western countries make full use of working-age women. The few that do, such as Sweden, where 86% of women with young children work (as opposed to 28% in Britain), have to rely on massive state subsidies for child care. The better route—companies adapting themselves to suit working mothers—is taking time to catch on.

16   Mrs Audrey Freedman of the Conference Board, a New York-based business think tank, says that to attract applicants from the 14m women who now stay at home to care for their children, more American companies are offering child-care schemes, generous maternity leave, flexible hours and part-time jobs. Britain's Midland Bank, 60% of whose staff are women, plans to establish 300 creches. At present Midland has only 11 creches, where parents typically pay £35 ($56) a week, half the cost, for dumping the children during working hours.

17   However, most companies do not want to be in the child-care business—particularly when it costs so much. According to ARA Services, an American provider of child-care services to other companies, many American employers still blanch at the cost of providing creches. They want the level of care that is provided by one professional for every four infants or toddlers in the creche, but they are not ready to pay more than what it costs merely to "warehouse" children.

18   One alternative is to give vouchers to women employees with children which could be used to purchase child care, in exchange for a reduction of other benefits. For example, a woman might opt for shorter holidays in return for better child-care provisions. Another alternative is to allow career-breaks and job-sharing. In Germany, Messerschmitt, BASF and Audi have introduced employment guarantees for female workers who leave work to have children.

19   Japan is the biggest waster of women. Though the proportion of its women in the labour force is rising rapidly, it still has the industrial world's deepest "M" shaped graph of female labour-force participation—the proportion rises to 70% by the age of 25, but then falls to 50% as women are forced to quit when they get married, rising again only after the age of 35.

20   Though some Japanese firms are catching on to women's potential, and many are hiring women as part-time factory workers, most have so far paid more attention to grey-haired males. Older people should be ideal targets for corporate recruiters everywhere. They are less likely to miss work, more polite to customers, and more loyal than their younger counterparts. In practice though, surely all they want to do is retire? The average age at which American men retire has declined from 65 in 1963 to 62 today and seems set to decline further. The few companies that are trying to halt that trend are an unconventional minority. On the Conference Board's reckoning, 62% of American companies offer early retirement plans and only 4% offer inducements to delay retirement.

21   That will change as American companies weigh the difficulties of recruiting new workers against the advantages of retaining old hands. Varian, a Silicon Valley company engaged in high-tech wizardry, is pioneering the way. Its phased-retirement plan permits employees who are 55 or older to work 20-32 hours a week for as long as they and the company wish. Retired people in America are allowed to work for 1,000 hours a year without affecting their pension and health benefits.

22   Japan's old people are, you guessed it, workaholics: most big firms have moved their retirement ages from 55 to 60 in recent years, to please their workers as well as to relieve the labour shortage. But there is a quid pro quo: many firms have adjusted their seniority systems so that the highest wages are paid at around 45 rather than just before retirement, in order to hold down labour costs. More than 60% of Japanese men over 55 are still working, compared with 40% in America. And Japanese women lead the world in one respect, at least: at 30%, their labour participation rate over the age of 55 is the industrial world's highest.

23   European companies are also waking up to the potential of hiring older workers. In the first six months of 1989 a British supermarket chain, Tesco, recruited around 1,500 people in their 50s and 60s with a "Life begins at 55" campaign. At a recent conference in West Germany on the country's greying society, sponsored by BDI, the employers' confederation, two-thirds of the

companies said they employed old-age pensioners part-time, and 75% said they expect to hire someone over 50 in the next year. With the youngest pensionable age in Europe, Germany has a huge reservoir of trained labour. All the signs are that it will need it.

4

Glossary

abounds	is plentiful, exists in large amounts
anecdotal	full of short stories or accounts of happenings
blanch	to become pale (from shock)
bolster	to strengthen, reinforce
boom	swift, vigorous growth or development
conglomerates	corporations formed by the merger of several companies
consternation	fear or shock, dismay
creches	day nursuries (in Europe)
demographic	distribution, density, vital statistics of populations
dismember	to cut to pieces, mutilate, divide up
dole	form of payment to the unemployed by the government
EC	European Community
fronts	specified areas of activity
gap	a lag or disparity between conditions
headhunters	agents specializing in recruitment of executives or highly skilled personnel
hovering	staying suspended
humiliated	degraded, hurt the pride or dignity of
inducements	incentives, motives
job-sharing	allowing one job to be performed by two persons, each responsible for half of the job
kidnapping	holding a person against his or her will by force
lure	anything that attracts or tempts, bait
milk round	yearly attempt by British employers to recruit the best graduates of British universities
OECD	Organization for Economic Cooperation and Development
opt	to make a choice
pensioners	persons who receive payments after reaching a certain age; former workers, no longer employed
project	to get across to others effectively
queues	lines of persons waiting to be served
raider	person who buys stock in a company in an attempt to take it over
recession	temporary falling off of business activity
recruit	to hire or engage the services of
remedial	special courses for helping students overcome deficiencies
reservoir	an extra or reserve supply
retain	to hold or keep
subsidies	grants of money from the government
trounced	defeated, beat
union-bashing	attacking or destroying unions (organizations of workers)
vouchers	papers serving as evidence or proof
warehouse	to place or store in a warehouse
whimper	cry, sound
wizardry	magic, sorcery
workaholics	persons having a compulsive need to work

Vocabulary

This exercise should be viewed as a recall task, to test your memory and understanding of the major ideas and vocabulary words in the article. Therefore, try to complete the exercise without looking back at the article. The sentences represent a brief summary of the article.

Without referring to the article, fill in the blanks in the following sentences with the correct words from this list. You may change the tense, number, or form of the words to fit the context. Use each word only once; not all the words on the list will be used.

subsidy	gap	conglomerate	reservoir	workaholic	kidnap
remedial	job-sharing	demographic	recruit	project	bolster

1. The labor* shortage will become more severe in the 1990s because of worldwide_____

   _____ factors.

2. In England and Japan, employers and management consultants are even _____ young college graduates to force them to sign job contracts.

3. As a result of the decrease in manufacturing jobs and the increase in service jobs, the skills

   _____ has grown more important.

4. Although there is a need for well-educated workers, few companies provide _____ education or training.

5. Companies will have to _____ workers from alternative labor markets such as older people or married women.

6. In addition, companies must _____ their departments of corporate affairs in order

   to _____ a better image.

7. The few western countries that have many working women with young children are depen-

   dent on large _____ from the state for child care.

8. Some American companies now offer child-care plans, maternity leave, flexible hours, and

   _____ or part-time jobs to attract applicants.

9. Having the youngest pensionable age in Europe, Germany faces less of a labor shortage

   since it has a huge _____ of trained workers.

---

* British English spelling = labour; American English spelling = labor

Idioms and Expressions

Idiomatic expressions are prevalent in contemporary business writing, and you will notice many in these articles. When completing the exercises, make a note of which idioms you are already familiar with and which are new to you. If the words are unfamiliar, try to guess the meaning from the context (sentence, paragraph) in which the idioms occur.

Read the paragraphs in which the following italicized idioms and expressions are found. Then circle the letter next to the answer that best describes the meaning of the idiom as used in the context of the article.

1. "Job-hopping in mid-career has also *caught on* there. . . ." (Paragraph 7)
   a. become a problem
   b. become popular
   c. become respected

2. "In Britain each spring Le Manoir aux Quat' Saisons, a fancy restaurant near Oxford, is *booked up.* . . ." (Paragraph 7)
   a reserved
   b. visited
   c. used

3. ". . . by management consultants also *bent on* kidnapping." (Paragraph 7)
   a. determined to do
   b. thinking about
   c. arranging

4. "Shell, an oil company, already admits that it can attract *high-flying* graduates only by promoting them above their less-gifted seniors." (Paragraph 11)
   a. risk-taking
   b. wealthy
   c. talented

5. ". . . more and more corporate recruiters are *plugging* the message 'here-is-a-nice-company-to-work-for.'. . ." (Paragraph 14)
   a. publicizing
   b. sending
   c. translating

6. ". . . to try to *drum up* job applicants." (Paragraph 14)
   a. secretly contact
   b. arouse interest in
   c. aggressively interview

7. "Mrs. Audrey Freedman of the Conference Board, a New York-based business *think tank* . . ." (Paragraph 16)
   a. a library specializing in current business theories and techniques
   b. a Board of Directors for large corporations
   c. an organization that does extensive research and problem solving

8. ". . . where parents typically pay £35 ($56) a week, half the cost, for *dumping* the children during working hours." (Paragraph 16)
   a. feeding
   b. getting rid of
   c. watching

9. "That will change as American companies weigh the difficulties of recruiting new workers against the advantages of retaining *old hands*." (Paragraph 21)
   a. experienced workers
   b. elderly laborers
   c. manual laborers

10. "But there is *a quid pro quo:* . . . ." (Paragraph 22)
    a. a response to a question
    b. one thing in return for another
    c. a related principle

11. "European companies are also *waking up to* the potential of hiring older workers." (Paragraph 23)
    a. accepting
    b. remembering
    c. realizing

Paraphrasing

Paraphrasing means restating an author's ideas in your own words by changing sentence structure, word order, and vocabulary. A good paraphrase is accurate—that is, true to the author's meaning—and complete. Paraphrasing tests both your knowledge of English grammar and vocabulary and your comprehension of the ideas in the article.

Read the following sentences carefully, and then rewrite them using your own words. Change the vocabulary and sentence structure, but do not change the author's intended meaning or paraphrase any technical terms. There are several ways of paraphrasing each sentence. (In this chapter, examples of possible paraphrases for each sentence are given.)

Original: "In most of the big OECD countries the total workforce will continue to grow, but there will be a shortage of young, skilled workers."

Paraphrase: Although the large OECD countries will see an increase in their overall labor supply, the number of young, trained laborers will decrease.

1. "A return to the mass-union power of the 1970s looks unlikely." (Paragraph 2)

   _____

   _____

2. "For a start a small recession in the early 1990s, should it come, will lengthen dole queues again." (Paragraph 3)

   _____

   _____

3. "Anecdotal evidence of a tightening labour market abounds." (Paragraph 7)

   _____

   _____

4. "Most companies will still prefer to have recent graduates." (Paragraph 11)

   _____

   _____

5. "Older people should be ideal targets for corporate recruiters everywhere." (Paragraph 20)

   _____

   _____

Examples of Possible Paraphrases

1. It does not seem probable that the 1970s mass-union strength will come back.

2. To begin with, unemployment lines will become long again if there is a minor recession in the early 1990s.

3. There are many stories that substantiate the shrinking workforce.

4. New college graduates will remain the first choice of the majority of business firms.

5. It would be advisable for corporate recruiters worldwide to hunt for elderly workers.

Comprehension

Your literal comprehension of the main idea, major points and supporting details in the article is shown by your ability to answer these questions. The answers can be found in the text, and you are asked to identify the paragraphs that contain the relevant information. The main idea is the central subject or unifying theme of the article and is often composed of several sentences stated in more than one paragraph.

Answer the following questions by finding the relevant information in the article. Give the numbers of the paragraphs that contain the answers.

1. What is the main idea of this article?
    Answer. "There will be a shortage of young, skilled workers . . . the shortage of younger workers will mean that companies in America will have to find new ways to attract, develop, motivate, reward and retain employees." (Paragraph 2) " . . . the labour shortage is sure to worsen in the 1990s." (Paragraph 3)

2. Why were the 1980s so good for employers?

3. How will the 1990s be different from the 1980s?

4. What will happen to the American, the European Community, and the Japanese workforces in the 1990s?

5. Study the graph entitled "Kid Shortage."
    a. Which country will show no increase in 15-to-19-year-olds between 1984 and 2000?
    b. Which countries will increase the most in 15-to-19-year-olds between 1984 and 2000?
    c. Which country will decrease the most in 15-to-19-year-olds between 1984 and 2000?

6. Why is the youngish labor pool in America and Western Europe unacceptable to most employers?

7. How will companies try to recruit talented workers?

8. What methods are companies using to recruit recent college graduates?

9. How are companies attracting women with children?

10. Why should older people be ideal targets for corporate recruiters?

11. What changes have Japanese firms made in regard to their workforce?

12. What advantage does Germany have?

Inference/Interpretation

In this exercise you are asked either to draw an inference about what you have read or to give an interpretation of a sentence or phrase. Drawing an inference means making a logical deduction based on information in the text. The answers are not stated explicitly (in so many words), but are strongly supported by the text. Look in the text for clues that can help you arrive at your conclusion.

Circle the letter next to the best answer. Choose your answer according to the meaning the author suggests but does not state explicitly. (In this chapter, the answers will be explained.)

1. What is the meaning of the following phrase: "the 'demographic time bomb'"? (Paragraph 3)
    a. The population density cannot be controlled.
    b. Population distribution is rapidly changing.
    c. The global population explosion is a serious problem.
    d. The shortage of young, skilled workers is becoming more and more serious.

Explanation 1

    a. This is not correct because density is not discussed in the article.

    b. This is too general to be the correct answer.

    c. This is incorrect. The global population explosion is not discussed.

    d. This is the correct interpretation of "demographic time bomb." The phrase implies that the labor shortage is like a bomb that is getting ready to explode in the 1990s.

2. What can be inferred from the following statement: "Six out of ten American 20-year-olds cannot add up their own lunch bills."? (Paragraph 8)

    a. Most Americans are poor in mathematics.

    b. Many young Americans lack the minimal proficiency in mathematics desired by today's corporations.

    c. Many Americans drop out of school by the 7th grade.

    d. Addition and subtraction are not taught properly in American schools.

Explanation 2

    a. This cannot be inferred from the text. The statement refers to young adults, not all Americans.

    b. This inference can be drawn from the statement. The previous sentence refers to a "youngish labour pool" that is "not the one most employers want."

    c. This cannot be inferred from the text. There is no discussion of the percentage of school dropouts or when students leave school.

    d. This cannot be inferred from the text. The quality of American education is not discussed.

3. It can be inferred that "merely to 'warehouse' children" (Paragraph 17) means

    a. to provide afterschool recreation for children.

    b. to give children minimal care and supervision.

    c. to give excellent care to large numbers of children.

    d. to provide care only for children who are in school.

Explanation 3

    a. This cannot be inferred from the text. Afterschool recreation is not mentioned.

    b. This inference can be drawn. Because of the cost, children are not receiving a high level of care. They are just being put in child-care situations where they are treated like items stored in a warehouse.

    c. This cannot be inferred from the text. The quality of care is not high because excellent care is expensive: "They are not ready to pay more than what it costs . . ."

    d. This cannot be inferred from the text. This aspect of child care is not discussed.

4. Explain the meaning of the following sentence: "Japan is the biggest waster of women." (Paragraph 19)

    a. Women in Japan are not encouraged to join the workforce.

    b. Japan is not taking advantage of a potential supply of women workers.

    c. Women are not considered the equal of men in Japan.

    d. Japan has fewer working women than any other industrial country.

Explanation 4

  a. This cannot be inferred since 70% of women join the workforce by age 25, and 30% of those over 55 remain in the workforce.

  b. This inference can be drawn because the 70% figure (working women) falls to 50% after Japanese women marry, so 20% of women who could work have quit.

  c. This cannot be inferred from the text. The position of women is not discussed.

  d. This cannot be inferred from the text. The total number of working women is not discussed.

5. From the article, what can we infer will cause the decrease in the number of young people in the workforce and the increase in the number of older people in the workforce in the OECD countries in the 1990s?

  a. Increasing life expectancies as a result of better health care

  b. Fewer births as a result of increasing use of birth control methods

  c. Large numbers of young people lacking basic job skills

  d. Young people's lack of interest in working

Explanation 5

  a. Even though this is a reasonable statement, this cannot be inferred from the text because the subject of life expectancies is not discussed.

  b. Even though this is a reasonable statement, this cannot be inferred from the text because the subjects of birth control and birth rate are not discussed.

  c. This can be inferred from the text. ("few bright young people available": Paragraph 10)

  d. This cannot be inferred from the text because the subject of young people's lack of interest in working is not discussed.

Structure

In this exercise, you will analyze the logical structure (form) in which the author has chosen to present the content. This includes identifying the overall method of development of the article, the various patterns of development used to organize paragraphs, and the location of the main idea. There are four basic types of organization:

1. Deductive: The main idea is stated at the beginning of the text.

2. Inductive: The main idea is stated at the end of the text.

3. Deductive-Restatement: The main idea is stated at the beginning and again at the end of the text.

4. Implied: The main idea is not stated explicitly in the text, but it is implied.

Methods of development include the following: analysis, argument, cause-effect, chronology, classification, comparison-contrast, definition, description, enumeration, exemplification (examples), problem-solution, process, and spatial order.

Circle the letter next to the correct answer(s). More than one answer may be correct. Be prepared to explain and justify your choices. (In this chapter, the answers will be explained.)

1. In which paragraph(s) is the main idea stated?
   a. Paragraph 1
   b. Paragraph 2
   c. Paragraph 3
   d. Paragraph 9
   e. Paragraph 22

Explanation 1

a. This answer is incorrect. This paragraph serves as an introduction and discusses the favorable conditions employers had in the 1980s.

b. This answer is correct. This paragraph contains the first part of the main idea: "There will be a shortage of young, skilled workers. But . . . companies will have to find ways to attract, develop, motivate, reward, and retain employees."

c. This answer is correct. This paragraph contains the second part of the main idea: "The labour shortage is sure to worsen in the 1990s."

d. This answer is incorrect. This paragraph discusses the increasing number of service jobs, which has made the skills gap more important.

e. This answer is incorrect. This paragraph discusses the older workers in Japan.

Write a paraphrase of the main idea in *one* sentence, using your own words as much as possible.

2. What is the purpose of the three examples in paragraph 1?
   a. To support the major point of paragraph
   b. To expand the idea in sentence 2 of paragraph 1
   c. To give a humorous tone to the introduction
   d. To get the attention of the reader
   e. To enumerate the names of famous persons

Explanation 2

a. This answer is correct. The examples support the major point that during the 1980s "employers never had it so good . . . imposed their will on the same organised labour that had often humiliated them in the 1970s."

b. This answer is correct. The examples show how businessmen and politicians "imposed their will . . . ."

c. This answer is not correct. The examples are not humorous.

d. This answer is correct. The examples get the reader's attention because most people have heard of Ronald Reagan, Margaret Thatcher, and perhaps Carl Icahn.

e. This answer is not correct. Simple enumeration is not the purpose of the examples.

3. Where is cause-effect development used to support the main idea of the article?
   a. Paragraph 2
   b. Paragraph 4
   c. Paragraph 5
   d. Paragraph 6
   e. Paragraph 9

Explanation 3

   a. This answer is correct. The cause is the shortage of younger workers. The effect is that companies will have to find new ways to attract, develop, motivate, reward, and retain employees.
   b. This answer is not correct. There is no cause-effect. The method used is comparison-contrast.
   c. This answer is not correct. There is no cause-effect. The method used is comparison-contrast.
   d. This answer is not correct. Comparison-contrast is used. There is also cause-effect development, but it does not support the main idea of the article.
   e. This answer is not correct. Comparison-contrast is used. There is also cause-effect development, but it does not support the main idea of the article.

4. What overall method of development is used in this article?
   a. Enumerating the steps in a process
   b. Presenting causes and effects
   c. Comparing and contrasting two methods
   d. Defining a technical system
   e. Analyzing a proposal

Explanation 4

   a. This answer is not correct.
   b. This answer is correct. The author discusses the causes of the shortage of young, skilled workers in the 1990s and the effects of this shortage. ("Companies in America, Japan, and Europe will have to find new ways to attract, develop, motivate, reward and retain employees.")
   c. This answer is not correct.
   d. This answer is not correct
   e. This answer is not correct.

Style

There are as many writing styles as there are writers. However, in business or technical writing, the author's choice of style is generally determined by three criteria:

1. The purpose of the document;

2. The audience for the document; and

3. The type of information in the document.

Analysis of an author's style is helpful in understanding the ideas conveyed by the writer. Styles may be formal or informal, technical or nontechnical, personal or impersonal, academic or journalistic, poetic or bureaucratic, literary or businesslike, legal or conversational, scientific or pictorial. (See Appendix A: Examples of Writing Styles.)

Style includes tone, the author's attitude toward the subject and the audience. Tone may be objective, subjective, humorous, serious, disapproving, approving, satirical, realistic, emotional, balanced, authoritative, tentative, positive, negative, polite, rude, hostile, friendly, analytical, or persuasive.

In this exercise you will analyze the style and tone of the author. Circle the letter next to the correct answer(s). More than one answer may be correct. Be prepared to justify your choices by giving specific examples from the article. (In this chapter, the answers will be explained.)

1. How would you describe the writing style of the author?
   a. Impersonal
   b. Personal
   c. Academic
   d. Technical
   e. Informal
   f. Formal

Explanation 1

   a. This answer is correct. The author writes in an impersonal style. There are no first person pronouns or personal opinions given.
   b. The author's style is not personal.
   c. The author does not have an academic or scholarly style. He or she writes casually and simply for an audience of laypersons, not scholars or academics.
   d. The author uses very few technical terms. ("Demographic" is one of the few.) He or she is writing for the average person, not a labor expert.
   e. This answer is correct. The author's style is informal. He or she uses several slang expressions and takes a colloquial (conversational) approach. ("Employers never had it so good.")
   f. The author's style is not formal.

2. What words best describe the tone of the article?
   a. Objective
   b. Subjective
   c. Optimistic
   d. Emotional
   e. Analytical
   f. Authoritative

Explanation 2

   a. This answer is correct. The tone is objective. The author presents nearly all the facts without personal comment. No "I" or "we" pronouns are used.
   b. The tone is not subjective. The author presents facts and statistics to substantiate the thesis about the workforce in the 1990s.
   c. The tone is not optimistic. The author emphasizes the worsening labor shortage.
   d. The tone is not emotional. In an unemotional, rational, and matter-of-fact manner, the author describes the problem of the labor shortage.
   e. This answer is correct. The tone is analytical and informative. Many facts and statistics are discussed objectively.
   f. This answer is correct. The author appears to be knowledgeable about the subject and has facts and statistics to support the major points. This gives the writing an authoritative tone.

3. The author's attitude toward the projected labor shortage is
   a. unconcerned.
   b. concerned.
   c. angry.
   d. negative.
   e. positive.
   f. realistic.

Explanation 3

   a. The author, although objective, is not unconcerned about the problem.
   b. This answer is correct. The author shows concern by referring to a "demographic time bomb" and using the adverb "sadly" in paragraph 8.
   c. The author shows no sign of anger in the article.
   d. The author does not have a negative attitude toward the labor shortage. Practical solutions are suggested.
   e. The author does not have a positive attitude toward the labor shortage.
   f. This answer is correct. The author's attitude is realistic. He or she realizes that the labor shortage will be a serious problem and that solutions will have to be found: "Companies . . . will have to find new ways to attract . . . employees" (Paragraph 2). In discussing Germany's "huge reservoir of trained labour," the author says: "All the signs are that it will need it" (Paragraph 23).

4. The author sets the conversational style of the article in the first sentence by using a slang expression: "During the 1980s employers never had it so good." Rewrite this sentence in a formal style.

_____

_____

Discussion

These questions encourage you to draw on your personal experience and knowledge and to express your point of view about the ideas in the article. Be prepared to explain your responses.

1. What is the unemployment rate in your country today?

2. What is the productivity growth rate in your country?

3. Do many women work in your country? Why or why not?

4. Should women with young children work? Why or why not?

5. What benefits should be offered to working women with children?

6. What is the average age of retirement in your country? Is there a mandatory retirement age? Should there be?

7. What is more important to you in choosing a job: financial reward, quality of life at work, or reputation of employers? Why?

Research Assignment

The following bibliography lists articles related to the topic in the main reading. These articles offer diverse points of view and further information on the subject.

Look up several of these articles in the library. Choose one article to read and take notes on.

"All in the Corporate Family." _Economist_ 315 (May 12, 1990): 19–20.

Becker, Gary S. "Opening the Golden Doors Wider—to Newcomers with Knowhow." _Business Week_ (June 11, 1990): 12.

"Economic and Financial Indicators." _Economist_ 314 (January 6, 1990): 103.

"Economic and Financial Indicators." _Economist_ 315 (May 26, 1990): 113.

Fraser, Jill Andresky. "The Making of a Work Force." _Business Month_ 134 (September 1989): 58–61.

Freedman, Audrey. "A Little Piracy Is Sometimes Called For." _Business Month_ 133 (April 1989): 121.

Friedman, Dana E. "Child Care for Employees' Kids." *Harvard Business Review* 64 (March-April 1986): 28–34.

Graham, Ellen. "Flexible Formulas." *Wall Street Journal* (June 4, 1990): R34–35.

Hoerr, John. "Business Shares the Blame for Workers' Low Skills." *Business Week* (June 25, 1990): 71.

"Italy: The Numbers Game." *Economist* 315 (May 26, 1990): 25–26.

Johnston, William B. "Global Work Force 2000: The New World Labor Market." *Harvard Business Review* 69 (March–April 1991): 115–27.

Kenworthy, Tom. "Senate Passes Bill Mandating Parental, Family Care Leave." *Washington Post* (June 15, 1990): A1, A17.

Lansing, Paul, and Kathryn Ready. "Hiring Women Managers in Japan: An Alternative for Foreign Employers." *California Management Review* 30 (Spring 1988): 112–27.

Machan, Dyan. "Cultivating the Gray." *Forbes* 144 (September 4, 1989): 126–28.

Macrae, Norman. "The Revenge of the Huddled Masses." *Business Month* 135 (March 1990): 19–21.

Rich, Spencer. "U.S. Isn't Only Place Where Modern Family Is Being Transformed." *Washington Post* (June 22, 1990): A25.

Rodgers, Fran Sussner, and Charles Rodgers. "Business and the Facts of Family Life." *Harvard Business Review* 67 (November-December 1989): 121–29.

Schwartz, Felice N. "Management Women and the New Facts of Life." *Harvard Business Review* 67 (January-February 1989): 65–76.

Sellers, Patricia. "What Customers Really Want." *Fortune* 121 (June 4,1990): 58–68.

Silver, Marc. "Hitting the Unretirement Circuit." *U.S. News & World Report* 108 (June 4, 1990): 76.

Skrzycki, Cindy. "Business Goes Back to the Three R's." *Washington Post* (June 3, 1990): H3.

Skrzycki, Cindy. "Getting the Attention of the Young Worker." *Washington Post* (May 27, 1990): H3.

Thomas, Linda Thiede, and James E. Thomas. "The ABCs of Child Care: Building Blocks of Competitive Advantage." *Sloan Management Review* 31 (Winter 1990): 31–41.

Oral Presentation

Oral communication skills are critical to success in the business world. This activity will give you practice in the preparation and presentation of an oral report. The articles listed in the research assignment should serve as the basis of your presentation. Guidelines for oral presentations are in Appendix B: Giving an Oral Presentation.

Give a ten-minute oral presentation to the class on the article that you chose in the research assignment. Include the author's main idea, major points, and some supporting data. Be prepared to answer questions on your topic.

Writing Assignments

Each chapter contains three different writing assignments that meet the needs of a variety of students and course objectives. Guidelines for and examples of writing assignments are presented in Appendix C: Writing a Summary: Example of Summary; Appendix D: Writing an Essay: Examples of Essay and Synthesis; and Appendix F: Writing Evaluation Form.

1. Make an outline of the article "Gone Fishing," indicating the major points and most significant supporting details. Use the following format:

I. The workforce in the 1990s in the OECD countries
   A.
   B.

II. Causes of the labor shortage in the 1990s
   A.
      1.
      2.
      3.
   B.
      1.
      2.
      3.
   C.
      1.
      2.
      3.
   D.
      1.
      2.

III.   Effects of the labor shortage in the 1990s
   A.
      1.
      2.
      3.
   B.
      1.
      2.
      3.
   C.
      1.
      2.
      3.

2. Discuss the workforce in your country. What is the unemployment rate? What percentage of the women work? Do women face any special problems? Is it easy or hard to find a job in a large company? Will there be a shortage of young workers in the 1990s? Develop a thesis and use enumeration to list the various characteristics of the workforce.

3. Describe the type of job you will search for after getting your degree. What are the qualifications for this type of job? How difficult will it be to find this job?

Case Study

This problem-solving activity offers the opportunity for students to work together in analyzing a case study and writing a case study report. Each case presents a dilemma that may be resolved in several different ways; no one solution is correct. Use brainstorming* to come up with as many suggestions as possible before choosing a preferred solution. The cases are built on the readings in each chapter and reinforce the vocabulary and major concepts. Appendix E: Case Study Report gives a suggested report format. (In this chapter, possible answers to the questions are given, and a case study report is provided as a model.)

---

* Brainstorming: The unrestrained offering of suggestions by all members of a group to seek solutions to problems. No idea is considered too absurd to mention. The purpose is to generate as many ideas as possible.

Case Study: A Labor Shortage Problem

Working in groups, read the following case study. Discuss the problem, answer the questions, and write a brief report on how your group would solve the problem. (Choose one member of the group to do the writing.) Follow the format in Appendix E (Case Study Report) in writing your report.

Tom Jacobson, President and Chief Operating Officer (CEO) of Equip, Inc., which designs and manufactures upscale kitchenware, is considering selling the company. Although Tom, the founder of Equip, Inc., has built a highly successful business over the years, today Equip is facing tough competition. And with the unemployment rate at 3%, the labor shortage in the state is getting quite severe. Tom cannot find enough qualified applicants to staff the distribution or the production departments. In addition, a number of longtime employees are reaching retirement age and planning to leave. To make matters worse, some employees have resigned from the company to go to work for his competitors. Tom has no idea why they left.

Recently, Tom has personally interviewed a large number of young job applicants, but he has found few qualified to work at Equip. These younger applicants are weak in basic job skills, such as reading, writing, and math. (The quality of the education system in the United States has certainly changed since Tom was in school.) The more qualified and experienced applicants, especially the women, seem to want all sorts of flexible scheduling and job options, such as family leave and child care.

For many years, Equip has had a reputation as a good company to work for because of its substantial benefits, like profit sharing, not to mention excellent working conditions. Of course, Tom is aware that he has taken a somewhat conservative approach by refusing to offer job options such as flextime and job-sharing. But Tom has never been convinced of the benefits of these flexible work arrangements. In fact, he tends to worry that they will lower productivity—and productivity is Tom's main goal and source of pride. The average productivity growth rate of Equip has been 4% for the past several years. However, with so many unfilled jobs, the productivity rate has begun to decrease rapidly, and Tom is feeling as if Equip has somehow fallen behind the competition.

Frankly, Tom is tired of arguing with Walter Harrington, who has been Director of Personnel for eleven years, about how to solve the labor and productivity problems. He and Walter used to see eye to eye about company policies and procedures, but lately Tom has begun to question Walter's judgment. It was Walter who would never consider instituting flextime or job-sharing at Equip. He was certain that such options would decrease productivity; he thought of them as benefits only for employees, not for management. His solutions to Equip's problems are to cut wages and de-skill jobs through automation. Walter believes that if Equip used automation to create very simple work tasks, they could hire employees at low wages and achieve cost competitiveness and better productivity—and with fewer workers.

Tom sees Walter's ideas as short-term solutions that would change the basic nature of his company and that could eventually lead to ruin. He wants a long-term solution that will be good for all involved: the company, the employees, and management. Since he is unsure about what to do, he has set up a meeting with a management consultant to get a new perspective on the situation and to help him decide on the strategic direction of the company.

Questions

1. What could Tom do to stop the decrease in productivity at Equip?
   — He could try to hire workers to fill the vacant positions.
   — He could institute a training program for the employees to improve their basic skills and to make them multiskilled and more adaptable.
   — He could add computers and robots and use automation to increase productivity.

2. What may be the causes of Equip's losing valued employees to competitors?
   — Equip is probably losing workers to competitors because it does not offer flextime, part-time jobs, job-sharing, or leaves.
   — Its pay scale may not be as good as those in other companies.
   — Its personnel director may be incompetent.

3. What should Tom ask the management consultant to do?
   — Tom should ask the consultant to conduct a survey of the employees to ask for their opinions on working conditions at Equip, on flexible scheduling, and on job options.
   — He should ask the consultant to interview the personnel director.
   — He should ask the consultant to conduct a needs analysis to determine what types of training programs Equip should offer.

4. What can Equip do to attract, develop, motivate, reward, and retain employees?
   — Equip can implement flexible job arrangements such as flextime, job-sharing, part-time jobs, leaves, and child care.
   — It can institute special training programs to improve the basic skills of both new and old workers and to make them multiskilled.
   — It can conduct a job audit, evaluate the wage scale, and possibly raise wages.

Solution: Case Study Report

   I. Define and analyze the problem.
  II. Suggest possible solutions.
 III. Evaluate possible solutions.
 IV. Select a solution.

Case Study Report

I. Statement of the Problem

  A. Definition: Tom Jacobson may have to sell Equip, Inc., if he cannot find skilled workers and increase productivity.

  B. Analysis: Equip, Inc., is facing a decrease in productivity because it has a labor shortage. Many jobs are unfilled, and several employees are leaving the company to go to work for competitors.

II. Suggestion of Possible Solutions

    A. Tom Jacobson could sell Equip.

    B. Tom Jacobson could purchase robots and computers to take the place of certain employees and to de-skill jobs through automation.

    C. Tom Jacobson could offer flexible work arrangements and training programs to the employees at Equip.

III. Evaluation of Possible Solutions

    A. Tom Jacobson could sell Equip.

        1. Advantages: No more business worries for Tom

        2. Disadvantages: Poor time to sell—may lose money

    B. Tom Jacobson could purchase robots and computers to take the place of certain employees and to de-skill jobs through automation.

        1. Advantages: Possible solution to the labor shortage and productivity decrease

        2. Disadvantages: Great expense, the technology may become quickly obsolete, and the workers' skills would be downgraded

    C. Tom Jacobson could offer flexible work arrangements and training programs to the employees at Equip.

        1. Advantages: Ability to recruit, develop, motivate, and keep workers and upgrade or diversify their skills

        2. Disadvantages: Need for restructuring of personnel policies and replacement of personnel director (which may not be a disadvantage)

IV. Selection of a Solution

    A. Choice: (C) Tom Jacobson should offer the employees flexible work arrangements at Equip (flextime, job-sharing, part-time jobs, family leaves, sabbaticals, child care) and training in basic skills.

    B. Justification: Equip will have to match the current work options offered by other companies if it wishes to remain competitive as an employer in the area. These job options will enable Equip to increase productivity and will therefore be cost effective. In addition, Equip can train its employees so they are multiskilled and can adapt to new conditions and technology, which will increase productivity.

Case Study Business Writing Assignment: Memorandum

This activity provides practice in writing business letters and memos with a communicative focus. Examples of the standard formats for business letters and memos are in Appendix G.

Write a memo from Tom Jacobson to the employees of Equip, Inc., describing the labor shortage and decrease in productivity and asking for their input on establishing flexible work arrangements and job options at the company. Tom should request that employees suggest the job options that they would prefer.

Format:
I. Introduction (Background and Main Idea)
II. Discussion (Request for Suggestions)
III. Closing (Thanks for Cooperation)

Style: Informal and personal
Tone: Friendly and optimistic

Additional Reading

The second reading presents the subject of the primary reading from a different perspective, thus broadening your knowledge of the topic.

"Hold That Body Count!"
A. Gary Shilling
Forbes 145 (January 22, 1990): 150

MONEY & INVESTMENTS

Here's why the much-heralded labor shortages of the 1990s won't happen.

HOLD THAT BODY COUNT!

By A. Gary Shilling

"Labor shortages in the 1990s," scream today's headlines. And why not, with the labor force likely to rise around 1% per year, only about half of the last decade's growth rate. The low-birthrate generation that followed the bulge of postwar babies are now the new job seekers. The pool of older women who entered the work force in droves in the last two decades is nearly exhausted.

But don't panic over finding enough people to staff your expanding business in the 1990s. The number of people available for work is only part of the story. The rest is how efficiently they work, their productivity.

Productivity growth was miserable in the 1970s. The postwar babies entered the labor force in droves as raw and inefficient recruits. The work ethic went to hell. The uncertain business environment and inflation lured many away from productivity-enhancing capital investments and into real estate and commodities speculation. From 1973 to 1980, manufacturing productivity grew only 1.2% per year,

A. Gary Shilling is president of A. Gary Shilling & Co., economic consultants and asset managers. His firm publishes Insight, *a monthly newsletter covering the business outlook and investment strategy.*

compared with the long-term trend of 2.8%. Service industries had even worse performance, 0.5% annually, versus the 2.2% trend.

That's changing. Productivity has been picking up again, at least in manufacturing. In the 1980s we had a more stable economy, less inflation, a reviving work ethic, more experienced postwar babies and, most of all, the challenge of intense international competition. These factors combined to stimulate the first major productivity-enhancing efforts since the 1930s in manufacturing. Productivity there has grown 4.1% per year in the current expansion that started in late 1982, well above trend.

Contrast this excellent 4.1% rate, however, with the far slower rate of productivity improvement in service businesses. Nonmanufacturing output per hour has languished at a pathetic 1.1% rate.

With little service productivity growth, the principal way of expanding output has been to add more bodies. Politicians love to take credit for an 18.2 million increase in jobs in this decade, but in the service businesses firms essentially have been digging the Grand Canyon with millions of people equipped only with picks and shovels—more production but achieved by the brute-force technique of adding bodies, rather than by improving efficiency.

The opportunities to improve service productivity through office automation, better management, etc. are tremendous, even without an increase in the skills of the rank and file. The pressures to get that improvement will come from the customers, themselves facing ex-

cruciating global competition. A manufacturer can be doing a bang-up job of raising his own productivity, but if hospitals and MDs have no productivity growth to hold down the costs of his medical benefits, he can't compete internationally.

Furthermore, with the globalization of almost everything, service industries from finance to airlines are now experiencing direct international competition. And the deregulation of banking, trucking, telecommunications and other service industries has freshened the bracing winds of competition, forcing companies like AT&T and U.S. West to slash their work forces to dramatically improve productivity.

A speedup in productivity growth means that fewer additional service workers will be hired. If nonmanufacturing productivity had grown on trend in the last decade, 7.6 million, not 18.2 million, jobs would have been created, and the current unemployment rate would be an incredible 13%, not 5.4%. And if overall productivity growth in the next ten years averages 2%, even a bit below the trend rate of 2.3%, the unemployment rate will still average about 10%. Wow!

So forget about labor shortages in the 1990s. Any slowdown in the labor supply will be more than compensated for by increased use of machinery and computers, and by people working better and smarter. Remember that in the 1950s and 1960s labor shortages were few despite a strong economy. Why? Because productivity was growing fast. We're in for a similar period in the Nineties.

If labor shortages are unlikely in the next decade, a lot of potential disruptions go away. A "Mommy Track" in your business will not become a necessity. Contrary to what feminist Felice Schwartz argues, you won't need to hire part-time or flex-time women who choose their own working hours in order to get enough skilled people to staff your business. And if your business is service oriented, you probably won't need as many people as you thought. Your customers and competitors will be applying so much heat that you will do everything possible to avoid adding more bodies, and getting more work out of those you already support. Every manager, every business person will be part of a great productivity enhancement machine. That or go out of business. ∎

Chapter 2

"Making Time to Manage"

Robert C. Dorney

Preview

Skimming. Skim the article quickly to find the following general information.

1. Read the author's name, the title, all headings, and graphic aids.

2. Read the first and second paragraphs, looking for the author's purpose and main idea.

3. Read the last paragraph, looking for a summary or conclusion.

Questioning. Answer the following questions and discuss your answers in class.

1. What does "making time" mean?

2. Do you know how you spend your time?

3. Are you always in a hurry, do you procrastinate, or are you in control of your time?

Scanning. Scan the article quickly to find the following specific information.

1. What did Charlemagne use to apportion his time as Holy Roman Emperor?

2. What is the most difficult part of managing one's time?

3. Who developed the 80-20 principle?

4. What is the executive's greatest need and privilege?

Vocabulary in Context. Read the following sentences and try to guess the meaning of the italicized words by using the context. Then replace the italicized words with synonyms (words or phrases that have nearly the same or similar meanings).

Harvard Business Review 66, no. 1 (January-February 1988)

1. "Most know what they ought to be doing; they may even *allocate* blocks of time to specified tasks. But that's not the same as *getting on with* them."

2. "I *submit* a *corollary*: most people don't know what their time is worth."

3. "I reflected that he was not only interrupting himself but also creating *chaos* in his office. That this could happen in Japan, that *exemplar* of efficiency and enlightened management, astounded me."

4. "It is a *truism* that many chief executives spend much of their time in their previous *function*."

5. "While marketing clearly bears directly on the company's future, the *criterion* for CEO involvement is not just importance. The *overriding* question is: Can someone do the job better?"

Making Time to Manage

by ROBERT C. DORNEY

Time management is more about management than about time.

1 Being a naturally disorganized person, I suppose it was inevitable that I should become president of a company dedicated to helping executives organize their work and plan their time.

2 I am no longer president, but in the 40 years I served in that capacity, time management became an accepted technique for focusing executive energy on the most important tasks. Hewlett-Packard AT&T, Marriott, Xerox, and a host of other companies give employees instruction in time management, particularly those moving into supervisory positions. The reason is very simple: the more responsibility people have, the more valuable their time and the more difficult the time-juggling act becomes.

3 The idea of time management is so widely accepted that it appears in many places. In the comics, Cathy tries it in an effort to bring order to her life. In Madonna's latest film, her suitor throws his diary into a ditch to symbolize his adoption of a more spontaneous life-style. *Money* magazine includes time management tools among the props that not-so-busy people use to create the opposite impression.

4 The idea goes far back in history too. Charlemagne is supposed to have used striped candles to help him apportion his time among his various duties as Holy Roman emperor. Napoleon habitually refused to answer his correspondence for six months on the assumption that it posed problems that would go away if he ignored them. Thus he saved himself untold hours solving problems for subordinates.

5 "Time management is a little like statistics," Stuart Smith, director of management development at Laventhal & Horwath, told me recently. "They're necessary and good, but only when linked to relevant functions. I find in teaching statistics that students cross the boredom barrier when I cross the relevance threshold. We therefore include time management in our training, but not as a separate discipline. We fold it into our curriculum of management skills. This connects it to the achievement of goals and the ordering of priorities."

6 Is it possible that some executives scorn time management because they fail to see its relevance? But if the achievement of goals and the ordering of priorities are managerial functions (and who would deny it?), the relevance is clear. The more valuable a person's time, the more carefully the spending of it needs scrutiny.

7 If asked, very few executives could say how they spend their time. Most know what they *ought* to be doing; they may even allocate blocks of time to specified tasks. But that's not the same as getting on with them.

8 I submit a corollary: most people don't know what their time is worth. It's simple enough to take your annual salary, add 40% or thereabouts for perks and benefits, and then divide the sum by 2,000 or some other number of hours to come up with an hourly rate. The *Exhibit* demonstrates the value – or at least the price – of executive time. Knowledge of the big numbers might encourage some executives to abandon trivial tasks and get on with running the enterprise.

Associated since 1947 with Day-Timers, Inc., a producer of self-organization systems for managers, Robert C. Dorney was president until early in 1987, when he stepped down to become senior vice president and director of product development. In 1972, Day-Timers was acquired by Beatrice Companies, then became part of E-II Holdings Inc. when that corporation was formed in 1986.

9 On the other hand, it might contribute to stress. An executive might say to herself anxiously, "Am I really worth $168.27 an hour when I'm reading a trade magazine?" The answer is "probably not." But I doubt that that realization would induce her to spend more time managing (whatever that means) if she were not already so disposed.

Focus on the second word

10 Time management is more about management than about time. Writing everything down in a planner or diary may inspire a feeling of ineffable virtue and even well-being. But if you're tracking activities you shouldn't be involved in at all, you aren't managing your time.

11 Unless you keep records, it's easy to think you are managing, planning, organizing, and setting goals, when in fact you may be spending most of your hours putting out fires, solving problems for subordinates, or worse, creating problems for your subordinates.

12 In Japan recently, I drove around Tokyo with an extremely successful Japanese businessman. Every time he had an idea, he called his office on his cellular phone. I reflected that he was not only interrupting himself but also creating chaos in his office. That this could happen in Japan, that exemplar of efficiency and enlightened management, astounded me.

13 As a student of Japanese business and culture, I'm emboldened to dispel my own astonishment: while the Japanese are very efficient in production, very precise in market analysis, and adept in statistical process control, they aren't very well organized. They make up for this deficiency by working extremely hard—harder, it's been noted often and with some asperity, than their American counterparts. Their keen interest in and enthusiasm for time management may have severe consequences for our trade deficit if it helps them further boost their efficiency.

Balancing act

14 Balancing is the most difficult part of managing one's own time. What meetings should I attend, which should I skip? Must I read all these reports? Should every important customer have access to my ear? What's important for me to know firsthand, and what can I delegate to others, is hard to pinpoint.

15 I used to set Saturdays aside for product development, the part of my job I liked most. So I enjoyed working Saturdays until my son started playing football at a university three hours distant. To see him play, I had to leave Friday afternoon. That ended Saturdays devoted to work. I had to rearrange my entire weekly schedule to include product de-

velopment, and that forced me to analyze where and how I was spending my time.

16 That analysis eventually brought me to place a value on my every activity. Some of them justified a valuation several times that of others. While product development justified five times my hourly rate, obviously I couldn't spend all my time on it. What was equally obvious, I had to limit the time I spent on less important work that didn't merit half my hourly rate.

17 The answer lay in allocating time to the various activities so that when I multiplied the hours devoted to each one by the hourly rate assigned to it, the total would be one that my board of directors and I could live with.

18 Most readers will recognize this as yet another application of Italian economist Vilfredo Pareto's 80-20 principle. Only instead of applying it to taxation of the "vital few" who pay 80% of the taxes, I apply it to the significant functions that produce 80% or more of the return while still giving the "trivial many" the time they are worth.

19 The arenas I operated in, besides product development, included these:

Selecting and training a successor
Long-range planning
Short-range planning
Reviewing budgets
Conducting staff meetings
Talking with customers
Reviewing senior staff performance
Delegating
Community activities
Facilities planning
Meeting suppliers
Reading mail
Reading professional journals
Recreation

20 I assigned the highest value (5) to those activities that have a

EXHIBIT	**What Is the Price of Executive Time?**					
Annual Salary	Weekly Salary	Benefits (40% of Weekly Salary)	Total Week	Value/ Hour*	Value/ Minute
$ 50,000	$ 961.54	$ 384.62	$1,346.16	$ 33.65	$0.56
60,000	1,153.85	461.54	1,615.39	40.38	0.67
75,000	1,442.31	576.93	2,019.24	50.48	0.84
100,000	1,923.08	769.23	2,692.31	67.31	1.12
250,000	4,807.70	1,923.08	6,730.78	168.27	2.80

*40-hour week

direct bearing on the company's future. They numbered only two: choosing and training my successor, and product development. Now, some might question the president's deep involvement in product development. And rightly so. But it depends on how important new products are to ensure the company's continued good health. The criterion I apply is: Can anyone else do it as well? Having settled that question with my usual modesty, I acknowledged that in an ideal world I would find and train a good engineer to direct product development.

21 It is a truism that many chief executives spend much of their time in their previous function. A president out of engineering tends to hang around the engineering department. A president from advertising tends to rewrite copy and fret over layouts—which is exactly where he or she should spend the least amount of time. Having expertise in the field

> **Delegating is the executive's greatest need—and greatest privilege.**

should enable the president to judge the work of that department with dispatch and precision. When an engineer-president reviews engineering, his or her expertise warrants assignment of the highest value to that time. But the instant the president sits down at a CAD terminal, the value drops to the rate paid those engaged in computer-assisted design.

22 And another point: the hourly value of an activity varies inversely with the amount of time spent. The reason is that as an ac-

tivity takes over a president's time, it tends to become an end in itself, an activity with little or no benefit. This applies even to a CEO's most important responsibility, planning. Plans should be blueprints for action, not a way to fill a bookshelf with impressive binders without issue.

Who can do it better?

23 Delegating is the executive's greatest need as well as greatest privilege. Most of it, of course, should happen automatically. Reviewing a market plan, say, is a function of the marketing vice president, not that person's boss. The act of delegating rates a value of 3, and that only when applying structure to a totally new responsibility.

24 While marketing clearly bears directly on the company's future, the criterion for CEO involvement is not just importance. The overriding question is: Can someone do the job better? Today, even strategic planning has become a delegated function. Value factors must therefore satisfy both criteria before the chief enters the picture.

25 Which brings me back to balancing. How can you control the demands made on you, the interruptions, the upward delegation, the unwanted invitations? There are ways to limit your involvement. Let me give an example. My name is known to many of our customers because it appears in most of our company literature. So I get myriads of phone calls from customers with suggestions or complaints. A certain amount of time I spend that way, though I assign it a value of 1, is productive. At some point, though, its value benefit vanishes.

26 I have a way to satisfy the customer and spare my time. The technique is less important than the purpose, which is to assign responsibility. When I learn what's

on the customer's mind, I say, "I want someone else to hear this too." I dial up a conference call, stay on for a few seconds, and then explain that Ms. So-and-So knows far more about this matter than I do and will take care of it.

27 The question of who can do it better also applies to the time-monitoring task. To focus on things they have identified as having the greatest impact on the future of their companies, many CEOs I have talked to keep detailed records of their daily activities. Some then dictate that record to a secretary or executive assistant. It's a laborious, boring, and time-consuming task. But they are convinced they have to do it to keep their priorities straight.

28 I'd go a step further. A CEO needs someone of unquestioned loyalty and discretion to monitor his or her activities against the template of differential values. I see two advantages to this tactic: it relieves the chief of the bothersome task of logging time and it offers the CEO a more detached view of how well the objective is being met.

29 While most companies have stated priorities and goals, it's a common lament that they are not consistently addressed. They become mere articles of faith, often repeated but not vigorously pursued.

30 Placing higher values on those activities that serve stated priorities and promise to achieve stated goals provides a means of measuring executive performance. Executives who consistently ask themselves, "Did I earn my salary today?" and have developed a quantitative method for answering that question should have the motivation necessary to make sure it is answered affirmatively. ▽

Reprint 88104

Glossary

adept	proficient, highly skilled
allocate	to distribute for a specific purpose, to apportion
apportion	to divide according to a plan—to make a proportionate distribution
asperity	harshness, roughness of manner
bearing	relation, connection
boost	to push upwards
chaos	state of confusion
corollary	a proposition that follows from another that has been proved; an inference or deduction
criterion	standard on which judgment is based
differential	difference between comparable things
discretion	ability to make responsible decisions, quality of being discreet
dispatch	efficient speed, promptness
dispel	to scatter, drive away
ditch	long narrow excavation dug in the earth
emboldened	filled with courage or boldness
enlightened	instructed, freed from ignorance
exemplar	an ideal model
expertise	skill, knowledge, judgment of an expert
fret	to worry
function	occupation, position
induce	to move by persuasion or influence, to cause
ineffable	incapable of being expressed in words, indescribable
inevitable	incapable of being avoided or evaded
inversely	opposite in effect, order
issue	result, consequence
juggling	keeping several objects in motion in the air at the same time
laborious	involving hard work
lament	complaint
logging	entering details of daily activities in a record book; keeping records of daily activities
merit	to be worthy of, to deserve
myriads	a great number
overriding	dominating, prevailing
perks	privileges above regular salary, resulting from one's position
pinpoint	to locate with great precision or accuracy
posed	presented for consideration
props	supports, things that sustain or support
spare	to avoid using, save
spontaneous	acting in accordance with natural feeling, impulse
submit	to suggest, propose, offer
suitor	a man courting a woman
template	pattern used as a guide
threshold	the point of beginning—point at which an effect begins to be produced

tracking	following, observing
trivial	of little importance, ordinary
truism	self-evident truth
untold	too numerous to count
warrants	guarantees, authorizes, justifies

Vocabulary

Without referring to the article, fill in the blanks in the following sentences with the correct words from this list. You may change the tense, number, or form of the words to fit the context. Use each word only once; not all of the words on the list will be used.

corollary   trivial   allocate   induce   chaos   apportion   laborious
discretion   merit   logging   criterion   myriad   adept   inversely

1. Although executives often _____ time to certain tasks, they may not actually do them.

2. Various techniques can be adopted by executives who are interested in _____ their time efficiently so that they do not spend valuable time on _____ tasks.

3. People may not be _____ to manage their time more effectively even if they know what their time is worth.

4. Having to answer _____ of phone calls can be unproductive, cause _____ in your daily schedule, and be a time waster.

5. It is surprising that the Japanese, who are very _____ in statistical process control and precise in market analysis, are sometimes disorganized.

6. You must learn to limit the time spent on activities that don't _____ your hourly rate of pay.

7. In delegation of responsibility, the _____ to be applied is: Can anyone else do this as well as I can?

8. A principle of time management is that the hourly value of an activity varies _____ with the amount of time spent.

9. The _____ task of _____ your time to analyze how it is being spent must be done if you want to improve time management.

Idioms and Expressions

Read the paragraphs in which the following italicized idioms and expressions are found. Then circle the letter next to the answer that best describes the meaning of the idiom as used in the context of the article.

1. "Knowledge of the big numbers might encourage some executives to abandon trivial tasks and *get on with* running the enterprise." (Paragraph 8)
   a. turn their attention to
   b. put off
   c. think about

2. "... you may be spending most of your hours *putting out fires*...." (Paragraph 11)
   a. refusing offers of help
   b. completing projects
   c. solving problems

3. "They *make up* for this deficiency by working extremely hard...." (Paragraph 13)
   a. apologize
   b. substitute
   c. compensate

4. "What meetings should I attend, which should I *skip*?" (Paragraph 14)
   a. emphasize
   b. not attend
   c. reschedule

5. "Should every important customer *have access to my ear*?" (Paragraph 14)
   a. be allowed to talk to me
   b. be allowed to telephone me
   c. be allowed to argue with me

6. "... the total would be one that my board of directors and I *could live with*." (Paragraph 17)
   a. could choose to ignore
   b. could accept as reasonable
   c. could understand

7. "A president out of engineering tends to *hang around* the engineering department." (Paragraph 21)
   a. stay in the location of
   b. criticize
   c. oversee

8. "Reviewing a market plan, *say,* is a function of the marketing vice president...." (Paragraph 23)
   a. I repeat
   b. I insist
   c. for example

9. "When I learn *what's on the customer's mind* ..." (Paragraph 26)
   a. what the customer is angry about
   b. what the customer wants to discuss
   c. what the customer forgot

10. "But they are convinced they have to do it *to keep their priorities straight*." (Paragraph 27)
    a. to know what is legal
    b. to know what is most important
    c. to understand the rules

Paraphrasing

Read the following sentences carefully, and then rewrite them using your own words. Change the vocabulary and sentence structure, but do not change the author's intended meaning or paraphrase any technical terms. There are several ways of paraphrasing each sentence.

Original: "If asked, very few executives could say how they spend their time."
Paraphrase: How their time is spent is a question most managers could not answer.

1. "The more valuable a person's time, the more carefully the spending of it needs scrutiny." (Paragraph 6)

   _____

   _____

2. "That this could happen in Japan, that exemplar of efficiency and enlightened management, astounded me." (Paragraph 12)

   _____

   _____

3. "I assigned the highest value to those activities that have a direct bearing on the company's future." (Paragraph 20)

   _____

   _____

4. "A CEO needs someone of unquestioned loyalty and discretion to monitor his or her activities against the template of differential values." (Paragraph 28)

   _____

   _____

Comprehension

Answer the following questions by finding the relevant information in the article. Give the numbers of the paragraphs that contain the answers.

1. What is the main idea of this article?

2. Why are companies giving supervisory employees instruction in time management?

3. In what way are time management and statistics similar?

4. Why is time management more about management than about time?

5. What is the 80-20 principle of Vilfredo Pareto?

6. Why should chief executives spend the least amount of time in their previous department?

7. Why does the hourly value of an activity vary inversely with the amount of time spent?

8. What are the two criteria for determining delegation?

9. What are the advantages of having a CEO's activities monitored by a loyal employee?

10. How can executives measure their performance?

Inference/Interpretation

Circle the letter next to the best answer. Choose your answer according to the meaning the author suggests but does not state explicitly.

1. It can be inferred from the article that writing all your daily activities down in a planner or diary (Paragraph 10)
   a. is essential to good time management.
   b. should be avoided at all cost.
   c. may not result in good time management.
   d. may help you feel good about yourself.

2. Which of the following statements about Vilfredo Pareto's principle can be inferred? (Paragraph 18)
   a. 80% of the functions produce 20% of the return.
   b. 80% of the people pay 20% of the taxes.
   c. 20% of taxes come from 20% of the people.
   d. 20% of your daily activities produce 80% of the return.

3. It can be inferred from the article that developing a quantitative method for answering the question "Did I earn my salary today" involves (Paragraph 30)
   a. determining the hourly value of an activity and how much time is spent on it.
   b. delegating responsibility to others.
   c. monitoring daily activities.
   d. planning and organizing.

4. Read the following sentence carefully: "*Money* magazine includes time management tools among the props that not-so-busy people use to create the opposite impression." (Paragraph 3) Explain what "the opposite impression" means.

   _____

   _____

Structure

Circle the letter next to the correct answer(s). More than one answer may be correct. Be prepared to explain and justify your choices.

1. In which paragraph(s) is the main idea stated?
   a. Paragraph 2
   b. Paragraph 6
   c. Paragraph 17
   d. Paragraph 22
   e. Paragraph 30
   Write a paraphrase of the main idea in *one* sentence, using your own words as much as possible.

   _____

2. Why does Dorney use irony in the first sentence of the article?
   a. To emphasize the main argument
   b. To establish the author's credibility
   c. To confuse the reader
   d. To make a humorous statement of contrast
   e. To establish an academic tone
   Rewrite this sentence in a direct way, without using irony.

   _____

3. Where does Dorney use specific examples to support a general idea?
   a. Paragraphs 3–4
   b. Paragraphs 7–8
   c. Paragraph 12
   d. Paragraph 22
   e. Paragraphs 25–26

4. Where is cause and effect development used to support a general idea?
   a. Paragraph 14
   b. Paragraph 15
   c. Paragraph 22
   d. Paragraph 23
   e. Paragraph 27

5. Where is comparison used to develop a paragraph?
   a. Paragraph 5
   b. Paragraph 8
   c. Paragraph 10
   d. Paragraph 14
   e. Paragraph 24

Explain what Stuart Smith means by "Students cross the boredom barrier when I cross the relevance threshold."

_____

6. What overall method of development is used in this article?
   a. Evaluating a controversial proposal
   b. Supporting an unusual argument
   c. Describing a chronological process
   d. Explaining a quantitative method
   e. Defining a technological problem

Style

Circle the letter next to the correct answer(s). More than one answer may be correct. Be prepared to justify your choices by giving specific examples from the article.

1. How would you describe the writing style of the author?
   a. Technical
   b. Literary
   c. Personal
   d. Conversational
   e. Bureaucratic
   f. Informal

2. How would you describe the tone of the article?
   a. Balanced
   b. Negative
   c. Disapproving
   d. Authoritative
   e. Humorous
   f. Positive

3. The author's attitude toward executives who look down on time management is
   a. unrealistic.
   b. realistic.
   c. critical.
   d. supportive.
   e. condescending.
   f. angry.

4. Dorney begins paragraph 22 with a sentence fragment rather than a complete sentence: "And another point:" Why does he use a fragment rather than a complete sentence? Rewrite this fragment as a complete sentence.

Discussion

1. Do you think that time management is a skill that needs to be taught, or can most people learn this skill by themselves?

2. Explain Dorney's statement that "balancing is the most difficult part of managing one's own time." How well do you balance your time?

3. The Pareto principle, commonly called the 80-20 rule, states that 80% of the value comes from 20% of the activities. Explain why the Pareto principle should be applied to time management and give an example of it.

4. Why is keeping a time log of daily activities a necessary step in becoming an effective manager of time?

5. How would determining the hourly value of every activity motivate an executive to be a better manager of time?

6. How does the American attitude toward time differ from the attitude toward time in your country in regard to business and social interactions?

Research Assignment

Look up several of these articles in the library. Choose one article to read and take notes on.

Allen, Jane Elizabeth. "Tips on Using Psychology to Deal with Disorganization." *Washington Post* (June 11, 1990): Washington Business Section, 6.

Ashkenas, Ronald N., and Robert H. Schaffer. "Managers Can Avoid Wasting Time." *Harvard Business Review* 60 (May-June 1982): 98–104.

Barkas, Jan L. "How to Stop Postponing Your Life." *Working Woman* (May 1985): 31–32.

Bartolomé, Fernando. "The Work Alibi: When It's Harder to Go Home." *Harvard Business Review* 61 (March-April 1983): 66–75.

Calonius, Erik. "How Top Managers Manage Their Time." *Fortune* 121(June 4, 1990): 250–62.

Calonius, Erik. "The Trouble with Time Management Courses." *Fortune* 121 (June 4, 1990): 262.

Colano, Jimmy, and Jeff Salzman. "How to Get More Done in a Day." *Working Woman* (April 1988): 99–100.

Collier, E. M. "Read This Article Immediately." *Nation's Business* 77 (October 1989): 68.

Dumaine, B. "How Managers Can Succeed through Speed." *Fortune* 119 (February 13, 1989): 54–57.

Jay, Antony. "How to Run a Meeting." *Harvard Business Review* 54 (March-April 1976): 43–57.

Jones, Curtis H. "The Money Value of Time." *Harvard Business Review* 46 (July-August 1968): 94–101.

Kiechel, W. "12 Reasons for Leaving at Five." *Fortune* 122 (July 16, 1990): 117–18.

Kiechel, W. "Workaholics Anonymous." *Fortune* 120 (August 14, 1989): 117–18.

Moore, Leo B. "Managerial Time." *Sloan Management Review* 10 (Spring 1968): 77–85.

Samuelson, Robert J. "Rediscovering the Rat Race." *Newsweek* 113 (May 15, 1989): 57.

Schaffer, Robert H. "Demand Better Results—and Get Them." *Harvard Business Review* 69 (March-April 1991): 142–49.

Symonds, W. C. "No, They Can't Stop Time, but They Can Help You Manage It." *Business Week* (May 22, 1989): 178–79.

Taylor, A. L., III. "How a Top Boss Manages His Day." *Fortune* 119 (June 19, 1989): 95–97.

Thompson, R. "Take Charge of Your Job." *Nation's Business* 77 (April 1989): 36–37.

Warshaw, Robin. "Why It's So Hard to Get Any Work Done." *Working Woman* (August 1986): 68–71.

Oral Presentation

Working with a partner, give a fifteen-minute oral presentation to the class on the additional reading in this chapter or the article that you chose in the research assignment. Include the author's main idea, major points, and some supporting data. Be prepared to answer questions on your topic. (See Appendix B: Giving an Oral Presentation.)

Writing Assignments

1. Analyze your allocation of time by keeping a time log for three days. Write down everything you do in twenty-four hours. After evaluating your activities, assign priorities to your responsibilities and tasks by numbering them 1 (least important) to 5 (most important). Then draw up a projected daily schedule based on allocating the most time to the most important tasks and using your most productive hours of the day for high-priority tasks.

2. Write an essay analyzing the problems of time management that were revealed by your time log (writing assignment 1) and offering solutions to these problems. List your greatest time-wasters and causes of inefficient time management. Organize your essay according to the problem and solution method of development. Also use cause and effect development.

3. Make a schedule of how you would spend an ideal twenty-four hours. List your activities and the length of time you would allocate to each of them.

Case Study: A Problem in Time Management

Working in groups, read the following case study. Discuss the problem, answer the questions, and write a brief report on how your group would solve the problem. (Choose one member of the group to do the writing.) Follow the format in Appendix E (Case Study Report) in writing your report.

Andrew Baker is the CEO (Chief Executive Officer) of Castle Computer Corporation, a successful computer company.* He is well known in the computer field as a brilliant and creative executive, but he is also known as a disorganized and last minute-type person, perhaps because he is a procrastinator. As a result, company employees are always in a state of confusion and instability, and deadlines for production schedules are almost never met. The fourth-quarter earnings statement has just come out, and profits are way down.

Deborah Jackson, who has been Mr. Baker's executive assistant for one year, recently attended a two-day time management workshop. She had hoped to discuss the concepts of effective time management with Mr. Baker, but when she brought up the subject, he laughed and said time management was the least of *his* problems. He was working on a plan for test-marketing the new Castle laptop computer, which Marcia Lee, the Marketing and Sales Vice President, had asked him to revise. In addition, he was redesigning the new laser printer that the Research and Development Division had just developed, and solving a personnel problem that the Director of Human Resources and Administration had brought to him.

Castle Computer Corporation Organization Chart

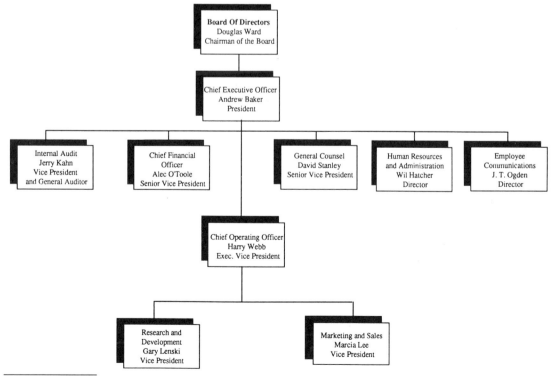

*See Organization Chart of Castle Computer Corporation.

Deborah knows that Mr. Baker, who has been with the company since its founding, likes to keep an eye on every department and stay in daily contact with all his division managers. However, she can see the results of Mr. Baker's "micromanagement" style and poor time management. In fact, she is considering asking for a meeting with the Chief Operating Officer of Castle Computer Corporation, Harry Webb, to voice her concerns about the future of the company under Mr. Baker's leadership. Although Deborah has a great deal of respect for Mr. Baker, she is completely worn out from her daily struggle to keep him on schedule. If only Mr. Baker would delegate some of his responsibilities and set priorities. In Deborah's eyes, Castle Computer Corporation is being under-led and overmanaged.

Questions

1. Should Deborah meet with the Chief Operating Officer?

2. Should Deborah talk to Mr. Baker once again about time management?

3. What methods could Deborah suggest to improve Mr. Baker's time management?

4. How could Deborah convince Mr. Baker of the importance of time management?

Solution: Case Study Report

  I. Define and analyze the problem.
 II. Suggest possible solutions.
III. Evaluate possible solutions.
IV. Select a solution.

Case Study Business Writing Assignment: Memorandum

Write a memo from Deborah Jackson to Andrew Baker, CEO of Castle Computer Corporation. The memo should summarize the major concepts Deborah learned from her time management workshop and convey her suggestion that more effective time management is needed at Castle Computer Corporation.

    Format:
           I. Introduction (Background and Main Idea)
         II. Discussion (Time Management Concepts)
      III. Closing (Suggestion)

    Style: Informal
    Tone: Conversational and enthusiastic

Additional Reading

"Management Time: Who's Got the Monkey?"
William Oncken, Jr., and Donald L. Wass
Harvard Business Review 52 (November-December 1974): 75–80

Management time: Who's got the monkey?

An analogy that underscores the value of assigning, delegating, and controlling

William Oncken, Jr. and Donald L. Wass

In any organization, the manager's bosses, peers, and subordinates–in return for their active support–impose some requirements, just as the manager imposes some requirements upon them where they are drawing upon his or her support. These demands constitute so much of the manager's time that successful leadership hinges on an ability to control this "monkey-on-the-back" input effectively.

Mr. Oncken is chairman of the board, The William Oncken Company of Texas, Inc., a management consulting firm. Mr. Wass is president of this company.

Why is it that managers are typically running out of time while their subordinates are typically running out of work? In this article, we shall explore the meaning of management time as it relates to the interaction between managers and their bosses, their own peers, and their subordinates.

Specifically, we shall deal with three different kinds of management time:

Boss-imposed time—to accomplish those activities which the boss requires and which the manager cannot disregard without direct and swift penalty.

System-imposed time—to accommodate those requests to the manager for active support from his or her peers. This assistance must also be provided lest there be penalties, though not always direct or swift.

Self-imposed time—to do those things which the manager originates or agrees to do. A certain portion of this kind of time, however, will be taken by subordinates and is called "subordinate-imposed time." The remaining portion will be his or her own and is called "discretionary time." Self-imposed time is not subject to penalty since neither the boss nor the system can discipline the manager for not doing what they did not know the manager had intended to do in the first place.

The management of time necessitates that managers get control over the timing and content of what they do. Since what their bosses and the system impose on them are backed up by penalty, managers cannot tamper with those requirements. Thus their self-imposed time becomes their major area of concern.

The managers' strategy is therefore to increase the "discretionary" component of their self-imposed time by minimizing or doing away with the "subordinate" component. They will then use the added increment to get better control over their boss-imposed and system-imposed activities. Most managers spend much more subordinate-imposed time than they even faintly realize. Hence we shall use a monkey-on-the-back analogy to examine how subordinate-imposed time comes into being and what the superior can do about it.

Where is the monkey?

Let us imagine that a manager is walking down the hall and that he notices one of his subordinates, Jones, coming up the hallway. When they are abreast of one another, Jones greets the manager with, "Good morning. By the way, we've got a problem. You see . . ." As Jones continues, the manager recognizes in this problem the same two characteristics common to all the problems his subordinates gratuitously bring to his attention. Namely, the manager knows (a) enough to get involved, but (b) not enough to make the on-the-spot decision expected of him. Eventually, the manager says, "So glad you brought this up. I'm in a rush right now. Meanwhile, let me think about it and I'll let you know." Then he and Jones part company.

Let us analyze what has just happened. Before the two of them met, on whose back was the "monkey"? The subordinate's. After they parted, on whose back was it? The manager's. Subordinate-imposed time begins the moment a monkey successfully executes a leap from the back of a subordinate to the back of his or her superior and does not end until the monkey is returned to its proper owner for care and feeding.

In accepting the monkey, the manager has voluntarily assumed a position subordinate to his subordinate. That is, he has allowed Jones to make him her subordinate by doing two things a subordinate is generally expected to do for a boss—the manager has accepted a responsibility from his subordinate, and the manager has promised her a progress report.

The subordinate, to make sure the manager does not miss this point, will later stick her head in the manager's office and cheerily query, "How's it coming?" (This is called "supervision.")

Or let us imagine again, in concluding a working conference with another subordinate, Johnson, the manager's parting words are, "Fine. Send me a memo on that."

Let us analyze this one. The monkey is now on the subordinate's back because the next move is his, but it is poised for a leap. Watch that monkey. Johnson dutifully writes the requested memo and drops it in his outbasket. Shortly thereafter, the manager plucks it from his inbasket and reads it. Whose move is it now? The manager's. If he does not make that move soon, he will get a follow-up memo from the subordinate (this is another form of supervision). The longer the manager delays, the more frustrated the subordinate will become (he'll be "spinning his wheels") and the more guilty the manager will feel (his backlog of subordinate-imposed time will be mounting).

Or suppose once again that at a meeting with a third subordinate, Smith, the manager agrees to provide all the necessary backing for a public relations proposal he has just asked Smith to develop. The manager's parting words to her are, "Just let me know how I can help."

Now let us analyze this. Here the monkey is initially on the subordinate's back. But for how long? Smith realizes that she cannot let the manager "know" until her proposal has the manager's approval. And from experience, she also realizes that her proposal will likely be sitting in the manager's briefcase for weeks waiting for him to eventually get to it. Who's really got the monkey? Who will be checking up on whom? Wheelspinning and bottlenecking are on their way again.

A fourth subordinate, Reed, has just been transferred from another part of the company in order to launch and eventually manage a newly created business venture. The manager has said that they should get together soon to hammer out a set of objectives for the new job, and that "I will draw up an initial draft for discussion with you."

Let us analyze this one, too. The subordinate has the new job (by formal assignment) and the full responsibility (by formal delegation), but the manager has the next move. Until he makes it, he will

have the monkey and the subordinate will be immobilized.

Why does it all happen? Because in each instance the manager and the subordinate assume at the outset, wittingly or unwittingly, that the matter under consideration is a joint problem. The monkey in each case begins its career astride both their backs. All it has to do now is move the wrong leg, and—presto—the subordinate deftly disappears. The manager is thus left with another acquisition to his menagerie. Of course, monkeys can be trained not to move the wrong leg. But it is easier to prevent them from straddling backs in the first place.

Who is working for whom?

To make what follows more credible, let us suppose that these same four subordinates are so thoughtful and considerate of the superior's time that they are at pains to allow no more than three monkeys to leap from each of their backs to his in any one day. In a five-day week, the manager will have picked up 60 screaming monkeys—far too many to do anything about individually. So he spends the subordinate-imposed time juggling his "priorities."

Late Friday afternoon, the manager is in his office with the door closed for privacy in order to contemplate the situation, while his subordinates are waiting outside to get a last chance before the weekend to remind him that he will have to "fish or cut bait." Imagine what they are saying to each other about the manager as they wait: "What a bottleneck. He just can't make up his mind. How anyone ever got that high up in our company without being able to make a decision we'll never know."

Worst of all, the reason the manager cannot make any of these "next moves" is that his time is almost entirely eaten up in meeting his own boss-imposed and system-imposed requirements. To get control of these, he needs discretionary time that is in turn denied him when he is preoccupied with all these monkeys. The manager is caught in a vicious circle.

But time is a-wasting (an understatement). The manager calls his secretary on the intercom and instructs her to tell his subordinates that he will be unavailable to see them until Monday morning. At

7:00 p.m., he drives home, intending with firm resolve to return to the office tomorrow to get caught up over the weekend. He returns bright and early the next day only to see, on the nearest green of the golf course across from his office window, a foursome. Guess who?

That does it. He now knows *who* is really working for *whom*. Moreover, he now sees that if he actually accomplishes during this weekend what he came to accomplish, his subordinates' morale will go up so sharply that they will each raise the limit on the number of monkeys they will let jump from their backs to his. In short, he now sees, with the clarity of a revelation on a mountaintop, that the more he gets caught up, the more he will fall behind.

He leaves the office with the speed of a person running away from a plague. His plan? To get caught up on something else he hasn't had time for in years: a weekend with his family. (This is one of the many varieties of discretionary time.)

Sunday night he enjoys ten hours of sweet, untroubled slumber, because he has clear-cut plans for Monday. He is going to get rid of his subordinate-imposed time. In exchange, he will get an equal amount of discretionary time, part of which he will spend with his subordinates to see that they learn the difficult but rewarding managerial art called, "The Care and Feeding of Monkeys."

The manager will also have plenty of discretionary time left over for getting control of the timing and content not only of his boss-imposed time but of his system-imposed time as well. All of this may take months, but compared with the way things have been, the rewards will be enormous. His ultimate objective is to manage his management time.

Getting rid of the monkeys

The manager returns to the office Monday morning just late enough to permit his four subordinates to collect in his outer office waiting to see him about their monkeys. He calls them in, one by one. The purpose of each interview is to take a monkey, place it on the desk between them, and figure out together how the next move might conceivably be the subordinate's. For certain monkeys, this will take some doing. The subordinate's next move may be so elusive that the manager may decide—just for now—merely to let the monkey sleep on the subordinate's back overnight and have him or her return with it at an appointed time the next morning to continue the joint quest for a more substantive move by the subordinate. (Monkeys sleep just as soundly overnight on subordinates' backs as on superiors'.)

As each subordinate leaves the office, the manager is rewarded by the sight of a monkey leaving his office on the subordinate's back. For the next 24 hours, the subordinate will not be waiting for the manager; instead, the manager will be waiting for the subordinate.

Later, as if to remind himself that there is no law against his engaging in a constructive exercise in the interim, the manager strolls by the subordinate's office, sticks his head in the door, and cheerily asks, "How's it coming?" (The time consumed in doing this is discretionary for the manager and boss-imposed for the subordinate.)

When the subordinate (with the monkey on his or her back) and the manager meet at the appointed hour the next day, the manager explains the ground rules in words to this effect:

"At no time while I am helping you with this or any other problem will your problem become my problem. The instant your problem becomes mine, you will no longer have a problem. I cannot help a person who hasn't got a problem.

"When this meeting is over, the problem will leave this office exactly the way it came in—on your back. You may ask my help at any appointed time, and we will make a joint determination of what the next move will be and who will make it.

"In those rare instances where the next move turns out to be mine, you and I will determine it together. I will not make any move alone."

The manager follows this same line of thought with each subordinate until at about 11:00 a.m. he realizes that he has no need to shut his door. His monkeys are gone. They will return—but by appointment only. His appointment calendar will assure this.

Transferring the initiative

What we have been driving at in this monkey-on-the-back analogy is to transfer initiative from superior to subordinate and keep it there. We have tried to highlight a truism as obvious as it is subtle. Namely, before developing initiative in subordinates, the manager must see to it that they *have* the initiative. Once he or she takes it back, they will no longer have it and the discretionary time can be kissed good-bye. It will all revert to subordinate-imposed time.

Nor can both manager and subordinate effectively have the same initiative at the same time. The opener, "Boss, we've got a problem," implies this duality and represents, as noted earlier, a monkey astride two backs, which is a very bad way to start a monkey on its career.

Let us, therefore, take a few moments to examine what we prefer to call "The Anatomy of Managerial Initiative."

There are five degrees of initiative that the manager can exercise in relation to the boss and to the system: (1) *wait* until told (lowest initiative); (2) *ask* what to do; (3) *recommend*, then take resulting action; (4) *act*, but advise at once; and (5) *act* on own, then routinely report (highest initiative).

Clearly, the manager should be professional enough not to indulge in initiatives 1 and 2 in relation either to the boss or to the system. A manager who uses initiative 1 has no control over either the timing or content of boss-imposed or system-imposed time, and thereby forfeits any right to complain about what he or she is told to do or when. The manager who uses initiative 2 has control over the timing but not over the content. Initiatives 3, 4, and 5 leave the manager in control of both, with the greatest control being at level 5.

The manager's job, in relation to subordinates' initiatives, is twofold; first, to outlaw the use of initiatives 1 and 2, thus giving subordinates no choice but to learn and master "Completed Staff Work"; then, to see that for each problem leaving the office there is an agreed-upon level of initiative assigned to it, in addition to the agreed-upon time and place of the next manager-subordinate conference. The latter should be duly noted on the manager's appointment calendar.

Care & feeding of monkeys

In order to further clarify our analogy between the monkey-on-the-back and the well-known processes of assigning and controlling, we shall refer briefly to the manager's appointment schedule, which calls for five hard and fast rules governing the "Care and Feeding of Monkeys" (violations of these rules will cost discretionary time):

Rule 1
Monkeys should be fed or shot. Otherwise, they will starve to death and the manager will waste valuable time on postmortems or attempted resurrections.

Rule 2
The monkey population should be kept below the maximum number the manager has time to feed. Subordinates will find time to work as many monkeys as he or she finds time to feed, but no more. It shouldn't take more than 5 to 15 minutes to feed a properly prepared monkey.

Rule 3
Monkeys should be fed by appointment only. The manager should not have to be hunting down starving monkeys and feeding them on a catch-as-catch-can basis.

Rule 4
Monkeys should be fed face to face or by telephone, but never by mail. (If by mail, the next move will be the manager's—remember?) Documentation may add to the feeding process, but it cannot take the place of feeding.

Rule 5
Every monkey should have an assigned "next feeding time" and "degree of initiative." These may be revised at any time by mutual consent, but never allowed to become vague or indefinite. Otherwise, the monkey will either starve to death or wind up on the manager's back.

Concluding note

"Get control over the timing and content of what you do" is appropriate advice for managing management time. The first order of business is for the manager to enlarge his or her discretionary time by eliminating subordinate-imposed time. The second is for the manager to use a portion of this new-found discretionary time to see to it that each subordinate possesses the initiative without which he or she cannot exercise initiative, and then to see to it that this initiative is in fact taken. The third is for the manager to use another portion of the increased discretionary time to get and keep control of the timing and content of both boss-imposed and system-imposed time.

The result of all this is that the manager's leverage will increase, in turn enabling the value of each hour spent in managing management time to multiply, without theoretical limit.

The woods are full of them.

Quoted by Alexander Wilson,
American Ornithology (1808);
preface

Chapter 3

"Ethics and Competitiveness— Putting First Things First"

John F. Akers

Preview

Skimming. Skim the article quickly to find the following general information.

1. Read the author's name, the title, and all headings.

2. Read the abstract and first and second paragraphs, looking for the author's purpose and main idea.

3. Read the last two paragraphs, looking for a summary or conclusion.

Questioning. Answer the following questions and discuss your answers in class.

1. What does *ethics* mean to you?

2. What does "Putting First Things First" mean?

3. How are ethics and competitiveness related?

Scanning. Scan the article quickly to find the following specific information.

1. Who said that all human beings are endowed with a moral sense?

2. What is the most powerful ethical buttress?

3. Why is a $30-million endowment being given to Harvard Business School?

4. Whose example should we never forget?

Sloan Management Review 30, no. 2 (Winter 1989)

Vocabulary in Context. Read the following sentences and try to guess the meaning of the italicized words by using the context. Then replace the italicized words with synonyms (words or phrases that have the same or similar meanings).

1. "First, we should *fortify* the practical ethical *buttresses* that help all of us—from childhood on—know and understand and do exactly what is required of us."

2. "It is *naive* to believe these buttresses will solve all our problems. But it is equally naive to expect ethical behavior to occur *in the absence of* clear requirements and consequences."

3. "What bothers me is that they have missed the *humane* lessons in individual ethical conduct that we find in the *annals* of world history, the biographies of great men and women, and the works of supreme imaginative literature."

4. "But the *good* of an entire society *transcends* that of any single corporation. The moral order of the world transcends any single nation-state."

5. "To something greater than themselves—to a new nation 'conceived in liberty and dedicated to the *proposition* that all men are created equal'— to that concept they pledged all *subordinate* things—their lives, their fortunes, and their sacred honor."

Ethics and Competitiveness — Putting First Things First

John F. Akers

IBM Corporation

JOHN AKERS, CHAIRMAN OF THE BOARD OF IBM, argues that business ethics are a key component of our competitiveness as a society. How can we ensure that we work in an atmosphere characterized by mutual trust and confidence? Although business schools can and should engage in some forms of ethical instruction, the work cannot begin — or end — there. Instruction must begin in childhood and encompass such practical devices as role models and codes of conduct; it must include a demanding study of history and literature; and above all it must recognize business's proper place within a greater hierarchy. *Ed.*

Sloan
Management
Review

Winter 1989

1 I SHOULD LIKE to consider a subject central to international economic competitiveness: ethics. Let me urge at the outset that all of us in management look at both these words — ethics and competitiveness — with a wide angle of vision. When we think of competitiveness we should think not just as Americans, Europeans, or Japanese seeking our own selfish beggar-thy-neighbor advantage, but as managers striving to succeed in an increasingly interdependent world, with the potential for improved living standards for all. And when we think of ethics, we should think not just as managers focusing on a narrow preserve labeled business ethics, but as citizens of a larger society.

2 Ethics and competitiveness are inseparable. We compete as a society. No society anywhere will compete very long or successfully with people stabbing each other in the back; with people trying to steal from each other; with everything requiring notarized confirmation because you can't trust the other fellow; with every little squabble ending in litigation; and with government writing reams of regulatory legislation, tying business hand and foot to keep it honest.

3 That is a recipe not only for headaches in running a company; it is a recipe for a nation to become wasteful, inefficient, and noncompetitive. There is no escaping this fact: the greater the measure of mutual trust and confidence in the ethics of a society, the greater its economic strength.

4 I do not say the sky is falling here in the United States. I do not think we had a great ethical height

in the good old days from which we've been tumbling downhill. We do face ethical and competitive problems, to be sure. We have all been reading about religious leaders who steal from their congregations, Wall Street brokers who profit from their insider status, assorted politicians and influence peddlers, law students who plagiarize, medical professors who falsify their research results, and Pentagon employees who sell classified information. But most of us can agree with Thomas Jefferson that all human beings are endowed with a moral sense — that the average farmer behind a plow can decide a moral question as well as a university professor. Like Jefferson, we can have confidence in the man in the street, whether that street is in Armonk, San Francisco, or Cambridge — or in London, Paris, or Tokyo.

5 That common moral sense, however, does not come out of nowhere or perpetuate itself automatically. Every generation must keep it alive and flourishing. All of us can think of means to this end. Here are three suggestions.

Ethical Buttresses

6 First, we should fortify the practical ethical buttresses that help all of us — from childhood on — know and understand and do exactly what is required of us. The simplest and most powerful buttress is the role model: parents and others who by precept and example set us straight on good and evil, right and wrong. Of all the role models in

Ethics and Competitiveness

Akers

John F. Akers is Chairman of the Board, President, and Chief Executive Officer of IBM Corporation. He is also Chairman of the Corporate Management Board and of IBM's Management Committee. Mr. Akers holds the B.S. degree from Yale University. He is a director of the board of the New York Times Company, co-chairman of the Business Roundtable, and a member of the board of trustees of the Metropolitan Museum of Art and of the California Institute of Technology.

my own life, I think perhaps the most durable is my grandfather—a flinty New England headmaster whose portrait hangs in my home. To this day, whenever I go by it I check the knot in my tie and stiffen my backbone.

7   There are many other ethical buttresses. Some, despite condescending sophisticates, are simple credos: "A Scout is trustworthy, loyal, helpful, friendly, courteous, kind, obedient, cheerful, thrifty, brave, clean, and reverent"; or "a cadet will not lie, cheat or steal or tolerate those who do." There are institutionalized buttresses like the honor system, by which college students police themselves—no plagiarism, no cheating on examinations. I find it ludicrous that even divinity schools and law schools and departments of philosophy—not to mention other parts of the university—have to pay proctors to pad up and down the aisles at examination time to make sure nobody is looking at crib notes or copying from a neighbor. A century and a half after Jefferson introduced the honor system at the University of Virginia, it is unfortunate that every college and university in America has not yet adopted it.

8   Finally there are professional standards and business codes of conduct, which spell out strict policies on such things as insider trading, gifts and entertainment, kickbacks, and conflicts of interest.

9   It is naive to believe these buttresses will solve all our problems. But it is equally naive to expect ethical behavior to occur in the absence of clear requirements and consequences.

Can Our Schools Teach Ethics?

10 The time has come to take a hard look at ethical teaching in our schools—and I don't just mean graduate schools of business. We know John Shad is giving the Harvard Business School most of a $30-million endowment to be devoted to studying and teaching ethics. And we know that MIT Sloan School dean Lester Thurow and other educators have openly disagreed with this undertaking.

11 Let's begin by defining what we are talking about. Many businesspeople facing student audiences have been appalled by knee-jerk assertions that it is open-and-shut immorality to do business in South Africa, to produce weapons for the military, to decide against setting up a day-care center, to run a nuclear power plant, or even to make a profit. An enormous amount of work needs to be done to help young people think clearly about complex

questions like these, which defy pseudomoralistic answers. They require instead incisive definition and analysis, and a clear-headed understanding of a company's sometimes conflicting responsibilities—to its employees, its stockholders, and its country. And these responsibilities often require some agonizingly difficult choices.

12 I wholeheartedly favor ethical instruction—in a business school or anywhere else in the university—that strengthens such analytical capabilities. I also favor ethical examination of workplace safety, consumer protection, environmental safeguards, and the rights of the individual employee within the organization.

13 But recall what Samuel Johnson once said: If a person doesn't know the difference between good and evil, "when he leaves our house, let us count our spoons." If an MBA candidate doesn't know the difference between honesty and crime, between lying and telling the truth, then business school, in all probability, will not produce a born-again convert.

14 Elementary, grass-roots instruction on why it is bad to sneak, cheat, or steal—such instruction in a school of business administration is much too little, far too late. That's not the place to start. The place to start is kindergarten.

15 There are, to be sure, vexing constitutional and other problems over prayer in the classroom. But we need not wait for the debate to end—if it ever does—before we begin to reinvigorate ethical instruction in our schools. We can start now, in kindergarten through twelfth grade, and not by feeding our children some vague abstractions called "values." I mean we should start with a clear-cut study of the past. Our ethical standards come out of the past—out of our inheritance as a people: religious, philosophical, historical. And the more we know of that past, the more surefootedly we can inculcate ethical conduct in the future.

16 If you want to know about Tammy Bakker, Senator Daniel Patrick Moynihan says, read Sinclair Lewis; if you want to know about insider trading, read Ida Tarbell. If you want to know what it is like to operate in a jungle where the individual predator profits as society suffers, read Thomas Hobbes and John Locke. If you want to understand the conflict between the demands of the organization and the conscience of the individual, read Thoreau on civil disobedience and Sophocles's *Antigone*. If you want to know about civility, read the words of Confucius. And if you want to know about cour-

We need not wait for the school prayer debate to end — if it ever does — before we begin to reinvigorate ethical instruction in our schools.

age, temperance, truthfulness, and justice, read Aristotle or the Bible.

17　When I hear reports that American high-school students know little or nothing about Chaucer or Walt Whitman or the Civil War or the Old Testament prophets, what bothers me most is not that they exhibit intellectual ignorance. What bothers me is that they have missed the humane lessons in individual ethical conduct that we find in the annals of world history, the biographies of great men and women, and the works of supreme imaginative literature.

18　A great classical writer once defined history as "philosophy learned from example." And a distinguished Brattle Street resident of Cambridge, Henry Wadsworth Longfellow, gave us this eloquent summary:

> Lives of great men all remind us
> We can make our lives sublime,
> And departing, leave behind us
> Footprints on the sands of time.

First Things First

19 My third suggestion is this: let's keep our sense of order straight. Let's put first things first.

20　We have all heard shortsighted businesspeople attribute a quotation to Vince Lombardi: "Winning is not the most important thing; it's the *only* thing." That's a good quotation for firing up a team, but as a business philosophy it is sheer nonsense. There is another, much better Lombardi quotation. He once said he expected his players to have three kinds of loyalty: to God, to their families, and to the Green Bay Packers, "in that order."

21　He knew that some things count more than others. Businessmen and women can be unabashedly proud of their companies. But the good

of an entire society transcends that of any single corporation. The moral order of the world transcends any single nation-state. And one cannot be a good business leader — or a good doctor or lawyer or engineer — without understanding the place of business in the greater scheme of things.

22　There is an incandescent example of a group who understood this fact: who saw life steadily, saw it whole, and saw it in a hierarchy — the delegates who drafted the U.S. Constitution in Philadelphia 200 years ago. What do we remember the oldest of them — Benjamin Franklin — for? Not for his vigorous advice on how to get up early in the morning, drive a business, make a profit, and win success in the marketplace, though he did all these things with gusto. We remember him and the others in Philadelphia — and those who signed the Declaration of Independence — because they did not see winning or self-advancement or even life itself as the *only* thing. To something greater than themselves — to a new nation "conceived in liberty and dedicated to the proposition that all men are created equal" — to that concept they pledged all subordinate things — their lives, their fortunes, and their sacred honor.

23　We should never forget their example.

So there are three suggestions:

• Fortify our ethical buttresses — role models, codes of conduct, the honor system.

• Reinvigorate our children's study of the past.

• Keep our priorities straight.

24　If we do these things, we shall go far toward discharging our responsibilities as managers and as human beings: contribute to our countries' strengths, heighten their capacity for leadership in an increasingly competitive and productive world, and keep them on the right track as we close out this century and enter the twenty-first. ■

Sloan
Management
Review

Winter 1989

Glossary

abstractions	ideas, unrealistic notions
annals	historical records
born-again	having a new, strong belief in some principle
buttresses	supports or reinforcements
cadet	student at a military school
civility	politeness
clear-headed	lucid, unconfused, rational
condescending	proud or haughty
credos	brief statements of beliefs or principles
crib notes	notes used dishonestly in doing school work or taking tests
durable	lasting, stable
eloquent	fluent, persuasive
endowment	gift that provides an income for an institution or person
ethics	code of morals of a person, religion, group, or profession; guidelines for conduct
flinty	extremely hard and firm
fortify	to make strong or stronger, strengthen
good	welfare, what is morally right
grass-roots	basic, fundamental
gusto	keen enjoyment
hierarchy	system in graded ranks
humane	civilizing, humanizing
in the absence of	without
incandescent	very bright, glowing
incisive	sharp, acute, penetrating
inculcate	to impress upon the mind
insider trading	trading of stocks and bonds based on confidential information from corporation employees who have private knowledge of financial developments before they become public knowledge
kickbacks	payments received as bribes
litigation	lawsuit
ludicrous	absurd or ridiculous
moral	relating to the principles of right and wrong
naive	foolishly simple, unsophisticated
notarized	certified by a notary public
pad	to walk with a soft step
perpetuate	to cause to continue or be remembered
plagiarism	taking ideas or writings from another person and passing them off as one's own
plow	farm implement to cut and break up the soil
police	to control, protect, keep orderly
precept	rule of moral conduct
predator	person who lives by capturing and feeding upon others
preserve	place treated as the special domain of a person or group

priorities	items of importance
proctors	persons who supervise examinations
proposition	proposal, statement
pseudomoralistic	falscly ethical
reams	great amount (500 sheets of paper = one ream)
reinvigorate	to fill with energy again, enliven
reverent	very respectful
role model	a person who is effective or inspiring in some social role and serves as a model for others
Scout	member of Boy Scouts or Girl Scouts
shortsighted	lacking foresight
squabble	petty quarrel or dispute
stiffen	to make or become rigid, firm, inflexible
sublime	noble, majestic
subordinate	secondary
surefootedly	not likely to make a mistake
temperance	moderation, self-restraint in conduct
transcends	surpasses, exceeds
tumbling	falling suddenly and clumsily
unabashedly	unashamedly, without shame
vexing	disturbing, annoying

Vocabulary

Without referring to the article, fill in the blanks in the following sentences with the correct words from this list. You may change the tense, number, or form of the words to fit the context. Use each word only once; not all of the words on the list will be used.

litigation	perpetuate	precept	ludicrous	kickback	naive
inculcate	priority	abstraction	transcend	hierarchy	incisive
ethics	insider trading				

1. Because of the decrease in honesty and trust among people, _____ has become a common method of solving disagreements in American society today.

2. We cannot expect morality and _____ to _____ themselves automatically without support from formal and informal education.

3. Our parents and other role models offer us many _____ about how to live life morally.

4. It seems _____ that so much cheating occurs, even in divinity and law schools in the United States.

5. Although it is illegal, taking _____ sometimes occurs in government contracting when a contractor gives money to the government official to influence his or her decision.

6. Only a(n) _____ person believes that ethical behavior is a natural part of human beings and needs no reinforcement from codes of conduct or education.

7. Vague _____ will not be effective in teaching ethical behavior to young people; on the contrary, concrete examples and _____ analysis are necessary.

8. Loyalty to our society as a whole should _____ loyalty to an individual company.

9. Businessmen and businesswomen must see life as a(n) _____ of moral values, not as pure competition.

10. People in the business world need to have their _____ in the right order if they want to succeed as managers and as human beings.

Idioms and Expressions

Read the paragraphs in which the following italicized idioms and expressions are found. Then circle the letter next to the answer that best describes the meaning of the idiom as used in the context of the article.

1. When we think of competitiveness we should think not just as Americans, Europeans, or Japanese seeking our own *beggar-thy-neighbor* advantage. . . ." (Paragraph 1)
   a. begging from others
   b. ruining others
   c. treating neighbors poorly

2. "No society anywhere will compete very long or successfully with people *stabbing each other in the back*. . . ." (Paragraph 2)
   a. cheating and deceiving each other
   b. murdering each other
   c. playing jokes on each other

3. ". . . government writing reams of regulatory legislation, *tying* business *hand and foot* to keep it honest." (Paragraph 2)
   a. tightly limiting
   b. pulling in several directions
   c. punishing

4. "I do not say *the sky is falling* here in the United States." (Paragraph 4)
   a. the economy is weakening
   b. the society is breaking down
   c. a catastrophe is occurring

5. "I do not think we had a great ethical height in *the good old days*. . . ." (Paragraph 4)
   a. the idealized past
   b. the recent past
   c. biblical times

6. "That common moral sense, however, does not *come out of nowhere . . . ."* (Paragraph 5)
   a. depend on location
   b. lack a connection
   c. have a connection with morality

7. ". . . parents and others who by precept and example *set us straight* on good and evil, right and wrong." (Paragraph 6)
   a. guide us
   b. tell us what is correct
   c. mislead us

8. "Many businesspeople facing student audiences have been appalled by *knee-jerk* assertions. . . ." (Paragraph 11)
   a. automatic and unthinking
   b. very strong
   c. very weak

9. ". . . that it is *open-and-shut* immorality to do business in South Africa. . ." (Paragraph 11)
   a. secret
   b. changeable
   c. unarguable

10. ". . . keep them *on the right track* as we close out this century and enter the twenty-first." (Paragraph 24)
    a. moving straight ahead
    b. behaving mechanically
    c. moving in the right ethical direction

Paraphrasing

Read the following sentences carefully, and then rewrite them using your own words. Change the vocabulary and sentence structure, but do not change the author's intended meaning or paraphrase any technical terms. There are several ways of paraphrasing each sentence.

Original: "And the more we know of that past, the more surefootedly we can inculcate ethical conduct in the future."

Paraphrase: If we understand our past history, we will be better able to teach moral behavior in the future.

1. "That common moral sense, however, does not come out of nowhere or perpetuate itself automatically." (Paragraph 5)

_____

_____

2. "But it is equally naive to expect ethical behavior to occur in the absence of clear requirements or consequences." (Paragraph 9)

   _____

   _____

3. "That's a good quotation for firing up a team, but as a business philosophy it is sheer nonsense." (Paragraph 20)

   _____

   _____

4. "He knew that some things count more than others." (Paragraph 21)

   _____

   _____

Comprehension

Answer the following questions by finding the relevant information in the article. Give the numbers
of the paragraphs that contain the answers.

1. What is the main idea of this article?

2. Why are ethics and competitiveness inseparable?

3. What three suggestions does Akers offer to keep the moral sense alive?

4. What are ethical buttresses and which ones does Akers describe?

5. When should instruction in ethical conduct begin, and on what should it be based?

6. Why should students study history, biography, and literature?

7. What does Akers mean by keeping our priorities straight and putting first things first?

8. Why is Vince Lombardi's quotation "Winning is not the most important thing, it is the _only_
   thing" nonsense as a business philosophy?

9. What do the delegates who drafted the U.S. Constitution exemplify to Akers?

10. What will result from following Akers's suggestions?

Inference/Interpretation

Circle the letter next to the best answer. Choose your answer according to the meaning the author
suggests but does not state explicitly.

1. What does Akers mean by the phrase "a wide angle of vision"? (Paragraph 1)
   a. A national perspective on business competition and ethics.
   b. A global perspective on business competition and ethics.
   c. A corporate perspective on business competition and ethics.
   d. A biased perspective on business competition and ethics.

2. Which of the following sentences about Samuel Johnson's statement can be inferred? (Paragraph 13)
   a. Human nature is basically good.
   b. All people have a tendency to steal and cheat.
   c. People don't know the difference between good and evil.
   d. People who haven't been taught moral behavior can't be trusted to behave morally.

3. What can we infer from a great classical writer's statement that history is "philosophy learned from example"? (Paragraph 18)
   a. History and philosophy are basically the same subjects.
   b. The past teaches us how to live ethically in the present.
   c. History involves a philosophical approach to life.
   d. Philosophy can only be developed from examples.

4. What is the main idea of Longfellow's poem? (Paragraph 18)
   a. The study of famous poetry is essential.
   b. The study of the past helps us solve our modern problems.
   c. The study of great men of the past can make us immortal.
   d. The study of great men of the past can enrich our lives.
   Explain the meaning of Longfellow's line of poetry: "Footprints on the sands of time." (Paragraph 18)

   _____

   _____

Structure

Circle the letter next to the correct answer(s). More than one answer may be correct. Be prepared to explain and justify your choices.

1. In which paragraph(s) is the main idea stated?
   a. Paragraph 1
   b. Paragraph 2
   c. Paragraph 3
   d. Paragraph 4
   e. Paragraph 5
   Write a paraphrase of the main idea in *one* sentence, using your own words as much as possible.

   _____

2. What techniques does Akers use to get the reader's attention in the introduction? (Paragraphs 1–5)
   a. Quotations
   b. Questions
   c. Negative statements
   d. Universalizing
   e. Repetition

3. Where does Akers use specific examples as a method of development of his general ideas?
   a. Paragraph 4
   b. Paragraph 5
   c. Paragraphs 6–7
   d. Paragraph 12
   e. Paragraph 22

4. Where does Akers use cause and effect development to support his thesis?
   a. Paragraphs 2–3
   b. Paragraphs 10–11
   c. Paragraph 16
   d. Paragraph 20
   e. Paragraph 24
   What are the causes and what are the effects?

   _____

5. What overall method of development is used in this article?
   a. Supporting an argument by enumerating specific proposals
   b. Attacking the assumptions of an argument
   c. Chronologically describing a problem
   d. Evaluating the advantages and disadvantages of a plan
   e. Defining a new method

Style

Circle the letter next to the correct answer(s). More than one answer may be correct. Be prepared to justify your choices by giving specific examples from the article.

1. How would you describe the writing style of the author?
   a. Very informal
   b. Somewhat formal
   c. Technical
   d. Poetic
   e. Bureaucratic
   f. Personal

2. What words best describe the tone of the article?
    a. Ironic
    b. Humorous
    c. Scholarly
    d. Serious
    e. Authoritative
    f. Tentative

3. The author's attitude toward today's high school students can be described as
    a. approving.
    b. disapproving.
    c. angry.
    d. condescending.
    e. positive.
    f. indifferent.

4. The author uses complex grammatical structures in the following sentence: "To something greater than themselves—to a new nation 'conceived in liberty and dedicated to the proposition that all men are created equal'—to that concept they pledged all subordinate things—their lives, their fortunes, and their sacred honor." (Paragraph 22) What contrast is the author making?
    a. "Something greater than themselves" is contrasted with "all subordinate things."
    b. "Their lives" is contrasted with "their sacred honor."
    c. "A new nation . . ." is contrasted with "their lives, their fortunes, and their sacred honor
    Rewrite this sentence in a simple style.

_____

_____

Discussion

1. Do you agree with Akers that ethics should be studied in school? Why or why not? Have you studied ethics in school?

2. When should the formal teaching of ethics begin—in elementary school, high school, or college?

3. Can someone who has a college degree in business be an ethical businessperson without having studied the history, philosophy, and literature of the past?

4. Is the study of religion sufficient for ethical behavior, or is the study of philosophy, history, biography, and literature also necessary? Why or why not?

5. Are all human beings born with a moral sense and, therefore, able to behave morally without formal education in moral values?

6. Akers mentions the following writers and philosophers in his article: Samuel Johnson, Sinclair Lewis, Ida Tarbell, Thomas Hobbes, John Locke, Henry Thoreau, Sophocles, Aristotle, Confucius, Chaucer, Walt Whitman, Henry Longfellow, and Benjamin Franklin. Which have you heard of? Which have you read?

Research Assignment

Look up several of these articles in the library. Choose one article to read and take notes on.

Andrews, Kenneth R. "Ethics in Practice." *Harvard Business Review* 67 (September-October 1989): 99–104.

Bruner, Robert F., and Lynn Sharp Paine. "Management Buyouts and Managerial Ethics." *California Management Review 30* (Winter 1988): 89–104.

Cadbury, Sir Adrian. "Ethical Managers Make Their Own Rules." *Harvard Business Review* 65 (September-October 1987): 69–73.

"Case Study in Caring." *Economist* 312 (September 30, 1989): 27.

Dolecheck, Maynard M., James Caldwell, and Carolyn C. Dolecheck. "Ethical Perceptions and Attitudes of Business Personnel." *American Business Review* (January 1988): 47–54.

Dolecheck, Maynard M., and Carolyn C. Dolecheck. "Ethics: Take It from the Top." *Business* 39 (January-February-March 1989): 12–18.

"Ethics Are Nice, but They Can Be a Handicap Some Executives Declare." *Wall Street Journal* (September 8, 1987): 1.

Finn, D. "Who Needs Poetry?" *Harvard Business Review* 67 (July-August 1989): 184–85.

Gellerman, Saul W. "Managing Ethics from the Top Down." *Sloan Management Review* 30 (Winter 1989): 73–79.

Gellerman, Saul W. "Why 'Good' Managers Make Bad Ethical Choices." *Harvard Business Review* 64 (July-August 1986): 85–90.

Goodpaster, Kenneth, and John Mathews. "Can a Corporation Have a Conscience?" *Harvard Business Review 60* (January-February 1982): 132–41.

Koepp, Stephen. "Having It All, Then Throwing It All Away." *Time* (May 25, 1987): 23.

Murphy, Patrick E. "Creating Ethical Corporate Structures." *Sloan Management Review* 30 (Winter 1989): 81–87.

Raelin, J. A. "Professional and Business Ethics: Bridging the Gap." *Management Review* 78 (November 1989): 39–42.

Robin, Donald P., and Eric Reidenbach. "Balancing Corporate Profits and Ethics: A Matrix Approach." *Business* 40 (October-November-December 1990): 11–15.

Silk, Leonard. "Does Morality Have a Place in the Boardroom?" *Business Month* 134 (October 1989): 11–13.

Sterngold, James. "Hardball on Wall Street." *New York Times Magazine* (August 16, 1987): 22ff.

Tidwell, G. L. "Here's a Tip—Know the Rules of Insider Trading." *Sloan Management Review* 28 (Summer 1987): 93–99.

Vitell, S. J., and T. A. Festervand. "Business Ethics: Conflicts, Practices and Beliefs of Industrial Executives." *Journal of Business Ethics* (May 1987): 116.

"Would You Blow Whistle on Wayward Colleague?" *American Banker* 153 (June 17, 1988): 16.

Oral Presentation

Give a ten-minute oral presentation to the class on the article that you chose in the research assignment. Include the author's main idea, major points, and some supporting data. Be prepared to answer questions on your topic. (See Appendix B: Giving an Oral Presentation.)

Writing Assignments

1. Write a 300-word summary of Aker's article. Be objective. Do not include your opinion or any extraneous information.

2. Discuss an ethical problem in business in your country. Use cause and effect organization of your ideas. What were the causes and effects of this problem? Did it have an impact on international competition?

3. Describe a person who has been an important role model for you. Why is this person important in your life? What have you learned from him or her?

Case Study: A Problem in Ethics

Working in groups, read the following case study. Discuss the problem, answer the questions, and write a brief report on how your group would solve the problem. (Choose one member of the group to do the writing.) Follow the format in Appendix E (Case Study Report) in writing your report.

Henry Lewis is the manager of the menswear department at Wallingham's. He prides himself on running an efficient department and considers himself an excellent judge of people. Currently, he is trying to fill the position of buyer for menswear, which has been unfilled since his buyer moved to California three months ago. However, he is having trouble deciding between the two finalists for the position. Both are his employees in the menswear department and have first-rate qualifications.

Mary O'Malley has been with Wallingham's for almost one year. She is highly motivated, hard-working, and experienced in the retail clothing business. She is the top salesperson in the department. John Conway has been with Wallingham's for two years and is very reliable, competent, and conscientious. He considers Henry Lewis his mentor at Wallingham's. Henry has been in a quandry for two weeks about whether to promote John or Mary to the buyer position.

Yesterday, John came to talk with Henry. He told Henry that he went out for a few drinks with Mary after work on Friday, and she revealed that she had been a drug abuser and had once been arrested for possession of cocaine, although now she was in a treatment program for recovering addicts. She said she had lied on her employment application to Wallingham's and begged John not to tell anyone about her secret. Nevertheless, John said he felt ethically compelled to tell Henry the truth about Mary because of the company's strict policy on maintaining a drug-free workplace.

Henry was shocked to hear this and told John that he would look into the problem. Then, because of his blinding headache, he took sick leave for the rest of the day and went home. But that night, Henry had trouble sleeping. Could John be spreading rumors about Mary in order to win the promotion? John knew that he and Mary were the two finalists for the position, and perhaps ambition was driving him to behave unscrupulously. Or was Mary really a drug addict, a person of weak character and immoral behavior? How could he have misjudged them? Henry had to find a way to settle this dilemma.

Questions

1. Should Henry Lewis ignore John's comments about Mary and consider them unfounded allegations?

2. Should Henry question John in more detail concerning his allegations about Mary?

3. Should Henry talk privately with Mary about her alleged drug use?

4. How can Henry decide on the best candidate to fill the position of buyer for the menswear department?

Solution: Case Study Report

   I. Define and analyze the problem.
  II. Suggest possible solutions.
 III. Evaluate possible solutions.
  IV. Select a solution.

Case Study Business Writing Assignment: Memorandum

Write a one-page memo from Henry Lewis, the manager of Wallingham's menswear department, to his employees, explaining the company policy on maintaining a drug-free workplace. The memo should state the policy and several possible courses of action that will be taken if violations are discovered. It should ask for cooperation from all employees in achieving a drug-free workplace.

Format:
      I. Introduction (Background and Main Idea)
     II. Discussion (Statement of Policy)
   III. Closing (Request for Cooperation)

Style: Formal
Tone: Authoritative and factual

Additional Reading

"Classroom Conundrum: Profits + Ethics = ?"
Max M. Thomas
Business Month 135 (February 1990): 6

SPEAKING OUT/MAX M. THOMAS

CLASSROOM CONUNDRUM: PROFITS + ETHICS = ?

THE BEST JOKES DURING MY COLLEGE DAYS EXposed contradictions in everday language: "Military intelligence," "responsible government," and "business ethics" were hilarious examples of social double-talk. Behind our love of oxymorons lay the idealistic conviction that in a more perfect world, business *should* be ethical. But times have changed.

America's youth today doesn't appreciate such ironies or their underlying idealism. Instead, there is a tragic conviction among students that business has no ethical responsibilities beyond the duty to make money.

The hardest job of all for Professor Thomas is convincing his students that there is such a thing as business scruples.

They are often alarmingly naive, assuming that businesspeople are as unconcerned with ethics as astronomers are with commodity prices. They don't even see *business ethics* sardonically, as a contradiction in terms, but innocently, as completely mismatched ideas.

Take the students who step into my business-ethics course on the first day. I commonly hear them say, "I never made a connection between business and ethical behavior" or, "Businesses just don't have the same moral obligations as people do"—as if businesses were divorced from the people who ran them.

Even those students who admit some affinity between business and ethics see the connection in a very limited way. They may venture that "business ethics involves my relationship only with coworkers and bosses" or that "ethics is important only as it affects me and my family." They confuse the affection they feel for their friends and families with ethical duties that apply to customers, the general public, and competitors.

In fact, there has been an explosion of ethical aware-

ness in the business community of late. More industries have created codes of conduct, hired ethics ombudsmen, and provided more ethics workshops for employees than ever before. A 1986 survey by the Center for Business Ethics at Bentley College shows that many corporations "listed the goal of being socially responsible as their primary reason for incorporating ethics into their organizations, rather than simply complying with state and federal requirements."

If today's students are eventually to abet management's new ethical outlook, they must first learn about it. The process of reinstating values education should begin in kindergarten and continue through MBA programs. We can discuss the importance of integrity, kindness, and charity without getting mired in the nastier controversies of abortion, euthanasia, and flag burning. Colleges and universities have a responsibility to make ethics courses a requirement for graduation, just as they do English and math courses.

My courses contain two primary messages. The first is that business professionals have a duty to be ethical. The best way I can get this across is through case studies focused on the difference between economic and ethical liabilities and obligations, which are easily confused in today's business world. The second message is that business leaders today *do* recognize their ethical obligations. Case studies serve me well here, too, to demonstrate just how executives meet ethical challenges.

Can teaching ethics make a discernible difference? I think so. Midway through my course, I distributed to my class copies of the BUSINESS MONTH FaxPoll on ethics. This is a group of students who came into my class with the typical mixture of apathy and innocence. Judging by their responses to the FaxPoll, at least, they have managed to grasp a few nuggets. Nearly all students (87 percent) agreed that "corporate ethics should be as important a priority as profits." More than 90 percent believed it is wrong to lie to the FDA; even the few dissenters argued that lying was acceptable only if it speeded approval of life-saving drugs.

If we are to continue to make ethics a central concern of business, executives must fortify the messages sent by educators. Some companies, such as Dow Corning, send speakers to schools to discuss their particular programs. Campus recruiters can do their part by distributing copies of their companies' codes of conduct. Imagine the impact personnel officers can have by asking prospective employees, Have you taken an ethics course?

Point is, this is a combined effort that needs constant attention. Business cannot underestimate its impact on young minds. Education should provide the framework for ethics, but corporations can add value to those ideas by making them ideals for their future coworkers. ∎

Max M. Thomas, Ph.D., is an assistant professor of philosophy at King's College in Wilkes-Barre, Pennsylvania.

LEIF SKOOGFORS

Chapter 4

"Let's Put Capitalists Back into Capitalism"

Lester C. Thurow

Preview

Skimming. Skim the article quickly to find the following general information.

1. Read the author's name, the title, and all headings.

2. Read the abstract and first and second paragraphs, looking for the author's purpose and main idea.

3. Read the last two paragraphs, looking for a summary or conclusion.

Questioning. Answer the following questions and discuss your answers in class.

1. What does capitalism mean?

2. What is a capitalist?

3. Do you live in a capitalist society?

Scanning. Scan the article quickly to find the following specific information.

1. What has U.S. productivity growth averaged over the past ten years?

2. Why do private firms exist in the United States?

3. What are merchant banks?

4. What do antitrust laws prohibit?

Sloan Management Review 30, no. 1 (Fall 1988)

Vocabulary in Context. Read the following sentences and try to guess the meaning of the italicized words by using the context. Then replace the italicized words with synonyms (words or phrases that have nearly the same or similar meanings).

1. "President Reagan has suggested some *modest* changes, but what's required is a *whole-sale* rethinking of these laws."

2. "How much they can *invest* in any one company is limited by law, as is how actively they can *intervene* in company decision making."

3. "They do not have the *clout* to change business decisions, corporate strategy, or *incumbent* managers with their voting power."

4. "Neither the manager nor the *shareholder* expects to be around very long. And neither has an *incentive* to watch out for the long-term growth of the company."

5. *"Proponents* of the takeover movement would argue that these criticisms miss the point: takeovers enrich shareholders, and firms exist *solely* to serve the interests of the shareholders, they would say."

Let's Put Capitalists Back into Capitalism

Lester C. Thurow   MIT Sloan School of Management

Sloan
Management
Review

Fall 1988

AS ALL THE ARTICLES in this anniversary issue attest, stagnant productivity rates are a major concern for American industry. Noted economist and MIT Sloan School dean Lester Thurow approaches the issue from an unusual angle in this paper. If the largest profits and highest incomes went to those who expanded output rather than to those who rejuggled financial assets, he argues, U.S. productivity levels would quickly rise. He proposes specific, broad-ranging changes in the regulatory framework governing industry and finance that would allow this to occur. *Ed.*

1 WE CALL OURSELVES a capitalist society, but there's something missing. We are rich in financial investors of every size and variety, from the man on the street to the giant pension funds to the get-rich-quick speculators and the takeover artists. We have more corporate managers than we know what to do with—in recent years, the number of private executives has grown far faster than the rate of output has. What we lack are genuine, old-style capitalists—those big investors of yesteryear who often invented the technologies they managed and whose personal wealth was inextricably linked to the destiny of their giant companies.

2 A successful economy is one that generates a rising standard of living for its citizens. To do this it must have a healthy rate of productivity growth. Ours does not. U.S. productivity growth has averaged 0.8 percent over the past ten years and was 0.8 percent in 1987. In our economy, private business is responsible for productivity growth. If productivity is not rising at a healthy rate, then American business is not doing its job.

3 To put it bluntly, American capitalism needs a heart transplant. The financial traders who now control American capitalism need to be taken out and replaced by real capitalists who can become the heart of an industrial rebirth. But the regulations governing industrial organization—mostly antitrust laws and banking regulations—stand in the way. President Reagan has suggested some modest changes, but what's required is a wholesale rethinking of these laws. Our economy must be restructured to regain some semblance of its old-style capitalist energy.

The Problem: No Incentives for Productivity Growth

4 Most big corporations were once run by individual capitalists: by one shareholder with enough stock to dominate the board of directors and to dictate policy, a shareholder who was usually also the chief executive officer. Owning a majority or controlling interest, these capitalists did not have to concentrate on reshuffling assets to fight off raids from financial vikings. They were free to make a living by producing new products or by producing old products more cheaply. Just as important, they were locked into their roles. They could not very well sell out for a quick profit—dumping large stock holdings on the market would have simply depressed the stock's price and cost them their jobs as captains of industry. So instead they sought to enhance their personal wealth by investing—by improving the long-run efficiency and productivity of the company.

5 Today, with very few exceptions, the stock of large U.S. corporations is held by financial institutions such as pension funds, foundations, or mutual funds—*not* by individual shareholders. And these financial institutions cannot legally become real capitalists who control what they own. How much they can invest in any one company is limited by

*Lester C. Thurow is
Dean and Gordon Y
Billard Professor of
Management and Eco-
nomics at the MIT
Sloan School of
Management. Dr.
Thurow holds the
B.A. degree from Wil-
liams College, the
M.A. degree from
Balliol College, Oxford
University, and the
Ph.D. degree from
Harvard University.
His research interests
include public finance,
income distribution eco-
nomics, and produc-
tivity.*

law, as is how actively they can intervene in company decision making.

6   These shareholders and corporate managers have
a very different agenda than dominant capitalists
do, and therein lies the problem. They do not have
the clout to change business decisions, corporate
strategy, or incumbent managers with their voting power. They can enhance their wealth *only* by
buying and selling shares based on what they think
is going to happen to short-term profits. Minority
shareholders have no choice but to be short-term
traders.

7   And since shareholders are by necessity interested
only in short-term trading, it is not surprising that
managers' compensation is based not on long-term
performance, but on current profits or sales.
Managerial compensation packages are completely
congruent with the short-run perspective of short-
run shareholders. Neither the manager nor the
shareholder expects to be around very long. And
neither has an incentive to watch out for the long-
term growth of the company.

8   We need to give managers and shareholders an
incentive to nurture long-term corporate growth—
in other words, to work as hard at enhancing
productivity and output as they now work at improving short-term profitability.

Why Minor Adjustments
Are Insufficient

9   The problem of slow productivity growth will not
be solved by enforcement of existing antitrust laws,
nor by throwing those laws out altogether, nor by
encouragement of aggressive acquisition. Instead,
the entire regulatory framework governing finance
and industry needs to be restructured so that the
biggest profits and highest incomes go to those who
expand output, rather than to those who rejuggle
financial assets.

10   Existing antitrust laws do not encourage productivity, as we have seen, and one could argue that
they are downright harmful. General Motors is permitted to engage in a joint venture with Toyota
that will attack Ford and Chrysler, but not in a
joint venture with Ford that might repel the Japanese auto invasion. Private antitrust suits are now
used as corporate blackmail—which was hardly
what the laws were intended for. And since the
current laws are not enforced by the Reagan administration anyway, no one is really even sure what

the effective antitrust laws *are*.

11   Simply letting the market function without rules
and regulations would not work, however. As the
nineteenth-century robber barons demonstrated,
there are all too often circumstances in which the
most profitable activities lead to contracted output and redistributed earnings. Left to themselves,
unregulated markets will inevitably focus on those
activities—we need look no further than the current financial merger wars for evidence of this pattern. Profit maximization (which firms automatically shoot for, with or without government
regulations) is not a synonym for output expansion.

12   Nor do financial speculations address the problem of slow productivity growth. In fact, they add
to it, since they focus the attention of American
businesspeople on highly profitable activities that
do not lead to industrial growth. When a company is acquired, its shareholders are certainly enriched, but the economy gains nothing. The
productivity assets that the company had are still
there—no bigger and no smaller. A redistributive
activity—not a productive activity—has occurred.

13   In theory the assets might be better managed
by the new owners and hence be more productive, but no one has ever demonstrated that mergers
lead to higher rates of productivity growth for the
assets being reshuffled. (If financial rearrangements
were the route to higher productivity, the United
States would have the highest rate of productivity
growth in the industrial world—not the lowest—
since it has rearranged more financial assets than
any other country in recent decades.)

14   Mergers also load firms up with debt. As a result, there are fewer funds available for investment
in new products, processes, or research and development. Companies are weakened financially and
made more vulnerable to financial collapse in the
next recession, when they might not be able to
meet their interest payments. Consequently, they
become more risk averse—less willing to bet the
company on new activities. The company has effectively already *been* bet.

15   Proponents of the takeover movement would argue that these criticisms miss the point: takeovers
enrich shareholders, and firms exist solely to serve
the interests of the shareholders, they would say.
The enrichment part of the argument is certainly
true—but do firms really exist solely to serve the
shareholders' interests? If this view had been taken
in the past, neither the antitrust laws nor the rules

Finance and industry should not be at arm's length.
They should be so entwined that their destinies
cannot be separated.

regulating the railroads would have been adopted. (There is no doubt that the activities being regulated in those instances enriched shareholders.)

16 Shareholders' rights are not paramount, in point of fact. Private firms exist in our society because collectively we have decided that they are the best way to expand the output available to everyone, shareholder and nonshareholder alike. If private firms fail to serve this social function, they will either be abolished and replaced with something that does serve it, or else they will be redirected (as they have been in the past) with new rules and regulations that attempt to set them off once again on a productive path.

17 To achieve this redirection, real capitalists must be put back into the U.S. economy. And they must be boxed in so that their profit-making energies are focused on activities that raise productivity and output. Realistically, this means creating institutional capitalists, not expanding the supply of individual capitalists. Occasionally a brilliant entrepreneur will nurture a corporation until it becomes one of America's largest, but within one or two generations that corporation, like the rest of U.S. industry, will be without dominant shareholders. Startups are not a substitute for giant corporations that retain their vitality.

Regulatory Changes That Will Improve Productivity Growth

18 Today's short-term financial traders must be remade into tomorrow's long-term capitalistic investors. To accomplish this task, the following major changes should occur.

Get Shareholders Involved . . .

19 • *The legal limits that now prevent financial institutions from acquiring a dominant or majority shareholding position should be removed.*

20 • *Institutions should be encouraged to sit on the boards of directors of companies in which they invest, to actively hire and fire managers, and to worry about the*

strategies that will make their investments successful.

21 • *The regulations that prevent U.S. commercial banks from becoming merchant banks—banks that own and control industrial corporations—should be lifted.* This proposed change deserves some discussion. In much of the rest of the world, the merchant bankers are the industrial capitalists who make the system work. When the Arabs threatened to buy a controlling interest in Mercedes-Benz a few years ago, for example, the Deutsche Bank intervened on behalf of the German economy and bought a controlling interest. The bank now controls the board of directors. It protects the managers of Mercedes-Benz from financial raiders. It frees them from the tyranny of the stock market, with its emphasis on quarterly profits. It helps plan corporate strategies and raises money to carry out those strategies. It also fires managers if the company slips in the auto market, and prevents them from engaging in self-serving activities (such as mergers or golden parachutes) that do not enhance the company's long-term prospects.

22 This path has not always been closed to us. Some of what were once America's most successful companies—General Electric, U.S. Steel, International Harvester—were founded by merchant bankers before this practice was outlawed during the Great Depression.

23 In recent years, small-scale merchant bankers have reappeared in the guise of venture capitalists. They play a vital role in helping companies get started, but when the firms become middle-sized and offer their shares for sale to the public, the venture capitalist drops out, sells the stock, and starts over again with a new company. Venture capitalists are no substitute for merchant banks.

24 • *Today's laws draw too sharp a distinction between loans and equity. The institutions that provide major long-term loans to companies should take an active role in their strategic direction. To bring this about, long-term loans should carry voting rights.* To avoid the appearance of conflict, executives from banks and other leading agencies may now sit on the boards of only those firms to which they have *not* loaned

Sloan
Management
Review

Fall 1988

much money. They are not supposed to be financially involved participants. This rule flies in the face of reason. Why not give long-term lenders voting rights? A $100-million long-term loan might, for example, entitle a lender to half the voting rights of a $100-million long-term equity investment. Major lenders, like equity investors, should not be absentee landlords.

25 As it now stands, bankers exert an influence on the management of a company to which they have loaned money only when the company is failing. How much better it would be if they were to help the corporation avoid mistakes that lead to failure.

Lock Them In . . .

26 We should also ensure that these institutions—or any shareholder with a dominant position in a company—cannot easily extricate themselves from that role. Finance and industry should not be at arm's length. They should be so entwined that their destinies cannot be separated. The United States needs an economy in which finance cannot succeed unless industry succeeds.

27 • *Anyone who holds a dominant position in any company—say, 20 percent or more—should be forced to give the public one day's notice of the intent to sell shares.* While the ownership of a large block of shares constitutes a substantial lock-in all by itself (it is difficult to sell a large number of shares without depressing one's own stock price), this natural lock should be reinforced by requiring notice of intent to sell. Unless the announced sale could be explained to the satisfaction of the investing public on grounds other than expected future failures, any such notice would inevitably trigger a general rush to sell the stock before the major investor could do so, leaving the big investor to sell at much reduced prices. Like the old-time capitalists, he or she would think long and hard before trying to bail out of a troubled company.

28 • *To reinforce the distinction between traders and investors, the voting rights of equity shareholders should increase the longer the shares are held.* Major investors subject to the 20 percent rule would become instant owners, but others would gain full voting rights only over a substantial period of time. No voting rights would be given to those who have owned shares for under two years, perhaps, and full voting rights would gradually be granted over the following three years: in year three, one-third

of a vote for each share held, in year four, two-thirds of a vote for each share held, and in year five, a full vote for each share held.

. . . And Take Away Their Quarterly Statements

29 • *The tyranny of the quarterly profit statement should be abolished.* When Japan resumed control of its economy after the U.S. occupation following World War II, it repealed the law requiring quarterly profit statements and substituted one requiring annual profit statements. The same should be done in the United States. Doing so might not change attitudes all by itself, but it would symbolize what needs to be done.

30 The importance currently granted quarterly profit statements puts managers in absurd and untenable positions. A recent example will illustrate this point. I was consulting for a firm whose cost-cutting program had substantially exceeded expectations. The firm had made 50 percent more money in one quarter than it had expected to make. This good news, learned too near the end of the quarter to be hidden by creative accounting, was treated as a disaster. Management was sure that stock prices would immediately rise and then plunge in the next quarter, since the firm could not possibly duplicate this quarter's performance and so maintain market expectations about future profits. News that was in fact good for the company—and the economy—became bad news because of the short-term focus that quarterly reports reinforce.

31 The quarterly profit statement is supposed to improve the information available to investors. It may do this for short-run stock speculators (although even this is open to doubt, given the volatility of short-run numbers), but from a social point of view there is no payoff to this availability. Not knowing current profits might force short-term investors to understand the firm's technologies and its market position—it might even persuade today's short-term traders that they could make more money by becoming tomorrow's long-term investors.

Conclusion

32 The antitrust laws prohibiting interlocking directorates, joint research, and trading companies were all designed to avoid monopolistic industrial combines. If the same people were planning strategy

in different firms, if products were being developed jointly, or if different firms were selling their products through a common sales organization, then the firms involved would not be totally separate and competitive. Strategies might be coordinated, joint development might lead to joint production, the common salesforce might eventually dominate the producing companies—in other words, de facto mergers might occur. There is some truth to such worries, but they are more than counterbalanced by the competition coming from abroad and the need to cooperate to meet that competition. National antitrust regulations are now simply obsolete. They don't recognize today's realities.

33 Merchant bankers, insurance companies, and pension or mutual funds managers should be encouraged to become capitalists who succeed or fail based on their ability to grow healthy industrial corporations. Their attention should be turned from something that is marginal to America's long-run success—the buying and selling of shares and the rearrangement of corporate financial assets—toward something that is central to U.S. success—the growth of productivity and output.

34 In any reformulation of our antitrust rules, one central goal must be kept in mind: put real capitalists back in charge of the American corporation and then box them in so that they have no choice but to improve the nation's productivity and competitiveness. Link their personal success to their corporation's productivity.

35 Without capitalists, capitalism can only fail. ∎

Sloan
Management
Review

Fall 1988

Glossary

abolished	done away with completely, ended
absentee landlords	landlords who live some distance away from the property they own
acquisition	companies, businesses being acquired
agenda	program of things to be done
antitrust laws	laws regulating trusts, business monopolies, or cartels
averse	reluctant, opposed to, unwilling
blackmail	payment extorted by threatening to disclose information that could bring ruin
bluntly	plainly, with candor
capitalism	economic system in which the means of production and distribution are privately owned and operated for profit under competitive conditions
capitalist	preferring or practicing capitalism
clout	power or influence
congruent	in agreement, harmonious
contracted	reduced, decreased
de facto	existing in actual fact though not by legal establishment
downright	thoroughly, utterly, absolutely
dumping	selling a stock or commodity in a large quantity at a very low price
duplicate	to copy, match, cause to happen again
enhance	to make greater, improve, augment, intensify
entrepreneur	person who organizes and manages a business undertaking, assuming the risk for the sake of a profit
entwined	twisted together
equity investment	investment of funds contributed by owners of a business
exert	to put into action, put forth
extricate	to separate, disentangle, release
fires	dismisses from a position, discharges
golden parachutes	financial incentive packages granted to senior managers as protection against job loss in the event of a merger or acquisition
granted	given or conferred formally
guise	pretense, false or deceiving appearance
incentive	motive, stimulus, something that stimulates one to take action
incumbent	person currently in a position
inevitably	certainly, unavoidably
inextricably	cannot be separated or untied
interlocking directorates	boards of directors having some members in common, so that the corporations concerned are more or less under the same control
intervene	to come between, as an influencing force
joint venture	business operation common to two or more organizations or corporations
lifted	revoked, rescinded, ended
lock-in	safeguard

marginal	not crucial, secondary; on the border between being profitable or nonprofitable
maximization	increasing to the maximum, raising to the highest degree
merger	combining of several corporations in one by issuing stock of the controlling corporation to replace the greater part of the others
modest	moderate, not extreme
monopolistic	having exclusive control or possession that makes possible the fixing of prices and elimination of free competition
mutual funds	trust or corporation formed to invest in diversified securities using funds obtained from its shareholders
nurture	to promote the development of
obsolete	out-of-date, old
outlawed	declared unlawful or illegal
paramount	dominant, ranking higher than any other, supreme
pension funds	mutual investment programs that pool participant payments for investing in common stocks, bonds, mortgages, or other financial instruments; the income from such investments provides payments for retired workers
plunge	to move rapidly downward
proponents	persons who support a cause or an idea
raids	sudden attacks—deliberate attempts by speculators to cause a quick, unexpected fall in stock market prices
recession	temporary decrease in business activity during a period when such activity has been increasing
redistributive	to distribute again or in a different way
rejuggle	to manipulate again to deceive or cheat
repealed	withdrew officially, revoked, canceled
repel	to drive or force back, hold off
reshuffling	rearranging or reorganizing
robber barons	U.S. capitalists of the late 19th century who ruthlessly acquired vast wealth
semblance	appearance, outward form, aspect
shareholder	a person who holds or owns a share or shares in a corporation
solely	only, exclusively, merely
sought	tried, attempted
speculators	persons who buy or sell stocks, commodities, land, hoping to take advantage of expected rise or fall in price
startups	new businesses
stock	capital invested in a company or corporation by the owners through the purchase of shares, entitling them to interest, dividends, voting rights
takeover artists	financial traders who assume control or possession of a company
takeover	assumption of control or possession of a company, often in a hostile manner
trigger	to initiate, set off
tyranny	harshness, severity

untenable	cannot be defended or maintained
venture capitalists	persons who invest funds (at considerable risk of loss) in potetially highly profitable enterprises
vikings	Scandinavian pirates who attacked and destroyed coasts of Europe from 8th to 10th centuries; powerful financial speculators
volatility	instability, unpredictability
wholesale	extensive, sweeping
yesteryear	past years

Vocabulary

Without referring to the article, fill in the following sentences with the correct words from this list. You may change the tense, number, or form of the words to fit the context. Use each word only once; not all of the words on the list will be used.

intervene	antitrust law	takeover	acquisition	entrepreneur	merger
untenable	venture capitalist	extricate	monopolistic	exert	obsolete
enhance	marginal				

1. Industrial organizations in the United States are governed by_____, which were

    designed to avoid _____ industrial combines.

2. The law limits how much a financial institution that owns stock in a company can _____

    _____ in that company's decision making.

3. Encouraging aggressive _____ and financial _____ is not the solution to the problem of slow productivity growth in the United States.

4. When a hostile _____ occurs, shareholders generally make a profit, but society does not benefit from expanded output or productivity.

5. Although successful and creative _____ may build new corporations, they cannot re-place the need for vital, profitable large-scale corporations owned by dominant shareholders.

6. Many companies are started with the financial support of _____, who do not remain with a company on a long-term basis and therefore cannot substitute for merchant banks.

7. Financial institutions should not be allowed to easily _____ themselves from their participation in the management of a company to which they have loaned money.

8. Quarterly profit statements are dangerous because they put managers in _____ posi-tions and reinforce short-term rather than long-term objectives.

9. Because of the realities of today's international competition, U.S. antitrust laws have become

    _____ and must be reformed.

10. The buying and selling of financial assets is _____ to the success of the United States and should be replaced by an emphasis on productivity and competitiveness.

Idioms and Expressions

Read the paragraphs in which the following italicized idioms and expressions are found. Then circle the letter next to the answer that best describes the meaning of the idiom as used in the context of the article.

1. "We are rich in financial investors of every size and variety from *the man on the street* to the giant pension funds. . . ." (Paragraph 1)
   a. pedestrian
   b. salesman
   c. average person

2. "Profit maximization, (which firms automatically *shoot for*) with or without government regulations . . ." (Paragraph 11)
   a. implement
   b. consider
   c. aim to achieve

3. "Proponents of the takeover movement would argue that these criticisms *miss the point*. . . ." (Paragraph 15)
   a. overlook the major aspect
   b. are not logical
   c. are not helpful

4. "And they [real capitalists] must be *boxed in* so that their profit-making energies are focused on activities that raise productivity and output." (Paragraph 17)
   a. enclosed
   b. restricted
   c. restructured

5. "This rule *flies in the face of* reason." (Paragraph 24)
   a. upholds
   b. goes against
   c. argues for

6. "Finance and industry should not be *at arm's length*." (Paragraph 26)
   a. far apart
   b. in disagreement
   c. near each other

Paraphrasing

Read the following sentences carefully, and then rewrite them using your own words. Change the vocabulary and sentence structure, but do not change the author's intended meaning or paraphrase any technical terms. There are several ways of paraphrasing each sentence.

Original: "If productivity is not rising at a healthy rate, then American business is not doing its job."

Paraphrase: American business must work well in order for productivity to show a strong increase.

1. "Our economy must be restructured to regain some semblance of its old-style capitalist energy." (Paragraph 3)

_____

_____

2. "Owning a majority or controlling interest, these capitalists did not have to concentrate on reshuffling assets to fight off raids from financial vikings." (Paragraph 4)

_____

_____

3. "In recent years, small-scale merchant bankers have reappeared in the guise of venture capitalists." (Paragraph 23)

_____

_____

4. "How much better it would be if they were to help the corporation avoid mistakes that lead to failure." (Paragraph 25)

_____

_____

5. "Link their personal success to their corporation's productivity." (Paragraph 34)

_____

_____

Comprehension

Answer the following questions by finding the relevant information in the article. Give the numbers of the paragraphs that contain the answers.

1. What is the main idea of this article?

2. Why must the American economy be restructured to regain its past capitalist energy?

3. How can the problem of slow productivity growth be solved?

4. What are the negative impacts of financial speculations such as acquisitions and mergers?

5. What social function are private firms supposed to serve in American society?

6. How can private firms be redirected to a more productive path?

7. How do venture capitalists differ from merchant banks?

8. Why should quarterly profit statements be abolished?

9. Why should national antitrust regulations be reformulated?

10. Why will capitalism fail without real capitalists?

Inference/Interpretation

Circle the letter next to the best answer. Choose your answer according to the meaning the author suggests but does not state explicitly.

1. It can be inferred from the article that the U.S. productivity growth rate (Paragraphs 1–2)
   a. is in a state of crisis.
   b. was higher in the days of the old-style capitalists.
   c. is not dependent on private business.
   d. has remained at 0.8% for the past ten years.

2. We can infer from the article that the nineteenth-century robber barons (Paragraph 11)
   a. maximized their profits without concern about raising the standard of living.
   b. increased output and earnings.
   c. reduced output and earnings.
   d. worked in an unregulated market.

3. What can be inferred from the following statements: "National antitrust regulations are now simply obsolete. They don't recognize today's realities"? (Paragraph 32)
   a. Cooperation between the United States and Japan is necessary.
   b. Antitrust regulations are out-of-date.
   c. U.S. firms should remain totally separate and competitive.
   d. U.S. industrial combines are necessary to meet the competition from abroad.

4. The first sentence of this article states: "We call ourselves a capitalist society, but there's something missing." (Paragraph 1) Why does Thurow say "We *call ourselves* . . ." instead of "We *are* . . ."? What does Thurow mean by "there's something missing"?

_____

_____

Structure

Circle the letter next to the correct answer(s). More than one answer may be correct. Be prepared to explain and justify your choices.

1. In which paragraph(s) is the main idea stated?
   a. Paragraph 3
   b. Paragraph 4
   c. Paragraph 18
   d. Paragraph 29
   e. Paragraph 35
   Write a paraphrase of the main idea in *one* sentence, using your own words as much as possible.

   _____

2. What is the purpose of the example given in paragraph 30? ("A recent example will illustrate this point.")
   a. To show how difficult it is to be a financial consultant
   b. To show how quarterly profit statements reinforce a short-term focus
   c. To support the importance of quarterly profit statements
   d. To reinforce the importance of managers' positions
   e. To explain why stock prices fluctuate

3. What is the primary purpose of the statement in paragraph 3: "To put it bluntly, American capitalism needs a heart transplant"?
   a. To surprise the reader by using a graphic image
   b. To support the previous sentence
   c. To develop a new idea
   d. To lead to the main idea of the article
   e. To add a touch of humor
   Rewrite Thurow's statement above, replacing the figure of speech "heart transplant" with nonfigurative language.

   _____

4. What is the overall method of development used in the article?
   a. Making proposals to solve a problem
   b. Testing the evidence supporting a theory
   c. Supporting a thesis with examples
   d. Explaining a series of steps in a process
   e. Enumerating the advantages and disadvantages of a plan

Style

Circle the letter next to the correct answer(s). More than one answer may be correct. Be prepared to justify your choices by giving specific examples from the article.

1. How would you describe the writing style of the author?
   a. Very formal
   b. Somewhat informal
   c. Personal
   d. Bureaucratic
   e. Very technical
   f. Somewhat technical

2. How would you describe the tone of the article?
   a. Discouraged
   b. Serious
   c. Humorous
   d. Emotional
   e. Persuasive
   f. Neutral

3. The author's attitude toward short-term financial traders can be described as
   a. enthusiastic.
   b. disapproving.
   c. sympathetic.
   d. indifferent.
   e. angry.
   f. critical.

4. In the conclusion (Paragraph 32), Thurow uses grammatical parallelism (similar grammatical structures) to convey his ideas effectively. List the parallel elements.

   _____

   _____

   _____

   _____

Discussion

1. Do you agree with Thurow that old-style capitalists are needed to revitalize the U.S. economy?

2. What is the best economic system for your country: capitalism, socialism, or a mixed economy? Why?

3. What are the advantages of an economic system based on incentives and private ownership?

4. What are the advantages of an economic system based on socialism and government ownership?

5. Why have U.S. productivity rates in industry declined in the past ten years?

6. What is the future of capitalism? Of socialism?

Research Assignment

Look up several of these articles in the library. Choose one article to read and take notes on.

Bolster, Paul J., and Jonathan B. Welch. "Why Takeovers Don't Hurt R & D." *Harvard Business Review* 68 (January-February 1990): 211–12.

"Capitalism's Visible Hand." *Economist* 315 (May 19, 1990): 11–12.

Copeland, James E., Jr., Maria Lombardi Bullen, and Roger H. Hermanson. "How CEOs View Hostile Takeovers." *Business* 39 (April-May-June 1989): 3–8.

Donham, Wallace B. "Can American Business Meet the Present Emergency?" *Harvard Business Review* 68 (May-June 1990): 62.

Fruhan, William E. "Corporate Raiders: Head 'em Off at Value Gap." *Harvard Business Review* 66 (July-August 1988): 63–68.

Fukuyama, Francis. "Are We at the End of History?" *Fortune* 121 (January 15, 1990): 75–78.

Gilder, George. "American Technology at Fire Sale Prices." *Forbes* 145 (January 22, 1990):60–64.

Haspeslagh, Philippe C., and David B. Jemison. "Acquisitions: Myths and Realities." *Sloan Management Review* 28 (Winter 1987): 53–58.

Kaplan, Roger. "Entrepreneurship Reconsidered: The Antimanagement Bias." *Harvard Business Review* 65 (May-June 1987): 84–89.

Mann, Charles C. "The Man with All the Answers." *Atlantic* 265 (January 1990): 45–62.

Mufson, Steven. "White House Seeks Easing Antitrust Law on Ventures." *Washington Post* (May 8, 1990): Cl, C8.

Novak, Michael. "How about Obscene Losses?" *Forbes* 143 (March 6, 1989): 76–77.

Novak, Michael. "A Revolution Restated." *Forbes* 143 (February 20, 1989): 86.

Podhoretz, Norman. "The New Defenders of Capitalism." *Harvard Business Review* 59 (March-April 1981): 96–106.

Robinson, Marshall. "America's Not-So-Troubling Debts and Deficits." *Harvard Business Review* 67 (July-August 1989): 50–58.

Rock, Arthur. "Strategy vs. Tactics from a Venture Capitalist." *Harvard Business Review* 65 (November-December 1987): 63–67.

Thurow, Lester C. "America Adrift." *Washington Post* (February 11, 1990): C1–C2.

"Trust the Trust, or Bust the Trust." *Economist* 312 (September 2, 1989): 63–64.

Webber, Alan M. "Acres of Diamonds." *Harvard Business Review* 68 (May-June 1990): 222–23.

Welles, Edward O. "The Tokyo Connection." *Inc.* 12 (February 1990): 52–65.

Work, Clemens P. "Return of the Big Stick." *U.S. News & World Report* 108 (June 4, 1990): 54–55.

Oral Presentation

Working with a partner, give a fifteen-minute oral presentation to the class on the articles that you chose in the research assignment. Include the author's main idea, major points, and some supporting data. Be prepared to answer questions on your topic. (See Appendix B: Giving an Oral Presentation.)

Writing Assignments

1. Write a 300-word summary of Thurow's article. Be objective. Do not include your opinion or any extraneous information.

2. Discuss the economy in your country. Is the standard of living rising? Is the productivity growth rate rising? What kind of regulatory framework governs your industry and finance? Develop a thesis about your country's economic growth, and support it with specific examples.

3. Imagine you are a successful entrepreneur. You own a company that manufactures high technology products for the home and office. What new product would you like to develop in your corporation? Explain your reasons for choosing this product.

Peer Critique

Choose a person to work with. After you have completed your writing assignment, let your partner read and critique your writing. Then you will read and critique his or her writing. Use the Writing Evaluation Form in Appendix F.

Case Study: A Problem of a Hostile Takeover

Working in groups, read the following case study. Discuss the problem, answer the questions, and write a brief report on how your group would solve the problem. (Choose one member of the group to do the writing.) Follow the format in Appendix E (Case Study Report) in writing your report.

International Airlines, which has never recovered from the October 1987 stock market crash, is struggling to stay alive. An IA stock selling for $28 one year ago now gets about $14, and IA appears to be vulnerable to a hostile takeover. In fact, the employees of IA have heard a rumor that Roland Crane, the infamous corporate raider and takeover artist, is preparing to stage a takeover of their once highly successful company. Crane is known as a cut-throat manipulator who treats his employees poorly and has little concern for the long-term growth and future of his companies. However, his wealth and power are so great that Crane usually gets whatever he goes after.

George Harris, the Chief Executive Officer (CEO) of IA, is determined to prevent the hostile takeover from succeeding. He is willing to use almost any tactics to achieve his goal. Harris has called an emergency meeting of the company's upper management to brainstorm a strategy to use in overpowering Crane's bid. The word on Wall Street is that Crane will make his move in the next ten days. Harris is leaning toward an Employee Stock Ownership Plan (ESOP), allowing IA employees to become employee-owners. IA could borrow money from a bank to establish an ESOP trust, which would buy shares of IA stock. Then the shares would be released to IA employees based on each employee's salary. By placing IA in an employee stock ownership plan, IA would change from a publicly owned to an employee-owned company, thus preventing takeovers. Now employees own about 10 percent of the stock, and with an ESOP, Harris thinks he could boost that to 55–60 percent. An ESOP would give employees an incentive because they would be working for themselves and taking a bigger role in running the company.

Patrick Fitzgerald, the Chief Operating Officer (COO) of IA, also has a proposal to present at the meeting, but it is quite radical. He wants to convince the company executives to attempt a last-minute merger with Worldwide Airlines, thus making Crane's takeover financially unfeasible. He knows, however, that he will face a great deal of resistance, especially from Paul Bergman, President of IA, and the senior executives. IA and WA went through an unsuccessful merger attempt last year, and there are hard feelings on both sides as a result. The merger failed because IA and WA executives couldn't agree on either the restructuring of the new organization or the company's long-term objectives, but Fitzgerald has reason to believe WA would be open to a deal.

Paul Bergman, President of IA, has rarely agreed with George Harris about anything, and now is no exception. Bergman has his own plan to present at the meeting. He and some other senior executives want to do a leveraged management buyout (MBO)* and buy IA themselves. Then IA would be a privately, not publicly, held corporation, which would protect it from any takeover attempts. Bergman knows their offer will have to be a fair one—and above the price of IA stock on the market—perhaps even $20 a share, but he thinks it's worth it. The only problem is how to raise the cash needed to buy the company. He is working on this and has already contacted several major banks that have tentatively agreed to provide financing at around 10 percent interest. Nothing has been settled, but he is hopeful that he'll have a viable solution by the time of the meeting. He heard that Harris will push for a merger with WA, which makes him angry. IA and WA have completely divergent long-term goals and company values. If they merge, he'll take early retirement. In Bergman's eyes, the only way for IA to stay alive is to go the MBO route.

---

* LBO = Leveraged Buyout; MBO = Management Buyout (Company's management and/or other private investors buy out ["buyout"] all the other shareholders, almost entirely with borrowed funds ["leveraged"].)

Questions

1. How should Harris present his ESOP plan at the meeting?

2. Should Fitzgerald contact executives at WA about a merger?

3. How should Bergman present his MBO plan at the meeting?

4. Should Bergman meet with Harris before the meeting to try to convince him of a leveraged management buyout (MBO)?

5. What other options do IA employees have?

Solution: Case Study Report

I. Define and analyze the problem.
II. Suggest possible solutions.
III. Evaluate possible solutions.
IV. Select a solution.

Case Study Business Writing Assignment: Memorandum

Write a memo from Paul Bergman, President of IA, to the employees of IA, announcing that the senior executives of IA intend to implement a management buyout (MBO). The memo should give the reasons for this action and justify it.

Format:
I. Introduction (Background and Main Idea)
II. Discussion (Reasons and Justification)
III. Closing (Restatement of Main Idea)

Style: Formal but personal
Tone: Persuasive and analytical

Additional Readings

"The Mind-Centered System"
Michael Novak
Forbes 143 (February 6, 1989): 44

"Greed Does Not Explain It"
Michael Novak
Forbes 143 (April 3, 1989): 56

Business people are not good at defending capitalism. Maybe it is because they don't quite understand it themselves.

THE MIND-CENTERED SYSTEM

By Michael Novak

Last fall I met an executive of a large American multinational, whom I shall call Robert Wilson. He told me with some dismay that his son had come home from university the preceding Christmas denouncing (to his mother) first "obscene profits" and "wicked multinational corporations" (Mrs. Wilson did her best to defend her husband's line of work), and then the entire capitalist system. Still, not having read the exact authors and books her son was citing, she knew she hadn't argued very well. Bob Wilson didn't do much better afterwards—even worse, since he lost his temper.

What *is* this thing called "capitalism," anyway? American dictionaries usually define it in a rather Marxist way. (Not surprising, since it was Marx who first defined what he opposed.) The *American Heritage Dictionary* defines capitalism as:

"An economic system characterized by freedom of the market with increasing concentration of private and corporate ownership of production and distribution means, pro-

Philosopher, novelist, journalist and ex-U.S. ambassador Michael Novak is now at the American Enterprise Institute in Washington, D.C. Among his most recent books are Taking Glasnost Seriously *and* Will It Liberate? Questions about Liberation Theology.

portionate to increasing accumulation and reinvestment of profits."

Not all definitions are quite so pejorative ("concentration," "accumulation"). Nonetheless, the emphasis in most does fall on private property, markets and profits.

But these three institutions cannot possibly provide an accurate definition of capitalism. For the word itself was invented to define a *new* economic system, which emerged fully only at the end of the 18th century. Its novelty is what drew attention to it—even Marx'.

What made this new system *different* could not have been private property, markets and profits. Biblical Jerusalem, at a crossroads of three continents, had all three. It was (economically) a market that respected private property and (aspiring to be a "land of milk and honey") smiled on profits.

These three characteristics do not capitalism make. They define the traditional economy in most times, at most places.

What is distinctive about capitalism is hidden in the word itself. What is the answer to Adam Smith's original inquiry into the cause of the wealth of nations? In one word, the cause is *wit*: invention, discovery, mind. (In Latin, *caput*, head.) In this respect, the word capitalism, which Marx intended as pejorative, is accurately chosen.

Simply put, the cause of wealth is human creativity. Smith dramatized this point in his example of the pin factory. Human ingenuity discovered a way to make pins quickly and in large multiples, whereas individual craftsmen had earlier required many laborious hours for each. To paraphrase

Hayek, capitalism didn't do much for duchesses, who already had pins, silk stockings and many other items, but it did a lot for working women who had never had them, but soon did.

Capitalism is the first social system organized around mind. It gives primacy to mind—to practical intellect, in the first place, but in the end also to intellectual research and contemplation for their own sakes. Systematic attention to the needs of mind begins in schools oriented to new discoveries and practicality. It continues in patent and copyright laws. It comes to flower through ease of incorporation, through habits of enterprise, favorable conditions for capital formation and access to the credit needed to bring creative ideas to realization.

Thus, a decisive moment in the history of capitalism occurred at the Constitutional Convention in Philadelphia in 1787, when the same right (the copyright) earlier extended to writers in Great Britain was here extended to patents for inventors and discoveries. Article 1, Section 8, of the Constitution listed among the limited powers granted to the Congress the following:

"To promote the progress of science and useful arts, by securing for limited times to authors and inventors the exclusive right to their respective writings and discoveries."

In this clause occurs for the first and only time in the Constitution proper the word "right"—a right grounded in the capacities of the human spirit for invention and discovery, and justified as a preeminent service to the common good.

In theological language, we can say that a capitalist system is founded on the Jewish and Christian belief that the Creator of all things made every man and every woman in His image. He thus endowed in each the right and the duty to be creative as He is creative: to invent and to discover, and thereby to serve the common good of all.

Capitalism is the system organized around creativity. That is what makes it different from the precapitalist economy, and also from the socialist economy. A system named for the human head (*caput*) is, like the human mind itself, forever open and inventive. If Bob Wilson and other business people want to mount an effective defense of capitalism, they should learn to explain it in these terms. ∎

Boldness in industrial undertakings, said Tocqueville, was the chief cause of America's rapid progress, power and greatness.

GREED DOES NOT EXPLAIN IT

By Michael Novak

Philip J. Freedenberg of Fairfax, Va. upbraids me in a letter recently published in FORBES for overpraising creativity as the cause of the wealth of the West, and for neglecting "the mechanism that . . . deserves equal billing: greed."

The enemies of capitalism ever have been quick to imagine that greed is the linchpin of capitalism. R.H. Tawney wrote of the "acquisitive" impulse, Marx of "accumulation," and recently the late Robert Lekachman, one of my favorite socialists, called his anti-Reagan book *Greed Is Not Enough.*

Trouble is, "the impulse to acquisition, pursuit of gain, of money, of the greatest possible amount of money, has in itself nothing to do with capitalism," Max Weber wrote in *The Protestant Ethic and the Spirit of Capitalism.* "It should be taught in kindergarten of cultural history that this naive idea of capitalism must be given up once and for all."

Greed did not begin with capitalism (late in the 18th century). Outbreaks of it are found from the earliest times, in the biblical ages, and in all cultures. Indeed, there are many reasons for believing that in the capitalist era greed (in its ancient meaning) has diminished as a motive force, or has in any case been deeply altered.

In a free society—both democratic and capitalist—there are lots of reasons why human beings do great deeds, build new industries, launch new inventions. Without judging personal motives, one can imagine many types of human energies being unleashed by liberty: the zest for life, ambition, challenge, excitement, conquest, self-determination, creativity, the will-to-power—yes, and greed.

Yet the word greed is always used to name a vice, never a virtue. The dictionaries say that it means an "excessive" hunger. Do those who insist that the driving mechanism of capitalism is greed want to prove that the system is inherently vicious? Yes, they do.

By contrast Adam Smith thought that the drive to "better one's condition" is an admirable natural impulse. But the most telling comment comes from Alexis de Tocqueville: "To clear, cultivate and transform the huge uninhabited continent which is their domain," he wrote, "the Americans need the support of an energetic passion; that passion can only be the love of wealth. So no stigma attaches to the love of money in America, and provided it does not exceed the bounds imposed by public order, it is held in honor."

In the zero-sum societies of the past, those who hoarded a portion of the common stock made others poorer. Not so, Tocqueville noted, in a country and an economy "limitless and full of inexhaustible resources." Wealth newly created takes from no one.

And the early Americans needed boldness: "For a people so situated the danger is not the ruin of a few, which is soon made good, but apathy and sloth in the community at large. Boldness in industrial undertakings is the chief cause of their rapid progress, power and greatness. To them industry appears as a vast lottery in which a few men daily lose but in which the state constantly profits. Such a people is bound to look with favor on boldness in industry and to honor it."

In ancient and medieval Europe, great landowners grew food not so much for markets as to feed their armies. Wealth for them was gold and precious objects to be seized from others. Not understanding how wealth is created and, as the book of Proverbs put it, "greedy of loot," they formed robber bands and pillaging armies to bring the booty home.

In those days greed typically meant "unlawful gain" and was expressed through armed might, brigandage and piracy. By contrast the proponents of a new type of society—"the commercial republic"—believed that commerce would tame ferocious manners.

Commerce, they thought, is better for society than war. Inherently, it requires peaceful ways, trustworthy personal relationships, long time horizons, voluntary contracts and international law. It teaches patience, discipline, a prudent watchfulness over small losses and small gains. It spurs vision, enterprise and grand designs. Proportionate to risk, it honors a reasonable return. Without such returns, indeed, there is no peaceful economic growth.

Thus the Americans regarded the warlike barons and lords of Europe as lawless, untamed and frenzied with greed. Their medieval ancestors would have called the American concern for steady material progress "base cupidity," Tocqueville noted. The Americans regarded economic enterprise as a "noble and estimable ambition," lawlike, respectful of public order, indispensable to national prosperity and boldly progressive.

Like our forebears, we should be careful to distinguish "boldness in industry" from "greed." The first is admirable, the second, not. ∎

Philosopher, journalist and ex-U.S. ambassador Michael Novak directs social and political studies at the American Enterprise Institute in Washington, D.C. Among his recent books are Taking Glasnost Seriously *and* Free Persons and the Common Good.

Chapter 5

"In Services, What's in a Name?"

Leonard L. Berry, Edward F. Lefkowith, and Terry Clark

Preview

Skimming. Skim the article quickly to find the following general information.

1. Read the authors' names, the title, and all headings.

2. Read the first and second paragraphs, looking for the authors' purpose and main idea.

3. Read the last paragraph, looking for a summary or conclusion.

Questioning. Answer the following questions and discuss your answers in class.

1. What is a service company?

2. What does "What's in a Name" mean?

3. What is branding?

Scanning. Scan the article quickly to find the following specific information.

1. Why is the brand name especially important for service companies?

2. What fabricated words have worked well as brand names?

3. What unflattering nickname does Montgomery Ward have?

4. What airline has gained powerful brand recognition in spite of an average name?

Vocabulary in Context. Read the following sentences and try to guess the meaning of the italicized words by using the context. Then replace the italicized words with synonyms (words or phrases that have nearly the same or similar meanings).

Harvard Business Review 66, no. 5 (September-October 1988)

1. "A name cannot make or break a product or company. It was not the name Edsel that *doomed* Ford's *ill-fated* car brand. . . ."

2. "A company that wishes to establish a *proprietary* position in the marketplace clearly should avoid a *generic*-sounding name. Words like 'Allied,' 'United,' and 'National' tell us little about what the enterprise delivers."

3. "A third option is to use *fabricated* words, which are becoming increasingly *prevalent*, in part because real words are getting harder to trademark."

4. "Humana suggests the human touch, personalization, *sensitivity*—positive *connotations* for a health-care organization."

5. "A word that *draws* its descriptive power from connotations is usually more flexible than one based on *literal* definitions."

The "branding" effect of a good corporate name is a potent marketing tool.

In Services, What's in a Name?

by Leonard L. Berry, Edwin F. Lefkowith, and Terry Clark

1 A name cannot make or break a product or company. It was not the name Edsel that doomed Ford's ill-fated car brand; the letters IBM, and the words they stand for, were not the critical ingredient in IBM's success. What matters is how well a company's goods or services meet its customers' needs.

2 Having said that, however, we contend that a well-chosen name can give a company a decided marketing edge over comparable competitors, and that the branding effect of a strong corporate name can be especially important for service companies. Why? Because in services the company name *is* the brand name.

3 Services do not lend themselves to individual branding the way tangible products do. Goods can be positioned and marketed with specific, appropriate brand names: Pampers, Alka Seltzer, Black Flag. Consumers may be loyal to such brands without ever knowing that the goods came from Procter & Gamble, Miles Laboratories, and American Home Products.

4 Although a service vendor may have a variety of offerings – first class, business class, and coach; or checking accounts and loan services – consumers tend to perceive all of them as components of a single brand. Think of such businesses as Avis, Federal Express, and Holiday Inns. Each conjures up an overall brand image.

5 For this reason, selecting a name for a service organization can be critical to a total marketing strategy, especially for new companies in very competitive markets and for companies expanding their range of services or their geographic reach.

6 Anyone can cite examples of successful companies with lackluster names; performance, after all, is primary. So how important, really, is a service brand name? The answer is that strong branding can accelerate market awareness and acceptance of a high-quality service, while weak branding can accelerate failure for a poorly conceived or delivered service.

7 Consider the difficulties of Allegis. Like Edsel, the name Allegis has probably come in for more than its fair share of criticism – a phenomenon that happens to support our thesis. The name itself was merely an extension of a flawed business strategy, a plan to create a systems concept in business travel by putting the well-known brands, United Airlines, Hertz, Hilton, and Westin Hotels, under the Allegis umbrella.

8 It was widespread skepticism about the *strategy* that turned the name into a lightning rod for criticism. To be sure, one can find flaws with the name. When introduced, it was defined as a combination of "allegiance" and "aegis," and the very fact that it needed to be explained – and its pronunciation made clear – signaled a problem. But this is hindsight. Had the strategy been sound and well executed, we obviously would not be citing Allegis as a flawed brand name.

9 Federal Express furnishes a contrasting example. We can now say that this is a strong and appropriate brand identity: Express delineates the nature and speed of the service, and Federal suggests a far-flung, perhaps governmentally sanctioned enterprise. But without its superlative ability to track and deliver parcels, and without its courteous employees and its professional-looking uniforms, trucks, envelopes, and advertising, the Federal Express brand would not be an example of excellence. The name was part of an overall operating strategy backed up by a sophisticated, cohesive branding program.

Four useful tests

10 Given the difficulty of judging brand names isolated from performance, are there any hard-and-fast rules for naming a service company? Beyond avoiding obvious negative connotations, there are no absolutes. But we have found four tests useful for assessing the branding potential of an existing or proposed name. A strong service brand should possess some, if not all, of these characteristics:

Leonard L. Berry is Foley's/Federated Professor of Retailing and Marketing Studies and director, Center for Retailing Studies at Texas A&M University. Mr. Berry's latest book is Service Quality – a Profit Strategy for Financial Institutions *(Dow Jones-Irwin, 1988). Edwin F. Lefkowith is president of a marketing and communications consultancy, Lefkowith Inc., in New York City. Terry Clark is assistant professor of marketing at the University of Notre Dame.*

1. Distinctiveness. It immediately identifies the service supplier and distinguishes it from competitors.

2. Relevance. It conveys the nature of the service or the service benefit.

3. Memorability. It can be understood, used, and recalled with ease.

4. Flexibility. It is broad enough to cover not just the organization's current business but also foreseeable expansions.

11 Let's take a closer look at the four tests and then examine how a cohesive branding and communications program allows a service company to exploit a brand image.

12 *Distinctiveness.* A company that wishes to establish a proprietary position in the marketplace clearly should avoid a generic-sounding name. Words like "Allied," "United," and "National" tell us little about what the enterprise delivers. They are empty baggage, and overused to boot. Allied who? Which United? National what? More words are needed (Van Lines, Stores, Airlines, Parcel Service) merely to identify the company's line of business. The day is past when a company added "National" to distinguish itself from local or regional competitors.

13 Years ago many financial institutions took names like "Commerce," "Merchants," "First National," and "First Federal." (In Texas alone, there are more than 60 S&Ls using "First Federal" in their name.) Now that financial services have become more competitive—financial institutions are expanding both geographically and in the services they offer—such names are inadequate to set a company apart from its rivals.

14 One way to set yourself apart is to use a word (or words) uncommon to the service category. Meridian is an example from financial services. Another approach is to use a proper name: Chase, Barnett, J.P. Morgan, McDonald's, Marriott. Names like these stand out in a competitive environment if well supported with distinctive marketing communication. They have the arbitrary (not literal or descriptive) quality that lawyers recognize as one ingredient of an effective trademark.

15 A third option is to use fabricated words, which are becoming increasingly prevalent, in part because real words are getting harder to trademark. Some have drawn fire for being too gimmicky, too obviously the product of a computer, but others serve their purpose well—names like Primerica, Exxon, Crestar.

16 *Relevance.* A name that conveys the essence of a service helps identify and position the company clearly in customers' minds—an important factor for companies selling intangibles. Ticketron suggests both the nature of the service and the electronic means by which it is delivered. Humana suggests the human touch, personalization, sensitivity—positive connotations for a healthcare organization. Visa is relevant for a worldwide financial service because it implies international access.

17 By relevance we do not mean that a name should give a simple, literal description of the service, because description leads to greater length and less distinctiveness. Overnight Delivery Services, for example, would be a relevant name but is weaker than Federal Express, Personal Touch Health Care, weaker than Humana. Names that resonate with indirect connotations, rather than literal descriptions, are also more likely to meet the third test, memorability.

18 *Memorability.* Several factors affect how memorable a service brand is. Distinctiveness is one. Pathmark is more memorable than Grand Union, NYNEX more memorable than U.S. West. But a name that is distinctive because it is complex or based on difficult or foreign words many consumers do not recognize, may flunk the memorability test.

19 Brevity and simplicity are generally assets. A name that is easy to understand when heard or read, and easy to pronounce, will encourage memorability; a short word also lends itself more easily than a long word to effective graphic treatment in a logo. Moreover, consumers tend to derive shorthand equivalents for long words. In some cases—like Pan Am—this does not pose a problem; but in other cases the nickname is unflattering, like "Monkey Ward" for Montgomery Ward.

20 While the name Aetna is brief and distinctive, one could argue that it is difficult to pronounce when first encountered. The company has addressed this problem through its "Aetna, I'm glad I met ya" advertising line, but companies contemplating new names should probably consider whether they want to expend their marketing resources on pronunciation (or on explanation, as with Allegis).

21 When it can be done with restraint, an unusual spelling immeasurably aids the memory. "Citibank," not much of a fabrication—but surely more distinctive than its former appellation, First National City Bank—stands out because of the unusual "i." Given the particular target audience, Toys "R" Us, with the "R" reversed, is inspired. Parents and grandparents who buy from this chain's stores evidently find the cute name and graphic appropriate. But for nearly all businesses, overdoing cuteness produces a brand name memorable only for its gimmickry.

22 *Flexibility.* Most companies change and expand over time, sometimes with the result that they outgrow their original names. In evaluating a name, a company would do well to consider any changes in direction it is likely to pursue, so that the name it selects is broad enough to grow with the lines of business.

23 Geographical references can be a limiting factor, and many companies have lived to regret their regional names. When "First National Bank of Hometown" expands into several states, it has a problem. Western Hotels became Western International (a confusing identity) and ultimately adopted Westin, a fabricated name with a less regional connotation. Allegheny Airlines changed to USAir as it expanded its system. (And while the carrier shed its derisive nickname "Agony Airlines," the newer name does not accommodate route

expansion beyond the national border.)

24 Delta, on the other hand, need not change its name to reflect its reach. For one thing, it has earned a strong brand position. For another, while "delta" has a regional association, the word has other meanings and is therefore not as limiting as "Air South" would have been, and as the more specific Allegheny was.

25 **PAN AM** Any purely descriptive term can become a straitjacket. A venture that has evolved into a total transportation enterprise will naturally have more trouble communicating the larger scope of its offerings to customers if its name still includes "trucking" or "rail." A name can also keep management from recognizing the company's opportunities; it can inadvertently become a kind of mission statement that limits its managerial perceptions.

26 A word that draws its descriptive power from connotations is usually more flexible than one based on literal definitions. "Sentry" can cover more territory—literally and figuratively—than Insurance Company of North America or Government Employees Insurance Company.

27 As important as the power of the name is the support and reinforcement the company gives its chosen name with an integrated, coordinated communications program, encompassing everything from forms to advertising. Indeed, some names that seem less than optimal on the basis of the four tests have nonetheless gained strong brand recognition because of a coordinated marketing effort. American Airlines is no better than an average name, yet it is a powerful brand. The most important element, of course, is the airline's service quality, but the carrier also has a disciplined branding program: well-designed uniforms, a consistent use of graphics in all tangibles—from planes to ticket jackets—and persuasive advertising.

Humana and Visa

28 The name Humana wins high scores on all four of our tests. Created in 1972 when Extendicare chose to sell its nursing homes and concentrate on hospitals, it is distinctive, unlike the names of many competitors. As noted earlier, it is relevant to the company's business of health care and carries positive connotations. It is short and easy to understand and remember. And it is flexible enough to apply to all the various services the company offers: hospitals, insurance plans, healthcare membership programs. The power of the name is evident in Humana's high ratings in market awareness surveys, and which is underscored by the company's performance record.

29 Another name with all four of the desirable characteristics is Visa. The credit card, originally called Bank-Americard by the Bank of America back in 1958, was rechristened in 1977. The name is distinctive compared with competitors MasterCard and American Express. It is relevant; the name suggests that the card will open doors internationally. **CITIBANK** It is easily understood and pronounced not just in the United States but all over the world. The limiting reference to banks, cards, and America are all gone, so it is flexible; the numerous services provided under the Visa banner include traveler's checks and an automated teller network. The brevity of the tag lends itself to effective graphic treatment.

30 The case of Visa also illustrates the importance of a service brand name in the context of a marketing communications strategy. Consumer research in the early 1980s showed that Visa's brand image was slipping against the competition. The company responded with an advertising program carrying the line "Visa—it's everywhere you want to be," which underlined the fact that more merchants worldwide accept the card than competitors' cards. The campaign worked in concert with the suggestions of access in the brand name. Recent research indicates that Visa's brand image is now much stronger.

31 A brand image is a total concept based on far more than a name alone. It includes the integration of words, colors, symbols, and slogans, and the consistent application of these elements to send a clear and cohesive message to consumers. An employee's uniform, the design of a sign, graphics on all materials, and an effective advertising campaign should work together to brand the intangible service.

32 Graphic symbols can help make a fair name better and a good name

> A well-chosen name can't save a company whose service is poor.

great. The red umbrella used by The Travelers—symbolizing protection and shelter—strengthens the brand image of a company that has outgrown the literal derivation of its name. Merrill Lynch's bull is another strong brand reinforcer. And who thinks of Prudential without picturing the rock?

33 Slogans can serve a similar purpose. "You're in good hands with Allstate" conveys with words and a visual image what consumers can expect from the company. Similarly, the concept of the "friendly skies of United" helps bring relevance to a dull name.

34 Brand image, of course, extends beyond name, logo, and advertising appeal. McDonald's supports its branding with everything from its M-like golden arches to menu items like Egg McMuffins and Chicken McNuggets. In short, a cohesive branding program requires effective blending of *all* communications elements and use of them consistently and imaginatively across services and media.

35 Still, at bottom, the quality of the service determines the success of the image. If you don't satisfy customers, the name won't help. But of course, if you combine good performance with a good name, you will generate the most powerful branding effect for your services.

Reprint 88502

More Ideas for Action on page 32

Glossary

accelerate	to increase the speed of
arbitrary	not fixed by rules but left to one's choice or preference
assessing	evaluating
cohesive	unified, holds together
conjures up	calls to mind
connotations	ideas associated with a word in addition to its explicit meaning
contend	to assert, argue
delineates	depicts, describes
derisive	ridiculous, ridiculing
doomed	ruined, destroyed
draws	gets or receives
exploit	to utilize productively, promote
fabricated	made up, invented
flunk	to fail
generic	inclusive or general
gimmickry	the use of superficially clever things
gimmicky	superficially clever, attention getting
graphics	drawings, visual artistic representations
hindsight	ability to see, after the event, what should have been done
ill-fated	unlucky
inadvertently	unintentionally
intangibles	things that have no material being or form
lackluster	dull, lacking brightness
literal	based on actual words in their ordinary meaning, not figurative or symbolic
logo	a graphic symbol used to represent an entire word; a distinctive company trademark
optimal	most favorable, the best
prevalent	widespread, widely existing
proprietary	belonging to an owner or company, privately owned and operated, held under trademark or patent
resonate	to resound, vibrate
sanctioned	approved, authorized
sensitivity	quality of being sensitive, highly responsive
slipping	losing strength, becoming worse
slogans	catch phrases used to advertise a product
straitjacket	device that restrains persons in a violent state
tangible	having actual form or substance
vendor	one who sells, seller

Vocabulary

Without referring to the article, fill in the following sentences with the correct words from this list. You may change the tense, number, or form of the words to fit the context. Use each word only once; not all of the words on the list will be used.

contend   accelerate   proprietary   connotation   delineate   exploit   generic
arbitrary   inadvertently   optimal   assess   tangible   cohesive   vendor

1. Companies in the service business do not offer _____ products to their customers; therefore, they are judged on performance.

2. Although service _____ usually provide a variety of services, consumers tend to perceive these services as one brand.

3. A strong brand name clearly and distinctively _____ the type of service offered by a company.

4. Branding must be interwoven with a(n) _____ business strategy in order to be powerful.

5. Since many words have both positive and negative _____, it is important to _____ the branding potential of a name carefully.

6. In the competitive business environment, each company tries to _____ its image to the fullest.

7. _____ names tend to be ineffective as brand names because they are so common; consequently, such names as "National" will not help a company gain a(n) _____ position in the marketplace.

8. Effective trademarks often use proper names like Chase that have a(n)_____ rather than descriptive or literal quality.

9. _____, a brand name can restrict not only a company's image but also managers' goals and plans.

10. The _____ strategy for business success combines the right name with excellent service.

Idioms and Expressions

Read the paragraphs in which the following italicized idioms and expressions are found. Then circle the letter next to the answer that best describes the meaning of the idiom as used in the context of the article.

1. ". . . turned the name into a *lightning rod* for criticism." (Paragraph 8)
   a. tool
   b. subject of attraction
   c system

2. ". . . are there any *hard-and-fast* rules for naming a service company?" (Paragraph 10)
   a. definite, unchanging
   b. difficult
   c. quickly changing

3. "Words like 'Allied,' 'United,' and 'National' . . . are *empty baggage,* and overused to boot."
   (Paragraph 12)
   a. outdated
   b. mysterious
   c. meaningless

4. "They are empty baggage, and overused *to boot.*" (Paragraph 12)
   a. for sure
   b. to kick out
   c. in addition

5. "Some have *drawn fire* for being too gimmicky. . . ." (Paragraph 15)
   a. stirred up criticism
   b. been redesigned
   c. been thrown away

6. "You're *in good hands* with Allstate. . . ." (Paragraph 33)
   a. getting along
   b. working
   c. safe

7. "Still, *at bottom,* the quality of the service determines the success of the image." (Paragraph 35)
   a. fundamentally
   b. finally
   c. surprisingly

Paraphrasing

Read the following sentences carefully, and then rewrite them using your own words. Change the vocabulary and sentence structure, but do not change the authors' intended meaning or paraphrase any technical terms. There are several ways of paraphrasing each sentence.

Original: "If you don't satisfy customers, the name won't help."

Paraphrase: A good name won't save a company whose customers are dissatisfied.

1. "A name cannot make or break a product or company." (Paragraph 1)

   _____

   _____

2. "Had the strategy been sound and well executed, we obviously would not be citing Allegis as a flawed brand name." (Paragraph 8)

   _____

   _____

3. "Given the difficulty of judging brand names isolated from performance, are there any hard-and-fast rules for naming a service company?" (Paragraph 10)

   _____

   _____

4. "American Airlines is no better than an average name, yet it is a powerful brand." (Paragraph 27)

   _____

   _____

5. "The campaign worked in concert with the suggestions of access in the brand name." (Paragraph 30)

   _____

   _____

Comprehension

Answer the following questions by finding the relevant information in the article. Give the numbers of the paragraphs that contain the answers.

1. What is the main idea of this article?

2. Why is choosing the right name so important for service companies?

3. What caused Allegis to fail as a brand name?

4. What caused Federal Express to succeed as a brand name?

5. What four tests can assess the branding potential of a name?

6. What is wrong with generic-sounding names for brands?

7. How can distinctive names be developed?

8. What makes a brand name relevant?

9. What characteristics make a name memorable?

10. Why should a brand name be flexible?

11. What makes Visa such a successful brand name?

12. What does a brand image depend on?

13. What is necessary for the most powerful branding effect?

Inference/Interpretation

Circle the letter next to the best answer. Choose your answer according to the meaning the authors suggest but do not state explicitly.

1. It can be inferred from the article that the Edsel was (Paragraph 1)
   a. a successful brand name for a weak product.
   b. an unsuccessful brand name for a strong product.
   c. a product that failed because of a flawed business strategy.
   d. a product that was criticized for its brand name alone.

2. It can be inferred from the article that (Paragraphs 3–5)
   a. service companies and production companies are the same.
   b. service companies are quite different from production companies.
   c. choosing a service brand name is easier than choosing a product brand name.
   d. choosing a product brand name is easier than choosing a service brand name.

3. What can be inferred about the quality of the service of American Airlines? (Paragraph 27)
   a. The quality is average.
   b. The quality is excellent.
   c. The quality is uneven.
   d. The quality is less than optimal.

4. Read the following sentences carefully:
   "Graphic symbols can help make a fair name better and a good name great. . . . Merrill Lynch's bull is another strong brand reinforcer. And who thinks of Prudential without picturing the rock?" (Paragraph 32) What does the bull symbolize for Merrill Lynch? What does the rock symbolize for Prudential Insurance?

Structure

Circle the letter next to the correct answer(s). More than one answer may be correct. Be prepared to explain and justify your choices.

1. In which paragraph(s) is the main idea stated?
   a. Paragraph 2
   b. Paragraph 3
   c. Paragraph 4
   d. Paragraph 6
   e. Paragraph 35
   Write a paraphrase of the main idea in *one* sentence, using your own words as much as possible.

   _____

2. What techniques do the authors use to get the reader's attention in the introduction? (Paragraphs 1–2)
   a. Quotations
   b. Questions
   c. Negative statements
   d. Reversal of point of view
   e. Humor

3. Where are specific examples used to support a general idea?
   a. Paragraph 1
   b. Paragraph 6
   c. Paragraph 9
   d. Paragraph 21
   e. Paragraphs 28–29

4. Where are comparison and contrast used to support a general idea?
   a. Paragraphs 7–9
   b. Paragraphs 10–11
   c. Paragraphs 22–23
   d. Paragraph 26
   e. Paragraph 31

5. What overall methods of development are used in the article?
   a. Describing causes and effects
   b. Enumerating characteristics
   c. Explaining a series of events
   d. Debating two sides of an issue
   e. Justifying a proposal

Style

Circle the letter next to the correct answer(s). More than one answer may be correct. Be prepared to justify your choices by giving specific examples from the article.

1. How would you describe the writing style of the authors?
   a. Technical
   b. Poetic
   c. Formal
   d. Informal
   e. Impersonal
   f. Personal

2. The tone of the article can best be described as
   a. witty.
   b. emotional.
   c. analytical.
   d. negative.
   e. strident.
   f. persuasive.

3. The authors' attitude toward the business strategy of Allegis can be described as
   a. critical.
   b. supportive.
   c. sympathetic.
   d. neutral.
   e. admiring.
   f. optimistic.

4. The following advertising line by Aetna Life and Casualty Company is informal in style: "Aetna, I'm glad I met ya." (Paragraph 20) What makes this slogan effective? Rewrite this sentence in formal English.

   _____

   What slogans do you know? Are they effective advertising?

Discussion

1. Do you agree with the authors that "a name cannot make or break a product or a company"? Why or why not?

2. Is a successful business strategy enough to make almost any brand name successful? Give examples to support your point of view.

3. How important is a brand name for companies engaged in global business?

4. What famous brand names can you think of from your country? What images do they conjure up?

5. What image does McDonald's have? Why?

6. How influenced are you by brand names? Which products or services do you use because of the brand names?

7. Explain Shakespeare's famous line in *Romeo and Juliet:* "A rose by any other name would smell as sweet." Would this quotation apply to brand names?

Research Assignment

Look up several of these articles in the library. Choose one article to read and take notes on.

Aaker, David. "Brand Extensions: The Good, the Bad, and the Ugly." *Sloan Management Review* 31 (Summer 1990): 47–56.

Freeman, L., and J. Lawrence. "Brand Building Gets New Life." *Advertising Age* 60 (September 4, 1989): 3.

Gruenwald, G. H. "New Thinking Is Required for Successful Brand Development." *Marketing News* 23 (May 8, 1989): 13.

Gubernick, Lisa. "No Brand Like an Old Brand." *Forbes* 145 (June 11, 1990): 178–80.

Heskett, James L. "Lessons in the Service Sector." *Harvard Business Review* 65 (March-April 1987): 118–26.

Maile, Carlton A., and Donna M. Bialik. "Rhyme, Rhythm, and Reason: The Three R's of Brand Name Selection." *Business* 39 (April-May-June 1989): 53–57.

McKenna, Regis. "Marketing in an Age of Diversity." *Harvard Business Review* 66 (September-October 1988): 88–95.

Onkvisit, Sak, and John J. Shaw. "Service Marketing: Image, Branding, and Competition." *Business Horizons* 32 (January-February 1989): 13–18.

Ono, Yumiko. "Designers Cater to Japan's Love of Logos." *Wall Street Journal* (May 29, 1990): B1.

Poole, Claire. "Sweating It Out." *Forbes* 144 (October 16, 1989): 274.

Salmon, Walter J., and Karen A. Cmar. "Private Labels Are Back in Fashion." *Harvard Business Review* 65 (May-June 1987): 99–106.

Schroer, James C. "Ad Spending: Growing Market Share." *Harvard Business Review* 68 (January-February 1990): 44–48.

Schutte, Thomas F. "The Semantics of Branding." *Journal of Marketing* 33 (April 1969): 5–11.

Weiner, Steve. "New Wine in Vintage Bottles." *Forbes* 145 (May 14, 1990): 122–23.

Wells, Bob. "An Idea Whose Time Has Come (Again)." *Marketing and Media Decisions* 24 (May 1989): 82–86.

Wells, Bob. "Branding: Order Out of Chaos." *Marketing and Media Decisions* 24 (June 1989): 99–100.

Wells, Bob. "A Strategic Weapon." *Marketing and Media Decisions* 24 (July 1989): 104–10.

"What's Your Slogan Quotient?" *Harvard Business Review* 66 (July-August 1988): 157.

"Will Bankers Look Good in Pink Spectacles?" *Economist* 315 (June 9, 1990): 79–80.

Oral Presentation

Give a ten-minute oral presentation to the class on the article that you chose in the research assignment. Include the author's main idea, major points, and some supporting data. Be prepared to answer questions on your topic. (See Appendix B: Giving an Oral Presentation.)

Writing Assignments

1. Write a synthesis using at least two of the articles listed in the research assignment and the additional reading in the chapter. After reading the articles, create a thesis based on relationships you develop among the readings, and support it with specific information from the articles you chose. Organize your synthesis according to one of the following methods: cause-effect, comparison-contrast, description, example, or process. (See Appendix D for an example of a synthesis.)

    Use parenthetical references in the author-date system for each of the sources you cite: (McKenna 1988). You may also choose to give the page number: (McKenna 1988, 90). List all sources at the end of your paper as References. Entries should be alphabetized according to the last name of the author: McKenna, Regis. 1988. "Marketing in an Age of Diversity." *Harvard Business Review* 66: 88–95.*

2. Discuss a product or a company that failed in your country. Did it fail because of weak branding, poor business strategy, or both? Use comparison and contrast organization for your ideas. Contrast the failed product or company with a successful product or company.

3. Working with a partner, create a new brand name for a major bank, using the four criteria of (1) distinctiveness, (2) relevance, (3) memorability, and (4) flexibility. Write a brief explanation of how the name meets each of the four criteria and justify your choice.

---

* There is variance in bibliography and reference formats. Also, the author-date system varies among different disciplines. The style used here is that suggested in the *Chicago Manual of Style,* 13th Edition (Chicago: University of Chicago Press, 1982).

Case Study: A Problem in Brand Names

Working in groups, read the following case study. Discuss the problem, answer the questions, and write a brief report on how your group would solve the problem. (Choose one member of the group to do the writing.) Follow the format in Appendix E (Case Study Report) in writing your report.

Joe Hernandez is Director of Marketing for XYZ Financial Company, which is in the banking industry. The company is very conservative and traditional in its image. Until recently, XYZ has largely ignored marketing, but now the company has begun to realize that many of its financial products are commodities that have to be sold to consumers, so the right brand name is critical. Since XYZ has never established itself as a strong brand name, Joe has been asked, as the head of marketing, to come up with a new brand name for the company, which has recently merged with another large financial institution. He is a young risk-taker who wants to get the company moving ahead in a highly competitive business environment. Furthermore, he knows that financial branding is difficult to achieve. Consequently, he thinks that the new brand name should be somewhat unusual and modern—a state-of-the-art name. His choice is *Americash.*

Joe's colleagues take a more conservative approach. They all disagree with Joe's philosophy of marketing, and the interpersonal relations among the employees in the marketing division are poor, if not actually hostile. However, upper management tends to think highly of Joe's ideas.

Joe has arranged a meeting to discuss his proposal and to hear suggestions and feedback from the others. He has prepared a lengthy presentation to justify *Americash* as the new brand name. Because almost all decisions in XYZ Company are made by consensus, Joe has to convince the other members of the marketing group that his proposal is sound.

Questions

1. How should Joe organize his proposal and presentation?

2. Should Joe work behind the scenes to persuade his colleagues?

3. Should Joe go to upper management before his meeting?

4. Should Joe ask for the others' suggestions before or after his presentation?

5. What alternative should Joe have ready to present if he fails to convince his co-workers of his proposal?

Solution: Case Study Report

    I. Define and analyze the problem.
   II. Suggest possible solutions.
  III. Evaluate possible solutions.
  IV. Select a solution.

Case Study Business Writing Assignment: Memorandum

Write a one-page memo from Joe Hernandez (Director of Marketing at XYZ Company) to the other members of the marketing division. The memo should outline and justify Joe's reasons for choosing *Americash* as the new brand name for XYZ Company.

Format:
     I. Introduction (Background and Main Idea)
    II. Discussion (Justification for Name)
   III. Closing (Restatement of Main Idea)

Style: Formal
Tone: Objective but persuasive

Additional Reading

"But in the Office, No"
Joshua Levine, editor
Forbes 144 (October 16, 1989): 272–73

Edited by Joshua Levine

How far can you stretch a brand image? To find out, you must discover what the brand means to consumers.

But in the office, no

RUBBERMAID, the Wooster, Ohio housewares company, has cashed in with its well-known brand name in some surprising places. Four years ago, for example, it started selling feed bins for hogs, horses and cattle to farmers and now markets 25 agricultural products.

But when it tried to market adjustable stands for computer workstations for secretaries, the product bombed.

Rubbermaid's blunder revealed that the brand had a very specific meaning for its customers. Market research discovered that the Rubbermaid name, above all, stands for rock-solid durability. That's a valuable asset for housewares, feed bins and office products like floor mats and desk pads, but not for computer tables, where ease and comfort are more important. Rubbermaid does not mean "comfort."

More and more companies with potent brand names, especially those in mature markets, where sales growth is slowing, are looking for fresh ways to market their still powerful but aging brands. Many have already exhausted the traditional brand line extensions—Oreo ice cream or Del Monte Cajun Style Tomatoes, for example. But they want more.

Dr. Scholl's, the foot pad people, having exhausted the possibilities for corn and bunion remedies, has successfully and logically licensed its name for a variety of foot products

Campbell's new line of cooking utensils
Conjuring images of hearth and home.

including shoes and socks.

Campbell Soup recently licensed its name to a subsidiary of American Home Products for a line of cooking utensils in Campbell's familiar red and white packaging. Research showed that the brand conjures up images of hearth and home.

Campbell doesn't see spoons and spatulas as a major new profit center, necessarily, but it gets free advertising, entrée to another aisle of the supermarket and, possibly, a way into other businesses. Campbell microwave ovens, anyone?

"We spent so many years establishing this brand, we figured let's see what else makes sense," says Donald Bart, Campbell's manager of corporate licensing. "We're just at the beginning, and we don't even know where the boundaries are."

Campbell is in good company. To unearth the hidden meaning and therefore the concealed sales and profit potential of brands, marketers are turning to a new kind of consultant. Many, but not all, of these newly minted brand consultants come from the package design field, since visual symbols and trademarks often carry the burden of a brand's meaning.

Landor Associates, a San Francisco-based designer, now grandly styles itself a "world leader in identity management," for instance, and peddles a process it calls "brandworth." The process covers extensive market surveys, including phone and shopping center canvassing, focus groups and a full range of free association and other tests. The aim is to find out how people feel about a brand.

This can be a useful exercise for executives in tradition-bound products companies, with closely focused and loyal managements. When you're a Dole executive toiling daily in the pineapple groves, it's natural to assume you're in the pineapple business. Landor re-examined the brand for parent Castle & Cooke three years ago and discovered Dole suggests "sunshine foods." When Dole came to Landor, its packaging sported a small pineapple-crown logo above the Dole "O." Landor turned Dole's "O" into a vivid yellow sunburst. This led Dole as far afield as fruit sorbet, carrots

An ad for Playboy shoes, on sale in the U.S.
The men's business suits were a flop.

Coke's name graced Murjani International's sportswear
Would the kids go for Domino's Pizza clothes, too?

and snack nuts, the latter a business Dole entered through its acquisition of Sun Giant Co. in 1987. Recently sales of Dole brand nuts grew almost 6%, to some $9 million, while the nut market as a whole fell 3.6%.

Pillsbury, Quaker and Jergens are currently sniffing out hidden meanings in their brands to see—in marketing lingo—where the consumer gives the brand permission to play.

For big brands, consumers can be awfully permissive. Playboy licensees sell $263 million worth of Playboy-brand merchandise—from shoes in the U.S. to wallpaper in Europe to cooking classes in Brazil. Many of these products don't sport Playboy's lecherous bunny logo and have nothing to do with bedroom shenanigans. William Stokkan, president of the magazine's licensing group, found that Playboy's name stands for swanky self-indulgence as well as sex.

Still, Playboy can't play everywhere. The company tested a line of Playboy-brand suits with Hart, Schaffner & Marx in 1978. No go. "A college graduate who gets a haircut and a new suit for his first job interview doesn't want to walk in in a Playboy suit," Stokkan discovered.

"Marketers always make the mistake of figuring that just having a salient brand name means they're home free," says Joseph Smith, head of the

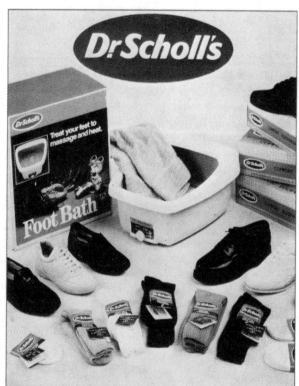

Scholl's socks, foot massager, shoes and hosiery
Trying to get beyond the traditional line extensions.

consumer research firm of Oxtoby-Smith. "It doesn't. Some of the strongest brand names aren't transferable, and they're often defeated by the very vigor and clarity of the brand in the consumer's mind."

Like Domino's Pizza. In 1985 Domino's asked Hamilton Projects, a licensing firm, to set up a deal for a line of Domino's sportswear. Domino's had seen the splash Coca-Cola made when it licensed Murjani International to slap the Coke logo on warm-up suits and sweatshirts, a deal Hamilton brokered. Murjani sold an impressive $500 million worth of Coke merchandise before the business dropped off and the license lapsed earlier this year.

In Domino's case, however, Hamilton president Michael Stone demurred. "Domino's means pizza," says Stone. "I told them nothing doing, unless maybe they wanted to do a tomato sauce."

Okay, maybe Domino's can't make the stretch beyond pepperoni, extra cheese and anchovies, but for most marketers these days, it's critical to find out just how far their brands can go.—J.L.

Chapter 6

"New Coke's Fizzle—Lessons for the Rest of Us"

Betsy D. Gelb and Gabriel M. Gelb

Preview

Skimming. Skim the article quickly to find the following general information.

1. Read the authors' names, the title, and all headings.

2. Read the abstract and first and second paragraphs, looking for the authors' purpose and main idea.

3. Read the last paragraph, looking for a summary or conclusion.

Questioning. Answer the following questions and discuss your answers in class.

1. Is Coca-Cola popular in your country?

2. What does *fizzle* mean?

3. What is the connection between New Coke and fizzle?

Scanning. Scan the article quickly to find the following specific information.

1. How much money and time did Coca-Cola spend on tests to measure consumer response to a new Coke?

2. What is the "80/20 rule"?

3. Which products are the riskiest to "improve"?

4. What did a Japanese observer say Coke represents to its American customers?

Sloan Management Review 28, no. 1 (Fall 1986)

Vocabulary in Context. Read the following sentences and try to guess the meaning of the italicized words by using the context. Then replace the italicized words with synonyms (words or phrases that have nearly the same or similar meanings).

1. "*Business Week* labeled the introduction of New Coke the 'marketing *blunder* of the decade.' It is difficult to quarrel with this *assessment*."

2. "Three different, but *compatible,* explanations can be offered. All three *assume* that a decision to buy is complex and that the basis on which it is made differs from buyer to buyer."

3. "To test a package designed for a new product, a researcher can present A, B, and C and ask *relevant prospects* which package they would buy."

4. "Coke apparently not only *quenches* thirst, but for its American customers *represents* in the words of a Japanese observer, 'an integral part of growing up [in the U.S.].'"

5. "Such a project should include testing the specific change *envisioned* with that change made *explicit* to those responding."

New Coke's Fizzle — Lessons for the Rest of Us

Betsy D. Gelb
Gabriel M. Gelb

University of Houston
Gelb Consulting Group, Inc.

THE NEW COKE FIASCO might have been avoided had market researchers concentrated more on consumers' emotional ties to the existing product. Coke drinkers *believed* that Coke stood for traditional values, as company ads had encouraged them to do, so they felt betrayed when the product changed radically overnight. Quantitative research often fails to uncover such fierce but unarticulated loyalties to the status quo. Researchers must use more qualitative methods, and they must acknowledge in advance that "improving" a popular product is a risky business. *Ed.*

Sloan
Management
Review

Fall 1986

1 CLASSIC COKE HAS BEEN with us for a year now, a red and white testament to the power of consumer resistance to change. Coca-Cola's 1985 decision to introduce a new formulation for its leading soft drink underscores a basic lesson: any marketer who plans a noticeable revision of a product must consider the possibility that buyers will rebel at the change. The prudent course of action, therefore, is to commission research sophisticated enough to detect whether such buyer resistance in fact exists.

2 Based on twenty years of research for consumer and industrial marketers in a wide range of fields, we argue that the resistance met by "new" Coke is by no means unique. And such resistance can be foreseen with research techniques more probing than the studies Coca-Cola performed. There are two basic steps. The first is to understand that balking at change is a customer characteristic independent of specific product preferences. Step two is to investigate, using qualitative as well as quantitative research, the nature and extent of resistance to a contemplated "improvement."

NEW COKE FIZZLES

3 *Business Week* labeled the introduction of New Coke the "marketing blunder of the decade." It is difficult to quarrel with this assessment. A.C. Nielsen recently reported that New Coke accounts for 3.4 percent of soft-drink sales in food stores. Classic (original) Coke holds a 14.5 percent share. Thus,

the combined share of the two brands is 17.9 percent — exactly equal to Coke's market share before the expensive and embarrassing introduction of a new formulation.[1]

4 How could a giant corporation, long admired for its marketing skill, so profoundly misjudge consumer reaction to a critical product decision? Our contention is not that Coca-Cola neglected market research. Rather, its research focused inadequately on the one issue that turned out to be crucial: indignation at change in a long-standing brand.

5 Coca-Cola spent $4 million and more than two years on tests designed to measure consumer response to a new formulation of its flagship soft drink. The firm tested three alternative formulations against "old" Coke and Pepsi on some 200,000 respondents. But only 30,000 to 40,000 of these tests involved the formulation that was actually introduced. Moreover, only a small fraction of the participants were told precisely what they were tasting; the vast majority of tests were "blind comparisons" between unnamed products. These tests determined that significantly more people (at one point, 53 percent versus 47 percent) preferred Drink A ("new" Coke) to Drink B (original Coke).[2]

6 The company also asked soft-drink consumers who had not tasted the new formulation a question on "the idea of changing the formulation." Basically, it was a yes/no question on whether the consumer favored the change as a concept. Next they asked whether the consumer would drink

*Betsy D. Gelb is
Professor of Marketing
at the University of
Houston-University
Park. Dr. Gelb also
holds the B.J. degree
from the University of
Missouri at Columbia,
and the M.B.A. and
Ph.D. degrees from the
University of Houston-
University Park. Her
primary teaching area
is in marketing
strategy, and she has
served as a consultant
in that field to both
for-profit and not-for-
profit organizations.
Dr. Gelb is the author
of numerous articles,
in such publications as
Harvard Business Re-
view, California
Management Review,
and Journal of Mar-
keting.*

more, less, or the same amount of Coke if there was a change. Also, they asked consumers who were soft-drink customers but not Coke customers whether they would be more likely, less likely, or equally likely to try Coke if a change were made.[3]

7 Results of the "change concept" study have never been made public. However, it seems unlikely that consumers' emotional ties to the past could have been discovered with a set of yes/no questions. Much the same shortcoming marked the taste tests. According to Ira Herbert, Coca-Cola's vice president for worldwide marketing, "We failed to tell the tasters graphically enough that their preference for the new would mean that they would never be able to taste the original Coke again." Thus, in the words of an *Advertising Age* commentator, Coca-Cola executives overlooked the symbolic meaning of their product and treated it as "simply a thirst-quenching liquid—period."[4]

8 Another problem was the "one man, one vote" nature of the results. With soft drinks, as with many other products, a relatively small proportion of buyers purchases the lion's share of all units. Marketers often refer to this phenomenon as the "80/20 rule"—20 percent of the buyers purchase 80 percent of the volume in a product category. These heavy users disproportionately preferred an unchanged Coke formula, according to a survey done for Pepsi soon after the change. Had every taste test vote been weighted by the respondent's weekly consumption of Coke, the results would have been a firm rejection of the new formulation.

UNDERSTANDING CONSUMER RESISTANCE

9 Why should a company assume that a change which appears to be preferred by a majority may meet resistance—and may be resisted most firmly by consumers most loyal to the company's brand? Three different, but compatible, explanations can be offered. All three assume that a decision to buy is complex and that the basis on which it is made differs from buyer to buyer.

10 The first explanation assumes that a brand choice results from a complex set of beliefs and weights attached to those beliefs.[5] For example, a consumer may think that buying a foreign-made car means high gas mileage, but he or she may also believe that high gas mileage is not very important. That same consumer may decide that it *is* important to "buy American," and be extremely motivated to do so, because his or her neighbors make snide remarks to those who drive foreign cars. A

researcher who simply asked such a consumer to compare Toyota and Ford on six characteristics might find Toyota preferred on five of the six, and fail to realize that those beliefs were not heavily weighted in the eventual decision-making process.

11 Similarly, someone responding to an interviewer can choose one company name, brand name, design, color, package, or flavor over the present name, design, etc., but do so without realizing that he or she has unintentionally voted for change. When that realization occurs, in an actual buying situation, the wish to retain the familiar may far outweigh what would otherwise be a preference for the unfamiliar. Familiarity, furthermore, may not be the entire issue. Emotional ties to a product are precisely what marketing professionals spend millions of dollars to establish. Consumers may not only become used to what they have—they may believe that, despite the superiority of a proposed new version, change would be impractical, startling, or just plain wrong.

12 A second explanation for resistance to change arises from the idea that buyers associate products with themselves. That is, they are likely to believe not only that "I am a Coke drinker" (or a Ford driver, or a Hyatt Hotel patron), but to some extent that *they actually resemble the brand they choose*.[6] In other words, people who consider themselves Coke drinkers are more prepared to tell a researcher that "Coke is like me" than they would be to make the same statement about Pepsi. Thus a product change may communicate to the consumer that he or she needs to change—a message that may be threatening, insulting, or both.

13 A study by the Ogilvy & Mather advertising agency reports that the "I use this, this is me" principle is most intense with products that are ingested or applied close to the skin. For example, the study found greater identification of men with their underwear than with their ties. Charlotte Beers, chief executive of Chicago's Tatham-Laird & Kudner agency, has pointed out that food products are the riskiest to "improve." She cites Velveeta cheese as an example. "Velveeta cheese has a distinct taste, but more than that, it is a part of childhood for a lot of people—the way it stirs and mixes and melts," Beers notes. "It would be very risky to change any of that."[7] Substantiating the qualms about food modifications are two other recent marketing missteps—a reformulation of Schlitz beer and a reshaping of Nestle's Chunky candy bar, which has since been changed back from an elongated shape

A product change may communicate to the consumer that he or she needs to change—a message that may be threatening, insulting, or both.

to its original trapezoidal "chunk."

14   A third explanation involves "psychographics," the art of segmenting groups of consumers by their activities, interests, and opinions, as well as by such demographic data as age, income, and residential location. In one well-known breakdown of the U.S. population into categories, the largest group is titled "belongers," more interested in fitting in with present conditions than in striving for novelty.[8] To the extent that a brand depends on purchases by this group, the company will be most likely to succeed by appealing to their traditional values (as Coke's advertising has consistently attempted to do). Of course, a taste test would not elicit aversion to change among this group if no one told a respondent that getting the preferred taste would mean abandoning something traditional.

HOW BETTER RESEARCH CAN HELP

15 We have tested proposed changes in corporate names, product names, logos, package designs, product formulations, and even a change in an invoice billing system. Results have convinced us that such testing of "improvements" simply is not the same process as testing new products or services.

16   To test a package designed for a new product, a researcher can present A, B, and C, and ask relevant prospects which package they would buy. Such tests generate measures of the dimensions participants consider as they evaluate the package, and the way in which designs A, B, and C are perceived to rank on those dimensions. For a package *change*, however, the task is different. Those packages in the abstract, even if they include the present package, cannot be taken into an area where the company does not market and be subjected to the same comparison. Instead, the company has to do what it is often greatly reluctant to do—ask its own customers to react to alternative changes and to no change. Frequently expressed concerns about "getting them all upset for nothing," or "telegraphing our plans to the competition," are simply unrealistic when the need to know is paramount. The essence of the research task is to confront one problem: expressing preference when forced by the research setting to try something new is far different from being willing to try it independently.

17 The basis of this resistance is not always emotional. Consider the case of a proposed condominium development in Monterrey, Mexico, during the mid-1970s. A developer had observed vigorous demand for luxury high-rise condominium buildings in Mexico City. Well-to-do men were buying the units for elderly parents or widowed mothers. This level of demand could have been interpreted as a universal indication of consumer preference. But the developer commissioned research specifically in Monterrey, where no condominium housing existed.

18 We interviewed a sample of individuals in the socioeconomic class that paralleled the Mexico City buyers, using focus groups and in-depth interviews as our qualitative research methods. We found great enthusiasm for the concept—sons would no longer have to build a small home for their parents on their own property, as was the tradition, but could nevertheless feel that they had provided a secure place to live. It would be a fine thing, said a typical respondent, for several families he knew. And how about himself? Well, we were told, one would not want to be the first to do such a thing. The problem, in other words, was change itself. The complex was never built—and at last report there were still no high-rise luxury condominiums in Monterrey.

19   Another example of nonemotional resistance to change concerns a national corporation that wanted to introduce an improved billing system. The system involved sending customers a computer-printed list of purchases, replacing individual hard-copy tickets for each purchase. The firm's customers were large organizations, which would now be able to process one sheet of paper representing fifty transactions, rather than fifty transaction tickets. When we talked to accounts payable managers, however, several pointed out that if their department's workload were to decrease, they would have to reduce their staffs. Thus, they opposed the "improvement."

Sloan Management Review

Fall 1986

WHAT DOES THE PRODUCT DO FOR THE BUYER?

20 What guidelines warn a manager that a change may be no improvement, even to those customers who in the abstract might concede its superiority? The key issues are what the product actually accomplishes for the user, and what emotional ties link that user to the brand.

21 Studying the actual use to which customers put products is valuable for many reasons, and assessing the desirability of improvement is surely one of them. Coke apparently not only quenches thirst, but for its American customers represents, in the words of a Japanese observer, "an integral part of growing up [in the U.S.]."[9] A billing method may be used by a manager to justify a staff of ego-gratifying size, or to avoid the trauma of layoffs. A "hacker" may use a computer to demonstrate that he can do something his parents cannot. Thus a company seeking to introduce a new level of cola sweetness, billing efficiency, or computer simplicity may not be helping buyers to accomplish their actual underlying purpose.

22 A closely allied issue concerns emotional ties between buyer and product – a relationship which qualitative research methods can assess. Such ties can be investigated unobtrusively, by observation. Do users talk to their computers, or prefer one brand to the other in an office setting where nearly identical machines sit side by side? If so, there is evidence of some kind of attachment to "a machine." Do customers at a trade show handle a product whose usefulness has nothing to do with its "feel"– supposedly? A trained observer may point out to management that these customers want to reassure themselves that their "old friend" hasn't changed.

23 A second research technique, focus group interviews, reveals emotional attachments through "conversations" among a product's users, led by an experienced moderator. As described by Weilbacher, the leader's role is to "appear charming . . . to establish and maintain substantial rapport within the group, and to ruthlessly probe and extract the respondents' fundamental attitude patterns toward the subject under discussion."[10]

24 The focus group technique can generate anecdotes, stories, and other comments that lead to valuable insights. In our experience, for example:

25 • A new owner of a small-town automobile dealership was considering changing its name to his own. Local focus group participants, who were offered a simple name change scenario, reacted by offering richly detailed reactions, purely from their own imaginations. Participants worried that after the proposed renaming the dealership would "jack up the prices," "stop carrying the economy cars in the line," and "hire salesmen from out of town."

26 • Before implementing a change in fan blade design, an industrial equipment manufacturer recruited a focus group from his customer list. Asked first about the pluses and minuses of the current design, participants described a number of flaws. Then asked about a pictorially displayed new design, these same customers worried that it was "too different" and, in effect, redesigned it to meet several of their objections about the current blade without changing it as drastically as had been proposed.

27 A more unusual research technique that may also help is the "animal" analogy.[11] Buyers are asked to attach animal names to brands of, say, computers. If Brand X turns out to be a turtle, the user is probably just labeling it as slow – emotional attachment to turtles being relatively rare in our society. But if it is called a dog or a cat, the marketer has a clue that some emotional bond has been created. When this technique has been used for cigarette brands, answers have clustered in nonrandom ways despite the many animals consumers could name.

28 A final example of a technique that goes far beyond the ordinary involves simulated "psychodrama." Consumers in one such study were given a questionnaire which listed eleven beverages, and were instructed, "Imagine, just for a moment, that you are a beverage, any liquid substance that can be safely consumed by a human being. . . . Please describe yourself and your behavior as this beverage."[12]

29 Results showed that the beverage an individual chose was, unsurprisingly, one which he or she drank more than others. More important, however, consumers were able to express *why* they imagined themselves as that particular beverage. To the extent that a parallel technique is used with brands of, say, coffee, a company may find that many of its buyers would like to be Maxwell House because "it's 'easy-going'– or 'friendly'–like me." If so, these buyers may have reached such a conclusion based

New Coke's Fizzle

Gelb & Gelb

Gabriel M. Gelb is President of Gelb Consulting Group Inc., a Houston-based marketing consulting and marketing research firm founded in 1965. He holds the B.S. degree from City College of New York and the M.A. degree from the University of Missouri at Columbia. He has been designated a certified management consultant by the Institute of Management Consultants, is a board member of the MIT Enterprise Forum of Texas, and is chairman of Houston's Research Roundtable. He is coauthor of Research at the Top: Better Data for Organizational Policy-Making, *published by the American Marketing Association, and has written extensively on survey research.*

Of course, a taste test would not elicit aversion to change . . . if no one told a respondent that getting the preferred taste would mean abandoning something traditional.

on a configuration of flavor and packaging cues that the company would therefore be well advised to leave unchanged.

APPLYING THE RESEARCH

30 Suppose research findings turn up an emotional attachment to the brand, or evidence that the product is being used in a way that the supposed improvement will not enhance. In either case, Coca-Cola's contingency strategy of parallel versions of a product—new and "classic"—may in fact be worthwhile. Alternatively, a change buyers cannot detect may be added without announcement. A third possibility, of course, is to position the brand as "traditional" and channel R&D funds elsewhere. Such a set of alternatives will not be considered unless consumer research has alerted management to the resistance that can be expected to accompany "improvements" in certain situations.

31 What might Coke have done differently? Some advice offered three months after the New Coke introduction illustrates how the kind of research we are advocating can lead to concrete marketing planning. The prescription, written after discussion with Mark Albion of the Harvard Business School faculty and with other marketing experts, reads:

> Okay, Coke, here's a strategy that might have worked. Using state-of-the-art market research . . . you could have found out how consumers felt about the new formula before the change. Here's what you would have discovered: Coke's largest and most loyal block of customers, mostly Middle Americans, are disturbed by changes. And the image of Coke as an American institution is just as special to them as its taste. Knowing this, a much more subtle approach was in order. The old brand should have reassuringly remained on the shelves far longer. And the ads were wrong:

better to tell consumers that New Coke is the same as the old, except for a couple of improvements to make it better. Finally, Bill Cosby was the wrong person to convince consumers that it's all right to tamper with an institution. That kind of pitch is more believable coming from someone like Walter Cronkite.[13]

32 For "the rest of us" who are not Coca-Cola, this specific advice represents one illustration of some excellent general guidelines. In brief, for any company considering a change in any facet of its offerings to the marketplace:

33 **1.** The possibility of consumer resistance to change must be recognized.

34 **2.** The likelihood of such resistance must be assessed, based on the kind of product involved, the kind of buyers involved, the use to which they actually put the product, and their degree of identification with it. Such an assessment is likely to be a research project in itself, with a number of creative techniques available for conducting it.

35 **3.** If it seems likely that resistance to change will be a problem, research to measure the extent and nature of that resistance should be undertaken. Such a project should include testing the specific change envisioned, with that change made explicit to those responding.

36 **4.** Once the degree and nature of resistance is determined, marketing plans can be designed to take the resistance into account. A change may be best explained, hidden, modified, delayed, abandoned, or only partially executed.

37 There is enough of a gap as it is between research results and actual purchases without compounding the problem by limiting research to conventional quantitative studies. If the possible gain from a product change is not sufficient to justify the risk and cost of the kind of research described here, a company may well be better off adhering to the

Sloan
Management
Review

Fall 1986

status quo. At least that way fewer buyers, evaluating a misguided "improvement," will decide: "My coffee just isn't me anymore." ∎

References

1
S. Scredon, "Roberto Goizueta," *Business Week*, 18 April 1986, p. 220.

2
J. Honomichl, "Missing Ingredients in 'New' Coke's Research," *Advertising Age*, 22 July 1985, pp. 1, 58.

3
Dr. Ray Suh, Manager, Custom Research, Coca-Cola USA, telephone interview, 11 June 1985.

4
Honomichl (July 1985), p. 1.

5
For a clear description and critique, see M.J. Ryan and E.H. Bonfield, "The Fishbein Extended Model and Consumer Behavior," *Journal of Consumer Research* 2 (1975): 118–136.

6
E.L. Landon, Jr., "Self Concept, Ideal Self Concept, and Consumer Purchase Intentions," *Journal of Consumer Research* 1 (1974): 44–51.

7
A.B. Fisher, "Coke's Brand Loyalty Lesson," *Fortune*, 5 August 1985, pp. 44–46.

8
"Belongers" are 38 percent of the U.S. population in the "VALS" typology developed by SRI International, Menlo Park, California. "VALS" is an acronym for "Values and Life Styles."

9
An excerpt from *Asbai Evening News*, a Tokyo daily, quoted in "Coca-Cola Makes Headlines Worldwide," *Advertising Age*, 5 August 1985, p. 36.

10
W. Weilbacher, *Marketing Management Cases*, 3rd ed. (New York: Macmillan, 1980), p. 64.

11
S.J. Levy, "Dreams, Fairy Tales, Animals and Cars," *Psychology and Marketing*, Summer 1985, pp. 67–81.

12
A.G. Woodside, N. Floyd-Finch, and E.J. Wilson, "Psychodrama and Beverage Consumption" (New Orleans, LA: Tulane University, Working Paper, 1985).

13
K. Foltz, "Wizards of Marketing," *Newsweek*, 22 July 1985, pp. 42–44.

New Coke's
Fizzle

Gelb & Gelb

Glossary

adhering to	staying attached, supporting
advocating	supporting, arguing for
analogy	comparison of, or similarity between, unlike things
anecdotes	short personal stories
aversion	strong dislike
balking	hesitating, refusing
blunder	error, mistake
compounding	increasing, intensifying
condominium	apartment building with individual ownership of units and joint ownership of common grounds
configuration	arrangement
contemplated	considered, planned, intended
contingency	emergency
drastically	extremely
elicit	to draw forth, cause to be revealed
feel	the nature of a thing perceived through touch
fizzle	an attempt that ends in failure, fiasco
flagship	the finest, largest, or most important
focus groups	market research technique using conversations among consumers to discover their attitudes toward products
gap	difference
graphically	vividly, realistically
hacker	talented user of computers, or one who tries to gain unauthorized access to files
indignation	anger
ingested	taken into the body by swallowing
integral	essential, necessary
missteps	mistakes
paramount	most important, dominant
pictorially	expressed in pictures
probe	to investigate, examine thoroughly
probing	thorough in investigating
prudent	wise, careful
qualms	doubts, uneasiness
R & D	Research and Development
rapport	close relationship, harmony
reluctant	hesitant, unwilling
ruthlessly	cruelly
scenario	outline of events
shortcoming	defect, deficiency
startling	surprising
status quo	the existing state of affairs
subtle	delicately skillful or clever, indirect
tamper	to interfere, meddle

testament	witness, affirmation
thirst-quenching	satisfying thirst
trapezoidal	shaped like a trapezoid (plane figure with four sides, only two of which are parallel)
trauma	shock, painful experience
underscores	emphasizes
unobtrusively	without being noticed
version	variation in form, modification

Vocabulary

Without referring to the article, fill in the blanks in the following sentences with the correct words from this list. You may change the tense, number, or form of the words to fit the context. Use each word only once; not all of the words on the list will be used.

| underscore | elicit | blunder | focus group | flagship | ruthlessly | probing |
| integral | contingency | reluctant | configuration | advocate | analogy | aversion |

1. The problem caused by the introduction of New Coke _____ the importance of accurate, extensive, and _____ market research before developing an "improved" product.

2. New Coke was considered a major marketing _____ by *Business Week*.

3. Coca-Cola's _____ soft drink, Coke, has had an enormous popularity for many years.

4. The purpose of market research is to _____ responses from consumers about desire for or _____ to change; this can help determine whether a company should produce a new or improved product.

5. One common market research technique uses _____ : conversations among consumers to discover their basic attitudes toward and emotional attachments to a product.

6. Drinking Coke appears to be a(n) _____ part of the American experience, according to a Japanese businessman.

7. A market research technique that is somewhat unusual involves the animal _____ ; buyers assign animal names to brands of products and thus reveal what if any emotional attachment they have to a product.

8. A successful food product is a(n) _____ of taste and packaging that appeals to the buyer because the product is not only useful but also emotionally appealing.

9. Even though Coca-Cola had a(n) _____ strategy of producing two versions of its product, New and Classic Coke, the New Coke was a major failure for the company.

10. Today, several marketing experts are strongly _____ both creative quantitative and qualitative studies of market research.

Idioms and Expressions

Read the paragraphs in which the following italicized idioms and expressions are found. Then circle the letter next to the answer that best describes the meaning of the idiom as used in the context of the article.

1. "Another problem was the '*one man, one vote*' nature of the results." (Paragraph 8)
   a. each person has one opinion
   b. only one man can vote
   c. only men can vote

2. ". . . a relatively small proportion of the buyers purchases *the lion's share* of all units." (Paragraph 8)
   a. the best portion
   b. the smallest portion
   c. the largest portion

3. ". . . the 'belongers,' more interested in *fitting in with* present conditions than in striving for novelty." (Paragraph 14)
   a. being part of [something]
   b. understanding
   c. rejecting

4. ". . . the dealership would '*jack up the prices.*'. . ." (Paragraph 25)
   a. correct wrong prices
   b. raise the prices
   c. lower the prices

5. "Using *state-of-the-art* market research . . ." (Paragraph 31)
   a. the most artistic, creative
   b. government- or state-sponsored
   c. the newest and best

6. "That kind of *pitch* is more believable coming from someone like Walter Cronkite." (Paragraph 31)
   a. sales talk
   b. point of view
   c. tone of voice

Paraphrasing

Read the following sentences carefully, and then rewrite them using your own words. Change the vocabulary and sentence structure, but do not change the authors' intended meaning or paraphrase any technical terms. There are several ways of paraphrasing each sentence.

Original: "Coca-Cola's 1985 decision to introduce a new formulation for its leading soft drink underscores a basic lesson. . . ."

Paraphrase: When Coca-Cola decided to change the form of its best-selling soft drink in 1985, it taught us a fundamental lesson.

1. "And such resistance can be foreseen with research techniques more probing than the studies Coca-Cola performed." (Paragraph 2)

_____

_____

2. "Substantiating the qualms about food modifications are two other recent marketing missteps. . . ." (Paragraph 13)

_____

_____

3. "A closely allied issue concerns emotional ties between buyer and product—a relationship which qualitative research methods can assess." (Paragraph 22)

_____

_____

4. "The possibility of consumer resistance to change must be recognized." (Paragraph 33)

_____

_____

Comprehension

Answer the following questions by finding the relevant information in the article. Give the numbers of the paragraphs that contain the answers.

1. What is the main idea of this article?

2. Why did Coca-Cola so greatly misjudge consumer reaction to a critical product decision?

3. What types of tests did Coca-Cola conduct to measure consumer response to a new Coke?

4. What were the problems with Coca-Cola's tests?

5. What three explanations are offered for understanding consumer resistance?

6. How does testing for new products differ from the testing of improvements in already existing products?

7. What is the essence of the market research task when testing for an improvement or change in a product?

8. What are the two key issues determining whether a product should be changed?

9. What four market research techniques can be used to study the emotional ties between buyers and products to assess the desirability of improving a product?

10. What three alternatives can a company consider if market research reveals consumer resistance to "improvements"?

11. What might Coca-Cola have done differently?

12. What type of market research should be conducted by any company considering a change in its product?

Inference/Interpretation

Circle the letter next to the best answer. Choose your answer according to the meaning the authors suggest but do not state explicitly.

1. What is conveyed by the authors' use of quotation marks around the word *improvement* in paragraph 2 and throughout the article?
   a. The unusual use of the word *improvement*
   b. The humorous use of the word *improvement*
   c. The authors' suggestion that the change is an improvement
   d. The authors' awareness that a change may not be an actual improvement

2. It can be inferred from the article that the "symbolic meaning" of Coke is (Paragraph 7)
   a. less important than its taste.
   b. equally as important as its taste.
   c. much more complex than just its use.
   d. a result of Coke's being thirst-quenching.

3. What is the meaning of the statement of a Japanese observer that Coke represents "an integral part of growing up" [in the U.S.]? (Paragraph 21)
   a. Almost all Americans drink Coke while growing up.
   b. Drinking Coke helps children grow tall.
   c. American children drink too much Coke.
   d. American consumers have an emotional attachment to Coke.

4. What can be inferred about conventional quantitative research studies? (Paragraph 37)
   a. They are the best research techniques to use to assess consumer resistance to change.
   b. They are unable to clearly assess consumer resistance to change.
   c. They are too creative to be effective.
   d. They should never be used to assess consumer resistance to change.

Structure

Circle the letter next to the correct answer(s). More than one answer may be correct. Be prepared to explain and justify your choices.

1. In which paragraph(s) is the main idea stated?
   a. Paragraph 1
   b. Paragraph 2
   c. Paragraph 3
   d. Paragraph 32
   e. Paragraph 37
   Write a paraphrase of the main idea in *one* sentence, using your own words as much as possible.

   _____

2. Why do the authors state in the introduction that they have conducted "20 years of research for consumer and industrial marketers in a wide range of fields . . ."?
   a. To contrast their experience with Coca-Cola marketers' experience
   b. To justify market research in all fields
   c. To establish their credibility in the field of market research
   d. To give an example of the importance of market research
   e. To support their argument that consumer resistance to change is common

3. Where do the authors use process as a method of development of their general ideas?
   a. Paragraph 2
   b Paragraphs 10, 12, 14
   c. Paragraph 16
   d Paragraph 30
   e. Paragraphs 33–36

4. Where do the authors use contrast as a method of development of their general ideas?
   a. Paragraph 4
   b Paragraph 9
   c. Paragraph 16
   d Paragraph 20
   e. Paragraph 29
   What words signal the contrast?

   _____

5. Where are specific examples used to support a general idea?
   a. Paragraph 13
   b Paragraphs 17–19
   c. Paragraph 23
   d. Paragraph 28
   e. Paragraph 30

6. Where do the authors use enumeration?
   a. Paragraph 5
   b. Paragraph 7
   c. Paragraphs 10, 12, 14
   d. Paragraph 17
   e. Paragraph 30

7. What overall methods of development are used in this article?
   a. Describing a study and its results
   b. Defining a problem and proposing a solution
   c. Supporting an argument by enumerating specific proposals
   d. Attacking an argument by comparing data
   e. Analyzing a scientific process

Style

Circle the letter next to the correct answer(s). More than one answer may be correct. Be prepared to justify your choices by giving specific examples from the article.

1. How would you describe the writing style of the authors?
   a. Technical
   b. Literary
   c. Informal
   d. Colorful
   e. Formal
   f. Businesslike

2. How would you describe the tone of the article?
   a. Objective
   b. Condescending
   c. Angry
   d. Analytical
   e. Emotional
   f. Approving

3. The authors' attitude toward the introduction of New Coke can be described as
   a. surprised.
   b. positive.
   c. critical.
   d. supportive.
   e. neutral.
   f. unrealistic.

4. The following statement contains a slang (informal) expression. Explain what this expression would mean to a market researcher: "My coffee just isn't me anymore" (Paragraph 37) Rewrite this sentence in a formal style.

Discussion

1. Do you agree with the authors that sophisticated market research is necessary to detect consumer resistance? Why or why not?

2. Is the decision to buy a product as complex as the authors argue? Why or why not?

3. What new food or drink products have recently been introduced in your country? Did they fail or succeed?

4. Do you have an emotional attachment to any product? Which ones? Why?

5. Do you consider yourself an educated consumer who shops carefully and knowledgeably?

6. Have you ever tried New Coke? If so, what was your reaction?

Research Assignment

Look up several of these articles in the library. Choose one article to read and take notes on.

"Coca-Cola Makes Headlines Worldwide." *Advertising Age* 56 (August 5, 1985): 36.

"An Embarrassment of Colas." *Economist* 310 (July 20, 1985): 25.

Foltz, K. "Wizards of Marketing." *Newsweek* 109 (July 22, 1985): 42–44.

Harvey, D. "Coke Changed Formula to Break from Old Habits." *Advertising Age* 56 (June 24, 1985): 24.

Honomichl, J. "Missing Ingredients in 'New' Coke's Research." *Advertising Age* 56 (July 22, 1985): 1, 58.

Johansson, Johnny K., and Ikujiro Nonaka. "Market Research the Japanese Way." *Harvard Business Review* 65 (May-June 1987): 16–22.

Landon, E. I., Jr. "Self Concept, Ideal Self Concept, and Consumer Purchase Intentions." *Journal of Consumer Research* 1 (1974): 44–51.

Lazarus, G. "Coke Is No. 1: Biggest Story, Biggest Goof." *Adweek* (December 23, 1985): 1.

Levy, S. J. "Dreams, Fairytales, Animals, and Cars." *Psychology and Marketing* (Summer 1985): 67–81.

McCarthy, Michael J. "New Coke Gets a New Look, New Chance." *Wall Street Journal* (March 7, 1990): B1, B8.

McCusker, Allen A. "Relaunching a Failure: The Job Ahead for Coke II." *Advertising Age* 61 (March 26, 1990): 20.

Potts, Mark. "New Coke to Try a New Name in Test." *Washington Post* (March 7, 1990): C1, C4.

Samli, A. Coskun, Kristian Palda, and A. Tansu Baker. "Toward a Mature Marketing Concept." *Sloan Management Review* 28 (Winter 1987): 45–51.

Scredon, S. "Brian Dyson Takes the New Coke Challenge." *Business Week* (May 26, 1986): 81.

Scredon, S. "Roberto Goizueta." *Business Week* (April 18, 1986): 220.

Scredon, S., and A. Dunkin. "New Coke Wins Round 1, but Can It Go the Distance?" *Business Week* (June 24, 1985): 48.

"Stepson of Coke." *Economist* 315 (May 26, 1990): 70–72.

Winters, P. "For New Coke, What Price Success?" *Advertising Age* 60 (March 20, 1989): 51–52.

Oral Presentation

Give a ten-minute oral presentation to the class on the article that you chose in the research assignment. Include the author's main idea and some supporting data. Be prepared to answer questions on your topic. (See Appendix B: Giving an Oral Presentation.)

Writing Assignments

1. Write a synthesis using at least two of the articles listed in the research assignment and the additional reading in this chapter. After reading the articles, create a thesis based on relationships you develop among the readings, and support it with specific information from the articles you chose. Organize your synthesis according to one of the following methods: cause-effect, comparison-contrast, description, example, or process. (See Appendix D for an example of a synthesis.)

   Use parenthetical references in the author-date system for each of the sources you cite: (Winters 1989). You may also choose to give the page number: (Winters 1989, 5). List all sources at the end of your paper as References. Entries should be alphabetized according to the last name of the author: Winters, P. 1989. "For New Coke, What Price Success?" *Advertising Age* 60:51–52.

2. Discuss a new product or an improved product that was recently introduced in your country. Did this product succeed or fail? Why? Use enumeration to present your ideas, as well as cause and effect organization.

3. You are the marketing director of a large soft drink company. You want to reformulate your best-selling soft drink into an "improved" version. Develop a questionnaire to be used as a market research instrument to measure consumer response to this new formulation. The questionnaire should have three parts: introduction, instructions, and questions. Include questions on the following subjects:

    I. Consumer loyalty to the particular soft drink;
   II. Consumer identification with the particular soft drink;
  III. Consumer use of the particular soft drink; and
  IV. Consumer resistance to change.

Peer Critique

Choose a person to work with. After you have completed your writing assignment, let your partner read and critique your writing. Then you will read and critique his or her writing. Use the Writing Evaluation Form in Appendix F.

Case Study: A Problem in Market Research

Working in groups, read the following case study. Discuss the problem, answer the qustions, and write a brief report on how your group would solve the problem. (Choose one member of the group to do the writing.) Follow the format in Appendix E (Case Study Report) in writing your report.

    Jack Novak works for Burt's Burgers, Inc., a fast-food company that has sold billions of Burt's Burgers all over the world. He is assistant to the Marketing Director and a recent business school graduate. Although most of his colleagues like him, they think he is too interested in marketing theory and lacking in practical knowledge and experience.

    Burt's Burgers, Inc. has shown increasing profits over the past five years, and the corporate headquarters has approved a budget to test market new products. Jack's boss, Mike Borowski, has suggested the introduction of the Burt's Barbecue Burger, an "improved" version of the standard Burt's hamburger. (It has spicy barbecue sauce mixed with the meat.) Mike did a little market research on the "improved" product, but only in the Southwest (Arizona, New Mexico, Colorado, and Texas). The consumer response was positive, so Mike is pushing for Burt's Burgers to introduce this "improved" product.

    Jack does not support Mike's position and has already told him why he disagrees. He feels that insufficient market research was done and only in a limited area. He is familiar with the New Coke fiasco and wants to do extensive market research before making the decision to go ahead with the Burt's Barbecue Burger. However, Jack is reluctant to speak out against his boss, who is a highly respected, longtime employee of Burt's Burgers.

    The final decision will be made at the corporate executive group meeting tomorrow morning. Both Jack and Mike will attend the meeting. Jack has already written a six-page memo analyzing the market potential for Burt's Barbecue Burger and justifying his position against introducing it. He has included a thorough market analysis and several statistical graphs and charts. In addition, Jack has come up with an idea of his own that he might mention at the meeting: if the company is ready to test market new products, he would like to suggest a low-fat hamburger, which would appeal to all the health conscious consumers who avoid eating at Burt's Burgers. He knows of two competitors that are already developing such a product. Why not try to beat them to it? Low-fat food is definitely the major trend of the times.

Questions

1. Should Jack present his point of view about the Burt's Barbecue Burger at the meeting, even though his boss strongly supports introducing the "improved" product?

2. Should Jack suggest further market research? If so, what specific types?

3. Where should the further market research be done and on how many respondents?

4. If the market research findings reveal an emotional attachment to the original Burt's hamburger, what alternatives could Jack suggest to the company?

Solution: Case Study Report

I. Define and analyze the problem.
II. Suggest possible solutions.
III. Evaluate possible solutions.
IV. Select a solution.

Case Study Business Writing Assignment: Memorandum

Write a memo from Jack Novak to his boss Mike Borowski. Explain why Jack does not support Mike's suggestion to introduce the Burt's Barbecue Burger.

Format:
I. Introduction (Background and Main Idea)
II. Discussion (Reasons)
III. Closing (Restatement of Main Idea)

Style: Informal and conversational
Tone: Friendly and persuasive

Additional Reading

"Coke's Brand-Loyalty Lesson"
Anne B. Fisher
Fortune 112 (August 5, 1985): 44–46

COKE'S BRAND-LOYALTY LESSON

Brand loyalty? Everyone knows Americans don't have much anymore. Or do they? Ask the folks at Coca-Cola who tampered with a 99-year-old national institution. Their marketing goof provides clues to what brand loyalty is—and how not to lose it. ■ *by Anne B. Fisher*

MARKETERS battling to keep competitors from grabbing off customers complain that there just doesn't seem to be as much brand loyalty around as there used to be. Yet when Coca-Cola Co. dared to tamper with a 99-year-old formula to bring out a "new" Coke, outraged U.S. consumers quickly forced the red-faced company to bring back the old brand. Coke's abrupt about-face, front-paged and prime-timed, raises questions about brand loyalty that every marketer has to ponder: how companies get it, how they keep it, and which products inspire such fierce loyalty that they're best left old and unimproved.

Brand loyalty—that certain something that makes a consumer keep buying over and over again—is an elusive quality. It begins with the customer's preference for a product on the basis of objective reasons—the drink is sweeter, the paper towel more absorbent. The brand name is the customer's guarantee that he will get what he expects. But when a branded product has been around a long time and is heavily advertised, it can pick up emotional freight: it can become a part of a person's self-image or summon fond memories of days gone by.

The sense of emotional attachment was palpable among consumers who for years had agreed with Coca-Cola that "Coke Is It." They wanted the Real Thing they had grown up with and in some cases grown old with. They inundated Coca-Cola's Atlanta headquarters with protests ("Dear Chief Dodo: What ignoramus decided to change the formula of Coke?"). In Seattle strident loyalists

RESEARCH ASSOCIATES *Wilton Woods and Robert Steyer*

Old new Coke *(left) and the new old Coke*

calling themselves Old Coke Drinkers of America laid plans to file a class action suit against Coca-Cola. They searched out shop owners, vending-machine owners, and others willing to claim that the company's formula change had cost them business. When June sales didn't pick up as the company had expected, bottlers too demanded old Coke's return—fast.

Coke thought it had moved cautiously in deciding to retire the old formula. The company spent about $4 million to taste-test the new soda pop on nearly 200,000 consumers. The tests took many forms. Some were blind tests without the emotion-laden brand name attached to them. Others posed such questions as, What if this were a new Coke taste? But Coca-Cola never disclosed that the product it was testing would replace the old favorite entirely.

So while it learned that more people liked the new, sweeter formula than the old, it failed to gauge how people would react once

they learned that old Coke was being replaced. Dennis Rosen, who teaches marketing at Indiana University's Graduate School of Business, thinks Coca-Cola unwittingly ran afoul of too many fond memories. "Taste tests," he says, "don't take into account the emotional tie-in with the old brand, which is all wrapped up with people's childhoods. Now that consumers are drinking out of cans labeled *new* Coke, naturally there is an emotional backlash."

When the new Coke hit the shelves in the U.S. in April, consumers felt that the company had broken the first promise of branding: that what you get today will be what you got yesterday. "All of the time and money and skill poured into consumer research on the new Coca-Cola could not measure or reveal the deep and abiding emotional attachment to original Coca-Cola," says Donald R. Keough, Coke's president and chief operating officer. He adds, "Some critic will say Coca-Cola made a marketing mistake. Some cynic will say that we planned the whole thing [for the publicity value]. The truth is we are not that dumb and we are not that smart."

Many marketing experts are sympathetic with Coke's giant misstep. "All research on brand loyalty is flawed," says John O'Toole, chairman of the Chicago-based advertising agency Foote Cone & Belding, "because you can't get at people's private motivations. In any kind of interview or questionnaire, they want to seem sensible and prudent. They aren't going to tell you how they *feel*." In Coca-Cola's case, consumers' feelings were not only unfathomable but fickle too. The company's research after the new formula hit supermarket shelves showed a curious turnaround. Before May 30, 53% of shoppers said they liked the new Coke, the rest said they didn't. In June the vote began to change, with more than half of all the people surveyed saying they didn't care for the new Coke. Says a Coke spokesman: "We had taken away more than the product Coca-Cola. We had taken away a little part of them and their past. They said, 'You had no right to do that. Bring it back.' " By the time the company decided it had erred in changing the formula, only 30% of the 900 consumers surveyed every week answered that they liked the new Coke.

With the old formula reintroduced as Coca-Cola Classic, complete with old-fashioned script logo, shoppers will now find six kinds of Coke on U.S. supermarket shelves—new, classic, caffeine-free, diet, diet caffeine-free, and cherry. (One more variety, the New York *Daily News* noted, and Coca-Cola "will have seven up.") Soft-drink

experts believe that the welter of Cokes will give the company a tough time keeping a clear identity in shoppers' minds. Some Coke executives are said to share that fear, though Chief Executive Roberto C. Goizueta called the lineup a "megabrand" and a marketing plus.

HE MAY BE right. Other products come in a variety of forms with no evident consumer befuddlement; Marlboro comes to mind, with its king-size and longs and low-tar lights in boxes and soft packs. Goizueta believes his megabrand gives the company an edge in supermarkets, where he who grabs the most shelf space wins. Wall Street seemed to share his confidence: in the week that the reintroduction of old Coke was announced, Coke's stock price jumped $5.50, closing at $73.75 a share.

Some consumers are quite capable of a kind of purchasing polygamy: they can be, and often are, faithful to more than one brand

at a time. The phenomenon, known as brand-cluster loyalty, has long been common in the soft drink aisle, and Coke in all its multiple guises is in the same brand cluster with Pepsi and all its variations. "In lots of stores, Coke and Pepsi are on special during alternate weeks," says Allen Rosenshine, president of the ad agency BBDO International. "So a lot of people switch back and forth regularly—even though they buy only Coke and Pepsi, and wouldn't buy any other colas." Pepsi executives, who have been crowing over Coke's embarrassment—Pepsi-Cola USA President Roger Enrico calls the new Coke "the Edsel of the 1980s"—might pause to consider that Coca-Cola now has more entries in that cola cluster.

For companies intent on changing a product without stirring up the natives, brand-loyalty pundits offer some advice. First, some products are safer to change than others. Brand loyalties seem to be most intense with products that are ingested or close to the skin; a study by the Ogilvy & Mather ad

A Coke loyalist *and co-founder of Old Coke Drinkers of America, Frank Olson, 41, says: "They took a great American tradition and turned it into just another soda pop." His Seattle group threatened to sue Coca-Cola if it didn't bring old Coke back.*

agency found that men care more about the brand name on their underwear than on their ties. The more closely a brand is bound to a person's image of himself, the more likely he will be to resist any change in it. This might be called the "I use this, this is me" principle, and it applies to things like cigarettes, perfume, and beer, all personal items that their users associate with particular ideas about status or even personality. It's not for nothing that Marlboro is the U.S. market leader in the high-loyalty cigarette category: the macho image of the Marlboro Man speaks volumes about how certain smokers see themselves.

Another high-loyalty market leader is Budweiser. "Anheuser-Busch would drop dead before they'd put 'new and improved' on that product," says Charlotte Beers, chief executive of the Chicago ad agency Tatham-Laird & Kudner. "Tradition is a big part of its appeal." Having the biggest market share, as Marlboro and Bud do, is helpful in establishing brand loyalty, simply because many people are most comfortable buying something that a lot of other people buy. But less ubiquitous products still attract ferocious loyalty. Asks Beers, "Can you imagine a new and improved Chanel No. 5?"

In their quest to make sense of the emotional side of brand loyalty, some marketers have devised quasi-scientific systems for measuring it. One of these is a model, in the form of a grid, that Foote Cone & Belding uses to pinpoint how emotionally involved a customer is likely to be with a given purchase. The higher the level of involvement, the stronger the brand loyalty—and the more hazardous it is to trumpet a big change in the product. At one end of the scale are products like hair coloring, where involvement is high partly because of the element of risk: you'd best get it right the first time, or buy lots of hats. According to John O'Toole of Foote Cone & Belding, consumers' loyalty to Clairol, a Foote Cone client, is "amazingly high."

At the other extreme, in this model, are products like cat litter, paper towels, and clothes pins, which are designed to get boring tasks done as inexpensively as possible. With these humdrum products, most consumers switch back and forth between brands with abandon, picking up whatever's on sale—although some will pay for quality when they come across a brand that they believe does the job better than any other. In any research designed to measure loyalty, cautions Morgan Hunter, vice chairman of Marketing Corp. of America, a Westport, Connecticut, marketing firm, it is important not to confuse a stated preference with what consumers actually do when they're in the store. They may not actually buy the brand they say they prefer if it costs too much more.

Marketers agree that food products, especially those that have been around a long time, are among the riskiest to "improve," as Coca-Cola has discovered the hard way. "You can make small improvements, but watch out," says Charlotte Beers. "Velveeta cheese, for example, has a distinct taste, but more than that, it is a part of childhood for a lot of people—the way it stirs and mixes and melts. It would be very risky to change any of that." If you must alter a product that reminds consumers of their salad days, brand-loyalty experts say, change it without a lot of hoopla.

WHETHER COCA-COLA could have gotten away with changing quietly is unknown. It might have succeeded had the change been less noticeable, as it was in Canada. Coke there was already sweeter than the U.S. version. When new Coke was introduced in Canada, shipments of concentrate reportedly jumped 42% in the first seven weeks over the year-earlier period. A Coke spokesman also notes that Canadians have less emotional attachment to Coke. Much of Coca-Cola's U.S. advertising has been steeped in Americana.

Over the past few years, marketers have worried that generic and other bargain products were making brand loyalty a thing of the past among increasingly savvy and recession-weary consumers. An annual study by the ad agency Needham Harper & Steers asks 4,000 heads of households, half of them men and half women, whether they agree with the statement: "I try to stick to well-known brand names." The percentage who answer "yes" has dropped from 77% in 1975 to 61% this year. Coke's debacle has shown decisively that, for some products at least, consumers would still rather fight than switch. **F**

WHO CAN BE LOYAL TO A TRASH BAG?

■ When generic products were coming on strong a few years ago, J. Walter Thompson, the New York-based ad agency, gauged consumers' loyalty to brands in 80 product categories. It found that the leader in market share was not necessarily the brand-loyalty leader. At that time, Bayer aspirin was the market share leader among headache remedies, but Tylenol had the most loyal following.

Thompson measured the degree of loyalty by asking people whether they'd switch for a 50% discount. Cigarette smokers most often said no, making them the most brand-loyal of consumers (see table). Film is the only one of the top five products that the user doesn't put in his mouth—so why such loyalty? According to Edith Gilson, Thompson's senior vice president of research, 35-mm film is used by photography buffs, who are not your average snapshooter: "It's for long-lasting, emotionally valued pictures, taken by someone who has invested a lot of money in his camera." Plenty of shoppers will try a different cola for 50% off, and most consumers think one plastic garbage bag or facial tissue is much like another.

HIGH-LOYALTY PRODUCTS	MEDIUM-LOYALTY PRODUCTS	LOW-LOYALTY PRODUCTS
cigarettes	cola drinks	paper towels
laxatives	margarine	crackers
cold remedies	shampoo	scouring powder
35-mm film	hand lotion	plastic trash bags
toothpaste	furniture polish	facial tissues

Brand names matter more in some products than in others, researchers find.

Chapter 7

"Image and Advertising"

Julia M. Collins

Preview

Skimming. Skim the article quickly to find the following general information.

1. Read the author's name, the title, all headings, and illustrations.

2. Read the first and second paragraphs, looking for the author's purpose and main idea.

3. Read the last paragraph, looking for a summary or conclusion.

Questioning. Answer the following questions and discuss your answers in class.

1. What does *image* mean?

2. What is the relationship between image and advertising?

3. Do you pay much attention to ads, or are you bored by them?

Scanning. Scan the article quickly to find the following specific information.

1. How much more money did the United States spend on advertising in 1986 compared with the total spent by the other 66 top-spending nations?

2. What was the name of the small car made by Volkswagen and advertised in the United States in the early 1960s?

3. A portrait of which English king was used in an ad for the Episcopal Church?

4. What do today's ads rely on even more than in the past?

Harvard Business Review 67, no. 1 (January-February 1989)

Vocabulary in Context. Read the following sentences and try to guess the meaning of the italicized words by using the context. Then replace the italicized words with synonyms (words or phrases that have nearly the same or similar meanings).

1. "Americans today are *barraged* by a greater *avalanche* of advertising than ever, making it tough for new products to establish memorable images."

2. "But the *parameters* of print advertising have changed, partly because of television's influence and partly because Americans simply don't read magazines and newspapers as they once did, *lingering* over the ads."

3. "In the early 1960s, Doyle Dane Bernbach's Volkswagen ads made Detroit move over by *exploiting* the Beetle's *novel* appearance to create an appealing nonconformist image."

4. "Strong images are emerging in previously *uncharted realms* of print advertising as well."

5. "Yet despite the emphasis on *compelling* images in today's print advertising, there are still occasions when the image must be *downplayed* or made more abstract."

Image and Advertising

by Julia M. Collins

1 The Toni twins. The Campbell Soup kids. The rugged Marlboro man heading on his horse into Marlboro country. The dashing man in the Hathaway shirt, jauntily sporting an eye patch. The Maidenform woman, proudly striding through city streets in her lingerie. For millions of Americans, many of these names conjure a vivid image. And behind that image lies a product.

2 In 1989, the money spent on advertising in America will likely reach $128 billion. According to *Advertising Age*, the United States spent $102 billion on advertising in 1986, compared with $71 billion spent by the other 66 top-spending nations combined. Americans today are barraged by a greater avalanche of advertising than ever, making it tough for new products to establish memorable images.

3 "The challenge now is to break through the clutter as well as public indifference," said Patrick Fallon of Fallon McElligott, a Minneapolis agency that has attained star status in recent years. "There are so many messages that the consumer tends to screen them and tune them out. We have to find out what matters—what the essence of the product or service is—and why it exists, and then build bridges between the product and the consumer."

4 Advertising's stronghold—the static, softer medium of print—was nudged aside in recent years by attention-grabbing television. Now, as more consumers zap TV ads with their remote controls or watch videos instead, print advertising is reemerging as a crucial form.

5 But the parameters of print advertising have changed, partly because of television's influence and

Julia M. Collins is a free-lance journalist and a consultant to the Harvard University Graduate School of Design.

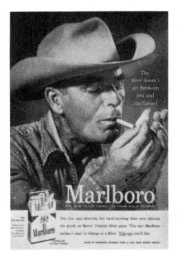

1960, Leo Burnett

1987, 1988, 1985, TBWA

partly because Americans simply don't read magazines and newspapers as they once did, lingering over the ads. Today ad copy is terser and compressed compared with the witty wordiness of classics like David Ogilvy's Rolls-Royce ad: "At 60 miles an hour, the loudest noise in this new Rolls-Royce comes from the electric clock." Images now take precedence over words and are more stylish, forceful, even stark. An effective print ad must pack enough graphic punch to arrest attention immediately and to avoid receding into the pages unnoticed.

6 "Today we really have to leap out at people to hold their attention," said Jerry Della Femina of New York's Della Femina McNamee WCRS. "If we don't shout, we're never going to be heard. We have to surprise consumers, stall them–almost reach out and pull them by the lapels to draw them into the ad."

7 Yet many of the effective visual themes in today's print advertising germinated in older campaigns. Virtually unchanged during its 20-year run, the Blackglama series demonstrates the potential of a single, dramatic image. The campaign was inaugurated in 1968 when representatives of the Great Lakes Mink Association–a group of 400 ranchers–went to New York City to seek an ad agency. They found Jane Trahey, who tapped the rich ore of Americans' star-struck fantasies. She came up with the product name Blackglama and the memorable slogan, "What Becomes a Legend Most." But it was each ad's striking, instantly recognizable image of a famous woman swathed in opulent black mink that quickly made the Blackglama label the most sought-after in the world.

1963,
Norman, Craig, and Kummel

1978,
Peter Rogers Associates

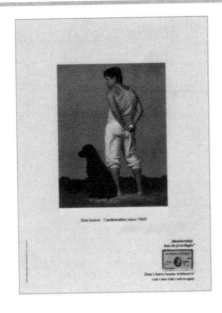

1987, 1988, Ogilvy & Mather

8 Today Ogilvy & Mather's "Portraits" series for American Express appeals to this same yearning for cachet. While each of Annie Leibovitz's photographs casts the individuality of a celebrity cardholder into sharp relief, at the same time the ad invites readers to rub elbows with the stars by applying for this exclusive green plastic rectangle.

9 In the early 1960s, Doyle Dane Bernbach's Volkswagen ads made Detroit move over by exploiting the Beetle's novel appearance to create an appealing, nonconformist image. Whether the Beetle was shrunken on the page to insectlike proportions with the slogan, "Think Small," or labeled as a rejected "lemon" to bluntly underscore Volkswagen's strin-

gent inspection standards, the campaign unblushingly starred the homely little auto.

10 In a similarly bold style, the international ad agency TBWA more recently took another ordinary object—a clear glass bottle—and gave it star status by placing it onstage, front and center. In ad after ad, TBWA has brilliantly showcased the pristine, gemlike bottle containing Absolut vodka, a newcomer to the overcrowded, competitive liquor market. The Swedish import's popularity has soared, becoming the best-selling imported vodka just six years after its introduction.

11 And as for that unflappable Maidenform woman, she is nowhere to be seen today. But when she first arrived on the scene in 1949, she was an immediate success and a titillating, sexy image. Right up until 1986, when the deluge of imitative, nothing-to-hide

Lemon.

1960, Doyle Dane Bernbach

2 in the afternoon. Breakfast. Lee jeans.

1988, Fallon McElligott

1987, 1988, Fallon McElligott

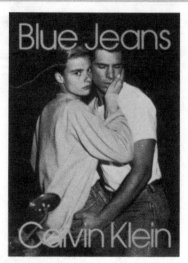

1986, CRK Advertising

lingerie ads finally drove the Maidenform woman off magazine pages, she casually displayed her unmentionables all over town. Her image even changed with the times—after 1969, the Maidenform woman no longer "dreamed" of roles to play, she was *doing* them. She was no longer the nurse—she was the doctor; no longer the stewardess—she piloted the plane.

12   Today a number of print advertisements are setting new limits for what is daring and suggestive, such as Calvin Klein's broodingly erotic "Obsession" perfume campaign, with its exotically tinted nudes.

13   Strong images are emerging in previously uncharted realms of print advertising as well. Fallon McElligott's campaign for the Episcopal Church acknowledges that today's churchgoers are choosier about where to worship and, in a sense, are consumers that the church must woo competitively. The ads are blunt, amusing, and reassuring. The image in one ad—a portrait of Henry VIII—is coupled with the slogan, "In a church started by a man with six wives, forgiveness goes without saying." As a result of this new open-arms image, many Episcopal churches have doubled enrollments.

14   Yet despite the emphasis on compelling images in today's print advertising, there are still occasions when the image must be downplayed or made more abstract. In 1987, one of the most controversial ads ever to appear in print confronted the American public with a painful subject that could not be graphically portrayed. Della Femina McNamee WCRS's

please do not lick this page!

ca.1960, Young and Rubicam

Perception.   Reality.

1987, 1988, Fallon McElligott

1986, CRK Advertising

1977, Christian Dior

1959, Ogilvy, Benson & Mather

understated ad for LifeStyles condoms broke new ground by offering an AIDS-prevention message. The ad simply depicted a young woman's serious face, with the quote, "I'd do a lot for love, but I'm not ready to die for it."

15 Many magazines and newspapers that covered the AIDS crisis in editorials and stories nevertheless rejected the condom ad. The ensuing furor was so intense, however, that these same publications reported on the controversy, and some ultimately ran the ad. Far more than the public's exposure to the ad itself, the widespread publicity it received helped break down resistance to ads addressing AIDS. Gradually, the images in advertisements dealing with this issue are becoming more forthright and arresting.

16 As these pages illustrate, yesterday's most enduring print advertisements drew on the impact of images—with memorable results. And today's ads rely even more on the visual. Whether the ad conveys a stark warning to young people about the realities of teenage pregnancy or trumpets a product breakthrough, print advertising today offers an array of eye-catching, sometimes eloquent images that—just like those Campbell Soup kids—may also linger in the public mind.

1986, Ammirati & Puris Inc.

1958, Ogilvy & Mather

Glossary

array	impressive display
arrest	to catch and keep
arresting	striking, interesting, attracting attention
avalanche	a large mass of loosened snow, earth, rocks suddenly sliding down a mountain
barraged	attacked heavily
breakthrough	strikingly important advance or discovery
broodingly	in a troubling way
cachet	distinction, prestige
celebrity	famous person
clutter	jumble, a number of things in disorder
compelling	forceful
condoms	devices used to prevent venereal infection or as contraceptives
conjure	to call to mind
dashing	bold, lively
deluge	great flood, overwhelming rush
downplayed	minimized
eloquent	vividly expressive, forceful and persuasive
ensuing	resulting, following
erotic	having to do with sexual love
exotically	strangely beautiful
exploiting	using productively, promoting
forthright	straightforward, direct, frank
forum	place for discussion, opportunity
furor	state of excitement, uproar
germinated	started developing
graphically	realistically and vividly
homely	not good-looking or handsome, plain or unattractive
inaugurated	formally begun, started
jauntily	stylishly, confidently, gaily
lingerie	women's underwear and night clothes
lingering	spending time slowly
nonconformist	not following established customs or beliefs
novel	new and unusual
nudged	pushed gently
opulent	rich, luxuriant
parameters	boundaries, limits, guidelines
pristine	pure, untouched, unspoiled
realms	areas, regions
receding	moving back, becoming indistinct
relief	distinctness of form, outline, contrast
rugged	strong, robust, vigorous, sturdy
screen	to separate
showcased	displayed to good advantage

shrunken	contracted in size, shriveled
sporting	wearing, displaying
stall	to bring to a stop
stark	unsoftened, bare, powerful
static	not moving, inactive, motionless
striding	walking vigorously, with long steps
stringent	strict, severe, rigidly controlled
stronghold	fortified place
swathed	surrounded, enveloped, enclosed
take precedence	to be more important
terser	more concise, succinct
titillating	exciting or stimulating pleasurably
trumpets	proclaims loudly
unblushingly	shamelessly
uncharted	unexplored or unknown
understated	restrained, stated weakly
unflappable	calm, not easily excited, imperturbable
unmentionables	undergarments, things improper to talk about
virtually	for all practical purposes
woo	to try to get, to seek
yearning	desire, deep longing

Vocabulary

Without referring to the article, fill in the blanks in the following sentences with the correct words from this list. You may change the tense, number, or form of the words to fit the context. Use each word only once; not all of the words on the list will be used.

forum	inaugurate	clutter	terse	nonconformist	virtually	arrest
take precedence	ensue	stronghold	screen	stringent	exploit	static

1. Because there is such a(n) _____ of ads today, consumers tend to _____ them or not even notice them.

2. In recent years, television had overtaken advertising's _____ , the print medium, which is _____ rather than active.

3. However, print advertising is regaining its position as an essential _____ for ads.

4. Today, ads have to be so powerful that the attention of the consumer is _____ quickly.

5. Therefore, effective ad copy is _____ than in the past, and images _____ over words.

6. The dramatic Blackglama ad campaign featuring famous women, which was _____

   _____ in 1968, has remained _____ unchanged throughout the years.

7. Humorous ads for the Volkswagen Beetle were successful in _____ its small,
   _____ appearance.

Idioms and Expressions

Read the paragraphs in which the following italicized idioms and expressions are found. Then circle the letter next to the answer that best describes the meaning of the idiom as used in the context of the article.

1. "There are so many messages that the consumer tends to screen them and *tune them out*." (Paragraph 3)
   a. pay no attention to them
   b. listen to them carelessly
   c. forget them

2. "We have to find out what matters . . . and then *build bridges* between the product and the consumer." (Paragraph 3)
   a. explain the difference
   b. see a similarity
   c. make a connection

3. "Now, as more consumers *zap* TV ads with their remote controls . . ." (Paragraph 4)
   a. choose
   b. destroy
   c. change

4. "An effective print ad must *pack enough* graphic *punch* to arrest attention immediately and to avoid receding into the pages unnoticed." (Paragraph 5)
   a. be short enough
   b. be shocking enough
   c. be powerful enough

5. "They found Jane Trahey, who *tapped the rich ore* . . ." (Paragraph 7)
   a. made use of
   b. discovered
   c. analyzed

6. ". . . of Americans' *star-struck* fantasies." (Paragraph 7)
   a. celebrity-loving
   b. astrological
   c. imaginary

7. "... the ad invites readers to *rub elbows with* the stars by applying for this exclusive green plastic rectangle." (Paragraph 8)
   a. imitate
   b. meet with
   c. mingle with

8. "In the early 1960s, Doyle Dane Bernbach's Volkswagen ads *made* Detroit *move over....*" (Paragraph 9)
   a. gave Detroit competition
   b. gave Detroit ideas
   c. gave Detroit trouble

9. "Whether the Beetle was shrunken on the page ... or labeled as a rejected *'lemon'...*" (Paragraph 9)
   a. unpopular car
   b. poorly built car
   c. old-fashioned car

10. "... 'In a church started by a man with six wives, forgiveness *goes without saying.*'" (Paragraph 13)
    a. is unnecessary
    b. is given automatically
    c. is not asked for

11. "As a result of this new *open-arms* image, many Episcopal churches have doubled enrollments." (Paragraph 13)
    a. modern
    b. interfaith
    c. welcoming

12. "Della Femina McNamee WCRS's understated ad for LifeStyles Condoms *broke new ground* by offering an AIDS-prevention message." (Paragraph 14)
    a. was an innovation
    b. caused a controversy
    c. began a trend

Paraphrasing

Read the following sentences carefully, and then rewrite them using your own words. Change the vocabulary and sentence structure, but do not change the author's intended meaning or paraphrase any technical terms. There are several ways of paraphrasing each sentence.

Original: "And behind that image lies a product."

Paraphrase: There is a product that can be found behind that picture.

1. "Yet many of the effective visual themes in today's print advertising germinated in older campaigns." (Paragraph 7)

   _____

   _____

2. "And as for that unflappable Maidenform woman, she is nowhere to be seen today." (Paragraph 11)

   _____

   _____

3. "In 1987, one of the most controversial ads ever to appear in print confronted the American public with a painful subject that could not be graphically portrayed." (Paragraph 14)

   _____

   _____

4. "As these pages illustrate, yesterday's most enduring print advertisements drew on the impact of images—with memorable results." (Paragraph 16)

   _____

   _____

Comprehension

Answer the following questions by finding the relevant information in the article. Give the numbers of the paragraphs that contain the answers.

1. What is the main idea of this article?

2. Why is it hard for new products to establish memorable images?

3. Why is print advertising reemerging as a crucial forum?

4. In what ways have the parameters of print advertising changed? Why?

5. What makes the Blackglama ad so successful?

6. Why are the American Express "Portraits" ads effective?

7. What drove the Maidenform woman off the magazine pages?

8. How did the Maidenform woman's image change with the times?

9. What is unusual about Fallon McElligott's ad campaign for the Episcopal Church?

10. What resulted from the publicity surrounding the LifeStyles Condoms ad?

Inference/Interpretation

Circle the letter next to the best answer. Choose your answer according to the meaning the author suggests but does not state explicitly.

1. What image does the Marlboro man project? (Paragraph 1 and ad)
   a. He is an independent outdoorsman.
   b. He is a traditional farmer.
   c. He is an intense intellectual.
   d. He is a country gentleman.

2. We can infer the following from Jerry Della Femina's statement: "If we don't shout, we're never going to be heard." (Paragraph 6)
   a. American consumers overlook starkly simple ads.
   b. American consumers respond best to forceful advertising.
   c. American consumers have become less influenced by ads.
   d. American consumers are turning against advertising.

3. What can we infer was the reason for the success of the ad for Absolut vodka? (Paragraph 10 and ad)
   a. More consumers are drinking vodka.
   b. Consumers are influenced by bold, beautiful visual images.
   c. Consumers are impressed by ads for Swedish products.
   d. Consumers prefer ads without images of people.

4. What major point in the article is supported by the 1958 Rolls Royce ad and the 1986 BMW ad?
   a. Ads rely more on the visual than they did in the past.
   b. Ads have become more daring than they used to be.
   c. Ads are more humorous than they used to be.
   d. Ad copy in the past was more clever than it is now.

Structure

Circle the letter next to the correct answer(s). More than one answer may be correct. Be prepared to explain and justify your choices.

1. In which paragraph(s) is the main idea stated?
   a. Paragraph 1
   b. Paragraph 3
   c. Paragraph 4
   d. Paragraph 5
   e. Paragraph 16
   Write a paraphrase of the main idea in *one* sentence, using your own words as much as possible.

2. Where is cause and effect development used to support the main idea?
   a. Paragraph 4
   b. Paragraph 5
   c. Paragraph 8
   d. Paragraph 13
   e. Paragraph 16

3. Why does the author begin the article with an enumeration of names in paragraph 1 (the Toni twins, the Campbell Soup kids, the Marlboro man, the man in the Hathaway shirt, the Maidenform woman)?
   a. To establish a context of familiarity for readers
   b. To give examples of famous ads from the past
   c. To support the main idea of the article
   d. To provide a humorous introduction
   e. To present a definition of advertising

4. What overall method of development is used in the article?
   a. Defining a process
   b. Refuting an argument through examples
   c. Comparing and contrasting two approaches
   d. Classifying and analyzing methods
   e. Outlining a problem and offering a solution

Style

Circle the letter next to the correct answer(s). More than one answer may be correct. Be prepared to justify your choices by giving specific examples from the article.

1. How would you describe the writing style of the author?
   a. Formal
   b. Informal
   c. Personal
   d. Technical
   e. Colorful
   f. Journalistic

2. What words would best describe the tone of the article?
   a. Scholarly
   b. Uncertain
   c. Emotional
   d. Balanced
   e. Factual
   f. Pessimistic

3. The author's attitude toward today's array of print advertising can be described as
   a. quite negative.
   b. completely neutral.

    c. rather admiring.

    d. harshly critical.

    e. very hostile.

    f. generally positive.

4. The author has a vivid, lively, and pictorial style, which matches her subject. She creates this style through the use of graphic nouns, adjectives, adverbs, and energetic verbs. Underline the pictorial nouns, verbs, adjectives, and adverbs in the first five paragraphs.

Discussion

1. Do you feel "barraged by an avalanche" of advertising in the United States?

2. How prevalent is advertising in your country? Which kinds of ads are most common?

3. Should ads be simple so that they appeal to the widest group of people, or should ads be tailored to specific markets (Hispanics, young women, etc.)?

4. In multinational marketing, should a company use a single advertising campaign or adapt it to local markets?

5. What is your reaction to the more daring and suggestive ads, such as Calvin Klein's "Obsession" perfume?

6. Which ads in this article do you find most effective, appealing, and memorable? Why?

Research Assignment

Look up several of these articles in the library. Choose one article to read and take notes on.

"Advertising Age's 1989 Global Media Lineup." *Advertising Age* 60 (December 4, 1989): 54.

"The Advertising Industry: The Proof of the Pudding." *Economist* 315 (June 9, 1990): Survey, 3–18.

"Best of 1989 Advertising." *Business Week* (January 8, 1990): 140.

"Bigness with a Smile." *Economist* 311 (May 20, 1989): 17–18.

Crumley, Bruce. "Whirlpool Striving to Clean Up Europe." *Advertising Age* 61 (March 5, 1990): 30.

"Eastern Europe Intrigues Shops." *Advertising Age* 60 (December 18, 1989): 14.

Endicott, R. Craig. "Newspapers Shine as Media Choice." *Advertising Age* 60 (December 4, 1989): S1.

Galen, M. "A Comeback May Be Ahead for Brand X." *Business Week* (December 4, 1989): 35.

"Global Gallery." *Advertising Age* 61 (February 5, 1990): 34.

"Global Gallery." *Advertising Age* 61 (February 26, 1990): 40.

"G'night, Mate." *Forbes* 144 (December 11, 1989): 286ff.

Graham, Judith. "AmEx 'Portraits' Stresses Values." *Advertising Age* 61 (January 1, 1990): 12, 38.

King, Thomas R. "American Express 'Portraits' Ads Take Aim at European Audience." *Wall Street Journal* (May 2, 1990): B7.

Landler, M. "Madison Avenue Takes to Perestroika." *Business Week* (March 5, 1990): 68.

McCauley, Lucy A. "The Face of Advertising." *Harvard Business Review* 67 (November-December 1989): 155–59.

Patton, Phillip. "Negativity and Product Advertising." *Marketing and Media Decisions* 25 (June l990): 72.

Randolph, Eleanor. "Comrades in Ads." *Washington Post* (May 18, 1990): F1.

Serafin, Raymond. "Doner Joining Global Rush." *Advertising Age* 60 (December 4, 1989): 22.

Sonfield, Matthew C. "Marketing to the Carriage Trade." *Harvard Business Review* 68 (May-June 1990): 112–17.

Vartorella, William. "Doing the Bright Thing with Your Company Logo." *Advertising Age* 61 (February 26, 1990): 31.

Oral Presentation

Working with a partner, give a fifteen-minute oral presentation to the class on the articles that you chose in the research assignment. Include the author's main idea, major points, and some supporting data. Be prepared to answer questions on your topic. (See Appendix B: Giving an Oral Presentation.)

Writing Assignments

1. Write a paper in which you develop an argument for one of the following points of view. Support your thesis with logical arguments, and discuss the counter argument.
   a. Print advertising should be censored by the government because it affects the moral standards and ethical behavior of a society and, thus, should not be suggestive, erotic, or contain pictures of nudes.
   b. Print advertising should not be censored by the government because ads are created to sell products or services and, thus, their influence on moral standards or ethical behavior is irrelevant.

   Format:
       I. Introduction and Thesis
      II. Pro Argument
     III. Pro Argument
     IV. Counter Argument
      V. Conclusion

2. Write an essay comparing and contrasting the Calvin Klein blue jeans ad with the Lee blue jeans ad as seen in this article. Discuss the visual images, the copy (words), and the type of consumer the ads are targeting. Analyze the difference in overall approach and message.

3. Look at various ads in several magazines. Choose one you react positively to and write an essay describing why the ad is effective, creative, and memorable. Use enumeration and cause and effect development. Attach a copy of the ad to your paper.

Peer Critique

Choose a person to work with. After you have completed your writing assignment, let your partner read and critique your writing. Then you will read and critique his or her writing. Use the Writing Evaluation Form in Appendix F.

Case Study: A Problem in Advertising

Working in groups, read the following case study. Discuss the problem, answer the questions, and write a brief report on how your group would solve the problem. (Choose one member of the group to do the writing.) Follow the format in Appendix E (Case Study Report) in writing your report.

Vince Biaggi, Vice President of Brand Marketing for Marshall Motor Company, is worried. Ever since January, when Marshall began a costly and aggressive ad campaign, Marshall's sales and market share have been plummeting. In the 1980s, Marshall was the number 3 U.S. carmaker, and its market share had risen above 18.0 percent. It ended 1989 with only a 12.0 percent share of the domestic new car market, and that plunged to 9.8 percent in May. That would be Marshall's lowest share of the car market since 1981. Why have things gone so badly?

Kate Saunders, Marketing Director for Marshall, thinks she knows the cause of the downturn in sales. The aggressive ad campaign has backfired, in her opinion, because it has mistakenly been aimed at the Japanese. In one series of print ads, Japanese cars are criticized for de-emphasizing safety. In another ad, a study shows that Marshall cars are superior to their Japanese competitors in five separate categories: cost, comfort, styling, service, and safety. These anti-Japanese ads, however, certainly do remind U.S. consumers about just how popular Japanese cars are. Kate argued vehemently against using these ads, but she was overruled by Vince. Now she's sure she was right; negative ads rarely work.

Vince's assistant, Alex Drummond, blames the loss of sales on the many blue-collar buyers Marshall attracts and the fact that those buyers are currently worried about the economy. He favors keeping the ad campaign going for at least another six months. Actually, he was the primary creator of the campaign strategy aimed at the Japanese, and he thinks it's great.

Vince has called a meeting for Wednesday to discuss whether to pull the ads and remake the ad campaign entirely or to stick with it. He is really not convinced that the ads are the cause of Marshall's decreasing sales and wants to ride out the downturn. He believes the ad campaign will eventually be successful and will have a positive cumulative effect on sales volume. He never expected the ads to reverse the downward trend overnight and thinks the anti-Japanese strategy is basically the way to go. "It will translate into higher sales in the long term," he keeps saying. But how can he prevent Kate from convincing the marketing managers and Marshall president that she was right and that Vince's ad campaign won't work? And whatever the cause, the sales downturn is giving Marshall Motor Company serious problems: earnings were slashed in the previous two quarters.

Questions

1. How can Vince justify his opinion about the ads?

2. How can Kate justify her opinion about the ads?

3. What factors could be affecting Marshall's sales?

4. What type of advertising campaign strategy should Marshall use?

Solution: Case Study Report

  I. Define and analyze the problem.
 II. Suggest possible solutions.
III. Evaluate possible solutions.
IV. Select a solution.

Case Study Business Writing Assignment: Memorandum

Write a memo from Kate Saunders, Marketing Director of Marshall Motor Company, to Vince Biaggi, Vice President of Brand Marketing. The memo should outline and justify Kate's reasons for opposing the anti-Japanese ad campaign.

  Format:
      I. Introduction (Background and Main Idea)
     II. Discussion (Reasons and Justification)
   III. Closing (Restatement of Main Idea)

  Style: Formal and concise
  Tone: Authoritative and balanced

Case Study Business Writing Assignment: Memorandum

Write a memo from Alex Drummond, Assistant to Vince Biaggi, to Kate Saunders, Marketing Director of Marshall Motor Company. The memo should outline and justify Alex's reasons for supporting the anti-Japanese ad campaign.

Format:
    I. Introduction (Background and Main Idea)
    II. Discussion (Reasons and Justification)
    III. Closing (Restatement of Main Idea)

Style: Informal and conversational
Tone: Subjective

Additional Reading

"Corporate Coats of Arms"
Ken Carls
Harvard Business Review 67 (May-June 1989): 135–39

Corporate Coats of Arms

by Ken Carls

The modern idea of corporate identity traces back to the Middle Ages and the military needs of knights. As armor became increasingly sophisticated, it protected more and more of the warrior's body. When it completely covered his face and totally obscured his identity, external markings became necessary: visual identity was born.

The need for clearly marked visual identities grew in the twelfth and thirteenth centuries when gunpowder entered the military arsenal. Because combatants could fight at greater distances, allies had a greater need to recognize each other instantly from afar. Then, in the age of chivalry, the idea of visual identity shifted in focus from military to political and economic: royalty used coats of arms markings to symbolize their aristocratic power.

In the early twentieth century, commerce appropriated visual identity, transferring the idea of an organized marking system from the aristocracy to the middle class. Peter Behrens, head of design of Allgemeine Electrizitäts Gesellschaft (AEG), a German manufacturer of electrical appliances, created the corporate prototype in 1908 when he began to experiment with a public image for the company. AEG had two divergent motivations: first, to unify the product line and consolidate its operation behind a single identity; second, to build a powerful, stable, conservative visual image to stem the rising tide of social revolution within the ranks of the employees.

In the United States, the idea of visual identity found some expression in the 1930s in the work of designers such as Raymond Loewy, who created the look of Studebaker cars and Greyhound buses. But it wasn't until the

1950s that designers such as Paul Rand for IBM and ABC, Chermayeff & Geismar Associates for the Chase Manhattan Bank and Mobil Oil, and Jay Doblin for J.C. Penney and Standard Oil made corporate identity an important and standard element of post-World War II corporate practice.

Global competition and sophisticated international players' need to present a strong, unified face worldwide fed this interest in a visible corporate identity. A typical corporate identity program included a logo, letterhead, business card, business forms, vehicle identification, signage, promotional materials, and interoffice applications. An annual report, featuring a consistent design theme, helped carry the message to shareholders. Companies sought an abstract image or symbol that would speak for the corporation's sense of itself. The style that emerged–drawn from the Swiss modernist school of design–was as much at home in Europe and Japan as in the United States: the typeface was helvetica; the colors were corporate grey or blue; the image was clinical; the message was power. By the 1960s, this was the international corporate style.

During the late 1970s and early 1980s, new images challenged this single standard of conservative corporate style. Smaller companies emerged as powerful competitors–and with them a new sense of corporate identity and the corporate message. Apple's user-friendly, postmodern design took on IBM's conservative Swiss modernism. Major corporations were no

Ken Carls is associate professor of graphic design at the University of Illinois at Urbana-Champaign.

IBM logo, Paul Rand, 1956
Chase Manhattan Bank logo,
    Chermayeff & Geismar
    Associates, 1960
Apple Macintosh logo,
    Apple Computer, 1985

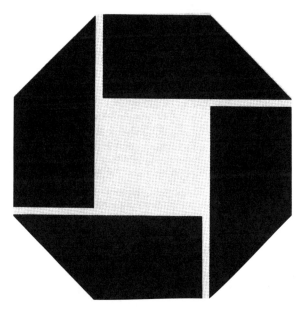

longer the only companies with well-developed identities; young, enterprising, mid-sized organizations now could make their marks with distinctive statements of corporate style. Most recently, the work coming out of some relatively young design firms such as Duffy Design Group in Minneapolis and Thirst in Chicago has introduced a more idiosyncratic, artistic flair to corporate identity, in sharp contrast to the cold rationalism of the older conservative approach. These younger rogues seek to restore humanism and populism to corporate images; they revel in the richness and complexity of American society; they seek to introduce human, nonelitist design that people can enjoy. Their work replaces overintellectualized abstract symbols with populist democratic images.

Today corporate design is broader in scope than ever before. Companies express their visual identity "passively" and "actively." In a passive program, the company develops a single and uniform mark for every application: the same logo with the same colors and the same typestyle appears on all company surfaces, from vehicles to

ESPRIT
COLLECTION

ESPRIT

Esprit logos, Esprit Graphic
Design Studio, 1985
Promotional book for
First Bank, Minneapolis,
Duffy Design Group, 1987
Identity Program for Medical
Innovation Capital Inc.,
Duffy Design Group, 1987

memos. An active program allows more flexibility – visual consistency is more an attitude than a rigid set of rules. In an active program, the company expresses its identity in a series of compatible, but not uniform, images. The program can change and evolve without requiring the company to scrap its entire visual identity for a total redesign.

Traditionally, the largest corporations have opted for the passive approach: for example, in the early 1980s, AT&T launched a new modernist corporate logo by Saul Bass and

has replicated it across all its applications. Increasingly, however, companies are moving toward active programs with more diverse imagery. Many current designers have lost faith in the old assumption of standardized corporate communication and the use of stiff methodology. Instead, they are embracing flexibility and individualization – a further expression of the way in which design thinking and corporate practice interact and change together.

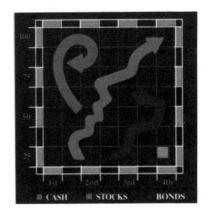

American Broadcasting
 Companies logo,
 Paul Rand, 1965
Morison Asset
 Allocation Fund logo,
 Duffy Design Group, 1987
The World Financial Center
 logo, Drenttel Doyle
 Partners, 1988
E.G. Smith, Inc. logo,
 Seth Jaben Studio, 1985

THE
HARTER
GROUP

Mobil

Imagine Grand Central made of glass, with sixteen stately palm trees, right on the Hudson. Welcome to the Winter Garden. Now imagine a promenade as individual as Park Avenue, overlooking the river. Welcome to the Esplanade. Imagine fine restaurants. Imagine excellent shops. Imagine free concerts and performances all over the place. Next, imagine civilized metropolitan fun. OK, now stop imagining.

Welcome.

Chapter 8

"Winging It in Foreign Markets"

Martin van Mesdag

Preview

Skimming. Skim the article quickly to find the following general information.

1. Read the author's name, the title, and all headings.

2. Read the first and second paragraphs, looking for the author's purpose and main idea.

3. Read the last paragraph, looking for a summary or conclusion.

Questioning. Answer the following questions and discuss your answers in class.

1. What does "winging it" mean?

2. What does the author mean by "winging it in foreign markets"?

3. How are foreign markets different from domestic markets?

Scanning. Scan the article quickly to find the following specific information.

1. What marketing approach do marketers use most often in taking a product across national boundaries?

2. What two products are the hardest to take global?

3. What company is the largest producer of Scotch-type whiskey?

4. What products were deliberately developed to sell in global markets?

5. What marketing strategy has proven the most difficult to implement?

Harvard Business Review 65, no. 1 (January-February 1987)

Vocabulary in Context. Read the following sentences and try to guess the meaning of the italicized words by using the context. Then replace the italicized words with synonyms (words or phrases that have nearly the same or similar meanings).

1. "When transcending national borders, marketers and product development people in all industries face a *host* of *constraints*."

2. "Our modern international communications have *proliferated*: we can look at each other daily on TV, so our newly emerging usage patterns *converge* and thereby enhance the globalizability of the new products that respond to those patterns."

3. "Even though a food or drink product that sells successfully in one country *theoretically* will not sell in another unless research *explicitly* predicts otherwise, many food products are, in fact, big successes globally."

4. "Moreover, the foreign supplier in a market may also have difficulty matching the value/price *framework* established by the *indigenous* competition."

5. "They did extensive research, testing, and reformulation before the international *rollout* of all these brands, but the product concepts had *domestic* origins."

6. "A target market *sector* characterized by long-established usage habits will require a product offering that is closely tailored to expectations about domestic product *attributes*, and marketers will have to choose a country-by-country development route."

Martin van Mesdag

Winging it in foreign markets

"The product you have may be just what they need."

1 What do hamburgers, hot dogs, soft cheeses, portion-packed yogurt, and Scotch whisky have in common besides that they're all edible or drinkable? They all sell like mad in global markets, and one strategy is responsible for their success. As marketers, we have three – and only three – available strategies for taking a product across national boundaries. The method behind these successful products is one of these three:

2 **Phased internationalization** appeals enormously to marketing people. It is what we all learned when we became marketers. You go to a foreign country with knowledge of your manufacturing capabilities but with no presuppositions about products. Next, you buy research to find out exactly what people there want within a product area you can cater to. Finally, you come home and get your development people to put together a product with which you can compete in that foreign market.

3 **Global marketing** is the trendiest and seemingly most promising approach. From a marketing point of view, it is a highly responsible strategy. Ignoring frontiers, you go out into a part of the world and try to discover newly emerging needs you might respond to with your manufacturing capabilities. You are particularly alert to consumer typology and to the behavior patterns into which your product offering will have to fit. You do a conscientious market segmentation job.

4 **The shot-in-the-dark method** is the seemingly crude, even sloppy, process of picking a product that is already successful in the home market and taking it abroad in the hope that it will sell there. It is an "unmarketing" approach since it makes what may be unwarranted assumptions about the behavior of a new and unfamiliar group of customers.

5 While we marketers are usually most comfortable with the first two approaches, the last – the shot-in-the-dark – is the one we use most often. Phased internationalization and formal global strategies are far less risky, but marketers who use them often miss the golden opportunities for taking products across national borders that may be right on our doorstep.

Constraints abroad

6 When transcending national borders, marketers and product development people in all industries face a host of constraints. Some of these are obvious. People in different countries speak different languages. Rules and regulations differ across national borders: in most countries you drive on the right, but in some you drive on the left. Then there are climate, economic conditions, race, topography, political stability, and occupations. The most important source of constraints by far, and the most difficult to measure, is cultural differences rooted in history, education, economics, and legal systems.

7 Because of all these differences, the international convertibility of products and services varies enormously from one product category to another. Pocket calculators, credit card facilities, and lubricating oils need few international adaptations, whereas toilet soap, phonograph records, and candy require rather more adjustment. I am intrigued by how slow simple

Martin van Mesdag is founder and president of Halliday Associates, a British consulting firm that focuses on policy-making, planning, and marketing management. He was previously marketing director at Van Houten, the Dutch chocolate company.

157

services like retailing and retail banking are to globalize and yet how standardization in some international hotel chains has gone so far that, as long as you stay inside the hotel, you cannot tell whether you are in Vancouver, Kuala Lumpur, Stockholm, or Torremolinos.

8   Of all the products I can think of, food and drink are probably the hardest to take global. Two constraints make globalizing food products especially difficult. The first, which is virtually unique to food products, is recognizability. People want to know what their food is made of, and they usually want to know how it's processed. They require recognizability in the appearance, the taste, and—in most cases—the texture of foods. Consumers impose no such requirements when they buy durables (except for textiles to some extent), personal care products, or household goods.

9   The recognizability constraint means that a food or a beverage product won't sell in countries where the people aren't familiar with its ingredients. It means that the amount of engineering and processing that companies can apply to food is limited. The recognizability requirement also means that extensive processing is more acceptable in countries where the product is not traditional than in countries where it is. Instant coffee is unpopular in Germany, France, and Italy, where people drink a lot of coffee and want it freshly brewed; it is more popular in non-coffee-drinking countries like Britain and Ireland.

10   The second main constraint on globalizing food products is what I call the age symptom. The

more a product is associated with long-standing usage habits, the less internationally marketable it is. Conversely, the more recent the usage pattern, the more likely it is that the product will be marketable in a variety of countries.

11   The age symptom does not apply just to food products, of course. Garden spades, which have been in use for ages, look quite different in Switzerland, England, and Holland. But gardeners in those countries use identical motor diggers. And although styles do evolve slowly, men's formal clothing is made in response to long-established usage habits. You don't need to be a tailor to tell a German, a Frenchman, and a Briton apart by the suits or the shoes they wear. But with the recent emergence of casual clothing, everybody wears the same jeans, T-shirts, and sneakers.

12   The reason for this phenomenon is not mysterious. Products that have been around a long time respond to long-established usage patterns because people in different countries, and indeed different regions, used to live in isolation. Our modern international communications have proliferated: we can look at each other daily on TV, so our newly emerging usage patterns converge and thereby enhance the globalizability of the new products that respond to those patterns. Some products that respond to long-established usage patterns are natural cheese, popular cuts of meat, and varieties of beers, wines, and spirits. Products that respond to more recent usage patterns are portion-packed yogurts, hamburgers, hot dogs, soft drinks, and light beers. These products have more global potential than those that respond to older usage patterns. Global products like these have often come from the needs or wishes of a new stratum of customers, or—it doesn't matter which way you put it—a new stratum of customers has come along as suppliers have produced low-cost, universally available, integrated products.

13   Even though a food or a drink product that sells successfully in one country theoretically will not sell in another unless research explicitly predicts otherwise, many food products are, in fact, big successes globally. Moreover, I would argue that their success is overwhelmingly due to a shot-in-the-dark marketing approach.

14   Look, for example, at British food consumption patterns over the past 20 years. The United Kingdom has a massive debit balance of trade in food. My estimate of the consumer value of products that were new to the U.K. market in the past 20 years is $4.5 billion—more than 10% of total consumer spending on food. Further estimates show that 85% of those new products have either been imported or based on existing product concepts in other countries. Evidently, Britons like to try foods they're unfamiliar with.

15   By far the most important source of new product ideas in Britain has been, and is likely to remain, existing products in other countries. In 1985,

for example, Britons ate $90 million worth of steaklets and grillsteaks – food products that, 20 years ago, were practically unheard of in Britain. The concept originated in America and is now meeting an enthusiastic response overseas. In the same year, Britons ate $260 million worth of yogurt – a product idea that came from Europe. Other nonindigenous foods popular in Britain now are low-fat cheeses, breakfast cereals, mineral water, pasta, and cookies.

16 Some of these products came to Britain through phased internationalization and through the formal global approach. Most of them, however, came by the shot-in-the-dark method. True, they were extensively researched and tested before their launch onto the British market. But the important fact is that they were products that had already established themselves in their respective home markets and were brought to Britain with a "let's try and see" attitude.

the concessions dictated by the need to maximize market penetration. You can afford to skim the cream off your markets. You sell not what the greatest number of consumers finds acceptable; instead you sell what a minority of consumers is very keen on. Some products that were deliberately developed to sell in global markets are margarine (though the originators of the product curiously never adopted a global brand strategy for it), IDV's Bailey's Irish Cream liqueur, Ferrero's Tic Tac candy, and Rocher chocolates. Some global brands have global strategies. Others – Coca-Cola, Kellogg's cornflakes, Heineken beer, and McDonald's hamburgers, for example – have not. In the food and drink arena, brands that succeed in using the global marketing approach are few and far between. The reasons are the low international convertibility of food and drink products mentioned earlier and the increasing difficulty of finding brand names for international use.

What doesn't work...

17 Phased internationalization works best with a single product in a particular market – the Dutch sell feta cheese in the Middle East, the Danes sell British-style bacon in Britain, and the Swiss chocolate makers carefully formulate their products to sell in America. Heinz and Unilever, among many others, have largely built their international business on this approach.

18 Phased internationalization, though, has a number of disadvantages. Because of the low international convertibility of food products, a product formulated for a single foreign country is unlikely to be salable in another. The Dutch do not sell their feta cheese outside the Middle East, nor do the Danes sell British-style bacon outside Britain. The North American Swiss chocolate recipes are unsuitable for other areas. Consequently, this strategy implies a country-by-country approach to international expansion.

19 Moreover, the foreign supplier in a market may also have difficulty matching the value/price framework established by the indigenous competition. Finally, the foreign supplier may have difficulty establishing credibility. While some German cheese makers produce a very good Camembert, I imagine they'd have trouble selling it to the French. And despite their status as the world's largest producer of Scotch-type whisky, the Suntory Company in Japan considers it unwise to sell its product in Britain.

20 To all appearances the global marketing approach solves all these problems. It looks, without a doubt, like the worthiest of the three strategies. It promises all the benefits of economies of scale without

...and what does

21 I have described the shot-in-the-dark strategy of selling abroad what you happen to be selling in your home market as a sloppy way to approach international marketing. Especially in food and drink products, with their notoriously low levels of international convertibility, you'd think that no responsible marketer would ever employ this strategy. But wait. This strategy, which may look casual, has resulted in an enormous worldwide export business. Practically all the world's wine export businesses and most of the exports of beer and spirits were built on this shot-in-the-dark approach. Dispatching nearly 340,000 tons of cheese per year, Holland is the largest exporter of cheese in the world; nearly all of that volume is in indigenous varieties. West Germany has been building a sizable food and drink export business. In the United Kingdom alone, Germany sold $2 billion of unfamiliar, expensive, high-quality products straight from its home market – a sixfold increase, in real terms, in 12 years. And there's more.

22 Earlier, I mentioned Bailey's Irish Cream and some Ferrero products as having been deliberately developed for a global market – and they were. Then I mentioned Coca-Cola, Kellogg, Heineken, and McDonald's as other global brands – which they are. Or, strictly speaking, which they became. Those brands and products were not deliberately developed for global markets. They were developed and, for many years, sold only in their home markets. Marketers did not take these domestically successful products to foreign markets willy-nilly. They did extensive research, testing, and reformulation before the international rollout of all these brands, but the product concepts had do-

mestic origins. It follows inescapably that the shot-in-the-dark strategy prompted the global growth of these brands. And when you think about it, the same applies to most global and international products and brands.

23   So while the shot-in-the-dark strategy is wholly reprehensible in theory, it has proved to be the most successful in practice. And the global marketing strategy – while the most laudable in theory – has proved the most difficult to implement.

Shots in the not-so-dark

24   While the shot-in-the-dark approach may be the most successful, marketers cannot afford to be lax about their planning and research methods. It is still important for marketers to examine and assess all three strategies since this choice will govern the entire product development process.

25   Once they've chosen a strategy, marketers can use the knowledge of their available technological resources to assess target markets not only for size and growth rate but also for age-of-usage and recognizability characteristics. A target market sector characterized by long-established usage habits will require a product offering that is closely tailored to expectations about domestic product attributes, and marketers will have to choose a country-by-country development route. The shot-in-the-dark and the global approaches are unlikely to work in this instance.

26   If, on the other hand, the company aspires after a global strategy, it will need to make a wide geographical sweep to ascertain whether it can discover any newly emerging need patterns that the company can respond to with its technological resources.

27   While the shot-in-the-dark approach has a high chance of failure, it can form the groundwork for either a phased internationalization or a global strategy; and it should certainly be tested against these possibilities.

28   No matter what strategy you choose, a rigorous knowledge-gathering program is in order. The resource investment in any serious sales expansion attempt is considerable, and appropriate knowledge can protect the investment. Getting ahold of that knowledge requires several types of inquiry skills:

29   **Scanning,** which is the collection of data, trends, judgments, and values that will – directly or indirectly – affect any envisaged marketing operation.

30   **"Inferencing,"** which is speculating about customer responses to environmental influences and about responses to related influences.

31   **"Propositioning,"** which is proposing a product offering in response to a particular customer need – whether assumed or ascertained – and measuring customers' assessment of that product offering.

32   Clearly, a formal global effort will initially concentrate on scanning and inferencing; a phased internationalization approach will start with a scanning exercise, soon to be followed by propositioning-type tests. The shot-in-the-dark approach will go straight to propositioning inquiries.

What about brands?

33   Of all the marketing mix elements, the product is the most restrictive when a global strategy is considered. Some brands are intrinsically linked with particular products: what applies to the product applies to the brand. Coca-Cola and Kaffee HAG are good examples. In these cases, the globalizability of the brand is confined to the product. Other brands are associated with broad ranges of products: all private-label brands and brands like Hero and Kraft are in that category. In these cases, the brand can be globalized to cover product ranges that are internationalized – that is, product ranges are formulated to local needs, country by country; brands are global.

34   In the case of food and drink, the opportunities for globalizing products are much more limited than the opportunities for globalizing brands – provided those brands leave enough latitude to encompass product ranges formulated to suit the needs of specific markets.

35   I have said that products that have actually been designed for global markets are very rare (especially in the food and drink sectors) and that many of today's "global" products were originally intended for, and confined to, their home markets. The success rate of the shot-in-the-dark approach – on top of the fact that it requires the least amount of imagination, time, and development effort – suggests that it will remain a popular strategy. If we evaluate products in *one* market for their ability to answer newly emerging trends and needs in *other* markets, we are, in fact, using a shot-in-the-dark approach to build a global strategy. All sorts of food – and other – products have become global in this way. They have turned out to be shots in the not-so-dark. ▽

Glossary

ascertain	to find out with certainty
attributes	characteristics, qualities
cater to	to try to gratify another's needs or desires
concessions	acts of yielding; things conceded or granted
conscientious	honest, showing care and precision
constraints	limits, restrictions
converge	to come together at a point
convertibility	change from one form to another, transformation
credibility	reliability, ability to be believed
crude	rough, not carefully made or done
debit	what is owing
domestic	native, made or produced in the home country
durables	goods usable for a relatively long time (machinery, cars, appliances)
encompass	to contain, include
enhance	to make greater, improve
evolve	to develop gradually by change
explictly	clearly, definitely
formulate	to develop in a systematic way
framework	structure, system
host	great number, multitude
indigenous	native
inescapably	certainly
integrated	unified
intrigued	fascinated, curious about
intrinsically	closely, naturally, essentially
latitude	freedom from narrow restrictions
laudable	worthy of being praised, commendable
lax	careless, inexact
nonindigenous	not native
notoriously	famously
presuppositions	assumptions, things taken for granted
proliferated	grown by multiplying quickly
reprehensible	deserving to be criticized or censured
respective	particular, separate
rollout	introduction
sector	section, segment, distinct area
segmentation	being divided into segments
shot-in-the-dark	an attempt made by guessing; imprecise strategy
sloppy	careless, messy
sneakers	tennis shoes, athletic shoes
speculating	thinking about various aspects of a subject
stratum	section, level, division, or socioeconomic group of society
theoretically	based on theory, hypothetically
topography	surface features of a region (rivers, lakes, roads)

transcending	going beyond the limits of
trendiest	most fashionable, in the latest style
typology	study of types, symbols
unwarranted	not justified
virtually	practically

Vocabulary

Without referring to the article, fill in the blanks in the following sentences with the correct words from this list. You may change the tense, number, or form of the words to fit the context. Use each word only once; not all of the words on the list will be used.

nonindigenous	credibility	latitude	proliferate	segmentation	indigenous
typology	theoretically	reprehensible	intrinsically	encompass	ascertain
speculate	stratum				

1. Global marketing is a strategy that carefully analyzes consumer _____ and market _____ .

2. Because modern international communications have _____, the newly emerging usage patterns of consumers all over the world are converging.

3. Marketers realize that a new _____ of consumer has developed in response to low-cost, global products.

4. Today Britons are eating millions of dollars of _____ foods such as steaklets, yogurt, breakfast cereals, and mineral water, mostly as a result of the shot-in-the-dark marketing method.

5. The marketing strategy of phased internationalization has several disadvantages, including matching the value/price framework of native products and establishing _____ with the consumers.

6. The shot-in-the-dark marketing strategy is _____ in theory; however, in practice it is extremely successful.

7. Marketers must plan and research in order to choose the best global strategy and to _____ _____ whether there are newly emerging consumer needs that the company can respond to.

8. Global marketers need inquiry skills such as "inferencing," which is _____ about consumer responses to environmental influences.

9. When brands are _____ linked to their products, like Coca-Cola, what applies to the product also applies to the brand.

10. Food and drink brands can be globalized if the brands have enough _____ to

_____ a range of products for specific markets.

Idioms and Expressions

Read the paragraphs in which the following italicized idioms and expressions are found. Then circle the letter next to the answer that best describes the meaning of the idiom as used in the context of the article.

1. "They all sell *like mad* in global markets, and one strategy is responsible for their success." (Paragraph 1)
   a. quite quickly
   b. in very large amounts
   c. for no clear reason

2. "The *shot-in-the-dark method* is the seemingly crude, even sloppy, process of picking a product that is already successful in the home market and taking it abroad in the hope that it will sell there." (Paragraph 4)
   a. a method based on guesswork, rather than careful analysis
   b. a secret method that is complicated
   c. a dangerous but exciting method

3. "Phased internationalization and formal global strategies are far less risky, but marketers who use them often miss the *golden opportunities. . . .*" (Paragraph 5)
   a. financial rewards
   b. once-in-a-lifetime experience
   c. excellent chances

4. ". . . for taking products across national borders that may be *right on our doorstep.*" (Paragraph 5)
   a. next door to us
   b. very close to us
   c. similar to us

5. "You sell not what the greatest number of consumers finds acceptable; instead you sell what a minority of consumers is very *keen on.*" (Paragraph 20)
   a. used to
   b. interested in
   c. fond of

6. "In the food and drink arena, brands that succeed in using the global marketing approach are *few and far between*." (Paragraph 20)
   a. not popular
   b. small in number
   c. small in size

7. "Marketers did not take these domestically successful products to foreign markets *willy-nilly*." (Paragraph 22)
   a. without planning
   b. in a hurry
   c. by mistake

8. "The success rate of the shot-in-the-dark approach—*on top of* the fact that it requires the least amount of imagination, time, and development effort—suggests that it will remain a popular strategy." (Paragraph 35)
   a. because of
   b. as a result of
   c. in addition to

Paraphrasing

Read the following sentences carefully, and then rewrite them using your own words. Change the vocabulary and sentence structure, but do not change the author's intended meaning or paraphrase any technical terms. There are several ways of paraphrasing each sentence.

Original: "They all sell like mad in global markets, and one strategy is responsible for their success."

Paraphrase: All these products have excellent international sales because of one method that has made them successful.

1. "The more a product is associated with long-standing usage habits, the less internationally marketable it is." (Paragraph 10)

   _____

   _____

2. "Even though a food or drink product that sells successfully in one country theoretically will not sell in another unless research explicitly predicts otherwise, many food products are, in fact, big successes globally." (Paragraph 13)

   _____

   _____

3. "Because of the low international convertibility of food products, a product formulated for a single foreign country is unlikely to be salable in another." (Paragraph 18)

_____

_____

4. "You sell not what the greatest number of consumers finds acceptable; instead you sell what a minority of consumers is very keen on." (Paragraph 20)

_____

_____

5. "It follows inescapably that the shot-in-the-dark strategy prompted the global growth of these brands." (Paragraph 22)

_____

_____

6. "While the shot-in-the-dark approach may be the most successful, marketers cannot afford to be lax about their planning and research methods." (Paragraph 24)

_____

_____

Comprehension

Answer the following questions by finding the relevant information in the article. Give the numbers of the paragraphs that contain the answers.

1. What is the main idea of this article?

2. Describe the differences in the three marketing methods for selling products in foreign markets.

3. What constraints do marketers face when selling products in foreign markets?

4. Why are food and drink products the hardest to take global?

5. What has resulted from the proliferation of our modern international communications?

6. What has been the most important source of new product ideas in Britain? Through what marketing approach have most of them been introduced?

7. What are the disadvantages of phased internationalization?

8. In the food and drink arena, how successful are brands that use the global marketing approach? Why?

9. What products that were originally developed for a domestic market have become successful globally through the shot-in-the-dark strategy?

10. What should the marketer do after choosing the correct marketing strategy?

11. Why will the shot-in-the-dark approach remain a popular strategy?

Inference/Interpretation

Circle the letter next to the best answer. Choose your answer according to the meaning the author suggests but does not state explicitly.

1. It can be inferred from the article that "winging it in foreign markets" means (title of article)
    a. using an unknown strategy to sell products in foreign markets.
    b. using a global approach to sell products in foreign markets.
    c. using phased internationalization to sell products in foreign markets.
    d. using an unstructured, imprecise, and risky strategy to sell products in foreign markets.

2. What can we infer about the motor digger? (Paragraph 11)
    a. Its form varies from country to country.
    b. It has a recent usage pattern.
    c. It has a long-standing usage pattern.
    d. It is used for gardening only in Europe.

3. What is the meaning of the following statement: "The United Kingdom has a massive debit balance of trade in food"? (Paragraph 14)
    a. The United Kingdom imports more food than it exports.
    b. The United Kingdom exports more food than it imports.
    c. The United Kingdom has incurred a large debt because of overconsumption.
    d. The United Kingdom exports no food products.

4. What is the meaning of the following statement: "All sorts of food—and other—products have become global in this way. They have turned out to be shots in the not-so-dark"? (Paragraph 35)
    a. The shot-in-the-dark approach is similar to global marketing.
    b. The shot-in-the-dark approach depends primarily on research.
    c. The shot-in-the-dark approach depends on scanning and inferencing.
    d. The shot-in-the-dark approach actually involves planning and evaluation.

Structure

Circle the letter next to the correct answer(s). More than one answer may be correct. Be prepared to explain and justify your choices.

1. In which paragraph(s) is the main idea stated?
    a. Paragraph 1
    b. Paragraph 5
    c. Paragraph 13

d. Paragraph 24

e. Paragraph 35

Write a paraphrase of the main idea in *one* sentence, using your own words as much as possible.

_____

2. Why does the author use the example of British food consumption patterns over the past 20 years? (Paragraphs 14–16)
   a. To prove that the shot-in-the-dark method is successful
   b. To prove that the United Kingdom has a massive debit balance of trade in food
   c. To prove that the British like to try unfamiliar foods
   d. To prove that global marketing is more successful than phased internationalization
   e. To prove that phased internationalization is more successful than global marketing

3. Where does the author use contrast to support his main idea?
   a. Paragraph 5
   b. Paragraph 6
   c. Paragraph 17
   d. Paragraph 20
   e. Paragraph 23
   Explain what the contrasts are.

_____

4. What overall methods of development are used in this article?
   a. Comparing and contrasting approaches
   b. Debating the value of a proposal
   c. Justifying a method with specific examples
   d. Describing causes and effects
   e. Enumerating the steps in a process

Style

Circle the letter next to the correct answer(s). More than one answer may be correct. Be prepared to justify your choices by giving specific examples from the article.

1. How would you describe the writing style of the author?
   a. Literary
   b. Academic
   c. Bureaucratic
   d. Formal
   e. Informal
   f. Conversational

2. The tone of the article can best be described as
    a. humorous.
    b. neutral.
    c. authoritative.
    d. subjective.
    e. objective.
    f. argumentative.

3. The author's attitude toward the global marketing approach for food and drink brands can be described as
    a. critical.
    b. pessimistic.
    c. optimistic.
    d. neutral.
    e. hostile.
    f. unrealistic.

4. Paragraph 34, which is written in a complex sentence structure, is one very long sentence (40 words). Rewrite paragraph 34 by dividing it into two sentences and using a simple style.

_____

_____

Discussion

1. Are Coca-Cola, Kellogg's cornflakes, Heineken beer, and/or McDonald's hamburgers sold in your country?

2. What nonindigenous foods and drinks are popular in your country?

3. What nonindigenous products have failed in your country?

4. What indigenous foods and drinks from your country could be successfully sold in global markets?

5. Do you believe that the shot-in-the-dark strategy is the most successful approach to global marketing? Why or why not?

6. What new products could be designed for global markets?

Research Assignment

Look up several of these articles in the library. Choose one article to read and take notes on.

Alden, Vernon R. "Who Says You Can't Crack Japanese Markets?" *Harvard Business Review* 65 (January-February 1987): 52–56.

Brown, Paul B. "Over There." *Inc.* 12 (April 1990): 105–6.

"Global Marketing and Media." *Advertising Age* 60 (December 4, 1989): S1, S4.

Hamel, Gary, and C. K. Prahalad. "Do You Really Have a Global Strategy?" *Harvard Business Review* 63 (July-August 1985): 139–48.

Henderson, Bruce D. "The Origin of Strategy." *Harvard Business Review* 67 (November-December 1989): 139–43.

Kashani, Kamran. "Beware the Pitfalls of Global Marketing." *Harvard Business Review* 67 (September-October 1989): 91–98.

Levitt, Ted. "The Pluralization of Consumption." *Harvard Business Review* 66 (May-June 1988): 7–8.

McKenna, Regis. "Marketing Is Everything." *Harvard Business Review* 69 (January-February 1991): 65–79.

Quelch, John A., and Edward J. Hoff. "Customizing Global Marketing." *Harvard Business Review* 64 (May-June 1986): 59–68.

Quelch, John A., Erich Joachimsthaler, and Jose Luis Nueno. "After the Wall: Marketing Guidelines for Eastern Europe." *Sloan Management Review* 32 (Winter 1991): 82–93.

Samli, A. Coskun, Kristian Palda, and A. Tansu Baker. "Toward a Mature Marketing Concept." *Sloan Management Review* 28 (Winter 1987): 45–50.

Star, Steven H. "Marketing and Its Discontents." *Harvard Business Review* 67 (November-December 1989): 148–54.

Wentz, Laurel. "After British Hit, Beecham Takes Beverage to U.S." *Advertising Age* 61 (February 26, 1990): 40.

Whitney, T. "An Agency with a Vision That Transcends Borders." *Marketing* 94 (December 11, 1989): 46.

Oral Presentation

Working with a partner, give a fifteen-minute oral presentation to the class on the article that you chose in the research assignment. Include the author's main idea, major points, and some supporting data. Be prepared to answer questions on your topic. (See Appendix B: Giving an Oral Presentation.)

Writing Assignments

1. Write a critique of van Mesdag's article in which you briefly summarize the argument, give your reaction to it, and evaluate it. Support your point of view with logical arguments and specific examples. A possible thesis for such a critique is: Although Martin van Mesdag's

article "Winging It in Foreign Markets" is informative, his choice of the "shot-in-the-dark" method as the optimal global marketing strategy is based on insufficient and unconvincing data.

Format:
  I. Introduction (Thesis)
  II. Summary
  III. Critique
  IV. Conclusion

2. Discuss an indigenous food or drink product from your country that could be successfully sold in global markets. Use enumeration and cause-effect to describe the reasons why the product would be successful, and explain the market research, testing, and reformulation that would be done before marketing the product.

3. Describe a product from your country that could be marketed successfully in the United States. What market would you target? Why is there a market for this product?

Case Study: A Problem in Global Marketing

Working in groups, read the following case study. Discuss the problem, answer the questions, and write a brief report on how your group would solve the problem. (Choose one member of the group to do the writing.) Follow the format in Appendix E (Case Study Report) in writing your report.

Universal Foods, Inc., a major company with offices throughout the United States, has made a decision to enter the international food market. Its food products include peanut butter, jellies, jams, cereals, and cookies. The Marketing Director, Wilbur Parks, wants to choose some of Universal Foods' best-selling products to export to several foreign markets. However, the marketing division has not yet decided which global marketing strategy to use. As a matter of fact, the division cannot come to agreement on this basic question, and, therefore, the product development process has not gotten off the ground.

The marketing division is divided into three camps in regard to marketing methods. Susan Stewart wants very much to use the phased internationalization strategy. She would like to visit various European and Asian countries and buy research to find out exactly what the people in those countries want in terms of new food products. Only after doing market research on product planning and development would she make a decision. Being a firm advocate of extensive consumer research and analysis, Susan likes to fine-tune the marketing strategy based on reactions from the marketplace.

Max Buchanon believes the global marketing approach is the only way to go. He wants to study the newly emerging needs of consumers in Europe and Asia, with special attention to consumer typology and behavior patterns. A market segmentation job would be his first priority. Max has always followed marketing trends, and he knows the global marketing strategy is certainly the trendiest today.

Isabelle Larsen has been arguing strongly for the shot-in-the-dark strategy. She has the feeling that foreign consumers will go for Universal Foods' peanut butter, and she is willing to use the "let's try and see" approach, even though it is much riskier than phased internationalization or global marketing. She is aware of the low level of international convertibility of food products, but she believes Universal Foods' peanut butter can be successful in the worldwide export business, just as Coca-Cola and McDonald's are. Isabelle is working day and night to convince Wilbur Parks, Susan Stewart, and Max Buchanon that Universal Foods' peanut butter should be developed for global markets. Unfortunately, she is seen as being somewhat irresponsible and unimaginative by the other members of the marketing division.

Questions

1. How can Universal Food's marketing division arrive at a sound decision about a global marketing strategy?

2. What global marketing strategy should Universal Foods choose? Why?

3. What should the marketing division do after choosing the marketing strategy?

4. How can Isabelle Larsen convince the other marketers that the shot-in- the-dark strategy is worth trying?

Solution: Case Study Report

I. Define and analyze the problem.
II. Suggest possible solutions.
III. Evaluate possible solutions.
IV. Select a solution.

Case Study Business Writing Assignment: Memorandum

Write a one-page memo of recommendation from Isabelle Larsen to Wilbur Parks, Marketing Director of Universal Foods. The memo should list, analyze, and evaluate the three marketing strategies that Universal Foods could implement in entering the international food market. It should recommend that UF choose the "shot-in-the-dark" marketing strategy.

Format:
I. Introduction (Background and Main Idea)
II. Discussion (Three Marketing Strategies)
III. Closing (Recommendation)

Style: Formal and somewhat technical
Tone: Balanced but persuasive

Additional Reading

"When in Rome Sell Like the Romans"
Edwin F. Lefkowith
Business Month 134 (December 1989): 89

MARKETING/EDWIN F. LEFKOWITH

WHEN IN ROME SELL LIKE THE ROMANS

AMERICAN MANAGERS ARE BEing challenged to think globally. However, amid all the discussion about foreign competition, product quality, currency fluctuations, and long-term commitment, a critical ingredient is missing: how to convey the right messages to the right audiences in the rapidly changing world marketplace. Many U.S. companies do not have a clue about what kind of corporate or brand identity will serve them best overseas. They're good at figuring out *where* they should be but not *what* they should be.

Many companies are sending the wrong messages—with disappointing results. Think of your chances if you were to go to market in the U.S. without a clearly articulated strategy for corporate communications and brand identification. Achieving success in unfamiliar foreign markets is even more problematic.

Why are otherwise successful and savvy companies making these marketing blunders? The causes are many. But two trends in particular are to blame:

☐ As U.S. companies decentralize to boost their profits, the identities of corporate and operating units diverge. The image that a company has worked so hard to establish becomes fractionalized.

☐ As both U.S. and foreign companies grow through acquisition, more and more corporate and brand identities affect the existing corporate culture. The effectiveness and efficiency of communications tend to deteriorate.

What's the solution? Here's a six-point plan that can help take most of the bumps out of the road to global marketing success.

1. Analyze the global com-

munications practices of the American and foreign brands that will be your toughest competitors. How are these products positioned, named, and identified?

2. Carefully assess the names and endorsement practices of your product lines. Have your brand names benefited from the parent corporation's endorsement, or do your brands do better on their own? What levels of recognition have your corporate and

---

Six ways to win the hearts and minds of foreign consumers.

---

brand names achieved in foreign markets? An analysis for the Chase Manhattan Bank revealed opportunities for strengthening market penetration by using the Chase name more consistently everywhere as a companion to the famous octagon symbol.

3. Evaluate the opportunities for a positioning strategy specifically tailored to the non-U.S. target market. A

key issue: How do your tactical marketing objectives fit into the overall strategic corporate communications plan? Recently, a global-identity umbrella was developed for Dow Chemical's $6.9 billion plastics operations. Up to then, these businesses had heavily promoted individual brand names. But an analysis showed that by marketing under a single, worldwide identity clearly linked to Dow, brand recognition could be preserved while providing the products with a strong competitive edge.

4. Think strategically. Start to build a strong single identity that can support global reach and boost the payback from marketing expenditures. Thomas & Betts Corp., a fast-growing $500 million electronic and electrical manufacturer, is expanding rapidly in international markets. It makes no sense for the company to try to support a basketful of different brand identities as its product lines battle for market share. So a single Thomas & Betts global identity has been created for all markets while retaining recognition in established brand names.

5. Explore which marketing communications media will best differentiate your products from those of the competition. In different countries, purchasers tend to respond to marketing approaches that are indigenous to their cultures.

6. Once you launch your marketing program, carefully monitor audience responses in case you need to fine-tune your strategy based on marketplace reactions.

International markets are going to be far more competitive three to five years from now. By resolving communications and identity issues at the outset, you can avoid the marketing "global glaucoma" that's afflicted many companies and move ahead with a clear and confident vision. ∎

Edwin F. Lefkowith is president of Lefkowith Inc., a marketing-communications consulting firm in New York.

KIMBERLEY BRY

Chapter 9

"Drugs: It Doesn't Have to Be Like This"

Preview

Skimming. Skim the article quickly to find the following general information.

1. Read the title and all headings and look at the illustrations.

2. Read the first three paragraphs, looking for the author's purpose and main idea.

3. Read the last paragraph, looking for a summary or conclusion.

Questioning. Answer the following questions and discuss your answers in class.

1. What does the title "It doesn't have to be like this" mean?

2. Do you think the drugs trade is increasing? Why?

3. Which drugs are classed as illegal and which are legal?

Scanning. Scan the article quickly to find the following specific information.

1. How much did the U.S. federal government spend in 1988 trying to keep heroin, cocaine, and marijuana out of its domestic market?

2. What is the most profitable article of trade in the world?

3. When was prohibition of alcohol tried in America?

4. In London, what costs more, a joint of marijuana or a pint of beer?

Economist 312, no. 7618 (September 2, 1989)

5. What country has applied social and medical remedies rather than criminal remedies to the drugs trade?

Vocabulary in Context. Read the following sentences and try to guess the meaning of the italicized words by using the context. Then replace the italicized words with synonyms (words or phrases that have nearly the same or similar meanings).

1. "The import, sale, and possession of cocaine are illegal in the United States, yet there was a *glut* of the *stuff*."

2. "The drugs trade is a fine *specimen* of unrestricted competition, which efficiently brings down prices and pushes up *consumption*."

3. "By the late 1980's deliveries had soared. To unload them, the middlemen had to *cut* their prices. They went down-market, hiring gangs to compete for distribution *monopolies* in poor areas."

4. "The demand for mind-changing drugs is irresistible although their effects are mysterious. Alcohol, for example, is *classed* as a *depressant*, but makes most drinkers happier."

5. "True, the *prospect* of time in jail must prevent prudent people from ever trying drugs at all. But it is not the *prudent* who need protection."

DRUGS

It doesn't have to be like this

Colombia is fighting a war against drugs. America is losing one. The rest of the world will lose too, if its weapon is prohibition. There are better ways

1 TOWARDS the end of 1988 a kilogramme of cocaine fetched about $12,000 in New York. A hard bargainer could get it for $8,000. Stockists were unloading and the price was falling fast. The import, sale and possession of cocaine are illegal in the United States, yet there was a glut of the stuff.

2 Back in 1980, one-kilogramme lots of cocaine hydrochloride cost about $60,000. In those days it was a foolish fashion for bankers and bond-salesmen, who sniffed it through rolled $100 bills after dinner while boasting of their good connections. Now it is sold adulterated at $10 or less for a cheap ten-minute thrill amid murder and mayhem in America's slums. Even that price still brings huge profits: a gramme makes four doses, so the kilogramme bought for $12,000 can fetch $40,000 on the street.

3 The drugs trade is a fine specimen of unrestricted competition, which efficiently brings down prices and pushes up consumption. Governments refuse to limit the trade by regulation, taxation and discouragement. Instead, by national laws and international conventions, they try to prohibit it. In 1980 the federal government of the United States spent just under $1 billion trying to keep heroin, cocaine and marijuana out of its domestic market. By 1988 it was spending almost $4 billion. Yet the retail price of drugs dropped even faster than the cost of policing rose. As prohibition failed, the volume of imports soared.

Funny figures

4 No one knows the arithmetic of the drugs trade. Retail prices can be fairly easily established by asking around in any American city. Since drugs traders do not declare their dealings to the customs or the tax-men, other figures on the trade are bogus. The American figures are especially odd, since 11 federal agencies (police, customs, coast-guard, Drug Enforcement Agency and so on), plus uncounted state bodies of one sort and another, competitively claim that the drugs problem is very serious, so give them more money and they can solve it. The first statement is true, the second false: either

way the "statistics" get swollen.

5 For example, a subcommittee of the United States Senate recently reckoned the global trade in banned drugs at $500 billion a year—an estimate credited to another estimate, in *Fortune* magazine. Of that, said the subcommittee, about $300 billion was earned in the United States, and about one-third of American drugs sales are of cocaine. So, hey presto, the American cocaine market is worth $100 billion a year, which, at $40,000 a kilo retail, implies imports of 2,500 tonnes of cocaine.

6 At a fair guess, it costs about $200 to produce one kilogramme. Transport from Colombia to North America costs about the same. Add a crude $1,000 for distribution expenses, including bribes and enforcement. Compare these costs even with the low 1988 street price, and it appears that along the distribution chain total American cocaine sales bring dealers tax-free profits of more than $95 billion.

7 Of such heroic arithmetic are scare-stories made. Yet—however uncertain the figures—cocaine is indeed clearly the most profitable article of trade in the world. In response to profitable American sales in the late 1970s, third-world producers planted extra acres, fitted out new laboratories and recruited better-armed sales forces. By the late 1980s deliveries had soared. To unload them, the middlemen had to cut their prices. They went down-market, hiring

gangs to compete for distribution monopolies in poor areas,

8 By early 1989 the slums of the District of Columbia, seat of the most powerful government in the world, saw—or rather, took care not to see—about ten murders a week. Half were associated with cocaine trafficking. Politicians and journalists could hear the shooting. It hugely reinforced the anti-drug propaganda that was already fashionable with everybody from First Ladies to the musicians selling rap and reggae and salsa tapes to the ghettoes. The war on drugs flooded the media. The drugs continued flooding the slums of Washington.

Now for Europe

9 American demand is probably falling (though not the murder rate: the fight for the remaining trade could well become still more vicious). So forward-looking drugs merchants are investing their profits in new markets. Japan's is potentially huge, and developing fast. The richest is Western Europe, even ahead of 1992. In drugs as in other leisure products, Europe's diverse countries have different tastes and offer different market opportunities. Spain's links of trade and culture with producing countries in Latin America make it a natural market for the Colombian cocaine industry. Italy is the native land of the mafia, which is losing its old grip on the North American drugs trade; heroin, the mafia speciality, is already rife in Italy, where it killed more than 800 people in 1988, half as many as in the United States.

10 In northern Europe, Chinese, Pakistani and West Indian gangs (not to mention the natives) have long competed for control of illicit markets. Imports are rising, prices dropping. European governments these days are spending much more on anti-drugs

law enforcement than they used to. Far higher is the price paid by the customers who die of overdoses or poisonous adulterants, by policemen, by ordinary citizens whose lives are intermittently put at risk and whose civil liberties sometimes curtailed in the losing battle to prohibit drugs.

Legal and illegal

11 Almost everybody takes some kind of stimulating drug. In 1988 the average Briton aged over 18 spent $50 on tea and coffee, $325 on tobacco and $750 on alcoholic drinks. These legitimate products please, or invigorate, or calm, or console; they change the taker's state of mind. So do various stimulants and tranquillisers that may (depending on local law) be available only on prescription. All are addictive, in varying degrees.

12 The demand for mind-changing drugs is irresistible, although their effects are mysterious. Alcohol, for instance, is classed as a depressant, but makes most drinkers happier. Alcohol abuse has been recorded ever since Noah, safe after his Flood, "drank of the wine, and was drunken", with awful consequences for race relations.

13 Cigarettes kill smokers by the million. Alcohol wrecks people's lives and livers, ruins families, helps cause most road accidents and most violent crimes in most western countries. Powerful advertising promotes its consumption, mild government campaigns (backed by discriminatory taxes) seek to diminish it. But outside the Muslim countries that forbid alcohol on religious grounds, nobody seriously suggests prohibition. That was tried in America between 1920 and 1933, and it failed.

14 Illegal drugs do much the same things as legal ones but more so; the difference that matters is legislative, not pharmacological. The law copes clumsily with "designer" drugs, invented by chemists and cheaply made in home laboratories. But the main traded products are easier targets, the traditional drugs derived from tropical plants:

15 ● **Marijuana** (ganja, bhang, dope) is made from the leaves and seeds of Indian hemp; its concentrated (and so more easily smuggled) form is hashish. It may be smoked, drunk as an infusion or baked in cakes. It produces euphoria, disorientation, a heightened sense of rhythm and music and a lack of motivation and aggression. It has no important medical use, and people do not feel ill when they stop using it. Many American students find marijuana milder, easier to conceal and harder to detect than beer, which is equally illegal for most people of college age there. Marijuana consumption is widely tolerated even where its sale and supply are banned.

16 ● **Cocaine** is the active ingredient of the coca plant, habitually used by Andean Indians against cold, hunger and fatigue. Medically, no good substitute has yet been found for coca derivatives in the relief of pain. Illegally, cocaine crystals are mixed with a neutral (sometimes harmful) powder and sniffed, smoked or sometimes dangerously injected. One eighth of a gramme in the bloodstream can intoxicate an inexperienced user into hyperactive euphoria. Regular users want more and more to get the same effect. Stopping its use may leave a craving as acute as that which some people feel after they stop smoking cigarettes. Regular use rots the nose and damages the muscles of the heart.

17 Cheap cocaine may contain traces of the damaging solvents used in extracting it from the original leaves. Tiny volumes of it, mixed with baking soda to make "crack", may be heated to give off hot and harmful intoxicating smoke. Crack is no more or less addictive than cocaine in other forms; but $10-worth of it can give impoverished youths ten minutes of reckless excitement, during which they do crazy things. They could get the same effect much more cheaply with synthetic amphetamines.

18 ● **Heroin** is a soluble powder derived from

poppies; opium is dried poppy sap, morphine an intermediate derivative, codeine is in every household. The opiates are medically irreplaceable painkillers, which work so powerfully on the central nervous system that stopping their use can cause physical distress as bad as a bad flu.

19 Prudently used, heroin need do no great physical harm: when doctors in Britain were free to prescribe it, some of them became addicts and still worked well at their jobs for decades. That was stopped because a few addicted doctors thought heroin so wonderful that they prescribed large quantities of it for others, profitably spreading their own addiction.

20 Most healthy people dislike heroin, but it can enslave the unhappy or the psychologically disturbed. As many as one in four of those who regularly use it feel ill if they do not take it, and will lie, cheat and steal for their supply; these are the addicts. Their craving may be chemically assuaged by synthetic methadone. Many doctors and prison officials think heroin addiction mainly a symptom of psychological disturbance, and try to treat it much as they treat alcoholism, gambling and other compulsions. But doctors are reluctant to treat addicts who, by admitting their addiction, are also confessing to a crime.

Addicted societies

21 Drug abuse may accompany social as well as personal disorder. Respectable citizens were scared by alcohol in England in the 1740s (and in Russia always), by opium in nineteenth-century China, by hashish in Egypt in the 1920s. North Europeans tend to drink rarely but in heavy binges, so Nordic countries tax strong drink hard. Southerners drink as much but more slowly, so Italians do not seem drunk and have weak anti-alcohol laws, but still damage their livers.

22 American politicians became convinced during the first world war that drink was wrecking the nation. In 1919 they amended the federal constitution to prohibit all dealings in alcohol, except for medical purposes. Drunkenness dropped, but a lot of people insisted on their beer or whisky. Some brewed the stuff at home, and brewed hangovers with it. Others bought certified liquor from Scotland via Canada, or from France via Cuba. The shippers, labelled as criminals, behaved as such. They "protected" truck-drivers and bar-owners, shot rivals, paid off local politicians and policemen.

23 The federal authorities caught the richest bootleggers mainly by tricks such as excessive income-tax assessments. As soon as they trapped one, another sprang up to satisfy the profitable demand. By 1933 the federal government gave up and legalised drinking again. The bootleggers, losing their tax-free profits, diversified into other illegal services such as gambling and abortion. As these too began to be made legal, so less profitable, the gangs went back to smuggling, and began with marijuana.

24 The Caribbean entrepots began to relive the bootlegging days that Hemingway recorded. Then in the 1960s the region acquired more small, poor, bribable governments. The marijuana transport and retail networks too made progress, brutally, by buy-outs and shoot-outs, into cocaine, which meant higher profits from smaller volumes easier to conceal and transport.

25 Britain's experience has been longer. In the eighteenth century cheap gin ravaged its crowded, already industrialising cities. Moralists were appalled at the degradation depicted by Hogarth, capitalists found that drink made their workers unproductive. So Parliament began to control the trade. Retail sales were limited to outlets supervised by local magistrates. The quality of spirits was stiffly controlled, to cut out poisonous adulterants. Taxes made strong drink much costlier than relatively harmless beer.

26 The system remains in place, modified (albeit too slowly) to match the changing

times. Now Britain certifies Scotch whisky that is smuggled to the prohibition countries of the Gulf, as though Colombia certified cocaine for export to New York. At home, alcohol's ravages increase when, as now, the government fails to keep taxes on drink ahead of inflation. Drinking remains a problem for private health and public safety. But the drinks trade is crime-free.

Crime-creating prohibition

27 Prohibition creates crime, and so gives rise to fiercer dangers than the medical and social ones it is intended to avert. True, the prospect of time in jail must prevent prudent people from ever trying drugs at all. But it is not the prudent who need protection.

28 The young and the foolish are exposed to special risks when several different drugs are classed together as illegal. The state says marijuana is much worse than alcohol, and must therefore be banned, with stiff penalties. Young people see their friends smoke it, and try it without much harm. They may therefore believe the whole law is an ass and imagine that heroin, subject to similar bans, is similarly harmless, which it is not.

29 Governments compel producers to indicate the alcohol content—and, for wine at least, the quality—of their drinks. Banned drugs are simply banned; their quality and purity depend on no more than the seller's good faith, which may not be great. Cheap crack, or the even cheaper cocaine sold as *basuco*, is often poisonously tainted by ethylene or even petrol used as a solvent in its making. That can kill. In southern Italy the mafia sells heroin at 10% concentration, in the north at 50%. Southern addicts visit the north and kill themselves with one injection, like a beer-drinker who might unknowingly gulp a pint of whisky.

30 Governments that ban drugs cannot also tax them; they thus abandon the most effective means of controlling their abuse. Britain's differing tax-rates divert demand from hard spirits to less harmful beer, but not from heroin to marijuana (nor from marijuana to beer, if you think that desirable, which many wouldn't, which a joint costs less

in London than a pint). Drugs impose public costs—for policing the trade, for treating its victims (such as the heroin users who get AIDS from shared needles), for warning the public against abuse. Governments decline the revenue that taxes could produce.

31 Drug-takers steal to pay for their illegal habit. Drug retailers fight it out for control of the streets. Drug wholesalers form protection squads, bribe policemen, tempt politicians. Drug shippers and exporters buy aircraft, arsenals and whole governments. America's covert agents, in South-East Asia and in Central America, have too often exchanged favours with them. The drugs business is the basis of much of the world's petty crime, and of some of the world's largest criminal conspiracies.

32 Vast untaxed profits amass in the conspirators' hands and trail off into peaceable tax havens. The latest intergovernmental fashion, enshrined in a new United Nations convention, is therefore to beat the conspirators by taking away their profits. That sounds good. But the world is awash with crypto-dollars, avoiding tax or evading exchange-controls; it is impossible to sort the drugs money out from the rest without attacking the banks that big countries protect. So far, the main target of America's prosecuting zeal is a bank owned by Saudis, inspired by Lebanese, managed by Pakistanis and blaming any regrettable misunderstandings on its outpost in Panama.

33 American politicians are frightened of drugs wars on their streets, and so they should be: they have the most heavily armed urban population in the world. Drugs wars in poorer, less resilient countries terrify their politicians with even better reason. Lebanon is awash with weapons, many of them paid for by the poppy crop whose precious sap keeps the Afghans fighting

too. In Colombia judges and newspaper editors have faced a choice: collaborate and get $100,000, resist and get a bullet in your son's head. Now it is the authority of the state itself that is at risk.

34 The ooze of corruption from the illegal trade threatens bigger nations such as Pakistan and Brazil. Hard-working Jamaicans can make money flying fresh flowers to the United States; but smugglers slip ganja into the flower-pots, so the American customs search the flowers for so long that they die.

Legalise and control

35 Drugs are dangerous. So is the illegality that surrounds them. In legitimate commerce, their sale controlled, taxed and supervised, their dangers proclaimed on every packet, drugs would poison fewer customers, kill fewer dealers, bribe fewer policemen, raise more public revenue.

36 For drugs as for alcohol, different societies need different remedies. The present international ban compels all to adopt the same blanket policy: to pretend that they can stop the trade, so forcing it into the evil ways that it now follows. Only the Dutch have had the courage to break away, treating different drugs differently and selectively applying social and medical remedies rather than criminal. Holland is permissive; yet few of its youngsters die of drug abuse (and hardly any get AIDS from infected needles). Drug-related crime is under control.

37 Legalising the drugs trade would be risky. Prohibition is worse than risky. It is a proven failure, a danger in its own right. *The Economist* advocates its replacement with more effective restrictions on the spread of drugs. In summary, we want to legalise, control and strongly discourage the use of them all. Give it 20 years, while today's drugs squads turn their energies to things that actually do some good like helping little old ladies cross the road.

Glossary

adulterants	substances that make something inferior or impure
adulterated	inferior, impure, not genuine because of addition of less valuable substances
advocates	supports, is in favor of
albeit	although, even though
amass	to accumulate, pile up
amended	changed, revised
arsenals	a large number of weapons; places for storing weapons
assuaged	lessened, satisfied
avert	prevent, keep from happening
awash	flooded with
banned	prohibited, forbidden
binges	completely unrestrained behavior, as drinking
blanket	uniform, covering a group of conditions
bogus	false, not genuine
bootleggers	people who make and sell liquor illegally
brewed	made
bribable	capable of being bribed
bribes	money given to make a person do something illegal or wrong
buy-outs	buying all the business rights, stocks
compel	to force
compulsions	irresistible, irrational impulses
console	to comfort, make feel less sad
consumption	the using up of goods or services by consumers
craving	intense desire
crude	rough, not analyzed
crypto-dollars	secret or hidden dollars
curtailed	reduced, shortened
degradation	corruption
depressant	a drug that lowers the spirits, rate of nervous activity; a sedative
derivatives	substances taken from another substance
diversified	expanded
divert	to turn aside, deflect
down-market	downward trend, less expensive
enshrined	held as sacred
enslave	to make a slave of, dominate
entrepots	distributing centers for goods
euphoria	feeling of well-being, vigor, high spirits
fatigue	tiredness, weariness, exhaustion
fetched	sold for, brought as a price
ghettoes	sections of a city in which minority groups live
glut	oversupply, supply greater than the demand
gulp	to swallow in a large amount
illicit	unlawful, unauthorized
impoverished	poor

infusion	liquid extract made by soaking a substance in water
intermittently	periodically; not continuous
invigorate	to fill with energy
irreplaceable	not replaceable
irresistible	cannot be resisted, too strong to be resisted
legitimate	legal, lawful
magistrates	civil officers who administer the law
mayhem	violence, destruction
middlemen	go-betweens, traders who buy from a producer and sell to retailers or consumers
monopolies	exclusive control of commodities or services in a given market
pharmacological	related to the qualities and uses of drugs
propaganda	systematic, widespread promotion of particular ideas
prospect	the mental view, examination
prudent	cautious, careful
ravaged	ruined, destroyed
reckoned	figured up, computed
remedies	solutions
resilient	able to recover strength, energy
rife	abundant, widespread, plentiful
risky	dangerous, hazardous
slums	heavily populated areas of city characterized by poverty, poor housing
smuggled	taken into or out of a country secretly, illegally
sniffed	breathed in through the nose
soared	rose very high
solvents	liquids that dissolve other substances
specimen	example
swollen	increased in size, blown up
synthetic	artificial, not naturally occurring
tainted	infected, spoiled, contaminated
zeal	intense enthusiasm, passion

Vocabulary

Without referring to the article, fill in the blanks in the following sentences with the correct words from this list. You may change the tense, number, or form of the words to fit the context. Use each word only once; not all of the words on the list will be used.

glut	illicit	adulterated	smuggle	legitimate	amend	divert
differential	degradation	compel	discretion	amass	curtail	soar

1. In 1988 there was a(n) _____ of cocaine on the market in the United States, so prices were falling, and the volume of imports was _____ .

2. Although it is quite dangerous and may even result in death, many people buy _____ cocaine for a cheap thrill at a cheap price.

3. In northern Europe, _____ markets for drugs are controlled by various ethnic groups in competition with each other.

4. The drug war has affected the lives of ordinary citizens, whose civil rights may be _____ _____ by anti-drugs law enforcement.

5. Most people take some kind of _____ drug, such as coffee, tea, or alcohol, which changes the taker's state of mind.

6. Large numbers of drugs are _____ into the United States every day in spite of the many law enforcement agencies working to prevent this from happening.

7. In 1919, the U.S. Constitution was _____ to prohibit all dealings in alcohol, unless for medical purposes.

8. After Hogarth's pictures showed the _____ caused by alcohol abuse, the British parliament decided to control alcohol trade in the 18th century.

9. To inform the consumer, liquor and wine producers are _____ by the government to indicate the alcohol content of their products.

10. As a result of Britain's differing tax-rates, consumer demand is _____ from hard liquor to beer.

11. Drug traders have become wealthy because they _____ vast untaxed profits and place these profits in tax shelters.

Idioms and Expressions

Read the paragraphs in which the following italicized idioms and expressions are found. Then circle the letter next to the answer that best describes the meaning of the idiom as used in the context of the article.

1. "So, *hey presto,* the American cocaine market is worth $100 billion a year. . . ." (Paragraph 5)
   a. by magic
   b. all of a sudden
   c. by accident

2. "The war on drugs *flooded* the media." (Paragraph 8)
   a. totally ruined
   b. completely covered
   c. strongly influenced

3. "Italy is the native land of the mafia, which is *losing its old grip on* the North American drugs trade. . . ." (Paragraph 9)
   a. no longer in control of
   b. no longer popular in
   c. no longer part of

4. "Heroin, the mafia specialty, is already *rife* in Italy. . . ." (Paragraph 9)
   a. widespread
   b. expensive
   c. available

5. "They 'protected' truck drivers and bar owners, shot rivals, *paid off* local politicians and policemen." (Paragraph 22)
   a. made regular payments to
   b. met the payroll of
   c. gave money as bribes to

6. "They may therefore believe the whole law is *an ass*. . . ." (Paragraph 28)
   a. foolish
   b. uncivilized
   c. old-fashioned

7. "The *ooze of corruption* from the illegal trade threatens bigger nations such as Pakistan and Brazil." (Paragraph 34)
   a. publicity
   b. spread of immorality
   c. bribery

Paraphrasing

Read the following sentences carefully, and then rewrite them using your own words. Change the vocabulary and sentence structure, but do not change the author's intended meaning or paraphrase any technical terms. There are several ways of paraphrasing each sentence.

Original: "As prohibition failed, the volume of imports soared."
Paraphrase: A great increase in the number of imports accompanied the failure of prohibition.

1. "Of such heroic arithmetic are scare-stories made." (Paragraph 7)

   _____

   _____

2. "These legitimate products please, or invigorate, or calm, or console . . . ." (Paragraph 11)

   _____

   _____

3. "Prudently used, heroin need do no great physical harm. . . ." (Paragraph 19)

_____

_____

4. "Prohibition creates crime, and so gives rise to fiercer dangers than the medical and social ones it is intended to avert." (Paragraph 27)

_____

_____

Comprehension

Answer the following questions by finding the relevant information in the article. Give the numbers of the paragraphs that contain the answers.

1. What is the main idea of this article?

2. Why is the drugs trade a fine specimen of unrestricted competition?

3. Why is it difficult to get accurate figures on the drugs trade?

4. What has resulted from the probable decrease in American demand for drugs?

5. What drugs are legal and what are the effects of legal drugs?

6. What drugs are illegal and what are their effects?

7. What were the effects of Prohibition in America?

8. How does Britain regulate alcohol trade?

9. How does prohibition of drugs create crime?

10. What benefits would result from taxing drugs?

11. What would happen if drugs were legalized and controlled?

12. What is the author's solution to the drug problem?

Inference/Interpretation

Circle the letter next to the best answer. Choose your answer according to the meaning the author suggests but does not state explicitly.

1. The article conveys the idea that the drug enforcement agencies have
   a. almost solved the problem of the drug trade.
   b. failed to solve the problem of the drug trade.
   c. contributed to the drug problem.
   d. asked for more money to solve the drug problem.

2. Which of the following sentences about marijuana can be inferred? (Paragraph 15)
    a. Marijuana has severely negative effects.
    b. Marijuana is more addictive than cocaine.
    c. Marijuana is used as an anesthetic.
    d. Marijuana has no severely negative effects.

3. What can we infer from the statement: "Prudently used, heroin need do no great physical harm"? (Paragraph 19)
    a. When used wisely, heroin is safe.
    b. Even when used wisely, heroin may cause some physical harm.
    c. When used wisely, heroin causes no mental harm.
    d. Heroin is not an addictive drug.

4. The author's tone is sarcastic in the last sentence of this article. Explain the meaning of this sentence: "Give it 20 years, while today's drugs squads turn their energies to things that actually do some good like helping little old ladies cross the road." (Paragraph 37)

_____

_____

Structure

Circle the letter next to the correct answer(s). More than one answer may be correct. Be prepared to explain and justify your choices.

1. In which paragraph(s) is the main idea stated?
    a. Paragraph 1
    b. Paragraph 3
    c. Paragraph 8
    d. Paragraph 35
    e. Paragraph 37
    Write a paraphrase of the main idea in *one* sentence, using your own words as much as possible.

_____

2. What is the main purpose of the statistics given in the first two paragraphs of the article?
    a. To show how expensive cocaine is
    b. To give an example of how a free market works
    c. To support the first sentence of paragraph 3
    d. To argue against the use of drugs
    e. To contrast past and present drug use

3. Where are examples used to support a general idea?
    a. Paragraph 5
    b. Paragraph 8
    c. Paragraph 12
    d. Paragraph 23
    e. Paragraph 33

4. Where is cause and effect development used to develop a paragraph?
   a. Paragraph 4
   b. Paragraph 6
   c. Paragraph 9
   d. Paragraph 28
   e. Paragraph 29

5. Where is chronological order used to develop a general idea?
   a. Paragraphs 5–6
   b. Paragraphs 7–8
   c. Paragraphs 15–16
   d. Paragraphs 22–23
   e. Paragraphs 32–33

6. What overall method of development is used in this article?
   a. Analyzing a technical proposal
   b. Defining a new policy
   c. Enumerating steps in a process
   d. Chronologically describing a problem
   e. Justifying an argument through analysis of causes and effects

Style

Circle the letter next to the correct answer(s). More than one answer may be correct. Be prepared to justify your choices by giving specific examples from the article.

1. How would you describe the writing style of the author?
   a. Conversational
   b. Formal
   c. Legal
   d. Literary
   e. Technical
   f. Informal

2. How would you describe the tone of the article?
   a. Witty
   b. Subjective
   c. Authoritative
   d. Sarcastic
   e. Angry
   f. Arrogant

3. The author's attitude toward the prohibition of drugs can be described as
   a. critical.
   b. indifferent.
   c. unrealistic.
   d. disapproving.
   e. approving.
   f. understanding.

4. Explain the purpose of the author's use of repetition and parallel sentence structures in paragraph 8: "The war on drugs flooded the media. The drugs continued flooding the slums of Washington."

Discussion

1. Do you agree with the author that drugs (marijuana, cocaine, heroin) should be legalized? Why or why not?

2. What are the effects of using marijuana? Can a person use marijuana on a regular basis and suffer no ill effects?

3. How does the use of cocaine or heroin on a regular basis affect a person's ability to be a responsible member of society?

4. How serious is alcohol abuse in comparison with drug abuse? Are they equally serious? Why or why not?

5. What are other alternatives to solving the drug problem besides prohibition or legalization?

Research Assignment

Look up several of these articles in the library. Choose one article to read and take notes on.

Baer, Donald. "A Judge Who Took the Stand: It's Time to Legalize Drugs." *U.S. News & World Report* 108 (April 9, 1990): 26–27.

Baker, T. L. "Preventing Drug Abuse at Work." *Personnel Administrator* 34 (July 1989): 56–59.

"Drugs: War Profiteers." *Economist* 311 (April 8, 1989): 35.

Du Pont, Robert L., and Ronald L. Goldfarb. "Drug Legalization: Asking for Trouble." *Washington Post* (January 26, 1990): A23.

Hentoff, Nat. "Random Drug Tests, Starting in the 7th Grade." *Washington Post* (July 7, 1990): A23.

Holthaus, D. "Employees Get Broader Power to Fight Drug Use." *Hospitals* 63 (August 5, 1989): 44.

"Ice Overdose." *Economist* 313 (December 2, 1989): 29–30.

McKee, Bradford A. "Small Firms Enlist to Fight Drugs." *Nation's Business* 78 (February 1990): 49–50.

"Mission Just Possible." *Economist* 312 (September 30, 1989): 72.

Morgan, J. P. "Employee Drug Tests Are Unreliable and Intrusive." *Hospitals* 63 (August 20, 1989): 64.

Moskowitz, Daniel B. "Court Decisions on Drug Testing Lack Guidance for Firms." *Washington Post* (July 2, 1990): Washington Business Section, 28.

Post, Tom. "You Said Yes But Santa Fe Knows How Tough It Is." *Business Month* 135 (March 1990): 42–45.

"Relief by Mail." *Economist* 313 (December 2, 1989): 35.

Riemer, B. "The Drug War—European Style." *Business Week* (October 2, 1989): 31–32.

Stodghill, R. "Will Fear Make Americans Kick the Drug Habit?" *Business Week* (September 11, 1989): 30.

Stuart, P. B. "Keeping Your Work Place Drug Free." *Business and Health* 7 (August 1989): 55.

Way, P. K. "Divergent Organizational Responses to Substance Abuse." *Labor Law Journal* 40 (August 1989): 521–26.

Wrich, James T. "Beyond Testing: Coping with Drugs at Work." *Harvard Business Review* 66 (January-February 1988): 120–33.

Wilson, James Q. "Legal Drugs? CEO's Should Just Say No." *Business Month* 135 (May 1990): 13–14.

Oral Presentation

Working with a partner, give a fifteen-minute oral presentation to the class on the article that you chose in the research assignment. Include the author's main idea, major points, and some supporting data. Be prepared to answer questions on your topic. (See Appendix B: Giving an Oral Presentation.)

Writing Assignments

1. Write a critique of this article in which you briefly summarize the author's argument, give your reaction to it, and evaluate it. Support your point of view with logical arguments and specific examples. A possible thesis for such a critique is: Although the author of "Drugs: It Doesn't Have to Be Like This" may be correct in asserting that the drugs squads are losing the war against drugs, the argument that drugs should be legalized is based on faulty reasoning.

Format:
    I. Introduction (Thesis)
    II. Summary
    III. Critique
    IV. Conclusion

2. Discuss the drug problem as it exists in your country or in the United States. Enumerate the major causes and effects that can be seen in a society that has a serious drug problem. Offer a solution to the problem.

3. Can a person use drugs responsibly? Make a list of all the legitimate drugs you have used (tobacco, alcohol, caffeine, etc.). How does each one affect you and change your state of mind? Do you want to stop using any of these drugs? (If you use none of these drugs, explain why you don't.)

Peer Critique

Choose a person to work with. After you have completed your writing assignment, let your partner read and critique your writing. Then you will read and critique his or her writing. Use the Writing Evaluation Form in Appendix F.

Case Study: A Problem in Drug Testing

Working in groups, read the following case study. Discuss the problem, answer the questions, and write a brief report on how your group would solve the problem. (Choose one member of the group to do the writing.) Follow the format in Appendix E (Case Study Report) in writing your report.

    ABC Corporation is implementing a War-on-Drugs Program. Margaret Heller has worked for ABC Corporation as a computer software expert for the past nine months. She has just received a memo from the President of ABC, Alan Black, stating that all ABC employees must take a random drug test every month in order to help achieve a drug-free workplace. Margaret does not take any drugs, and never has, but she does not want to submit to random drug testing. She believes it would be an invasion of her privacy and a denial of her right to due process since she probably could not fight the results of the tests. She also thinks that it is a violation of the Fourth Amendment to the U.S. Constitution, which protects against "unreasonable searches and seizures."

    Margaret has talked to her supervisor, Ms. Wallace, and expressed her opinion about drug testing being unconstitutional—an erosion of her civil liberties. Her supervisor advised Margaret to comply with the order in the memo, especially as Margaret is a new employee and "shouldn't be causing trouble." Ms. Wallace warned Margaret that she could be reprimanded or possibly even terminated for refusing to take the drug tests.

    Margaret loves her job with the ABC Corporation. Although she feels strongly about the issue of involuntary drug testing, she does not want to lose her job. Nevertheless, she has always stood up for what she believes in. Of course, she is aware that in 1989 the Supreme Court upheld random drug tests for some employees of the U.S. Customs Service even though the testing infringed upon the employees' rights to privacy. But Margaret knows that the law is still not settled, and there are many drug-testing cases in the federal courts.

Questions

1. Should Margaret take the drug tests and then file a protest?

2. Should Margaret refuse to take the drug tests?

3. Whom should Margaret talk to about this issue?

4. What other alternatives does Margaret have?

Solution: Case Study Report

I. Define and analyze the problem.
II. Suggest possible solutions.
III. Evaluate possible solutions.
IV. Select a solution.

Case Study Business Writing Assignment: Business Letter

Write a letter from Margaret Heller to the editor of the local newspaper. The letter should explain Margaret's position on the policy of random drug testing of ABC Corporation's employees.

Format:
    I. Introduction (Background and Main Idea)
    II. Discussion (Position on Drug Testing)
    III. Closing (Restatement of Main Idea)

Style: Informal
Tone: Emotional and angry

Case Study Business Writing Assignment: Memorandum

Write a memo from Alan Black, the President of ABC Corporation, to all employees. The memo should state that ABC will be implementing a random drug-testing program for all employees and give the reasons for taking such an action. It should request everyone's cooperation.

Format:
    I. Introduction (Background and Main Idea)
    II. Discussion (Reasons for Action)
    III. Closing (Request for Cooperation)

Style: Formal
Tone: Authoritative and objective

Additional Reading

“Uncivil Liberties?”
Tom Morganthau
Newsweek 114 (April 23, 1990): 18–20

Uncivil Liberties?

Debating whether drug-war tactics are eroding constitutional rights

Chalk one up for "L.A. Law." Only a week after the hit TV series aired a new episode involving a wrong-address drug raid by pumped-up television narcs, the District of Columbia police force managed to act out the real thing. The victims were George and Katrina Stokes, who live in a crack-infested neighborhood of southeast Washington. The Stokeses were home watching television early one evening when a heavily armed D.C. SWAT team came crashing through their door. George Stokes was ordered to the floor at gunpoint, somehow sustaining a gash on his head in the process. His wife, understandably terrified, fell down the cellar stairs as she tried to run away from the band of black-uniformed intruders.

Like their television counterparts, the D.C. drugbusters soon found they had the wrong house. Worse yet, a camera crew from a local television station was on hand to record the whole event. The newsies,

assigned to cover a neighborhood anti-drug protest, had their camera rolling as the SWAT team charged into the Stokeses' living room—and they were still taping when the cops, looking sheepish, trooped back outside, apologized and drove off to find the right address. The denouement was just like "L.A. Law," too: the victims got a lawyer, who said his clients are now considering a lawsuit against the city.

As "L.A. Law" and the nightly news suggest, America is beginning to confront the true cost, in terms of civil liberties and the rights of the individual, of the nationwide war against drugs. SWAT-team raids, stop-and-frisk tactics and a wide variety of aggressive surveillance techniques are the hallmarks of the police offensive against drug trafficking in cities from coast to coast. Elsewhere—in suburban schools, in the workplace and throughout the electronic banking system—government is steadily broadening its monitoring of private citizens' affairs. If drugs and drug-

related crime pose a danger to the nation—and most Americans believe that they do—such measures may be the price of civil order. But the corollary is a threatened erosion of constitutional safeguards that deeply troubles leading civil libertarians. "Throughout [American] history, the government has said we're in an unprecedented crisis and that we must live without civil liberties until the crisis is over," says Yale Kamisar of the University of Michigan School of Law. "It's a hoax."

The broad and cautious view from many constitutional scholars is that the core values of the Bill of Rights are still intact. But some are concerned by what they see as a gradual erosion of civil liberties on a case-by-case or situation-by-situation basis. A short list of emerging issues that worry civil libertarians includes:

■ **Drug Testing.** Despite continued concern about the accuracy of urinalysis, the national trend toward pre-employment and on-the-job drug testing is well established.

For all the controversy over tough procedures, many inner-city residents are behind the cops: *Suspected gang members in Los Angeles*

The law, however, is still unsettled. Last year the Supreme Court narrowly upheld random drug tests for some Customs Service personnel. "In my view, the Customs Service rules are a kind of immolation of privacy and human dignity," Justice Antonin Scalia wrote in a blistering dissent. Meanwhile, in cases from Indiana and Texas, the federal courts are tackling the new craze for drug-testing programs in the nation's public schools. The rule so far: drug tests can be required for athletes, though not for all students. (In effect, the courts have held that athletics are optional activities and that schools can enforce special eligibility rules. But since school attendance is compulsory, drug tests for all students would infringe on individual rights.)

ALON REININGER—CONTACT PRESS IMAGES

■ **Stop and Frisk.** After a series of Supreme Court decisions reaching back to 1968, the law on stop-and-frisk searches has been settled—mostly in favor of the police. But the drug war, with its climate of pervasive violence, has forced authorities in many cities to rely on stop-and-frisk tactics as never before. That trend, immediately obvious to residents of south-central Los Angeles or Boston's Dorchester and Roxbury sections, has triggered new controversies about police harassment of minorities. After community complaints in Boston, for example, five youths backed by the Civil Liberties Union of Massachusetts filed suit to limit stop-and-frisk searches. Still, many inner-city residents have solidly backed the cops. "I think the police really have to kick butt right now," said anti-drug activist Georgette Watson. "We're under siege."

■ **Drug-Courier Profiles.** Increasingly used by federal, state and local cops, drug-courier profiles (chart) are criticized by civil libertarians because they are based on a person's looks or behavior rather than on some reasonable suspicion that a crime has been committed. As a result, critics say, they may lead to groundless searches of blacks and other minorities who police believe are more likely to be carrying drugs. Last year the Supreme Court upheld the use of profiles by the Drug Enforcement Administration. The DEA, which uses its profiles in surveillance at U.S. airports, trains and bus stations, says these "investigative techniques" lead to some 3,000 arrests a year—but it keeps no statistics on the number of travelers who are questioned and let go. "It's not like they throw you to the ground and handcuff you," an agency spokesman says. "It is strictly conversation: what's your name, how are you doing today? People shouldn't be alarmed."

■ **Housing-Project Sweeps.** After discovering that federal regulations made it difficult and time-consuming to evict known drug dealers from public-housing projects, Jack Kemp, the Bush administration's secretary of Housing and Urban Development, decided to junk the regulations. Since then HUD has authorized 39 states and the District of Columbia to waive the hearings process that Kemp said protected the druggies. The results so far have been mixed, and some civil-liberties lawyers say the new rules don't guarantee due process. In Chicago, however, the ACLU is cooperating with the city housing authority and the police. The goal: to protect law-abiding tenants while enabling police to drive the

Alarm Bells

Drug-courier profiles vary around the country and are tailored to the mode of transport—car or plane—a suspected trafficker is using. What sets off alarms:

Airports

Passengers who appear nervous and in a hurry, and are traveling alone without luggage. Also those who buy tickets at the last minute with cash and are traveling to and from Miami, Detroit and Houston. Nigerians are frequently stopped and searched.

Interstate Highways

Young people driving late-model cars at the speed limit (to avoid tickets) in high drug-traffic areas and near international borders. Cars with license plates from Florida and Texas are often suspect.

drug dealers out. "What we found is that the problem really wasn't with the occupied apartments but with gangs selling drugs out of the unoccupied apartments," the ACLU's Jay Miller says. The sweeps, under guidelines drawn up with the ACLU, are continuing, and tenants say they want more. "We will do anything we have to do to put an end to the murders and the drugs," says tenant leader Helen Finner.

But it is the get-tough national mood that alarms civil libertarians most. While recognizing that drugs are a serious social issue, particularly in the inner city, defense attorneys and legal scholars are increasingly concerned by what they view as indiscriminate support for repression. They are worried by politicians' drug-bashing demagoguery, and they are appalled by polls that show the public would give up "a few of the freedoms we have in this country" in return for suppressing drug abuse. "Our privacy rights are being eroded," says William Genago, a professor at Boston University School of Law. "The fact that people in the neighborhoods support [drug crackdowns] is most alarming. They're willing to

RALF-FINN HESTOFT—SABA

Rules: *Student athletes check schedule for random drug tests*

sacrifice their rights without asking whether these measures are effective."

There is no doubt that the urge to control drug abuse has led to instances of excess. In Chicago, all sixth, seventh and eighth graders at St. Sabina's elementary school are required to participate in random urinalysis—and the Rev. Michael Pfleger, pastor of St. Sabina's Roman Catholic Church, boasts that his is the only elementary school in the nation with such a program. (No child has yet tested positive for drugs.) In Los Angeles, the ACLU went to court to block a campaign against a notori-

ous street gang known as the Playboy Gangster Crips. City officials sought to bar gang members from loitering, wearing gang regalia or gathering in groups of more than two. Worse, residents of the Cadillac-Corning area of L.A., where the Playboy Gangsters allegedly hang out, would have been required to carry proof that they lived at a particular address—a rule that seemed frighteningly reminiscent of South Africa's notorious "pass laws." The ACLU won its case.

It can be argued that the drug-war trend toward tougher law enforcement was inevitable—that it represents, in the long view of constitutional scholars, a cyclical balancing of the rights of the individual with the rights of society at large. It is also true, as drug czar William Bennett maintains, that government has an overriding obligation to secure the civil peace for all its citizens. But the question for drug-warriors and private citizens is the same: how much law and order is really necessary, and at what price?

TOM MORGANTHAU *with* MARK MILLER *in Washington,* DAVID A. KAPLAN *in New York,* TODD BARRETT *in Boston,* LYNDA WRIGHT *in Los Angeles and bureau reports*

Chapter 10

"The 9 to 5 Underground: Are You Policing Computer Crimes?"

Jeffrey A. Hoffer and Detmar W. Straub, Jr.

Preview

Skimming. Skim the article quickly to find the following general information.

1. Read the authors' names, the title, all headings, and graphic aids.

2. Read the abstract and first and second paragraphs, looking for the authors' purpose and main idea.

3. Read the paragraph labeled *Conclusion,* looking for a summary or conclusion.

Questioning. Answer the following questions and discuss your answers in class.

1. What does "underground" mean?

2. What is the meaning of "policing"?

3. What are the most common computer crimes?

Scanning. Scan the article quickly to find the following specific information.

1. What percent of major U.S. firms may have lost money because of computer fraud?

2. How are most computer abuses discovered?

3. Where is most abuse directed?

4. Which industries are more susceptible to computer abuse than others?

5. How can computer viruses be prevented?

Sloan Management Review 30, no. 4 (Summer 1989)

Vocabulary in Context. Read the following sentences and try to guess the meaning of the italicized words by using the context. Then replace the italicized words with synonyms (words or phrases that have nearly the same or similar meanings).

1. "For all their *intricacy* and mystique, computer systems are just as subject to abuse as *manual* systems are."

2. "We found that organizations respond in a variety of ways to the potential threat from abuse and the need to *uncover* abuse; in general, security staff practices such as educating users on proper system use and stressing penalties for misuse are good *deterrents.*"

3. "In program abuse, a program might be *altered* to juggle accounts, for example, placing money in a newly created account for purposes of *embezzlement.*"

4. "Hackers are a threat, but *insiders* are a more *pressing* threat."

5. "Large organizations *experience* more significant and frequent computer abuse than small organizations do, even though they generally have proportionately larger security staffs. What explains this apparent *anomaly?*"

6. "From one standpoint, this *finding* is reassuring; it underscores the security function's perceived efficacy. This high level of support is appropriate, given the *empirical* evidence of security measures' effectiveness in lowering abuse."

The 9 to 5 Underground: Are You Policing Computer Crimes?

Jeffrey A. Hoffer
Detmar W. Straub, Jr.

Indiana University
University of Minnesota

NOBODY REALLY KNOWS HOW MUCH MONEY is lost every year as the result of computer system abuse. The authors' research indicates that the losses could be substantial — and that many of them could be avoided if firms were more serious about deterrence and prevention. Their article is a call for proactive computer security administration: it outlines the most common forms of abuse, the most effective countermeasures, and the steps that can lead to effective security management. *Ed.*

Sloan
Management
Review

Summer 1989

1 FOR ALL THEIR INTRICACY and mystique, computer systems are just as subject to abuse as manual systems are; indeed, abusive activities are seriously threatening computer system integrity and the businesses these systems serve. There is growing evidence that new, management-directed countermeasures will be needed to shore up system defenses.

2 According to a variety of case histories and surveys, organizations report a significant impact from computer-related losses.[1] A high percentage of major U.S. firms — between 25 and 50 percent, in fact — uncover one or more serious abuses each year; and, according to an Ernst and Whinney study, as many as 50 to 90 percent may have lost money because of computer fraud.[2] Some of these incidents were catastrophic; others were substantial and had the potential to be even worse. A task force sponsored by the American Bar Association estimated annual losses at a half-billion dollars for seventy-two Fortune 500 organizations.[3]

The Need for Greater Executive Awareness

3 Since the early 1980s, information systems managers have cited security as a key management issue in opinion surveys, but other managers may be less concerned than they should be.[4] In one study, general managers did not rank security among the top twenty management issues in the systems domain.[5] The value of systems documen-tation, backup and recovery procedures, and access controls is not self-evident until a major loss occurs, so until that happens concern with security is generally quite low. Ironically, legislators have paid more attention than managers to media reports of computer abuse and crime; all fifty states and the federal government now have statutes dealing with computer crime, but this trend still has not raised the security-consciousness of the general population.[6]

4 Why don't managers pay more attention to warnings about protecting information resources?[7] A number of plausible explanations for this complacency emerged during the fieldwork for our study. First, information about large-scale losses is often suppressed because of management embarrassment. The effect is to promote a false sense that systems are more secure than they really are. Second, it is not clear to managers how to assess costs and benefits of system security. Generally speaking, it is difficult to quantify the benefits of security, because no one knows exactly how much computer abuse is avoided or deterred by having a security team in place. In addition, the actual loss from an abusive act is often intangible.

5 How can the potential for data system abuse be effectively managed? Our research, as well as lengthy discussions with managers, led us to break that question down into several interrelated, more specific questions:
- To whom is data system abuse being reported?
- How are systems being abused?

Jeffrey A. Hoffer is Professor of Operations and Systems Management at the Graduate School of Business, Indiana University. He holds the B.S. degree from Miami University and the Ph.D. degree in operations research from Cornell University. His research interests include data management, computer and data security, information technology planning, and management of information technology.

Computer
Abuse

Hoffer
& Straub

Detmar W. Straub,
Jr., is Assistant Profes-
sor of Management
Information Systems
at the Curtis L. Carl-
son School of Manage-
ment, University of
Minnesota. Dr.
Straub holds the B.A.
degree from Hobart
College, the M.A. de-
gree from CUNY, the
M.B.A. degree from
Gannon College, the
Ph.D. degree from
Pennsylvania State
University, and the
D.B.A. degree in
management informa-
tion systems from In-
diana University. His
research interests in-
clude computer secu-
rity, group decision
support, research
methods, and manage-
ment of information
technology.

- Who are the abusers, and what motivates them?
- Are privileged personnel more prone to abus-ing systems than other users?
- Is organizational size a factor in how much abuse occurs?
- Are certain industries more susceptible to abuse than others?
- What measures can be taken to deter abuses?
- Can administrative as well as operational mea-sures be effective?

6   Our study included a large-sample mailed sur-vey asking about incidents of computer system abuse, as well as face-to-face interviews with numer-ous systems professionals and general managers. (For more about methodology, see the Appendix.) It addressed each of the questions above.

A Serious Problem

7   The study reinforced earlier findings that *computer abuse is a serious and underreported problem*. Of the 1,211 organizations that returned our survey, 211 firms reported 259 separate incidents of abuse. Five of the 211 organizations reported dollar losses of more than $100,000 at the local level; in the pilot study, one organization reported a $2,000,000 loss. These results, which are similar to results from ear-lier studies, indicate that one out of five organiza-tions experiences one or more security breaches in a three-year period. This figure is undoubtedly an underestimate, since no single manager is aware of all the abuse uncovered in an organization. Based on our validation studies, a single manager may be aware of less than 50 percent of the abuse actu-ally discovered in a firm. Uncovered abuse, more-over, is probably only a portion of actual abuse. Several studies have found that half of all known computer-related crimes are discovered by accident.[8]

Security Staff Practices

8   This part of our study was based on the crimino-logical theory of general deterrence; it tested whether increased levels of security, especially deterrents, actually decreased levels of computer abuse.[9] We found that organizations respond in a variety of ways to the potential threat from abuse and the need to uncover abuse; in general, security staff practices such as educating users on proper system use and stressing penalties for misuse are good deterrents.

9   In around 60 percent of the responding organi-zations, staff members were assigned to administer computer security on a full- or part-time basis. Their roles differed significantly from organization to organization, but their tasks can be classified into four general areas: information (data) security, phys-ical security, disaster recovery, and user awareness training.

10 • **Information (data) security** attempts to con-trol access to electronic assets like data files and programs so that deliberate abuse of the system is minimized.

11 • **Physical security** deals with the physical pro-tection of all system resources.

12 • **Disaster recovery** is concerned with backup procedures and alternate system sites required in the event of an emergency.

13 • **User awareness training** consists of training em-ployees in proper system use. Security officers re-view topics such as system authorizations, condi-tions for use, methods for changing passwords, and penalties for security breaches.

14   Currently, most security efforts are preventive: for example, the assignment of passwords and read-write-delete privileges. Few organizations take a sys-tematic approach to abuse detection. As a result, only one in eight abuses is now detected by secu-rity officers or auditors, as shown in Table 1. Most abuses are discovered by accident or by normal sys-tem controls.

Table 1	Means of Discovery of Computer Abuse
Discovery by accident	32.0%
Normal system controls	45.0%
Computer security officers	8.0%
All auditors	4.5%
Other	.5%

15   On several tested dimensions, the percentage of abuses detected by security investigations and other administrative practices did not differ from those discovered by accident, so undiscovered abuse may not be intrinsically different from the abuse we al-ready know about. Our data also revealed that strengthening and improving detection procedures may not simply uncover more abuses; it may also have a deterrent impact.

16   Respondents in this and earlier studies advocated vigorous detection activities.[10] Strategies range from the simple to the complex. One large financial in-stitution encourages its system auditors to "browse" once a day through corporate data files for suspi-

cious activity. (Personal privacy and intellectual property rights must, of course, be contractually prespecified when such a strategy is employed.) In one year, they uncovered abuses that resulted in the termination of one employee and the reprimand of another. The public knowledge that random surveillance is occurring has a deterrent effect. On the more complex side, sophisticated surveillance technology that can capture keystrokes for all users on the system is now available.[11]

17 Survey results showed that fewer than 10 percent of uncovered abuses were reported to the authorities. This result did not surprise us since, in field interviews during the survey pretest, respondents showed reluctance about reporting abuse for fear of revealing their systems' security inadequacy. In actual fact, tests reveal that potential violators are deterred when abuse is reported and perpetrators are prosecuted.[12] Given the amount of media attention lavished on computer abuse in recent years, this underreporting is particularly discouraging. Reporting offenses to the authorities and prosecution to deter future abuses is extremely important when one considers the dollar amounts involved.

18 Security software effectively deters computer abuse. Respondents indicated that using operating system controls (such as passwords), database management system controls (such as security locks and integrity rules), or specialized security access controls (such as extra security software) does, in fact, cut down on computer abuse.

How Are Organizations Vulnerable?

19 Respondents identified five categories of computer abuse: unauthorized use of computer service, disruption of computer service, and abuse affecting data, programs, and hardware. A single offense could fall into more than one of these categories. As Figure 1 shows, abuse is directed mainly at computer service, although programs and data are also at risk.

20 The single largest category of reported abuse was misuse of computer service. Examples of such misuse include maintaining data about a personal videotape collection, producing invoices for an unrelated business, and playing computer games. Such misuse can cause a computer system to run slower or delay the execution of legitimate computer work, thus costing the organization time and money. In

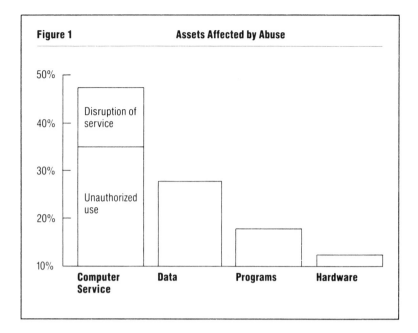

Figure 1   **Assets Affected by Abuse**

many cases, misuse of service directly violates clearly stated policies.

21 Program and data abuses together represent a significant part of the reported abuse. In program abuse, a program might be altered to juggle accounts, for example, placing money in a newly created account for purposes of embezzlement. Data abuse might involve creating dummy vendors and false orders and receipts. Data abuse can also involve stealing data, such as company trade secrets.

Offenders

22 Table 2 shows offenders' occupations. Application programmers abuse systems most frequently; they are followed by three categories of frequent system users (clerical personnel, system users, and managers) that together account for two out of five abuses in business organizations.

23 We found no significant relationship between users' system privileges and their propensity to abuse the system. This nonfinding counters the common belief that users with special privileges – auditors, computer security specialists, controllers, top executives, and system programmers – expose the organization to higher risk.

24 The overwhelming majority of offenders were employees or ex-employees, which reinforces the notion that those with direct system contact are more likely to commit abuses. Hackers are a threat, but insiders are a more pressing threat.

25 Offenders appear to have been motivated almost

Table 2	Offenders' Occupations	
Application programmers		18%
Clerical personnel		14%
Other system users*		14%
Students		12%
Managers		11%
Systems analysts		6%
Machine operators		6%
Top executives		4%
Other EDP staff		3%
Data entry staff		3%
Systems programmers		3%
Consultants		3%
Accountants		2%
Security officers		1%
Controllers		0%
Auditors		0%

*"Other" stands for a general category of nonclerical and non-managerial users.

equally by desire for personal gain, ignorance of proper professional conduct, and misguided playfulness; a smaller group was motivated by maliciousness (see Figure 2). Security administrators may be able to deter the first three types of abuse, but they probably cannot deter malicious abuse.[13] Since malice is "expressive" (like a crime of passion), it is more difficult to deter using the rational inhibitors available to security administrators.

Size and Industry-Specific Nature of Abuse

26 Large organizations experience more significant and frequent computer abuse than small organizations

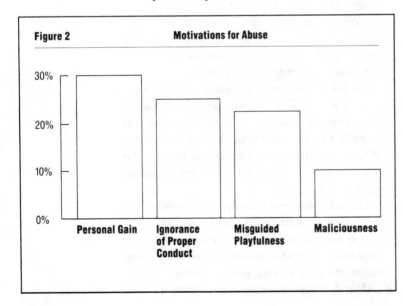

Figure 2   Motivations for Abuse

do, even though they generally have proportionately larger security staffs.[14] What explains this apparent anomaly? We don't yet have a good answer to that question. In the field interviews, respondents from smaller organizations argued that their relatively light security was viable because they knew their employees well and could trust them.

27 Certain industries are more susceptible to abuse than others. Educational institutions, wholesale and retail trade, and utilities are especially vulnerable. (Financial institutions, contrary to popular belief, do not experience abuses at an abnormally high rate.) Why would these three groups be especially susceptible? Academic institutions are at risk because of their large, computer-literate student population, and because of the relative openness of their computer systems. Wholesale and retail trade businesses do an enormous number of transactions without the level of protection that financial institutions, for example, enjoy. The higher level of abuse in utilities may reflect a reporting bias: utilities are more accustomed than other businesses to tracking and reporting their performance.

How Do Organizations Assess Security Effectiveness?

28 The number of organizations wholly without security (excluding standard file backup procedures) is alarmingly high by virtually any standard, as Table 3 shows. In many cases, security may be neglected because no incidents of abuse have yet been uncovered. Of those who reported incidents, approximately one-fifth had initiated security *after* an abuse occurred—usually shortly after the abuse came to light.

29 Organizations that did have security administrators were asked to assess the effectiveness of their efforts. In general, managers believed security functions did prevent some breaches, but they were not convinced that security efforts could deter abuse. Fortunately, this sense that deterrence does not work was not supported by the data in our study.

30 About a fifth of the respondents indicated that their current security effort was largely the result of past computer abuses. To determine if this was the case among those who had experienced abuses within the last three years, we calculated frequencies for that group as well. About a third agreed that abuses were likely to result in increased security. Among those who had not experienced abuses within the last three years, we could not infer that

earlier abuses were sufficiently serious to merit a new security effort.

31 More than half the respondents with security measures in place believed security administrators' activities were highly visible. Three-fourths believed security was tight and effective. The group that had experienced abuses did not answer these questions much differently than the entire respondent group did. These figures suggest that, among those with security units, the majority of organizations have active, highly visible administrators and that these security efforts are supported. From one standpoint, this finding is reassuring; it underscores the security function's perceived efficacy. This high level of support is appropriate, given the empirical evidence of security measures' effectiveness in lowering abuse.[15]

32 Slightly more than half of all respondents were not convinced that security efforts *did deter* abuse. These figures may indicate that security is conceived by many as a preventive function — administrative procedures designed to restrict abusive activities. The empirical evidence shows, to the contrary, that specific security efforts *can* be effective in deterring abuse.

33 Table 4 shows the administrative practices that respondents favored most as deterrents. Many security officers favored informal administrative measures, but organizations with software security in place also used security violations reports. Organizations tended to use multiple channels — four methods on average — to distribute this information.

Implications for Managers

34 Computer abuse causes major losses in every kind of organization. A single incident of abuse can cost hundreds of thousands of dollars. Of even greater concern, much abuse is probably never uncovered. When abuses are discovered, they are generally not reported to legal authorities because of a mistaken impression that publicity will encourage future crimes.

35 Many organizations put themselves at risk by committing no resources whatsoever to system security; even among those with security administrators, use of security software is low. There is a widespread — and inaccurate — perception among administrators that security efforts do not deter abuse. Further, there is evidence that many firms do not introduce security measures until a major abuse has occurred; this pattern, obviously, is reac-

Table 3   Percentages of Industrial Groups without Security Administration and with Abusive Incidents

Industrial Type	Percent without Security	Percent with Abusive Incidents*
Medical/legal services	62	17
Construction	55	9
Wholesale and retail trade	53	11
Transportation	52	19
Petroleum	50	16
Manufacturing	47	11
Financial institutions	36	8
Educational institutions	34	31
Government at all levels	34	19
Computer and data-processing services	33	15
Chemical and pharmaceutical	33	8
Utilities	33	26
Overall	41	18

*This column includes organizations with one or more abuses. Wholesale and retail trade groups tended to have multiple incidents per organization.

Table 4   Favored Deterrents

Informal discussions	26%
Periodic departmental memos and notes	23%
Distributed guidelines	23%
Organizational meetings	14%
Vital records classification program	11%
Computer security violations reports	9%
Distributed statements of professional ethics	8%
Computer security awareness training sessions	7%

tive rather than proactive.

36 The data is encouraging in that a high percentage of the measures that do exist focus on data security, and these have proven instrumental in controlling abuse. Moreover, respondents with security administrators are, on average, satisfied with the effectiveness of their security efforts.

37 Security administration is gradually being incorporated into the mainstream of American business. This evolution is lagging in certain industrial groups (for example, medical, legal, wholesale and retail trade, and transportation), which need to reevaluate their position on security.

38 This study dramatically indicates that certain actions effectively deter computer abuse. These include the following:

39 • establishing a *data and system security organization* to monitor system use and disseminate information about improper use and its consequences;

40 • *communicating clearly* that appropriate penalties

will be imposed on abusers (civil prosecution, criminal prosecution, and firing, for example);

41 • *defining and communicating to all personnel, using a wide variety of means,* what the organization considers improper behavior. These means might include distributed system guidelines, data sensitivity classifications, professional ethics statements, reports on discovered violations, computer security awareness training sessions, employee sign-off on data responsibilities, and informal discussions; and

42 • *using security software packages* and making users aware that these mechanisms are in place.

43 Let us stress that deterrent measures have proven effective, even though many organizations lack confidence in them. Organizations need to realize that deterrents as well as access-limiting controls are effective; resources should be allocated to both types of activities. Educational institutions, wholesale and retail trade businesses, and utilities should especially heed this point, since they are particularly vulnerable to computer abuse. In addition, larger organizations are evidently more vulnerable and need to embrace these options more enthusiastically.

44 Security administrators play an important role as *controllers*. In addition, they spend substantial time doing *contingency planning*: planning for system recovery in the event of natural, accidental, or abuse-caused disasters. These individuals can also manage other functions, such as *user awareness training*: in this role, administrators sensitize users to dangers from careless accidents as well as from intentional breaches of security.

45 The process of formulating a computer security administrative function includes the following steps:

46 • *Develop a plan for security and disaster recovery.* A high-level risk assessment may help set priorities about which data, transactions, and computer programs most need protection.

47 • *Develop and distribute system guidelines.* These should state rules for computer operation and use; in addition, they should specify which departments are owners or custodians for which pieces of data, which data access and manipulation actions are permitted by owners and others, and which safeguards are to be followed to limit risk.

48 • *Conduct regular orientation programs that communicate policies and penalties for violations.* Simply raising the workforce's awareness of security issues is, in itself, an effective deterrent. Face-to-face communication of guidelines reinforces the seriousness

with which the organization treats computer abuse. Public recognition of good security practices is also a positive step.

49 • *Classify information, programs, and all vital records.* Knowing an activity is classified will deter some potential abusers. Reminders and periodic reconsideration of classifications help keep attention focused on security procedures.

50 • *Design (or select) and implement security software packages for monitoring and preventing abuses.* Security software can consume considerable computer resources, and additional computer hardware may be required. User access rights must be carefully specified.

51 • *Constantly monitor the effectiveness of security policies, procedures, software, and training.* Security practices must be reassessed when abuses are discovered or when policies disrupt business operations.

52 There is every reason to believe that efforts such as these can reduce organizational exposure. As in other technology-intensive areas, however, managers must respond proactively to emerging threats. One recent—and very serious—threat has come from *computer viruses*, to which we address special attention now.

The Threat from Computer Viruses

53 A computer virus is a set of instructions introduced surreptitiously into an information system by hackers, terrorists, or saboteurs. Viruses are dangerous because, once introduced, they attach themselves to legitimate programs. They take on all the legitimate program's characteristics, including its security privileges. If the program is authorized to delete transactions or files, for example, then the virus may instruct the computer to delete all files or records in its authorized domain. Viruses can remain dormant for months before their destructive work is activated by the computer's internal clock or calendar. They can also copy themselves into master software and operating systems, hiding copies inside numerous other, legitimate programs. All infected programs in the information system become contagious, and the virus passes to other programs and systems. A single strategically placed virus can infect thousands of other systems; in one case, approximately 350,000 illegal copies had been made within two months of a virus's introduction.[16]

54 How rapidly viruses are spreading has not yet

been studied systematically. It is clear, though, that large-scale attacks have occurred, including the virus that shut down IBM's E-mail system just before Christmas in 1987 and the one that threatened to destroy all information on the network at Hebrew University in May 1988. While the most virulent outbreaks seem to be occurring in personal computers, the threat to mainframes and minicomputers is clear. In fact, an operating system attack perpetrated by a Cornell graduate student in the fall of 1988 spread rapidly through the nationwide VAX minicomputer network.

55 The extent of the damage from computer viruses is also unclear because we have no generally accepted sources of information about the frequency of occurrence. There have been some highly publicized cases, but estimates from antivirus software vendors claiming more than 300,000 separate instances cannot be substantiated.[17] Prosecutors will undoubtedly note the conviction of a virus abuser in Fort Worth, though: in this case a fired employee of the USPS & IRA Company planted a virus that destroyed 168,000 sales commission records.[18]

56 A general lack of clarity in this area is compounded by the difficulty of placing a dollar value on the corruption of data caused by a virus. For example, if a file with $100,000 worth of customer orders is erased, is that a $100,000 loss, or a $20 loss for destroying the magnetic tape on which the data is stored? There certainly is the material damage to the magnetic tape, but the last orders (even if only temporary) could result in canceled orders, overtime to reenter and check the orders, extra computer time to reprocess, and potential loss of customer confidence. What is the cost of all this?

57 Since most virus offenders appear to have strong antisocial tendencies, administrative deterrents may not have the same impact they do on people who abuse systems out of ignorance or for personal gain. Nevertheless, there will be some deterrent effect from administrative procedures. Clearly, as the prosecution described above shows, computer abusers who infect organizational information systems with harmful viruses can be convicted. For their deterrent effect alone, these prosecutions should be pursued to the full extent of the law.

58 Unless the information system is completely isolated, it is not possible to guarantee a viral-free system using any existing protection scheme.[19] Viruses, in fact, have been introduced by perfectly legitimate sources: there are a number of documented cases where commercial software houses unintentionally spread viruses simply by selling their products.[20]

59 There are some relatively straightforward controls that organizations can introduce to protect themselves in case administrative deterrents do not work. Write tabs that prohibit erasing or changing a computer file should be placed on all program software. Policies on the use of electronic bulletin boards and public domain software should be articulated and disseminated to employees. These policies can specify that software acquired from outside sources should either be restricted or independently certified as virus-free before being loaded onto computers.

60 Security staff or corporate management responsible for protecting information resources should also investigate the possibility of antiviral software. A virus filter, for example, theoretically detects viruses before they can infect data or programs. Where properly designed and used, cryptographical authentication systems can also detect viruses before they enter the system.

61 No antiviral software package offers a comprehensive antidote for all viruses, however. Further, computer insurance policies are likely to offer inadequate protection or specifically exclude virus protection. Backup copies of files and programs can also become infected with a virus, making cleanup a long-term issue. Only eliminating file sharing and downloaded programs can prevent viruses.

Conclusion

62 Computer viruses notwithstanding, the evidence is clear: security measures deter computer abuse. When managers do not undertake such efforts, they place their organizations at great risk of financial loss or public embarrassment. As the probability of detection and the severity of penalties are made clear to employees, abusive actions decrease. Used in tandem with abuse prevention software, these practices can constitute a viable security program and keep the risk of major loss to a minimum. ∎

Appendix: Methodology

63 We gathered incidents of computer abuse by surveying 5,489 randomly selected managers in the spring of 1986 under the auspices of International DPMA (Data Processing Management Association).[21] We validated the questionnaire first through a series of face-to-face interviews with 35 systems

Sloan
Management
Review

Summer 1989

professionals, then with 44 interviews and matched questionnaire responses from managers working in industries of all sizes and types. Finally, we conducted a pilot survey of 1,000 randomly selected DPMA members.

64   Questionnaires were returned by 1,211 separate organizations in the final study survey. They were tested to ensure that respondents were not systematically different from nonrespondents. Since response bias did not prove to be an issue, the results of the randomly selected sample can be generalized with some confidence to the entire DPMA membership of 36,000. (DPMA is a professional organization that represents every type of organization in the private and public sectors.)

65   The definition of computer abuse in the survey is restricted to abuse perpetrated by individuals against organizations. We asked respondents to report incidents of purposeful misuse of system resources including violations against hardware, programs, data, and computer service. We gave examples of abuses that would qualify; these included alternation or modification of computer programs or data, electronic embezzlement, and disruption of computer service on the information system.

References

1
AICPA, "Report on the Study of EDP-Related Fraud in the Banking and Insurance Industries" (New York: American Institute of Certified Public Accountants, pamphlet, 1984);
D.W. Straub, "Computer Abuse and Computer Security: Update on an Empirical Study," *Security, Audit, and Control Review*, Spring 1986, pp. 21–31; and
T. Whiteside, *Computer Capers* (New York: New American Library, 1978).

2
A. LaPlante, "Computer Fraud Threat Increasing, Study Says," *Infoworld*, 18 May 1987, p. 47.

3
"Report on Computer Crime" (Washington, DC: pamphlet prepared by the Task Force on Computer Crime, American Bar Association, Section on Criminal Justice, 1984);
AICPA (1984).

4
L. Ball and R. Harris, "SMIS Member: A Membership Anal-ysis," *MIS Quarterly*, March 1982, pp. 19–38;
E. W. Martin, "Information Needs of Top MIS Managers," *MIS Quarterly*, September 1983, pp. 1–11;
G. W. Dickson et al., "Key Information Systems Issues for the 80's," *MIS Quarterly*, September 1984, pp. 135–159.

5
J. Brancheau and J.C. Wetherbe, "Key Issues in Information Systems–1986," *MIS Quarterly*, March 1987, pp. 23–45.

6
R.C. Hollinger and L. Lanza-Kaduce, "The Process of Criminalization: The Case of Computer Crime Laws," *Criminology*, February 1988, pp. 101–126.

7
S. Madnick, "Management Policies and Procedures Needed for Effective Computer Security," *Sloan Management Review*, Fall 1978, pp. 61–74.

8
AICPA (1984);
Straub (Spring 1986).

9
The affirmative results in support of this hypothesis were tested through four types of sophisticated statistical analysis: Linear Structural Relations Causal Modeling (LISREL), canonical correlation, Kruscal-Wallis nonparametric tests, and chi-square contingency tables.

10
S.T. Dunn, "Methodology for the Optimization of Resources in the Detection of Computer Fraud" (Tucson: University of Arizona, unpublished doctoral dissertation, 1982).

11
A. Clyde, "Insider Threat on Automated Information Systems" (Bethesda, MD: Proceedings of the Fourth Conference on Insider Threat Identification Systems, August 1987).

12
D.W. Straub, "Deterring Computer Abuse: The Effectiveness of Deterrent Countermeasures in the Computer Security Environment" (Bloomington: Indiana University School of Business, unpublished doctoral dissertation, 1986);
D.W. Straub and W.D. Nance, "The Discovery and Prosecution of Computer Abuse: Assessing IS Managerial Responses" (Bloomington: Indiana University, Institute for Research on the Management of Information Systems, working paper W708, 1987).

13
D.W. Straub and C.S. Widom, "Deviancy by Bits and Bytes: Computer Abusers and Control Measures" in *Computer Security: A Global Challenge*, J.H. Finch and E.G. Dougall, eds. (Amsterdam: Elsevier Science Publishers and International Federation of Information Processing Societies, 1984), pp. 91–102.

14
These results are not surprising because the rate of abuse (per 1,000 employees) is approximately the same in both large and small organizations.

15
Straub (1986).

16

"Is Your Computer Secure?" *Business Week*, 1 August 1988, pp. 64–72.

17

John McFee of the Computer Virus Industry Association as cited in "Computer 'Infections' are Invisible, Deadly," *USA Today*, 22 September 1988, p. 8A.

18

T. Loff, "Conviction in Computer 'Virus' Case May Be U.S. First," *Detroit News*, 21 September 1988, p. 3A.

19

A.E. Brill, "Computer Fraud: What You Can Do to Prevent It," *Computers in Accounting*, June 1988, pp. 78–86;

F. Cohen, "Computer Viruses: Theory and Experiments," *Computers & Security*, February 1987, pp. 22–35.

20

D. Picard, "Thoughts and Opinions on Online Services and Computer Communications," *Link-up*, May-June 1988, pp. 3, 8;

R. Francis, "Apple-Microsoft Suit Raises Issue of Vague Copyright Laws," *Datamation*, 15 May 1988, pp. 22, 26.

21

This research was underwritten by grants from IRMIS (Institute for Research on the Management of Information Systems, Indiana University Graduate School of Business) and the Ball Corporation Foundation.

Sloan
Management
Review

Summer 1989

Glossary

advocated	supported, defended, proposed
allocated	set apart for a specific purpose
anomaly	abnormality, departure from the general rule
antidote	something that prevents or counteracts; a remedy for poison
antisocial	hostile or harmful to organized society; behavior deviating from the norm
articulated	explained clearly and effectively
assets	property, resources, advantages
auditors	persons authorized to examine and verify accounts
auspices	kindly patronage, guidance
authentication	proof of authenticity, verification
breaches	violations of a law
browse	to look over or through things casually
catastrophic	tragic, disastrous
complacency	unconcern, self-satisfaction and unawareness of danger
conceived	understood, believed to be
contagious	infectious, communicable by contact, catching
contingency	emergency
contractually	relating to a contract or constituting a contract
controllers	persons in charge of finances or expenditures in a business
counters	opposes, is contrary to
criminological	relating to crimes and criminals
cryptographical	relating to secret writing, codes
deterred	discouraged, prevented from acting
deterrence	the act of preventing an action from occurring
deterrents	preventions of action, the acts of prevention
disaster	great misfortune, catastrophe
disrupt	to disturb or interrupt
disruption	break down, disorder
disseminate	to distribute widely
domain	territory, sphere of influence or activity
dormant	temporarily lacking activity, inactive
dummy	imitation, secretly acting as a front for another
efficacy	effectiveness, power to produce intended results
embezzlement	taking by fraud for one's own use
embrace	to adopt eagerly, accept readily
empirical	based on experiment and observation rather than theory
formulating	expressing in a formula or in a systematic way
hackers	talented users of computers; computer users who try to gain unauthorized access to files
heed	to pay close attention to
in tandem	working together
inhibitors	restraints, methods of prevention
instrumental	helpful in bringing something about
intangible	(something) not corporeal

integrity	honesty, adherence to moral values; soundness, completeness
intricacy	complication, complexity
intrinsically	belonging to the essential nature of a thing
invoices	itemized lists of goods or services, with a request for payment
ironically	sarcastically, with incongruity
juggle	to manipulate in order to cheat or deceive
keystrokes	acts of depressing keys on keyboard
lagging	developing more slowly than expected, falling behind
lavished	bestowed with profusion, squandered
legitimate	lawful, sanctioned by law or custom, conforming to the law
mainframes	large, centralized computers; central processing units of computers
mainstream	major or prevailing part
maliciousness	intentionally harmful behavior
merit	deserve, be worthy of
misguided	led by error, mistaken
mystique	the special skill essential in an activity; mystical attitudes surrounding something
notwithstanding	although
passwords	words that must be typed into a computer before the system will open
perpetrated	committed
perpetrators	people who commit crimes
pilot study	trial study, sample of proposed study
plausible	believable, reasonable
pressing	urgent
proactive	acting ahead of or before the event
prone to	having a tendency to
propensity	natural inclination or tendency
proportionately	in proper proportion (of parts to the whole)
quantify	to measure the quantity of
random	without definite aim, plan, pattern, method, rule; haphazard
reactive	tending to react, showing reaction
reevaluate	to evaluate again
reluctance	unwillingness, holding back
reprimand	censure, severe reproof
saboteurs	persons who engage in intentional sabotage (destruction and damage of materials)
safeguards	safety devices, methods of protection against loss or injury
sensitize	to make someone sensitive to or aware of
shore up	to give support to
statutes	laws
suppressed	subdued, kept secret, stopped revelation of
surreptitiously	secretly
surveillance	close watch kept over someone; supervision
susceptible	subject to some influence or action
termination	ending of employment
tracking	keeping track of, recording data

validation	proof, determination of degree of validity
vendors	sellers, people who sell
viable	workable
violates	breaks a law or rule
virulent	extremely poisonous, full of malice
viruses	infective agents that cause diseases and are capable of multiplying
visible	apparent, evident, perceptible by the eye
whatsoever	whatever, at all

Vocabulary

Without referring to the article, fill in the blanks in the following sentences with the correct words from this list. You may change the tense, number, or form of the words to fit the context. Use each word only once; not all of the words on the list will be used.

contingency	safeguard	disseminate	articulate	contagious	deter
catastrophic	perpetrator	susceptible	statute	proportionately	proactive
termination	surveillance				

1. Today, computer crimes have become so prevalent that all fifty U.S. states as well as the federal government have _____ regulating computer abuse.

2. Since the loss caused by computer crimes is often intangible, it is hard to know how much abuse is _____ by having a security team.

3. All industries are not equally _____ to computer abuse; in fact, educational institutions and utilities are among the most vulnerable.

4. One method of deterrence is random _____ of corporate data files; another, more complex method involves the use of sophisticated technology that captures the keystrokes of all users.

5. Although many people are reluctant to report computer crimes, they should report all crimes in order to deter potential _____ .

6. Large companies usually have _____ larger security staffs than small companies; nevertheless, computer crimes occur more frequently in large companies.

7. Organizations must take a(n) _____ and systematic approach to the problem of computer abuse by introducing security measures *before* any major abuse occurs rather than after.

8. The study results indicate that it is effective for organizations to establish security systems that monitor computer system use and to widely _____ information about improper use and its consequences.

9. _____ planning is a major responsibility for security administrators, who must plan for system recovery after abuse-caused disasters.

10. In addition, security administrators should develop and distribute system guidelines that outline the _____ to be followed to limit risk.

11. Because computer viruses are so _____, one virus can infect thousands of computer systems.

12. Therefore, controls should be introduced for protection against viruses, and policies on the use of public domain software should be clearly _____ to all employees.

Idioms and Expressions

Read the paragraphs in which the following italicized idioms and expressions are found. Then circle the letter next to the answer that best describes the meaning of the idiom as used in the context of the article.

1. "There is growing evidence that new, management-directed countermeasures will be needed to *shore up* system defenses." (Paragraph 1)
   a. explain
   b. repair
   c. support

2. "Data abuse might involve creating *dummy* vendors and false orders and receipts." (Paragraph 21)
   a. fake
   b. unintelligent
   c. imaginary

3. "A computer virus is a set of instructions introduced surreptitiously into an information system by *hackers,* terrorists, or saboteurs." (Paragraph 53)
   a. thieves who attempt to steal computers from companies
   b. computer users who attempt to gain unauthorized access to files
   c. cheaters who attempt to sell computers at unfair prices

4. "Used *in tandem* with abuse prevention software, these practices can constitute a viable security program and keep the risk of major loss to a minimum." (Paragraph 62)
   a. secretly
   b. carefully
   c. together

Paraphrasing

Read the following sentences carefully, and then rewrite them using your own words. Change the vocabulary and sentence structure, but do not change the authors' intended meaning or paraphrase any technical terms. There are several ways of paraphrasing each sentence.

Original: "Ironically, legislators have paid more attention than managers to media reports of computer abuse and crime."

Paraphrase: It is ironic that executives have been less concerned about media reports of computer crime than lawmakers have.

1. "A number of plausible explanations for this complacency emerged during the fieldwork for our study." (Paragraph 4)

2. "Given the amount of media attention lavished on computer abuse in recent years, this underreporting is particularly discouraging." (Paragraph 17)

3. "Such misuse can cause a computer system to run slower or delay the execution of legitimate computer work, thus costing the organization time and money." (Paragraph 20)

4. "When abuses are discovered, they are generally not reported to legal authorities because of a mistaken impression that publicity will encourage future crimes." (Paragraph 34)

5. "How rapidly viruses are spreading has not yet been studied systematically." (Paragraph 54)

6. "Computer viruses notwithstanding, the evidence is clear: security measures deter computer abuse." (Paragraph 62)

Comprehension

Answer the following questions by finding the relevant information in the article. Give the numbers of the paragraphs that contain the answers.

1. What is the main idea of this article?

2. What two reasons explain managers' lack of attention to warnings about protecting information resources?

3. What statistics support the finding that "computer abuse is a serious and underreported problem"?

4. What four tasks does a computer security system include?

5. Why are most abuses discovered by accident or by normal system controls rather than by security officers?

6. What methods and strategies can be used to detect or cut down on computer abuse?

7. Who is most likely to commit computer abuses?

8. Which type of abuser may be the most difficult to deter and why?

9. What security measures effectively deter computer abuse?

10. Why are computer viruses so dangerous?

11. Why is it difficult to determine the extent of damage caused by computer viruses?

12. What methodology was used by the authors of this study?

Inference/Interpretation

Circle the letter next to the best answer. Choose your answer according to the meaning the authors suggest but do not state explicitly.

1. It can be inferred from the article that information systems managers and general managers (Paragraph 3)
   a. disagree about the importance of information system security.
   b. agree about the seriousness of the computer crime problem.
   c. have difficulty working together.
   d. need to pay more attention to computer abuse.

2. According to the article, abuse of computer hardware (Figure 1 and Paragraphs 19–20)
   a. is an extremely rare occurrence.
   b. is very difficult to detect.
   c. is always underreported.
   d. may not be a major problem.

3. What can be inferred about malicious abusers? (Paragraph 25)
   a. Malicious abusers are motivated by passionate emotion.
   b. Malicious abusers are easy to deter.
   c. Malicious abusers are similar to abusers motivated by misguided playfulness.
   d. Malicious abusers do not respond to typical security measures.

4. What can we infer about the administrative practices that survey respondents favored most as deterrents? (Table 4 and Paragraph 33)
   a. Organizational meetings are less popular than informal discussions.
   b. Oral communication is much more favored than written communication as a method of deterrence.
   c. Formal administrative practices are less favored than informal ones.
   d. Periodic departmental memos and notes and distributed guidelines are similar methods of deterrence.

5. Read the following sentence carefully: "For their deterrent effect alone, these prosecutions should be pursued to the full extent of the law" (Paragraph 57). Explain what the authors mean by "For their deterrent effect alone."

Structure

Circle the letter next to the correct answer(s). More than one answer may be correct. Be prepared to explain and justify your choices.

1. In which paragraph(s) is the main idea stated?
   a. Paragraph 1
   b. Paragraph 7
   c. Paragraph 19
   d. Paragraph 48
   e. Paragraph 62
   Write a paraphrase of the main idea in *one* sentence, using your own words as much as possible.

---

2. Where is classification used as a method of organization of ideas?
   a. Paragraph 4
   b. Paragraph 9
   c. Paragraph 19
   d. Paragraph 26
   e. Paragraph 34

3. Why do the authors use questions as the topic sentences for paragraphs 4 and 5?
    a. To involve the reader in the subject matter
    b. To develop a logical argument
    c. To present their major points
    d. To show various viewpoints on an issue
    e. To express a lack of certainty

4. Paragraph 53 contains a formal definition of a computer virus. Write a formal definition for the following terms:
    a. Information (data) security (Paragraph 10)
    b. Physical security (Paragraph 11)
    c. Disaster recovery (Paragraph 12)
    d. User awareness training (Paragraph 13)

5. What overall method of development is used in the article?
    a. Comparing and contrasting two methods
    b. Defining a new system
    c. Supporting an argument with specific data and evidence
    d. Arguing the pros and cons of an issue
    e. Explaining the steps in a complex process

Style

Circle the letter next to the correct answer(s). More than one answer may be correct. Be prepared to justify your choices by giving specific examples from the article.

1. How would you describe the writing style of the authors?
    a. Technical
    b. Academic
    c. Informal
    d. Formal
    e. Colorful
    f. Journalistic

2. How would you describe the tone of the article?
    a. Emotional
    b. Objective
    c. Humorous
    d. Ironic
    e. Analytical
    f. Persuasive

3. The authors' attitude toward organizations without system security administration can be described as
   a. supportive.
   b. critical.
   c. hostile.
   d. concerned.
   e. disapproving.
   f. neutral.

4. Sentence connectors are coherence devices in writing. In paragraph 1, the authors use a sentence connector: "For all their intricacy and mystique, computer systems are just as subject to abuse as manual systems are; *indeed,* abusive activities are seriously threatening computer system integrity and the businesses these systems serve." What effects are achieved through use of *indeed*? What other sentence connector could be used here?

Discussion

1. Are you computer literate? Do you use computers? Can you write a computer program?

2. What is fair punishment for computer criminals who infect information systems with viruses: criminal or civil prosecution?

3. Do you believe that an organization's random surveillance of an employee's data files is an invasion of personal privacy? Why or why not?

4. Would you ever be tempted, out of misguided playfulness, to introduce a computer virus into an information system?

5. To what extent is computer crime a problem in your country?

Research Assignment

Look up several of these articles in the library. Choose one article to read and take notes on.

Alexander, Michael. "It's the Flu Season for Viruses." *Computer World* 23 (September 1989): 39–49.

Brill, A. E. "Computer Fraud: What You Can Do to Prevent It." *Computers in Accounting* (June 1988): 78–86.

Buss, Martin D. J., and Lynn M. Salerno. "Common Sense and Computer Security." *Harvard Business Review* 62 (March-April 1984): 112–21.

Cohen, F. "Computer Viruses: Theory and Experiments." *Computers and Security* (February 1987): 22–35.

"Computer 'Infections' Are Invisible, Deadly." *USA Today* (September 22, 1988): 8A.

Dennis, Terry L., and Daniel A. Joseph. "Protecting Your PC Data." *Business* 39 (April-May-June 1989): 9–13.

Loff, T. "Conviction in Computer 'Virus' Case May Be U.S. First." *Detroit News* (September 21, 1988): 3A.

Madnick, S. "Management Policies and Procedures Needed for Effective Computer Security." *Sloan Management Review* 20 (Fall 1978): 61–74.

"MIS Talk." *Business Month* 134 (March 1989): 78.

Moskowitz, Daniel B. "Court Decisions on Drug Testing Lack Guidance for Firms." *Washington Post* (July 2, 1990): Washington Business Section, 28.

Robinson, Phillip. "New Programs Can Provide Good Medicine for Computer Viruses." *Washington Post* (November 20, 1989): Washington Business Section, 26.

Schatz, Willie. "Software Pioneer Eyes Legal Aid for Hackers." *Washington Post* (May 31, 1990): E1, E4.

Schatz, Willie. "The Terminal Men." *Washington Post* (June 24, 1990): H1, H6.

Schwartz, John. "The Hacker Dragnet." *Newsweek* 114 (April 30, 1990): 50.

"Vengeance by Virus." *U.S. News & World Report* 105 (October 3, 1988): 10.

Wiener, Daniel P. "When a Virus Makes Your P.C. Sneeze." *U.S. News & World Report* 108 (February 26, 1990): 62.

Oral Presentation

Working with a small group, give a fifteen-minute oral presentation to the class on the additional readings in this chapter and the articles that you chose in the research assignment. Include the authors' main ideas, major points, and some supporting data. Be prepared to answer questions on your topic. (See Appendix B: Giving an Oral Presentation.)

Writing Assignments

1. Conduct an interview on the topic of computer crime with a person who works in the computer center of your school or organization. Use a tape recorder during the interview, if possible. Then write up the interview. Include questions such as: (1) Is there a security system? (2) Have abusive incidents taken place? (3) Which assets have been affected?

   Format:
   I.   Introduction (Purpose of Interview and Position of Person Being Interviewed)
   II. Questions and Answers
   III. Conclusion

2. Analyze *Motivations for Abuse* (Figure 2) and *Favored Deterrents* (Table 4). Then write an essay about the *three* deterrents that you believe would be most effective against computer abuse. Organize your essay according to problem-solution format. Justify your choices with specific reasons.

3. Design a questionnaire to determine how vulnerable an organization's information system is to computer abuse. The questionnaire should have three parts: introduction, instructions, and questions. Include questions on the following subjects:
   I.   Past problems of abuse;
   II. Types of reported abuse;
   III. Methods of deterrence; and
   IV. Abuse prevention software.

Case Study: A Problem in Computer Crime

Working in groups, read the following case study. Discuss the problem, answer the questions, and write a brief report on how your group would solve the problem. (Choose one member of the group to do the writing.) Follow the format in Appendix E (Case Study Report) in writing your report.

Karen Hanley works as an applications programmer for E&G Utilities Corporation. She is known as a computer whiz and is a valued and professional employee. Recently, Karen has been coming to work much earlier than usual and staying much later. David Burnside, her friend and office mate, noticed Karen's longer hours and was thinking of asking Karen why she wanted to work so hard. But David was also working longer hours because of the special project he was assigned to, and he got so busy that he forgot about Karen and her unusual work schedule.

One night, David stayed late to finish a progress report for his project. When he tried to open his data file to work on the report, his computer had a system error that he could not correct; therefore, he decided to use Karen's computer to finish up the report. In a rush, David turned on her terminal and accidentally opened the wrong file: he found himself looking at a series of invoices for a company called Hanley Associates. He was confused at first, but gradually everything became clear. Karen had started her own computer programming business and was keeping her records on the business in E&G's computer. As the truth dawned on David, he felt shocked. Karen, his friend and colleague, was a computer criminal.

While David continued "browsing" through the file, he saw what a highly successful business Karen had. She was actually earning more than her salary at E&G. Now David began to wonder how many of the hours Karen spent at E&G were really devoted to her job. David was concerned. What should he do, if anything? He knew E&G had strict system guidelines that stated the rules for computer operation and use and the penalties that would be imposed on abusers. In fact, he knew Karen would be fired if he revealed her actions to his supervisor. Maybe he should talk to Karen and point out to her the risk she was taking with her professional career. Or maybe he should ask her if she needed a partner for Hanley Associates. What a team they would make!

Questions

1. Should David talk to Karen and warn her of the penalties for computer abuse?

2. Should David talk to Karen and suggest becoming her partner in Hanley Associates?

3. Should David tell his supervisor about Karen's computer abuse?

4. Should David forget he opened that file on Hanley Associates and not get involved?

Solution: Case Study Report

I. Define and analyze the problem.
II. Suggest possible solutions.
III. Evaluate possible solutions.
IV. Select a solution.

Case Study Business Writing Assignment: Memorandum

Write a memo from Drew Jarvis, Manager of Information Systems, to all employees of E&G Utilities. The memo should state that the problem of computer abuse is increasing at E&G. It should list the guidelines for computer operation, safeguards that should be followed to limit risk, and penalties for abusers.

Format:
    I. Introduction (Background and Main Idea)
   II. Discussion (Guidelines and Safeguards)
  III. Closing (Penalties)

Style: Formal
Tone: Authoritative and impersonal

Additional Readings

"Is Your Computer Secure?"
Katherine M. Hafner
Business Week (August 1, 1988): 64–72

"A German Hackers' Club That Promotes Creative Chaos"
Gail Schares
Business Week (August 1, 1988): 71

IS YOUR COMPUTER

HACKERS, HIGH-TECH BANDITS, AND DISASTERS COST BUSINESS BILLIONS—AND AS

Donald Gene Burleson resented authority. He denounced federal income taxes as unconstitutional and boasted that he hadn't paid any since 1970. The pudgy, 40-year-old programmer also complained that his salary at USPA & IRA Co., a Fort Worth securities trading firm, was too low. He often had heated arguments with superiors. "He was so fanatical about everything," says former co-worker Patricia Hayden. But she adds: "He could do anything with a computer."

Evidently he could. Two days after USPA fired him in 1985, the company alleges, Burleson entered its headquarters and planted a program that once each month would wipe out all records of sales commissions. USPA discovered the break-in two days later. But it lost 168,000 records before disabling the pro-

gram. Burleson is now awaiting trial on charges of "harmful access to a computer," a felony in Texas. If convicted, he faces up to 10 years in jail.

VIOLENT SHUTDOWN. The Burleson caper is just one in a string of recent events that point to the alarming vulnerability of computer systems—and the businesses and government agencies that rely on them. Hackers have invaded sophisticated data networks—even those at the Pentagon. Accidents, such as the May 8 fire at an Illinois Bell switching station outside Chicago, have disrupted communications in entire towns for weeks at a time. But experts agree that the No. 1 threat, which accounts for at least 80% of security breaches, is internal: "The real problem is errors, omissions, or well-thought-out acts by individuals who have authorized access to data," says

Lawrence L. Wills, who's in charge of selling data security software for IBM.

Whether the fault lies with a disgruntled employee, a hacker, simple human ineptitude, or a natural disaster, disabling a vital computer and communications system can be as easy as cutting a critical power line or typing a few commands on a keyboard. The threat is eloquently simple: Computer networks and the information they handle are assets a company can't do without. But often they aren't adequately protected, and the consequences of that exposure can be disastrous. Without computers, "we cannot run our plants, we cannot schedule, we cannot bill or collect money for our product, we can't design our product," says G. N. Simonds, executive director of management information systems at Chrysler Corp. "In essence, we

VIRUSES AND OTHER MALICIOUS SOFTWARE
These potentially devastating programs are usually planted by means of a "Trojan Horse"—a seemingly normal package hiding a destructive program that can wipe out a computer's data files. Use antiviral programs to detect viruses. Prohibit employees from loading untested software into the system.

FIRES, FLOODS, POWER FAILURES, EARTHQUAKES
A few precautions can prevent acts of God from becoming data disasters. Store copies of data at another site. Set up a backup computer. Disaster recovery services guarantee restoration of normal data processing within hours of a crisis.

SNEAK ATTACKS BY OUTSIDE HACKERS
Simple passwords won't stop these techno-terrorists from breaking in by phone. Encrypt data and program the computer to accept calls only from authorized phones. At night, shut down disk drives containing sensitive data.

SECURE?
PCs PROLIFERATE, THE PROBLEM CAN ONLY GROW WORSE

PHOTOGRAPHS BY TED MORRISON. ILLUSTRATION BY RALPH WERNLI

very quickly shut the company down."

The potential for trouble is even greater in the service industries that now dominate the economy. Every workday, U. S. computer networks transmit close to $1 trillion among financial institutions, an amount equal to 25% of the gross national product. When a software problem fouled up record-keeping in Bank of New York's government securities trading operations in 1985, other banks temporarily stopped trading with it. The Fed had to lend the bank $24 billion to keep operating until the problem was fixed. An airline the size of American Airlines Inc. could lose as much as $34,000 in booking fees each hour its reservation system is down.

Little wonder that businesses are worried—and reacting. To protect its vast reservations system in Tulsa, American built a $34 million underground facility with foot-thick concrete walls and a 42-inch-thick ceiling. Anyone who scales the barbed wire faces a security system that includes a retina scanner, a James Bondian device that detects unauthorized personnel by the unfamiliar pattern of blood vessels in their eyeballs. Indeed, a booming industry has developed to help protect computers, ranging from scores of consultants to sellers of hardware and software impediments to intruders.

'HELL OF A MESS.' Despite such defenses, however, systems remain vulnerable. High-tech thieves steal $3 billion to $5 billion annually in the U. S. alone, according to consultants at accounting firm Ernst & Whinney in Cleveland. And computer crime pays well: In an average stickup, security experts say, a bank robber grabs $5,000. By contrast, the average electronic heist nets $500,000. In electronic funds networks, "you have $15,000-a-year clerks transferring $25 million a day," says Ronald Hale, research manager at the Bank Administration Institute in Chicago. For some, the temptation is too great.

In early July, a group of insiders wired $54 million from the London office of Union Bank of

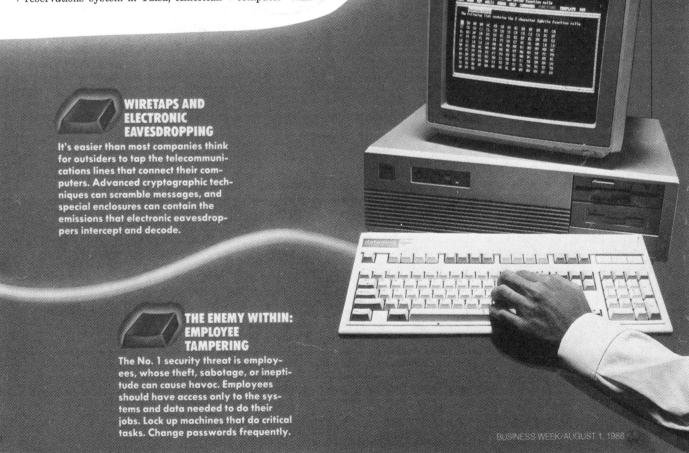

WIRETAPS AND ELECTRONIC EAVESDROPPING

It's easier than most companies think for outsiders to tap the telecommunications lines that connect their computers. Advanced cryptographic techniques can scramble messages, and special enclosures can contain the emissions that electronic eavesdroppers intercept and decode.

THE ENEMY WITHIN: EMPLOYEE TAMPERING

The No. 1 security threat is employees, whose theft, sabotage, or ineptitude can cause havoc. Employees should have access only to the systems and data needed to do their jobs. Lock up machines that do critical tasks. Change passwords frequently.

BUSINESS WEEK/AUGUST 1, 1988

Switzerland to another Swiss bank, complete with the correct authorization codes. A malfunction in the second bank's computer delayed the transaction, and auditors discovered it and froze the funds before they could be collected. First National Bank of Chicago foiled a $70 million embezzlement scheme last May only because the two employees who masterminded it made a dumb mistake: They tried to overdraw on the accounts they were stealing from.

Often, even hackers depend on inside help. A band of teenage programmers, calling themselves "phrackers," has been giving fits to Pacific Bell and other phone companies with a simple con game. Posing as fellow employees, they call phone company representatives and cajole them into releasing computer passwords. Says one 17-year-old phracker: "It works surprisingly well." Inside the phone company computer, phrackers cause mayhem by disconnecting service to customers or changing work orders.

Now changes in computer technology are making mischief easier. Increasingly, minicomputers and personal computers are being spread through offices and networked together. Such "distributed processing" multiplies the potential points of access. "When computerization was centralized, the computers were in one room behind locked doors," says Edwin B. Heinlein, a computer security consultant in San Rafael, Calif. "Now it's a hell of a mess." With 33 million desktop machines in use, hundreds of thousands of individuals have acquired the technical skill to "penetrate most systems," says Gerald E. Mitchell, director of data security at IDS Financial Services Inc. in Minneapolis.

Using international phone links, a group of West German hackers took repeated strolls through NASA computers last summer, as well as through several U.S. military networks. NASA spent three months changing passwords and clearing out "trap door" programs that the intruders had planted to give them access. Another German hacker spent nearly two years cruising through unclassified data in U.S. Defense Dept. and other research computers around the world until he was stopped last year. And last May, NASA's Jet Propulsion Laboratory in Pasadena, Calif., was invaded by hackers yet to be identified.

Even companies with good security have run into a new and insidious problem: the computer virus. Like microorganisms, these replicate and spread. They're tiny bits of software, often

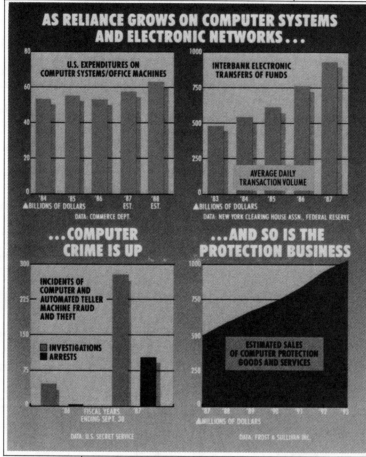

AS RELIANCE GROWS ON COMPUTER SYSTEMS AND ELECTRONIC NETWORKS . . .

U.S. EXPENDITURES ON COMPUTER SYSTEMS/OFFICE MACHINES
▲BILLIONS OF DOLLARS
'84 '85 '86 '87 EST. '88 EST.
DATA: COMMERCE DEPT.

INTERBANK ELECTRONIC TRANSFERS OF FUNDS
AVERAGE DAILY TRANSACTION VOLUME
▲BILLIONS OF DOLLARS
'83 '84 '85 '86 '87
DATA: NEW YORK CLEARING HOUSE ASSN., FEDERAL RESERVE

. . . COMPUTER CRIME IS UP
INCIDENTS OF COMPUTER AND AUTOMATED TELLER MACHINE FRAUD AND THEFT
☐ INVESTIGATIONS ■ ARRESTS
'86 FISCAL YEARS ENDING SEPT. 30 '87
DATA: U.S. SECRET SERVICE

. . . AND SO IS THE PROTECTION BUSINESS
ESTIMATED SALES OF COMPUTER PROTECTION GOODS AND SERVICES
▲MILLIONS OF DOLLARS
'87 '88 '89 '90 '91 '92 '93
DATA: FROST & SULLIVAN INC.

quickly written, that hide in larger programs and then pounce unpredictably. Some simply deliver a surprise message on the screen. Others can wipe out every shred of information in a computer.

What especially worries corporate computer managers is that somehow these destructive programs could migrate to mainframe computers and do serious damage to the most sensitive corporate data. Says Jeffrey M. Hoffman, a computer specialist at Atlantic Richfield Co.: "The PC world is the lightly protected gateway to the host computer world." Although most large computer systems employ mechanisms that isolate computer code, reducing the opportunity for a virus to spread, the threat exists—even for Big Blue. Although the company plays down the incident, last December a virus-like program infiltrated IBM's 145-country electronic mail network, forcing the entire system to be shut down.

When such incidents occur, the victim company often has failed to employ some surprisingly simple measures. Experts say, for instance, that companies should outlaw such mundane passwords as a birthday or a spouse's name. NASA concedes that it was using "inappropriate" passwords that were easy to guess. IBM's Wills urges companies to remind workers not to log on to a computer and then leave it unattended, nor share passwords with co-workers. He is also a proponent of written computer security policies, complete with security clearances.

NEED TO KNOW. IBM has five classes of data, from unclassified, with no restrictions, to "registered IBM confidential," available only to employees with a predetermined need to know. After last year's incident, which began when a West German law student sent a self-replicating Christmas greeting into a European academic research network, IBM tightened controls over its electronic networks.

It's crucial, say experts, to treat computer security as a management, not a technology, problem. For example, programs running on Marine Midland Bank's central computer are "encapsulated" so that employees can use only what's needed to perform their jobs—and can't browse through the system.

Physical barriers are important, too, and there are lots of new ones. Electronic card keys, or "smart cards," with embedded microchip memories and processors, are starting to be used as I.D. cards for workers. They can be programmed with volumes of personal data and authorization codes that are hard to fake. Some smart cards change passwords every 60 seconds. But even such cards have a flaw: They can be stolen. More secure, some experts think, are biometric devices, which identify people according to physical quirks. Machines

ERIC HOFFMAN

can now scan voice inflections, hand prints, even typing habits.

Still, common sense may be the best protection—and less intrusive. For example, USPA could have thwarted Donald Gene Burleson by thinking faster. The company procrastinated before changing its computer passwords, a crucial mistake: As a computer security officer, Burleson was one of three people at the company who knew everyone's password.

COVER-UP. A similar mistake caught up with Wollongong Group, a software company in Palo Alto, Calif. Ming Jyh Hsieh, a 38-year-old Taiwanese émigré who worked as a customer support representative, was fired in late 1987. Two months later, Wollongong noticed that someone was logging on to its computers at night via modem. Some files had been copied or damaged. After tracing the calls to Hsieh's nearby home, police seized her personal computer, along with disks containing Wollongong's proprietary software, estimated to be worth millions of dollars. She was arrested, charged with illegal access to computers, and if convicted faces up to five years in prison.

Wollongong had crippled Hsieh's access code but the company suspects that she somehow obtained another worker's. Since the incident, Wollongong periodically changes passwords and account numbers. "Any company that doesn't is asking to be kicked," says Norman Lombino, Wollongong's marketing communications manager.

One advantage for computer crooks is that their victims often keep quiet, notes consultant Robert H. Courtney Jr. Statistics are hard to come by. But experts estimate that only 20% to 50% of computer crimes are ever reported. Particularly for banks, a successful fraud is a public relations disaster. Burleson's

IBM'S WILLS (ABOVE) RECOMMENDS STIFF SECURITY POLICIES—BUT BIG BLUE'S OWN ELECTRONIC MAIL NETWORK TOOK A HIT LAST YEAR. JOURNALISTS BRANDOW AND ZOVILE LOOSED A 'BENIGN' VIRUS ON MAC USERS LAST SPRING

break-in at USPA might never have come to light had he not sued for back pay—thus encouraging a countersuit. "No one wants to display their managerial shortcomings," says Courtney. In one extreme case, Courtney says, an insurance company executive used his PC to scan claim records needed to commit a $13 million fraud. The company found out and fired him. But to avoid a scandal, it gave him a lavish going-away party.

Bringing the problem into the open may be the only way to improve security, however. Take viruses. These wily programs most often find their way into corporate computer systems when an employee inadvertently introduces them. Computer enthusiasts from New York to New Delhi use electronic bulletin boards on communications networks such as The Source to "chat" by computer. One of their favorite pastimes is swapping programs—any one of which can include a virus that attaches itself to other programs in a computer.

No one knows how many viruses have been planted. But John D. McAfee, a virus expert at InterPath Corp., a security consulting firm in Santa Clara, Calif., says there have already been 250,000 outbreaks. He estimates that 40 of the nation's largest industrial companies have been infected.

PAKISTANI FLU. Worldwide computer networks take viruses on some remarkable journeys. Recently, *The Providence Journal-Bulletin* was infected by the Pakistani Brain—two years after that program began circulating. Nobody knows how it got to Rhode Island. But before it was through, it had infected 100 of the paper's personal computer hard disks. Basit Farooq Alvi, a 19-year-old programmer from Punjab province, says he wrote the virus not to destroy data but as a warning to would-be software pirates. The virus would interfere only with bootlegged copies of his package, a program for physicians. Other programmers, however, have given it a pernicious twist: Now versions of the brain often carry instructions to wipe out data files. And some of these versions have spread to Israel, Europe, and the U. S.

Even a well-meant virus can have unfortunate side effects. Richard R. Bran-

219

A COMPUTER VIRUS: WHAT IT IS AND HOW IT SPREADS

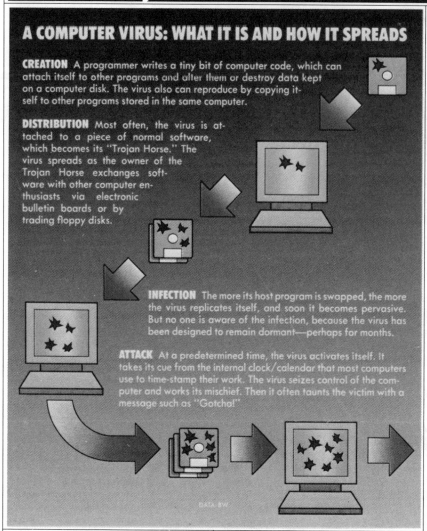

CREATION A programmer writes a tiny bit of computer code, which can attach itself to other programs and alter them or destroy data kept on a computer disk. The virus also can reproduce by copying itself to other programs stored in the same computer.

DISTRIBUTION Most often, the virus is attached to a piece of normal software, which becomes its "Trojan Horse." The virus spreads as the owner of the Trojan Horse exchanges software with other computer enthusiasts via electronic bulletin boards or by trading floppy disks.

INFECTION The more its host program is swapped, the more the virus replicates itself, and soon it becomes pervasive. But no one is aware of the infection, because the virus has been designed to remain dormant—perhaps for months.

ATTACK At a predetermined time, the virus activates itself. It takes its cue from the internal clock/calendar that most computers use to time-stamp their work. The virus seizes control of the computer and works its mischief. Then it often taunts the victim with a message such as "Gotcha!"

DATA BW

dow, the 24-year-old publisher of a Montreal computer magazine, and co-worker Pierre M. Zovilé created a benign virus to dramatize the pervasiveness of software piracy. Point proved: In two months, Brandow says, illegal copying had transferred the virus to 350,000 Macintoshes around the world. When the internal clocks on these machines hit last Mar. 2, the first birthday of the Mac II computer, each machine displayed Brandow's "universal message of peace to all Macintosh users."

'SAFE SEX.' It was a nice thought. But Marc Canter, president of a small Chicago software publisher, says that Zovile's virus wasn't innocuous. It caused Canter's computer to crash and infected disks that he supplied to software producer Aldus Corp. in Seattle. For three days, Aldus unwittingly transferred the virus onto copies of its Freehand illustration program on its assembly lines. Aldus pulled back the tainted disks, but not before some got to customers.

As with many computer security problems, the chief weapon against viruses is employee awareness, says Arco's Hoffman. After a virus invaded Macs at Arco's Dallas office, then spread to another Arco office in Anchorage, the company told employees not to use software of questionable origin. "It's the PC equivalent of safe sex," says Hoffman.

There also are more than a dozen "vaccine" programs, including Interferon, a package that Robert J. Woodhead, an Ithaca (N.Y.) author of computer games, offers free. Woodhead says each virus has a unique pattern, which his software can identify. It then erases the virus. Another method, in use at Lehigh University's computer labs since a virus struck there last winter, is to test suspicious software by setting the computer clock to Christmas, New Year's, or April Fools' Day—dates on which many viruses are set to detonate.

Viruses have caused such consternation that Congress is mulling tougher federal laws. A House bill introduced on July 14 would make it a federal crime to

insert a malicious virus into a computer. Basic computer-crime laws are already on the books in 48 states, and business and industry leaders are looking for government agencies to set guidelines for security standards. Under the Computer Security Act of 1987, the National Bureau of Standards is charged with doing that. But agency budget cuts are expected to slow the process, industry officials say. In Japan, meantime, the government gives a tax break to companies purchasing facilities and hardware to guard their systems.

Even without such incentives, U.S. companies are spending huge sums on computer chastity belts. They can be anything from software to control access to the mainframe, costing $35,000 a copy, to hardware that scrambles data so it can't be understood if a phone line is tapped. In 1982 only 10% of IBM mainframes had data security software, according to a survey by market researcher Computer Intelligence. Now the figure is 35%.

To foil hackers, many companies are installing dial-back systems on computers. These ensure that an incoming call is from an authorized number. A large mainframe may have hundreds of "ports" for remote computers—with call-back units costing $600 to $700 per port. Additional encryption hardware can cost $1,200 per communications line. With the most to lose, banks are a big market for such equipment. They disguise data by encrypting it, and many use message-authentication techniques to ensure that what is received over phone lines matches what was sent.

MODEM MELTDOWN. In the wake of the Chicago fire, there's also new interest in "disaster recovery"—restoring operations after fires, floods, earthquakes, or sabotage. For years, companies have shipped computer tapes with sensitive records to vaults such as that run by Data Mountain Inc. in Phoenix, where gun-toting guards watch over a 2,000-square-foot room chiseled out of rock.

But the phone company blaze in the Chicago suburb of Hinsdale lent a new urgency to such planning. "The story has gotten out to Europe, Asia, and Australia," says Dave Haeckel, a principal with Arthur Andersen & Co., a Big Eight accounting firm that does computer consulting. That's been a boon for disaster recovery specialists such as Comdisco Inc. "I've never seen anything like this," says Raymond Hipp, president of Comdisco Disaster, which collects fees of $100 million annually from 1,000 customers to maintain backup systems. Comdisco says it can restore computer service in 24 hours.

Such a promise may be worthless if

phone lines have melted, as they did in Hinsdale. "Nobody had really focused on the lack of redundancy in the Bell operating companies' networks," notes Hipp. Local phone companies relay computer signals to a long-distance carrier such as American Telephone & Telegraph Co. or a data network such as Tymnet, which relays the signal to a local phone company that picks it up for the customer. Without that last link, the most sophisticated computer network may be useless.

Most of the time, phone company backup systems route calls around trouble spots. But in Hinsdale, a worst-case scenario occurred. The automated phone switching facility was unstaffed and lacked the kind of fire-suppression system used in computer centers. There was no alarm at the local fire station, because Illinois Bell feared that the fire department couldn't put out a computer fire without causing excessive damage.

The result: Thousands of homes and businesses, including headquarters offices of McDonald's Corp. and Motorola Corp., were cut off. Large businesses restored communications with emergency microwave radio systems. But seven local businesses have filed lawsuits to recover losses caused by the outage.

Computer customers, as well, want better security features from hardware and software suppliers. Many companies are considering making AT&T's Unix software—or its derivatives—a standard to smooth the connections between different brands of machines. But since Unix was designed to make it easy for computers to share files and programs, it's also susceptible to break-ins, says Judith S. Hurwitz, editor of *Unix in the Office*, a newsletter.

For instance, phrackers in California, after cracking the password system on

A GERMAN HACKERS' CLUB THAT PROMOTES CREATIVE CHAOS

West German computer hacker Bernd Fix holds the economic equivalent of a nuclear bomb in his head. The University of Heidelberg astrophysics student claims it took him only 20 hours to write a virus that could destroy all information in a mainframe computer—erasing tens of thousands of pages in minutes. In the wrong hands, it could cripple companies, the IRS, even the Pentagon. Fix has no such plans: He says he wrote the program as an intellectual exercise—"for the experience of doing it." He has since encrypted it so that it can't be used by others.

Welcome to the oddball world of hacking, German style. Fix, 26, is a member of the Hamburg-based Chaos Computer Club, a group of 300 hackers who, says Herwart "Wau" Holland, the club's founder and leader, are a far cry from the teenage thrill-seekers who prowl U.S. computer networks. Despite the club's name, Holland, 36, says it's against electronic mischief. His goal is more serious: increasing the flow of public information. In West Germany, environmental and scientific data, census figures, and government reports are costly and difficult to get. "It's not a very democratic system," Holland says. Not until Chaos gets involved.

Holland's weekly newsletter, circulation 3,000, and his "Hacker's Bible," 25,000 copies sold, are filled with tips on breaking into computer systems around the world. "We believe we have the right of access to information, and we take it," says Holland. During the Chernobyl nuclear disaster, he says, German officials "fed the public a lot of false [reassuring] statements." By purloining hidden data, "we made sure the press was well informed"—a claim that German reporters confirm.

FORBIDDEN FUN. Chaos members, who meet weekly, hold an annual convention, and pay dues of $66 a year, revel in showing up West Germany's obstinate bureaucracies. In 1984, Chaos uncovered a security hole in the videotex system that the German telephone authority, the Deutsche Bundespost, was building. When the agency ignored club warnings that messages in a customer's private electronic mailbox weren't secure, Chaos members set out to prove the point. They logged on to computers at Hamburger Sparkasse, a savings bank, and programmed them to make thousands of videotex calls to Chaos headquarters on one weekend. After only two days of this, the bank owed the Bundespost $75,000 in telephone charges. Uncaught, Chaos revealed its stunt on Nov. 19, the birthday of Bundespost Minister Christian Schwartz-Schilling. Both the bank and

HOLLAND: "WE HAVE THE RIGHT OF ACCESS TO INFORMATION"

the Bundespost now say the break-in was a fluke.

The incident fits with Holland's goal "of changing structures in society. Everything in Germany is so overly organized." He adds: "Some people throw bombs. It's more effective to find the absurdities and make people laugh."

Like hackers everywhere, however, Chaos members can't resist a challenge. And that sometimes means treading near the edge of West German law, which prohibits manipulating or destroying data, both foreign and domestic, or breaking into "extra secure" systems, which are undefined. Holland denies that the club was behind a NASA break-in last year. Chaos members may have done it, he concedes, though none has confessed. But he adds: "We do not encourage illegal acts."

That's an assertion that critics often discount, given the club's key role in promoting hacking—and its record of never having expelled anyone for unsportsmanlike conduct. Still, Holland, who traded his blue jeans for blue suits when he started a typesetting business 18 months ago, knows that hacking can hurt. Three years ago, fellow enthusiasts stole his password to a German data network and published it in the tabloid *Bild Zeitung*. Soon gleeful computer fanatics had racked up $1,500 in charges to Holland's account. "I was broke at the time, and this incident made an impression on a lot of hackers who knew me," he says.

Nonetheless, there's still the matter of all that closely held government information. And until it's more public, Chaos most likely will fill the void.

By Gail Schares in Heidelberg

one Unix computer last year, used the same approach to unlock Unix-based systems at phone companies all over the country. Now AT&T is making Unix more secure. Similarly, Digital Equipment Corp. says it has patched software holes that let West German Chaos Club members break into its VAX computers.

HIGH-TECH HIJACKING. Concern over computer security will mount as companies do more electronic transactions. In the $55 billion textile business, for instance, sales data, new orders, shipment information, inventory receipts, and invoices are beginning to flow directly from one company's computer to another's via a pipeline called Electronic Data Interchange. Other companies, such as auto parts makers, are using EDI to send items directly to customers, bypassing warehouses. The potential for fraud and theft is huge. "There have always been attempts to divert products," says Peter Browne, president of Profile Analysis, a Ridgefield (Conn.) consulting firm. "Now it can be done electronically."

Corporations are left in a bind: They need to expand computerized information and transaction-processing systems to compete. But the more they do, the greater their risk. "Our society must do something to control the problem," says Ernest A. Conrads, director of corporate security at Westinghouse Electric Corp. "If not, our information system can't grow the way technology will allow us to." In the long run, that could have more profound economic consequences than all the hackers, viruses, and disaster-induced computer failures combined.

By Katherine M. Hafner in New York, with Geoff Lewis in New York, Kevin Kelly in Dallas, Maria Shao in San Francisco, Chuck Hawkins in Toronto, Paul Angiolillo in Boston, and bureau reports

WALTER CALAHAN

Chapter 11

"How to Go Global—And Why"

Jeremy Main

Preview

Skimming. Skim the article quickly to find the following general information.

1. Read the author's name, the title, all headings, and illustrations.

2. Read the first and second paragraphs, looking for the author's purpose and main idea.

3. Read the last paragraph, looking for a summary or conclusion.

Questioning. Answer the following questions and discuss your answers in class.

1. What does "How to Go Global" mean?

2. Why should a company "go global"?

3. How should a company "go global"?

Scanning. Scan the article quickly to find the following specific information.

1. What is another name for the global corporation?

2. How many of ICI's 180 top people are non-British?

3. How many of American Express's 33.3 million card holders are non-U.S.?

4. In how many countries does Citicorp have investment banks?

Vocabulary in Context. Read the following sentences and try to guess the meaning of the italicized words by using the context. Then replace the italicized words with synonyms (words or phrases that have nearly the same or a similar meanings).

Fortune 120, no. 5 (August 28, 1989)

1. "For many major companies, going global is a *matter* of survival, and it means *radically* changing the way they work."

2. "Managers can find it tough to *discard* national preferences in making decisions about such *charged* matters as promotions or capital investment."

3. "Every would-be global company has its own pace and approach, but common *imperatives* stand out—as *exemplified* by several major world players."

4. "When he went to England, he couldn't get any respect with his direct Australian *manner*, so he learned the *oblique* ways of the English."

5. "Ford's claim that Escort is the world's biggest-selling car is somewhat *disingenuous*. Although the U.S. and European Escorts bear a *superficial* resemblance, they share very few common parts."

6. "But how do you market a credit card to different nationalities with *clashing* values and tastes? The *trick* is to design a global strategy and then create ads that are strictly local."

HOW TO GO GLOBAL —AND WHY

Why? To survive. How? Look at the whole world as one market. Buy, borrow, hire, and manufacture wherever you can do it best. And get local allies. ■ *by Jeremy Main*

1 **G**LOBALISM—that word is everywhere. But before dismissing the business buzzword of the moment as globaloney, be aware that it's serious stuff. For many major companies, going global is a matter of survival, and it means radically changing the way they work.

2 Haven't companies like Exxon and GM been global all along? No. They are internationals or multinationals. They happen to do business around the world or are export minded but remain firmly anchored in their home countries with offspring in others. Building a few plants here and there the world over doesn't make you global either.

3 Running a global company is an order of magnitude more complicated than managing a multinational or international firm. The global corporation—or transnational corporation, to use the tag some academics prefer—looks at the whole world as *one market*. It manufactures, conducts research, raises capital, and buys supplies wherever it can do the job best. It keeps in touch with technology and market trends all around the world. National boundaries and regulations tend to be irrelevant, or a mere hindrance. Corporate headquarters might be anywhere.

4 Why the rush to take on the daunting task of going global? The rules for survival have changed since the beginning of the 1980s. "Domestic markets have become too small," says Wharton professor Stephen Kobrin. "Even the biggest companies in the biggest countries cannot survive on their domestic markets if they are in global industries. They have to be in all major markets." That means North America, Western Europe, and the Pacific Rim countries.

5 Take, for example, the pharmaceuticals business. In the 1970s, developing a new drug cost about $16 million and took four to five years, says David Friend, head of the pharmaceuticals division of British-based Imperial Chemical Industries. The drug could be produced in Britain or the U.S. and eventually exported. Now developing a drug costs about $250 million and takes as long as 12 years. Only a global product for a global market can support that much risk. Says Friend: "No major pharmaceuticals company is in the game for anything other than global products." That helps explain a series of mergers of major drug companies, most recently the marriage of Bristol-Myers and Squibb.

6 Not every industry should view the world as one. Some packaged goods, for example, don't gain much from economies of scale and need to be marketed differently in each country. Strong niche players, such as the makers of luxury cars, can survive nicely. Mercedes is hardly threatened by global mass producers. And many resourceful

REPORTER ASSOCIATE *Karen Nickel*

1 A.M. in New York: Citicorp's traders keep foreign exchange lines open 24 hours each day.

companies are likely to prosper by doing things faster or better than the big boys.

7 But Howard Perlmutter of Wharton identifies 136 industries, from accounting to zippers, where you may have to play world chess or get out. They include autos, banking, consumer electronics, entertainment, pharmaceuticals, publishing, travel services, and washing machines. Perlmutter sees a shakeout in each industry during the 1990s, leaving three to five key actors per sector.

8 Adapting to the new global format won't be easy. Managers can find it tough to discard national preferences in making decisions about such charged matters as promotions or capital investment. The Japanese face a special challenge in rethinking the centralized model that has served them so well, says Hirotaka Takeuchi of Hitotsubashi University. An adviser to companies trying to go global, Takeuchi tells Japanese managers that they can no longer afford to be what he calls "soles"—flat fish with both eyes on one side of their heads fixed on headquarters. They will also need to

British-based ICI spans the planet. Its directors come from five countries. The executives go everywhere. Case in point: Australian Ben Lochtenberg, above, runs ICI Americas from Wilmington, Delaware.

start hiring and using more non-Japanese. Honda, one of the companies he advises, hired six non-Japanese, mostly Americans, straight out of college two years ago to work in Japan, and more than ten last year. Sony this year appointed an American and a West German to its board.

9 No company has yet reached a state of pure globality. Even with its worldwide net of products, plants, offices, and labs, IBM still has a long way to go. Others are just starting. Whirlpool bought control of Philips's $2-billion-a-year appliance business in Europe last winter and is beginning to integrate the two to create a worldwide appliance business.

10 Every would-be global company has its own pace and approach, but common imperatives stand out—as exemplified by several major world players:

IMPERIAL CHEMICAL INDUSTRIES

11 ■ The archaic name is entirely appropriate: The sun never sets on ICI's far-flung nerve centers, and the company has probably

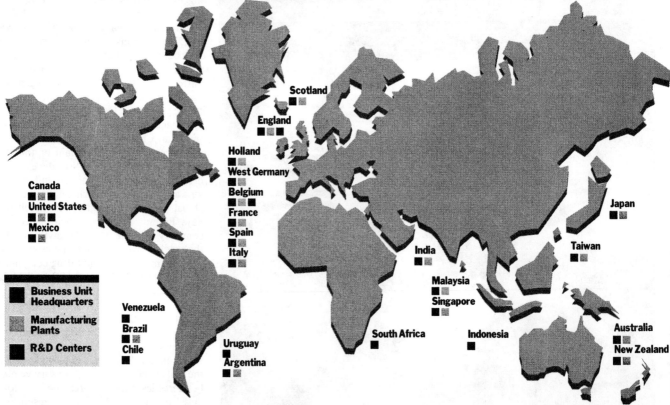

A COMPANY WITHOUT BORDERS: ICI's MAJOR OPERATIONS

moved as near as any to being truly global. The world's 38th-largest industrial corporation, ICI sells $21 billion a year of pharmaceuticals, film, polymers, agricultural chemicals, explosives, and other products.

12 In 1983, ICI began to abandon its traditional country-by-country organization and establish worldwide business units. The company concentrated its resources on its strongest ones. Within each, it focused activity where the most strength lay. Four of the nine new business units are headquartered outside Britain. Two are in Wilmington, Delaware—ICI is growing 20% a year in the U.S. but only 2% to 3% at home. A factory in Britain or Brazil producing advanced materials or specialty chemicals answers to a boss in Wilmington.

13 To avoid overlapping research around the world, labs were given lead roles near the most important markets. Advanced materials research went to Phoenix to be near clients in defense industries, while leather dye research went to the south of France, the heart of the market.

14 The strategic shift created wrenching changes. ICI reduced its manufacturing jobs in Britain by 10,000, to 55,000; other people were transferred or taken off pet projects. "It's a major change," says Hugh Miller, the American who heads the advanced materials and electronics group. "It's hard on people who have built national empires and now don't have such freedom. We are asking people to be less nationalistic and more concerned with what happens outside their country." The upheaval has been especially worrisome to British employees, since ICI's stronger growth rate elsewhere attracts more resources.

15 The payoff, says Miller, is better decision-making. "Before, each territory would work up projects and you'd have warring factions competing in London for the same money. Now with one man responsible for a global product line, it becomes immaterial where a project is located. His profits will be the same. When you start operating in this manner, it takes a lot of steam out of the defense of fiefdoms." In pharmaceuticals, for example, better—and quicker—decision-making has helped ICI reduce the time lag in introducing new drugs to different markets from half a dozen years to one or two. ICI hopes eventually to make the introductions simultaneous.

16 A global company needs a world view at the top. Until 1982, ICI's 16-person board was all British. Now it includes two Americans, a Canadian, a Japanese, and a German. Among the 180 top people in the company, 35% are non-British.

17 British or non-British, they may go anywhere. Ben Lochtenberg, the new chairman of ICI Americas Inc., is an Australian who also has worked for ICI in Britain and Canada. He quickly learned that a common language is no insurance against cultural shocks. When he went to England, he couldn't get any respect with his direct Australian manner, so he learned the oblique ways of the English. For example, he says, if an English boss reacts to a pet project by saying, "Perhaps you ought to think about this a little more," what he really means is "You must be mad. Forget it." In the U.S., Lochtenberg had to unlearn the lesson. He told a manager, "Perhaps you ought to think about this a little more." The manager

American Express ads are local, but the message is universal.

took him literally. Asked why he had gone ahead, the man replied, "Well, I thought about it, like you said, and the idea got better."

GENERAL ELECTRIC

18 ■ Claude Benchimol, 39, jovial, open, and multilingual, was made to be a global manager. Born of Jewish parents in Morocco, he attended school in France, got his Ph.D. at UCLA, married an American, and went to work for Thomson CGR in Paris. His specialty is computed tomography, or CT, a

diagnostic scanning system. Today he runs GE's global effort to develop premium CTs, working in Waukesha, Wisconsin, near the headquarters of GE Medical Systems.

19 Benchimol moved after Thomson acquired GE's consumer electronics business in a swap in 1987 and in return gave GE cash and Thomson's diagnostic imaging business. At the same time, GE established GE Medical Systems Asia (Gemsa) in Tokyo, anchored on Yokogawa Medical Systems, which is 75% owned by GE. With this triad, GE secured its place as a world player in the business of making X-ray, CT, magnetic resonance, ultrasound, and other diagnostic imaging devices. The move fits Chairman Jack Welch's plan to be first or second in the world in a business or to get out. GE is No. 1, ahead of Siemens, Philips, and Toshiba.

20 "Rationalizing" the business, to use a phrase favored when job losses are involved, was painful but productive. Each leg of the new triad became exclusively responsible for products in which it was the volume leader. General Electric CGR in France got primary responsibility for X-rays, Waukesha took over premium CTs and magnetic resonance equipment, and Tokyo got the cheaper lines. Thomson CGR's U.S. headquarters in Columbia, Maryland, was eliminated, and 15% of the employees in France lost their jobs. But the pain was distributed fairly. GE had previously cut the number of Medical Systems employees around Milwaukee from 5,500 to 3,500 and is considering a 10% to 15% cut in the X-ray division there.

21 GE puts a lot of effort into helping the survivors and drawing them together. For example, it adapted what it calls a Global Leadership Program, developed and run by an international business school faculty directed by Noel Tichy of the University of Michigan. Over a period of ten months, the top 55 people from GE, CGR, and Gemsa met once on each of the three continents for several days at a time to learn about one another. In between these meetings they worked on three-way task forces assigned to deal with specific medical system problems. The purpose was as much to get them to understand one another as to solve the problems. The second group of some 57 managers has just begun its program.

A Japanese engineer works with an American and an Indian at Texas Instruments in Dallas.

22 Claude Benchimol seems to be taking the merger in stride. It left him without a job in France, but GE needed someone to run CT development in Wisconsin. Benchimol looked like the best candidate—worldwide—so he got the job.

23 There were culture shocks. He can't get used to his windowless office in the Waukesha plant where GE turns out several hundred $1 million CT devices a year. In France he always had a pleasant view. The French are surprised the American parking lots empty out as early as 5 P.M.; the Americans are surprised the French don't start work at 8 A.M. Benchimol feels the French are more talkative and candid. Americans have more of a sense of hierarchy and are less likely to criticize. But they may be growing closer to the French. Says Benchimol: "It's taken a year to get across the idea that we are all entitled to say what we don't like to become more productive and work better."

FORD MOTOR

24 ■ Unlike ICI, Ford is making its bid to be global without a major reorganization. Two years ago it unified all foreign and domestic auto operations under Philip Benton, head of international auto operations, and gave him a newly created title, president of the Ford Automotive Group. A small worldwide planning office was added to his staff. Otherwise the organization remains the same. The big difference is in the manner of developing products.

25 Compare the creation of the subcompact Escort a decade ago with a current project to replace the compact Tempo-Topaz-Sierra line. The Escort was billed as a world car, developed in Europe for Ford to sell everywhere. It was indeed developed in Europe, but as Ford now acknowledges, matters got out of hand when the European engineers turned their designs over to the Detroit engineers. Engineers were created to design things, and the Detroit crowd couldn't keep its hands off plans made elsewhere. Result: Ford's claim that Escort is the world's biggest-selling car is somewhat disingenuous. Although the U.S. and European Escorts bear a superficial resemblance, they share very few common parts.

26 For the follow-up to the Tempo-Topaz-Sierra cars, due in the early 1990s and designated the CDW27 for now, Detroit again gave lead responsibility to Ford Europe. But this time David Price, the Englishman in charge of the project, will coordinate all features of the new car for both sides of the Atlantic. If the skin is shaped differently for American tastes, he will have the final say. Kenneth Dabrowski, program manager for small cars in Dearborn, provides Price with a liaison service with designers and suppliers in the U.S. Unlike the Escort, both versions of the CDW27 will have the same platform, engines, and other parts.

27 Even if the will to make the Escort a true world car had been there ten years ago, the technology wasn't. With the CDW27, Ford is using new communications methods, such as teleconferencing and CAD/CAM links to Europe, as well as plenty of travel, to manage the complex task of meshing car companies on two continents.

28 European and American engineers don't automatically work together in harmony. Benton admits cultural differences—meaning that American engineers may think their British counterparts are idiots and vice versa—may be delaying the program by months. A bigger problem is that manufacturing has evolved differently on each side of the Atlantic.

29 In the European Sierra, for example, side panels are one stamping. For the Topaz, the American equivalent, several panels are welded together on the line. If Ford succeeds in designing a single CDW27, the same plans and processes will be used in Europe and the U.S. So it will cost more than usual to tear up and retool U.S. factories for the new car. Ford believes the savings in design costs and time, as well as the standardization of parts, will easily justify the one-time expense.

30 To its regret, Ford has no plants of its own in Japan. Instead, like other global companies, it has constructed a complex array of alliances to compensate for geographic holes, to fill niches, and to produce mass-market cars like the Escort. For instance, Ford owns 25% of Mazda. Mercury sells the Tracer, based on a Mazda design and built by Ford in Mexico. Ford sells the Festiva, made by Kia in Korea to Ford's design. And Ford will build a Nissan-designed minivan in Ohio, to be sold by both Nissan and Ford. Mazda leads the development of the Escort successor, now designated the CT20 and due out next year.

31 Though Ford has made several complex arrangements, Benton says, "We haven't yet learned how to make a three-way deal." He means getting Japan, Europe, and North America all behind one competitive world car. The three-way deal may be a necessary competitive step. Benton sees an overca-

pacity of nine million cars coming soon in the world's auto plants and predicts "competition in this car-clogged market will escalate to previously unheard-of levels."

AMERICAN EXPRESS

32 ■ Only 9.3 million of American Express's 33.3 million card holders are non-U.S., but they bring in 31% more revenue per card than Americans. As the world's GNP grows, the company will find many more potential members out there than at home.

33 But how do you market a credit card to different nationalities with clashing values and tastes? The trick is to design a global strategy and then create ads that are strictly local. With its worldwide ad agency, Ogilvy & Mather, American Express sends themes like "Don't leave home without it" and "Membership has its privileges" around the world. The ads are created for specific countries, and even specific cities, by local agencies, usually the office of Ogilvy & Mather.

34 In Japan the "privileges" slogan translates to "Peace of mind only for members." A typical ad shows a young couple visiting the drift ice in the north—a remote and exclusive place that appeals to the crowded Japanese—and rejoicing that their American Express card allows them to stay two days longer. In Australia an exuberant young couple has a blast on their card. So it goes around the world.

35 Until the mid-1980s, most of American Express's foreign revenue came from traveling Americans. Then, says Rick Thoman, president of American Express International, the company realized that services are inherently global and switched from an export mentality to a global mentality. A recent report by Sanford C. Bernstein & Co., the New York investment research firm, cites Amex's high-quality, upscale image as "possibly the most potent asset in all financial services" and predicts the company's international business will generate 40% of the growth in card profits over the next five years.

CITICORP

36 ■ Global companies with high-tech links can mobilize resources quickly around the world to help a client. Until a couple of years ago, a potential borrower approaching a Citicorp office in Australia or Hong Kong could get only the services of that office. He might even visit several Citicorp locations to get competing offers. Today, for a single deal, the bank can seek out the best rates and terms offered by its offices

anywhere in the world. It might draw funds from outposts in several countries, in different currencies, involving several tax jurisdictions. Such deals take a lot of time, but they are becoming more common as Citibank's clients spread around the world.

37 The bank began sprinkling branches around the world in 1902 but only recently began to link them in a global business, using strength in one market to gain advantage in another. Michael Callen, who runs Citicorp's investment banking worldwide, says that the technology to operate globally didn't exist at the beginning of the decade. For instance, Citicorp's investment banks in 90 countries could quote only their own exchange rates. Now they can give a client the best rate in any one of the 90. Citicorp

YOUR GLOBAL CHECKLIST

There's no handy formula for going global, but any company serious about joining the race will have to do most or all of the following:

■ Make yourself at home in all three of the world's most important markets—North America, Europe, and Asia.

■ Develop new products for the whole world.

■ Replace profit centers based on countries or regions with ones based on product lines.

■ "Glocalize," as the Japanese call it: Make global decisions on strategic questions about products, capital, and research, but let local units decide tactical questions about packaging, marketing, and advertising.

■ Overcome parochial attitudes, such as the "not-invented-here" syndrome. Train people to think internationally, send them off on frequent trips, and give them the latest communications technology, such as teleconferencing.

■ Open the senior ranks to foreign employees.

■ Do whatever seems best wherever it seems best, even if people at home lose jobs or responsibilities.

■ In markets that you cannot penetrate on your own, find allies.

is testing automatic tellers that would serve a client anywhere in the world.

38 Part of Citicorp's global thrust comes from the sheer growth in volume of international business—the world's daily trade in currencies has reached $400 billion. The volume now justifies keeping Citicorp's trading rooms in New York, London, and Tokyo running 24 hours a day.

39 But a new mind-set is more important. Officers are required to work through ad hoc international teams to assemble deals. To make sure Citibankers help one another, says Callen, the company has adopted a system of cross-evaluations. A manager in New York who is supposed to work with a colleague in Tokyo gets rated by the fellow in Tokyo and vice versa. Their bonuses are based partly on how well they collaborate.

TEXAS INSTRUMENTS

40 ■ Globalization is helping Texas Instruments fight back against the Japanese in memory chips—the product TI pioneered. Under Chairman Jerry Junkins, TI has designated a single design center and manufacturing organization for each memory chip. TI has also gone for help to the source of its problems, the Pacific Rim. Two of its four new $250 million memory chip plants are in Taiwan and Japan, where it can cut capital costs because interest rates are half U.S. rates. To reduce high research costs, it has made an alliance with Hitachi to develop a 16-megabit chip. And the TI boss in Japan, Akiro Ishikawa, runs worldwide strategy for the company's whole memory business.

41 So far TI's strategy has worked. The company has grabbed 5.2% of the world market for memory chips; their sales helped boost earnings by 69% to $368 million last year.

42 Like GE's Jack Welch, executives in other global industries, as well as academics, see a stark choice between being right at the top or playing in a different league—if at all. Citibank's Callen thinks the three biggest contenders in each banking specialty will pick up as much as 90% of the earnings to be made in that business, while the rest will get nothing but crumbs. Says Perlmutter of the Wharton School: "Unless a unit in your company has a shot at being a global leader, you'll probably have to get rid of it." That may be stating the choices too starkly—many survivors with large niches will doubtless survive handily. But the competitive pace is increasingly being set by emerging global giants. ∎

Glossary

alliance	close association for a common objective
anchored	settled in one place
archaic	old-fashioned, belonging to an earlier period
array	arrangement
bid	to attempt or try
boost	to raise, push up, increase in amount
buzzword	word used by member of some group, having little meaning but sounding impressive
candid	frank, direct, honest
car-clogged	obstructed by cars
charged	explosive
cites	refers to; mentions by way of example
clashing	conflicting
collaborate	to work together
contenders	competitors
daunting	intimidating, discouraging
designated	specified, indicated
discard	to throw away, abandon, get rid of
disingenuous	not straightforward, not frank; insincere
dye	substance used to give color to something; coloring matter or solution
entitled	had the right
escalate	to grow or increase rapidly, often to the point of becoming unmanageable
evolved	developed gradually by a process of growth
exuberant	full of life, good health, high spirits
factions	groups working against other groups within an organization
far-flung	extending over a wide area
fiefdoms	areas belonging to a particular group
globalism	policy or outlook that is worldwide in scope
grabbed	seized suddenly
handily	easily, with no trouble
hierarchy	group of persons arranged in order of rank or grade
hindrance	obstacle, impediment
idiots	very foolish or stupid persons
immaterial	unimportant
imperatives	compelling rules or requirements
inherently	basically, innately, naturally
irrelevant	not relevant, not relating to the subject
jovial	full of good humor, genial
jurisdictions	ranges of authority
leg	branch, part
literally	word for word, in a literal manner, not figuratively
magnitude	importance
mentality	mental power, activity, capacity, or outlook
meshing	fitting closely together, interlocking

mind-set	fixed mental attitude formed by experience and education
mobilize	to bring into readiness, organize for active service, put into use
niche	specific place in the market occupied by a product
oblique	indirect, evasive, not straightforward
offspring	children
open	frank, direct, honest
outposts	offices away from the home country
overlapping	coinciding with
payoff	reward, recompense
pet	favorite, especially liked
pharmaceuticals	drugs
polymers	naturally occurring or synthetic substances
potent	effective, powerful, influential
quote	to refer to or cite; to state the price of
rejoicing	feeling full of joy, happiness, delight
retool	to reorganize to meet new or different needs; to adapt machinery to manufacture a different product
shakeout	any drop in economic activity that eliminates unprofitable or marginal businesses or products
sheer	absolute, unqualified
simultaneous	occurring together or at the same time
sprinkling	scattering, distributing at random
stamping	piece of metal or other material that has been cut, shaped, or bent by a stamp or die
stark	bleak, unsoftened
starkly	bleakly, harshly
switched	changed, shifted
tag	label
thrust	push, impetus, forward movement
time lag	slowness in time, interval between two events
triad	group of three
upheaval	sudden, violent change or disturbance
upscale	for people who are educated, affluent, and stylish
warring	fighting, conflicting
welded	joined by heating until fused
worrisome	causing worry or anxiety
would-be	wishing or pretending to be
wrenching	sudden and violent

Vocabulary

Without referring to the article, fill in the blanks in the following sentences with the correct words from this list. You may change the tense, number, or form of the words to fit the context. Use each word only once; not all of the words on the list will be used.

warring	stark	hierarchy	candid	faction	collaborate	magnitude
mentality	escalate	inherently	shakeout	evolve	buzzword	imperative

1. The new _____ for business is globalism, which is a serious strategy, not a minor trend.

2. During the 1990s, a(n) _____ is predicted for major industries that will have to either enter the world market or get out of business.

3. Although each company is different, several common _____ exist in regard to running a successful global business.

4. Taking a global approach to research and production often results in eliminating _____ _____ in competition for the same money.

5. Global companies have to deal with cultural differences among their employees, such as Americans' strong sense of _____ and less _____ natures, compared to the French.

6. Unless Japan, Europe, and North America can form a three-way deal to make a world car, the competition in the automobile market may _____ to extremely high levels.

7. American Express realized in the mid-1980s that its services were _____ global, so it adopted a global _____.

8. Operating as a global company with offices around the world means that managers from distant countries will have to learn to _____ with each other as international teams.

9. Many executives believe that companies have to make a _____ choice between attempting to become global leaders or losing their share of the market.

Idioms and Expressions

Read the paragraphs in which the following italicized idioms and expressions are found. Then circle the letter next to the answer that best describes the meaning of the idiom as used in the context of the article.

1. "It [the global corporation] *keeps in touch with* technology and market trends all around the world." (Paragraph 3)
   a. studies in detail
   b. disseminates information about
   c. stays in contact with

2. "Why the rush to *take on* the daunting task of going global?" (Paragraph 4)
   a. begin managing
   b. accept
   c. experiment with

3. "And many resourceful companies are likely to prosper by doing things faster or better than *the big boys*." (Paragraph 6)
   a. older companies
   b. industry executives
   c. major companies

4. "*The sun never sets on* ICI's far-flung nerve centers, and the company has probably moved as near as any to being truly global." (Paragraph 11)
   a. work is going on around the world at
   b. employees work night shifts at
   c. work is thoroughly enjoyable at

5. "When you start operating in this manner, it *takes a lot of steam out of* the defense of fiefdoms." (Paragraph 15)
   a. encourages
   b. weakens
   c. improves

6. ". . . what he really means is '*You must be mad*.'" (Paragraph 17)
   a. You must be crazy.
   b. You must be angry.
   c. You must be worried.

7. "Claude Benchimol seems to be *taking the merger in stride*." (Paragraph 22)
   a. reacting negatively to the merger
   b. reacting emotionally to the merger
   c. adjusting well to the merger

8. "The Escort was *billed as* a world car, developed in Europe for Ford to sell everywhere." (Paragraph 25)
   a. built as
   b. promoted as
   c. financially evaluated as

9. "It was indeed developed in Europe, but as Ford now acknowledges, matters *got out of hand.* . . ." (Paragraph 25)
   a. went out of control
   b. became difficult
   c. were reorganized

10. ". . . the Detroit crowd *couldn't keep its hands off* plans made elsewhere." (Paragraph 25)
    a. could not accept
    b. could not understand
    c. could not avoid interfering in

11. "In Australia an exuberant young couple *has a blast* on their card." (Paragraph 34)
    a. has an accident
    b. has a wonderful time
    c. has a vacation

12. "Officers are required to work through *ad hoc* international teams to assemble deals." (Paragraph 39)
    a. temporary
    b. complex
    c. large

13. "Unless a unit in your company *has a shot at being* a global leader, you'll probably have to get rid of it." (Paragraph 42)
    a. has the experience to be
    b. has a chance to be
    c. has a desire to be

Paraphrasing

Read the following sentences carefully, and then rewrite them using your own words. Change the vocabulary and sentence structure, but do not change the author's intended meaning or paraphrase any technical terms. There are several ways of paraphrasing each sentence.

Original: "Running a global company is an order of magnitude more complicated than managing a multinational or international firm."

Paraphrase: A global company is more complex to manage than a multinational or international business.

1. "Why the rush to take on the daunting task of going global?" (Paragraph 4)

   _____

   _____

2. "Not every industry should view the world as one." (Paragraph 6)

   _____

   _____

3. "Managers can find it tough to discard national preferences in making decisions about such charged matters as promotions or capital investment." (Paragraph 8)

   _____

   _____

4. "Even if the will to make the Escort a true world car had been there ten years ago, the technology wasn't." (Paragraph 27)

_____

_____

5. "Officers are required to work through ad hoc international teams to assemble deals." (Paragraph 39)

_____

_____

Comprehension

Answer the following questions by finding the relevant information in the article. Give the numbers of the paragraphs that contain the answers.

1. What is the main idea of this article?

2. What differentiates a global corporation from a multinational or international firm?

3. Why are many companies becoming global?

4. What kinds of industries may have to go global?

5. What changes will the Japanese have to make in order to adapt to the new global format?

6. How did ICI become a global company?

7. What problems has Ford Motor Company faced in becoming global?

8. How does American Express market its one credit card to different nationalities?

9. What accounts for Citicorp's development as a global company?

10. What strategy has Texas Instruments adopted to compete with the Japanese in memory chips? Has it worked?

11. What choice is facing companies in global industries?

Inference/Interpretation

Circle the letter next to the best answer. Choose your answer according to the meaning the author suggests but does not state explicitly.

1. It can be inferred from the article that "globaloney" means (Paragraph 1)
   a. the global food business.
   b. a global joke.
   c. a global rumor.
   d. global nonsense.

2. What can we infer about the following statement: "Not every industry should view the world as one"? (Paragraph 6)
   a. Not all companies want to become global.
   b. The world is not really one large market.
   c. Some companies can succeed without becoming global.
   d. Most companies should become global.

3. The phrase "'rationalizing' the business" means (Paragraph 20)
   a. laying off employees.
   b. hiring employees.
   c. training employees.
   d. counseling employees.

4. What can be inferred from the following statement: "Only 9.3 million of American Express's 33.3 million card holders are non-U.S., but they bring in 31% more revenue per card than Americans"? (Paragraph 32)
   a. American Express should do more international marketing.
   b. American Express should do more marketing in the United States.
   c. American Express should not market in the United States.
   d. American Express should not market internationally.

Structure

Circle the letter next to the correct answer(s). More than one answer may be correct. Be prepared to explain and justify your choices.

1. In which paragraph(s) is the main idea stated?
   a. Paragraph 1
   b. Paragraph 3
   c. Paragraph 10
   d. Paragraph 40
   e. Paragraph 42
   Write a paraphrase of the main idea in *one* sentence, using your own words as much as possible.

   _____

2. What is the purpose of the example of developing a new drug in the pharmaceuticals business, which is discussed in paragraph 5?
   a. To explain why it is expensive to develop a new drug
   b. To explain why many big companies must become global
   c. To explain why major drug companies have merged
   d. To explain what pharmaceutical companies do
   e. To explain the success of ICI as a global company

3. Why does the author describe Australian Ben Lochtenberg's experience working for ICI in Britain and the United States? (Paragraph 17)

    a. To show how similar the British and Australians are

    b. To show how different the Australians and Americans are

    c. To show how the use of English varies from one English-speaking country to another

    d. To show why cultural shocks are difficult to avoid

    e. To show how hard it is to communicate in English

4. What overall method of development is used in this article?

    a. Comparing and contrasting two approaches

    b. Choosing and describing one alternative out of several

    c. Defining a technical system

    d. Supporting an argument by giving specific examples

    e. Explaining a complex process

Style

Circle the letter next to the correct answer(s). More than one answer may be correct. Be prepared to justify your choices by giving specific examples from the article.

1. How would you describe the writing style of the author?

    a. Technical

    b. Impersonal

    c. Bureaucratic

    d. Informal

    e. Formal

    f. Academic

2. How would you describe the tone of the article?

    a. Negative

    b. Subjective

    c. Factual

    d. Uncertain

    e. Authoritative

    f. Scholarly

3. What is the author's attitude toward Howard Perlmutter's statement: "Unless a unit in your company has a shot at being a global leader, you'll probably have to get rid of it"? (Paragraph 42)

    a. Complete disagreement

    b. Partial disagreement

    c. Surprise

    d. Admiration

    e. Complete agreement

    f. Anger

4. Read the following sentence carefully: "Benton admits cultural differences—meaning that American engineers may think their British counterparts are idiots and vice versa—may be delaying the program by months" (Paragraph 28). Why does the author use the insulting word *idiots* in his explanation of cultural differences?

Discussion

1. What is the likelihood of survival for a major company that does not go global?

2. What, if any, are the advantages for a large company in not becoming a global business?

3. How much influence do multinational or transnational corporations have on the political systems in foreign countries where they are located?

4. Would the joint production of a competitive world car by Japan, Europe, and North America be a benefit to the consumer? Why or why not?

5. Do you have an American Express Card? How is it marketed in your country?

6. Would you like to work for a global corporation? What type of training would you need?

Research Assignment

Look up several of these articles in the library. Choose one article to read and take notes on.

Agins, Teri, and Yumiko Ono. "Japanese Market Lures, Vexes Retailers." *Wall Street Journal* (May 29, 1990): B1, B6.

Aurbach, Stuart. "Schools Learn to Go Global." *Washington Post* (May 6, 1990): H1ff.

Aurbach, Stuart. "Georgetown Students Learn to Deal in Marks and Bahts." *Washington Post* (May 6, 1990): H6.

Boyle, Rosemarie. "McDonald's Gives Soviets Something Worth Waiting For." *Advertising Age* 61 (March 19, 1990): 61.

Chandler, Seth. "The Nordic Market: Swedish Marketers Going Global." *Advertising Age* 61 (April 16, 1990): 38.

Hax, Arnoldo C. "Building the Firm of the Future." *Sloan Management Review* 30 (Spring 1989): 75–82.

Hayes, John P., and Gregory Matusky. "Franchising Abroad . . . American Companies Look East." *Inc.* 11 (September 1989): 108–13.

Nelton, Sharon. "Family Firms' Global Reach." *Nation's Business* 78 (February 1990): 51–52.

Ohmae, Kenichi. "Managing in a Borderless World." *Harvard Business Review* 67 (May-June 1989): 152–61.

Ohmae, Kenichi. "Planting for a Global Harvest." *Harvard Business Review* 67 (July-August 1989): 136–45.

Porter, Michael. "Europe's Companies after 1992." *Economist* 315 (June 9, 1990): 17–19.

Rudolph, Stephen. "Sometimes the Best Solution Is in Someone Else's Lab." *Business Month* 134 (October 1989): 91.

Ruffin, William R. "Wired for Speed." *Business Month* 135 (January 1990): 57.

Schatz, Willie. "D.C. Area Firms Look to International Markets." *Washington Post* (November 20, 1989): Washington Business Section, 5–6.

Stewart, Thomas A. "How to Manage in the New Era." *Fortune* 121 (January 15, 1990): 59–72.

Sugiura, Hideo. "How Honda Localizes Its Global Strategy." *Sloan Management Review* 32 (Fall 1990): 77–82.

Tannenbaum, Jeffrey A. "Franchisers See a Future in East Bloc." *Wall Street Journal* (June 5, 1990): B1–B2.

Trinter, Susan. "Planning Your Strategies: A Tale of Three Companies." *Washington Business Journal* (April 30, 1990): 12–13.

Woolley, Suzanne. "Going Global? Here's How." *Business Week* (July 2, 1990): 88–89.

Yip, George S. "Global Strategy in a World of Nations." *Sloan Management Review* 31 (Fall 1989): 29–41.

Oral Presentation

Working with a partner, give a fifteen-minute oral presentation to the class on the articles that you chose in the research assignment. Include the author's main idea, major points, and some supporting data. Be prepared to answer questions on your topic. (See Appendix B: Giving an Oral Presentation.)

Writing Assignments

1. Write a short report in which you analyze and evaluate the factors that lead to failure or success as a global company. Use the additional reading in this chapter and the articles listed in the research assignment. In the report, consider the following: (1) the type of company that should become global; and (2) the best potential markets to enter. Include a 100-word abstract (very short summary) as the first section of the report.

   Use parenthetical references in the author-date system for each of the sources you cite: (Ruffin 1990). You may also choose to give the page number (Ruffin 1990, 57). List all sources at the end of your report as References. Entries must be alphabetized according to the last name of the author: Ruffin, William R. 1990. "Wired for Speed." *Business Month* 135:57.

Purpose Statement: The purpose of this report is to analyze and evaluate the major factors that determine the success of a global business.

Thesis: It is evident that the following factors are critical to the success of a global company: . . .

Format:
      I. Abstract (Purpose, Thesis, Conclusions)
     II. Introduction (Background, Purpose, Thesis)
   III. Discussion (Success Factors)
   IV. Discussion (Failure Factors)
    V. Conclusion (Summary)

2. Discuss a multinational corporation with offices in your country. What products does it produce? Does it employ natives of the country in which it is located? What markets has it penetrated? Should this corporation go global? If so, describe the process it should follow in order to become a global corporation.

3. Create a specific advertisement for the American Express credit card in your country. Develop a slogan and a picture.

Peer Critique

Choose a person to work with. After you have completed your writing assignment, let your partner read and critique your writing. Then you will read and critique his or her writing. Use the Writing Evaluation Form in Appendix F.

Case Study: A Problem in Going Global

Working in groups, read the following case study. Discuss the problem, answer the questions, and write a brief report on how your group would solve the problem. (Choose one member of the group to do the writing.) Follow the format in Appendix E (Case Study Report) in writing your report.

    BCB Corporation, a high-technology company, produces central processing units, video display terminals, and other computer hardware. It is a large multinational company headquartered in Dallas, Texas. While BCB has a solid technology and distribution network, orders have gone soft, competition has intensified, and profit margins have decreased recently. BCB seems to be caught in a business downturn.

    Consequently, several of the top executives of BCB have been pushing for the company to go global. They believe BCB can compete more successfully against U. S. and Japanese producers of computer hardware if it forms a joint venture in Japan with Omada Corporation and also builds some new factories in locations outside of the United States where capital and overhead costs are lower. However, in order for BCB to globalize, a complete restructuring of the organization will be necessary, and some of its offices in the United States will have to be eliminated. Thousands of employees will be laid off, as a result.

Charles Chambers, President and CEO of BCB, is the one member of upper management who is adamantly against the plan to globalize. He does not see the necessity to reshape the company and is especially averse to the idea of eliminating so many jobs. Chambers has a strong commitment to his employees and also does not believe in letting one central office make decisions about a global product line. Instead, he wants to maintain the country-by-country organization of BCB and the standardized products, marketing, and advertising that BCB has always had. Why should BCB restructure just because market dynamics have changed?

The first quarter earnings statement has just come out, and BCB is not doing well, compared to last year at this time. Its major competitors all appear to be eating into BCB's markets. A meeting of the Board of Directors has been called for Tuesday at 4 P.M. to discuss BCB's future and its possible reorganization as a global business. Larry Thomas, Chairman of the Board of Directors, will run the meeting. He wants Chambers to go along with the globalization plan, but he knows how stubborn Chambers can be. Therefore, he has asked Anne Shaw, Director of Finance, to prepare a detailed financial analysis of the projected globalization plan and bring copies of it to the meeting. He has seen Anne's preliminary figures, and they look good.

Questions

1. What could Chambers do to change the minds of those who favor globalization of BCB?

2. What could Thomas do to change Chamber's mind?

3. Should BCB remain a multinational corporation or become a transnational corporation?

4. How can BCB make the transition from multinational to transnational?

Solution: Case Study Report

    I. Define and analyze the problem.
   II. Suggest possible solutions.
 III. Evaluate possible solutions.
 IV. Select a solution.

Case Study Business Writing Assignment: Memorandum

Write a memo from Larry Thomas, Chairman of the Board of Directors of BCB Corporation, to Charles Chambers, President and CEO. The memo will contain Thomas's reasons for wanting BCB to become a global company, his analysis of the marketing situation, and a justification of his position.

    Format:
        I. Introduction (Background and Recommendation)
      II. Justification of Recommendation

III. Discussion of Alternatives
IV. Closing (Restatement of Recommendation)

Style: Formal and somewhat technical
Tone: Objective and analytical

Additional Reading

"Taking the Grief Out of Going Global"
Kurt Weidenhaupt
Business Month 135 (February 1990): 72–73

THE CEO/KURT WIEDENHAUPT

TAKING THE GRIEF OUT OF GOING GLOBAL

IT'S EASY TO SAY YOU'RE TAKING your company global. Doing it right—especially when you're buying a foreign subsidiary—is hard.

Since my company, AEG, moved into the United States in 1986, we have learned a few basic principles of management, communication, and cultural diplomacy that may be instructive for American CEOs contemplating a foreign acquisition.

Here are some pointers:

Respect the market. When contemplating a move into a foreign country, first determine whether there is a well-regarded company for sale in that nation that makes products similar to yours. AEG's experience has convinced us that the most effective way to enter a foreign market is through acquisition.

Sure, we have great products in the automation field. But few people in the U.S. have ever heard of them. To try to introduce our equipment in America would have been a long and expensive struggle against some very tough competitors. So we acquired MODICON and MODCOMP, American companies whose lines were very familiar to American consumers of automation products. As a result, we were not perceived as foreign big shots trying to impose new products poorly suited to American tastes.

Our first and most crucial decision concerned whether to change the brand names of the products—or the names of the companies—that we acquired. We decided we were better off selling the product under a tried-and-true, recognizable, local name rather than our own. In the end, we took a balanced approach. MODICON is "an AEG company," and its products are all sold under the well-respected MODICON name. So when you make a foreign acquisition, remember that it's very important to keep the old familiar brand name.

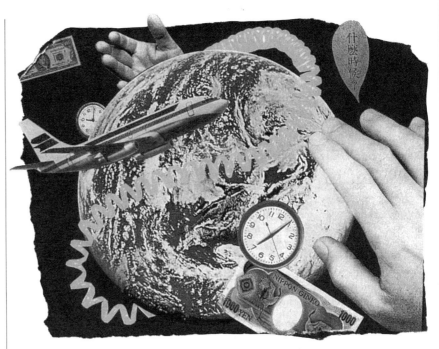

Communicate with customers. Introduce your company to customers as soon as possible. Meet one-on-one with key accounts to discuss your credentials and your business plans. Be open about your business and your goals, particularly if this is your first foray into a specific national market.

> ## A company should be led by its strongest unit, whatever the nationality.

Changes in ownership prompt significant uncertainties in customers' minds—and opportunities for competitors to exploit those uncertainties, often with nationalistic overtones. Your accessibility and candor can help dispel customer concerns.

Consider running a series of advertisements in the trade and business press in order to reach those in the marketplace with whom you can't interact personally. The ads we ran were reprinted and used as direct-mail pieces, giving additional exposure to our message. We also held a three-day conference for several hundred MODICON sales managers and representatives where they met their AEG counterparts and learned the benefits of the combined operation.

Accept leadership wherever you find it. Learn to treat overlapping product lines not as competitors but as worldwide partners. Play to the strengths of the partnership and avoid the tendency of acquirers to assume that they automatically dominate the relationship. A truly international company should champion leadership from its strongest unit, independent of nationality.

When AEG acquired MODICON and MODCOMP, we already had industrial-automation products and computer operations elsewhere in the company, principally in Europe. We knew we wanted to integrate each line of business into a global product division. And we could have simply folded the new companies into the existing business with a complete loss of identity and focus. Instead, we recognized that our American partners should be the undisputed centers of technological competence for all of AEG's efforts worldwide in those markets.

At the same time, we have balanced this business leadership with clear lines of management control. Our American companies do not direct our business worldwide, even though they drive some aspects of it, because AEG's corporate office in Frankfurt, Germany, is still in command. And while U.S. market strategy is developed in close cooperation with each individual business unit, that strategy is under central guidance through my office.

This is not an easy relationship for some U.S. managers to live with. But we believe it permits maximized strength and a more productive use of joint resources than is possible when companies choose the extremes of hands-off management or total dominance of acquired units.

Forge close relationships. To the extent possible, close the cultural gaps between your company and the newly acquired foreign subsidiary. At AEG we encourage daily personal contact with our foreign subsidiaries in order to develop strong working relationships. On the simplest level, we start our workday earlier in the U.S. so our American executives have more time to stay in touch by phone with their German counterparts.

There are other ways to get closer to an overseas business partner. One, of course, is to encourage employees of both the acquirer and the acquiree to learn each other's language. Another is to develop opportunities for employees to work overseas. I think we will see more short-term business exchange programs than in the past, and they will be aimed at employees at all levels, not just managers.

There are also some less formal approaches that help form close relationships. Employees of both the parent firm and the subsidiary should be encouraged to read a book or two about the other's country, and maybe even spend a vacation there. They should consider sending their children on summer exchange visits with the children of their business counterparts. Such efforts could all be encouraged through company subsidies. ■

Kurt Wiedenhaupt is president of AEG Corporation.

Chapter 12

"Global Managers for Global Businesses"

F. T. Murray and Alice Haller Murray

Preview

Skimming. Skim the article quickly to find the following general information.

1. Read the authors' names, the title, and all headings.

2. Read the abstract and first and second paragraphs, looking for the authors' purpose and main idea.

3. Read the last two paragraphs, looking for a summary or conclusion.

Questioning. Answer the following questions and discuss your answers in class.

1. What are some well-known global businesses?

2. What would a global manager have to know in order to be effective?

3. What characteristics should a global manager have?

Scanning. Scan the article quickly to find the following specific information.

1. What percentage of U.S. businesses reported that they had to recall or dismiss overseas personnel because of poor performance?

2. How much does it cost to maintain a U.S. family overseas?

3. What is the primary requisite for success in an overseas assignment?

4. What percent of American companies have formal training programs to prepare personnel for overseas work?

Soan Management Review 27, no. 2 (Winter 1986)

5. Why are Japanese companies willing to invest more heavily in training and supporting over-seas personnel?

Vocabulary in Context. Read the following sentences and try to guess the meaning of the italicized words by using the context. Then replace the italicized words with synonyms (words or phrases that have nearly the same or similar meanings).

1. "If we look closely, however, at the success rate of American *expatriates* compared with Japanese expatriates, we find that American managers and technicians assigned overseas *run* a poor second."

2. "From the *moment* of arrival in the country of assignment, the new Japanese manager or technician has a *mentor* who is reponsible for helping the newly arrived manager with any problem."

3. "The primary *requisite* for success in an overseas assignment is managerial or technical job *competence*. There are, however, two other requisites for success in working overseas."

4. "In our increasingly competitive global economy and market, an effective worldwide pres-ence is a necessity for any company that is not ready to *relinquish* the *field* to the Japanese and others."

5. "What these needs are can be determined by a person well grounded in intercultural affairs and familiar with the situations and frustrations likely to *plague* expatriates upon being *immersed* in another culture."

SMR Forum:
Global Managers for Global Businesses

F.T. Murray   **FAM Associates**
Alice Haller Murray   **FAM Associates**

The increasing global-ization of business pro-duces a need for effec-tive overseas managers. Among Japanese over-seas managers the fail-ure rate is quite low, while failures among American expatriate managers are quite common. What is the reason for this? What can be done about it? In this paper, the authors review the factors that make expatriate man-agers successful and outline how targeted training programs, modeled after the sys-tematic and thorough approach of Japanese companies, can reduce the failure rate and im-prove performance. Training in effective-ness and coping skills not only produces suc-cessful overseas man-agers, but successful overseas businesses as well. *Ed.*

1 Price, quality, a strong dollar. These are the reasons given for Japan's awesome penetra-tion of world markets. They're valid ones. But there's another factor that's fundamental to the Japanese success in becoming a global economic power: their understanding of and response to the needs and opportunities of foreign markets. Not by chance do they have this understanding; they've acquired it through a concerted effort to develop a corps of international managers and technicians adept at doing business in alien countries and cultures.

2 To date American companies have shown little evidence of realizing how much Ja-pan owes its phenomenal success to high-performing international managers. From the Japanese we've been willing to borrow techniques such as quality circles and just-in-time assembling, but we haven't asked ourselves if there's a lesson to be learned from the thoroughness with which Japanese companies go about equipping their expa-triate personnel for the exacting task of work-ing and living in an alien culture.

Costs of Failure

3 In the years since World War II American corporations have compiled an enviable record in penetrating foreign markets and building global businesses. A large share of the credit for globalizing the scope of Amer-ican business belongs to U.S. overseas man-agers, who have learned the ins and outs of doing business in a world of unfamiliar cus-toms and markets. If we look closely, how-ever, at the success rate of American expa-triates compared with Japanese expatriates, we find that American managers and techni-cians assigned overseas run a poor second.

4 A recent survey of large multinational corporations revealed the following: more than three quarters of the eighty U.S. corpora-tions responding reported that 10 to 40 per-cent of their personnel assigned overseas had to be recalled or dismissed because of poor performance — most of them people whose performance previous to the overseas assignment had been excellent. Only a quar-ter of the corporations reported a failure rate below 10 percent. Of the thirty-five Japanese companies responding, however, 86 percent reported a failure rate of less than 10 percent; no more than 14 percent stated their failure rate was over 10 percent; in no case did it reach 20 percent.[1]

5 The costs of the high American failure rate extend beyond the $150,000 to $250,000 per annum it costs to maintain a U.S. family overseas. Expatriate managers and techni-cians are key people. When a crisis makes it necessary to replace them, company opera-tions are disrupted and a period of lost op-portunities and profits ensues. At the same time valuable human assets are permanently lost to the company; even those whose per-formance prior to an overseas assignment was quite good rarely stay with the company after failing as expatriates.

6 In addition, it is safe to conclude that the same factors causing failures also act as a drag on the performance of those who man-age to complete overseas assignments. Typi-fying this is the remark of an American engineer who, after three years in Venezuela, said: "Here I'm only able to work at 30 per-cent of my effectiveness in the U.S."[2]

7 Is there something that can be done to re-duce this failure rate, and at the same time improve the performance of expatriate per-

F.T. Murray is President of FAM Associates and Adjunct Professor of Management at Connecticut State University. Dr. Murray holds the B.S. degree from Manhattan College, the M.P.A. degree from New York University, and the Ph.D. degree from California Western University. His consulting interests extend over a wide spectrum of organizational issues, including productivity, motivation, reorganization, managing change, and accelerated development of managers. He specializes in diagnosing the roots of unsatisfactory performance. Dr. Murray's articles have appeared in such journals as *Business and Society Review*, *Human Resource Management*, and *Training and Development Journal*.

sonnel who don't fail? A look at what Japanese multinationals do to keep their failure rate so low provides food for thought.

The Japanese Approach

8 Japanese managers and technicians do not set out on foreign assignments before their companies have thoroughly prepared them for the demanding task of working and living in an alien culture.[3] Japanese, like Americans, are attached to their homeland and enjoy living there. Leaving Japan to work and live elsewhere, their companies recognize, is much more than a relocation; it's a change with the impact of a dislocation. Therefore, with the same thorough, systematic approach used in attacking issues of quality and productivity, most Japanese companies have worked out comprehensive programs that ease this transition and equip their expatriate personnel to perform well in unfamiliar surroundings.

9 Normally Japanese companies make overseas assignments at least a year before actual departure. Assignees, in the year previous to departure, as part of their work, learn the culture, customs, and ways of doing business in the country for which they are destined. Generally they learn the language as well.

10 Such thorough pre-departure preparation is only the beginning. From the moment of arrival in the country of assignment, the new Japanese manager or technician has a mentor who is responsible for helping the newly arrived manager with any problem. Mentoring is not limited to the first few months of the assignment; it stretches out over a year or two until the new manager has become well acclimated.

11 In a person's performance appraisal at the end of the first year overseas, the company demonstrates its understanding that most of the first year is consumed in learning about the new country and adjusting to the way business is done there.

12 Meanwhile, the Japanese manager on a foreign assignment doesn't have to worry about his future in the company and wonder about whether or not they've forgotten about him back in corporate headquarters. He knows that his foreign assignment is an integral and necessary step in a career plan preparing him for future responsibilities.

13 Japanese managers and technicians, despite their insularity and strong attachment to their homeland, perform well on overseas assignments. What their companies do for them is:

— Equip them with the intercultural skills necessary to maintain a high level of performance in a different and demanding environment.

— Minimize the personal stress that results from encountering unanticipated situations and strains.

— Reduce the feeling of alienation from the company that inevitably accompanies foreign assignments.

— Ease the readjustment of both employees and family upon their return to Japan.

Success Factors

14 The primary requisite for success in an overseas assignment is managerial or technical job competence. American and Japanese companies, as their actions demonstrate, agree on this. There are, however, two other requisites for success in working overseas. One can be called *effectiveness* skills, which empower the expatriate to successfully translate his managerial and technical competence; in effect, this means that he reshapes his skills so that they fit a different set of relations with subordinates, business associates, and customers — as well as dealings with the regulatory, political, and market environment.[4]

15 No one is born with such skills. Everyone has to learn them. Proficiency in the home country constitutes a good groundwork for learning them, but skills that get the job done in one country lose something when transplanted to a country with different values,

Alice Haller Murray is a principal in FAM Associates. Ms. Murray holds the B.S. degree from Rogers College and the M.A. degree from St. Louis University. She has had twenty years' experience in consulting and administration, specializing in organizational improvement and training for intercultural understanding and competence. Ms. Murray has worked on such projects as equipping U.S. professionals for overseas assignments, analyzing language learning needs, designing and setting up language and orientation centers, team building, and resolving intergroup conflicts. She has lived and worked in Latin America.

customs, ways of doing business, and socioeconomic systems. Success for the expatriate, who has grown up and been socialized in a different culture, comes only after he has built an understanding of this new context and made adjustments in his previous way of working.

16 Also requisite for success overseas are *coping* skills, which enable a person to become reasonably comfortable, or at least survive, in a foreign environment. Not only the expatriate employee, but also his family, need these. Unless they learn to do without things easily available in the home country and to accept, respect, and eventually even enjoy unfamiliar and inconvenient customs and procedures, "culture fatigue" plays havoc with personal and family life and saps the energies of the expatriate employee.

17 Japanese companies, we have seen, recognizing the importance of effectiveness and coping skills, make a considerable investment to enable their expatriates to acquire them. American companies seem to ignore the critical importance of these skills, and evidence of this is their record of preparing expatriates for the transition to living and working overseas. Roughly 68 percent of American companies have no formal training programs to prepare personnel for overseas work. Of the 32 percent who do have formal training programs, the majority limit the training to informational briefing that provides a basic understanding of the country's sociopolitical history, geography, state of economic development, cultural institutions, and living conditions.[5]

Training That Pays

18 American companies have their reasons for not investing more heavily in preparing expatriates and their families for overseas assignments. Many, because of a policy of replacing expatriate personnel with host country nationals, send fewer people overseas than formerly. Also, since people assigned overseas frequently go out one or two at a time, it becomes awkward or impractical to

assemble a group for training, which many companies mistakenly assume can only be done in a group. But apparently it is the skepticism of many companies regarding the value of training for overseas that principally explains their neglect of it. These companies have learned by experience that informational briefing on a country makes little difference in the subsequent performance of overseas personnel.

19 Research corroborates the logic of their view. Informational briefings don't come to grips with the principal causes of failure. These, as mentioned above, are the entire family's inability to be comfortable in a new environment and the employee's inability to relate effectively to business and business associates in a foreign environment. Obviously, therefore, training for overseas, if it is to be worthwhile and cost effective, has to go beyond mere informational briefing. It needs to be training that targets the real needs of the expatriate, both job-related and familial, and focuses on the acquisition and practice of the special skills requisite for making a successful transition to working and living in an unfamiliar country.

20 The need for such training will not end soon. Although many expatriate personnel are being replaced by host country nationals, the increasing globalization of business and the need for effective links with corporate headquarters is producing an increase in the total number of Americans working overseas. Obviously there's a place for training programs that can reduce the high failure rate among American expatriates along with its concomitant costs.

21 More is at stake than reducing the number of failures. In our increasingly competitive global economy and market, an effective worldwide presence is a necessity for any company that is not ready to relinquish the field to the Japanese and others. Upgrading host country nationals to higher level positions is an important part of establishing a truly global, transnational presence. But it is not enough. For an American company to properly manage overseas operations, it needs American managers and technicians

who are at home in and can work effectively in other cultures.

Three Kinds of Expatriates

22 A growing number of expatriates are involved in technical assistance or the transfer of technology. It is common for their overseas stay to last no more than several months. The needs of such people may not be the same as those of longer term people. Short termers, provided their projects are tightly structured and their assignments clearly defined, can usually get by with a minimum of coping or survival skills — enough to stay out of trouble and remain whole. Such survival skills include:

— Some understanding of the uniqueness of the culture in which one works and what it means to live in it.

— A sufficient knowledge of self to recognize one's limitations and engage in activities that will make life in an alien land tolerable.

Long-term expatriates, on the other hand, need more than survival skills. They are required to operate in a variety of open-ended situations. Therefore only effectiveness skills will enable them to know what to expect, how to read cues and subtleties correctly, how things get done, how problems are handled, and how to adjust their personal and managerial style to the foreign culture. In addition, if, over the long run, they are going to avoid succumbing to culture fatigue, they will have to acquire the ability not only to respect and appreciate the "differentness" of another culture, but also recognize its value and enjoy it. Some short termers, those working in difficult projects with tight time schedules and a variety of open-ended situations, will need the same effectiveness skills as long-term people.

23 Another type is the expatriate in the U.S. As part of technology transfer contracts, American companies often bring citizens of other countries to the U.S. for training. These expatriate trainees also need help in making the transition to life in another country. While living in the U.S. is usually a welcome experience for them, they too face the problem of crossing a cultural threshold and adjusting to a country where people behave differently.

Targeting the Needs

24 Each of the three groups mentioned above has distinct needs, and individuals in each of the groups have their own special ones. Providing generalized preparation on the assumption that all have identical needs satisfies only in small measure the needs of any. To ensure that individuals get what they need and are not exposed to time-consuming activities of little use, they must be given customized training that is based on a sound analysis of individual needs.

25 What these needs are can be determined by a person well grounded in intercultural affairs and familiar with the situations and frustrations likely to plague expatriates upon being immersed in another culture. Such an interculturally skilled person — after conducting interviews with those destined to go overseas, with people who have already worked in the country of assignment, and with executives of the company — can sketch out two profiles for each person assigned. One profile will project the know-how and skills requisite for success in the new job; the other will indicate the assignee's ability to cope and adjust. The guidance provided by the two profiles makes it possible to design and implement training that fits the assignee and equips him with the understanding and skills required to close the gap between the demands of the new job and his present state.

26 Assignees can be directly involved in making up the profiles that will determine the focus of their training by having them do a personal self-assessment. This active participation in diagnosing one's own needs starts the training on the right foot. While making the assignee co-responsible for his

own training, it gives him a clear understanding of the skills he must acquire to be successful.

27 To have optimal impact the training should be problem-centered and particularized to the country of assignment. Problems encountered in France are not the same as those met in Zimbabwe. To fit in with Saudis and do business with them a person doesn't act as with the Japanese. With the profiles previously mentioned the training effort can focus on the situations and problems that will actually be encountered in Japan, Saudi Arabia, or Cameroon.

28 What will this training look like? Good training concentrates on the acquisition and practice of skills. It incorporates conceptual and attitudinal training only insofar as necessary to underpin and reinforce the skills that ultimately determine whether a person performs satisfactorily or not.

29 The diagnostic profiles provide trainers with the information needed to develop customized training activities, which permit trainees to learn and practice the coping and effectiveness skills their assignment requires. The profiles indicate whether the skills needed are in listening, negotiation, consensual decision-making, etc. The best training methodology to use in developing such skills consists of analysis and role play of critical incidents, case studies, reality practice, and group discussions.[6]

30 For the most part, the American companies who do have programs to train expatriate personnel limit the training to pre-departure orientation. Japanese companies, however, not only begin training personnel destined for overseas long before departure, they keep a close watch on their expatriate personnel and continue to support them after they have reached their overseas posts. Naturally American companies are not going to blindly imitate the Japanese. But seeing how the Japanese extend the training and support of their expatriate personnel over a protracted period prompts us to question whether pre-departure training by itself can adequately sustain an expatriate through a whole assignment.

31 Usually about six months to a year after arrival in an unfamiliar country, the newness of an assignment has worn thin. The expatriate, feeling more acutely the strain of working in a different environment, has reached a personal low in his adjustment cycle. This is the time, especially in the case of very difficult and trying assignments, when expatriates and their families can benefit from a fresh infusion of support to help them cope with isolation, loneliness, and disappointment.

32 By giving them an opportunity to gather together and talk about their successes and failures in adjusting to the country, the people, and the customs, they get a new lease on life overseas. They come to a fuller understanding of what has been happening to them and discover new insights on how to cope. With actual experience behind them, they are now ready to sharpen and refine the effectiveness skills specific to their own situation in a specific culture. They may, for example, need to learn more about how to communicate and develop a unified work group. At this juncture, work sessions dealing with problems encountered on the job are a very effective training method.[7]

Conclusion: Investing for a Future

33 Japanese companies are willing to invest more heavily in training and supporting their expatriates because they stay longer in overseas assignments than Americans. Certainly, the shorter an assignment, the less sense it makes to invest substantially in training for it. If, however, American expatriates were better trained for overseas assignments, they might stay longer. The training would enable them to adjust more successfully to another culture. Thanks to getting a good start through appropriate skills training, they would find themselves progressing in effectiveness and perhaps become willing to prolong their stay — particularly if they were given assurance that a prolonged stay would not jeopardize their future career. And companies will benefit from

the superior performance that only comes with time and experience in another culture.

34 What we've outlined here is an approach, not a blueprint. Each company has to work out and implement programs that fit its own special circumstances and limitations. This, though not a simple task, is doable. And considering the stakes involved, doing a good job in preparing and maintaining expatriate personnel will easily produce a good return on investment. Perhaps it is later than we think. Unless the training of expatriates is upgraded, American companies may soon discover that their life expectancies as global businesses are limited.

References

1
R.L. Tung, *Key to Japan's Economic Strength: Human Power* (Lexington, MA: D.C. Heath, 1984), pp. 15–16.

2
J. Seward, "Speaking the Japanese Business Language," *European Business*, Winter 1975, p. 40ff. shows that this is not an isolated case.

3
Described in *Japan Economic News*, June 24, 1982.

4
For a discussion of what causes failure, see R.D. Hays, "Expatriate Selection: Insuring Success and Avoiding Failure," *Journal of International Business Studies*, 5 (1974): 25–37.

5
R.L. Tung (1984), p. 13.

6
Examples of such methodologies are found in: D.S. Hoopes and P. Ventura, *Intercultural Sourcebook: Cross-Cultural Training Methodologies* (Chicago, IL: Intercultural Press, 1979).

7
Another time of transition and stress occurs when the expatriate completes a foreign assignment and comes back home. A company concerned about developing and maintaining high caliber international personnel will not neglect the problems of this re-entry. The familiar has now turned into the unfamiliar. The returning expatriates have to adjust to doing the job the way it's done in the U.S. They need to relearn old work values, practices, and customs, and also familiarize themselves with new ones introduced during their absence. It helps if they can discuss the expectations and problems associated with returning home.

Glossary

acclimated	accustomed to different climate, environment, or circumstances
acquisition	acquiring, getting
acutely	sharply, severely
alien	foreign, belonging to another country or people
alienation	separation
awesome	great, superior
blindly	recklessly, without sound logic
competence	condition of being well qualified, capable, fit
compiled	put together
conceptual	of concepts, ideas, thoughts
concerted	mutually agreed upon, combined
concomitant	accompanying
consensual	involving mutual consent, agreement
constitutes	makes up, composes
consumed	used up, spent
corroborates	confirms, supports
cues	indirect suggestions, hints
customized	made according to individual or personal specifications
destined	intended, headed for
diagnosing	carefully examining and analyzing facts
dislocation	disruption, upsetting the order
disrupted	disturbed, interrupted
doable	can be done
ease	to make easier, facilitate
empower	to give power or authority to, give ability to, enable
encountering	facing
ensues	follows immediately, happens as a consequence
exacting	arduous, demanding great effort, making severe demands
expatriate	living outside one's native land
familial	involving a family
fatigue	exhaustion, weariness
field	area where competitive activity is taking place
grounded	educated
groundwork	foundation, basis
immersed	deeply absorbed, engrossed
implement	to carry out, accomplish
inevitably	cannot be avoided, certainly
infusion	inspiration, instilling
insights	clear understandings of the inner nature of certain things
insularity	narrow-mindedness, provincialism, isolation
integral	essential, necessary for completeness
jeopardize	to endanger, put at risk
life expectancies	expectation of remaining alive or useful
mentor	wise, loyal advisor or teacher

multinational	a corporation with branches in a number of countries
open-ended	having no set limits, unrestricted, open to change
optimal	most favorable or desirable, best
per annum	by the year, annually
performance appraisal	evaluation of how well a person meets the requirements of a job or carries out responsibilities
plague	to trouble, annoy
project	to propose a plan of action for the future
prolong	to lengthen or extend in time
protracted	prolonged, extended
regulatory	relating to regulations, rules, laws, systems
relinquish	to give up, abandon, surrender
relocation	moving to a new location
requisite	requirement
saps	weakens, exhausts
skepticism	doubting attitude
sound	accurate, reliable, sensible
stakes	reward, prize
subsequent	later, following
substantially	considerably, heavily
subtleties	fine distinctions in meaning, delicate suggestions
succumbing	giving way to, yielding, submitting
sustain	to support, strengthen the spirits of
tolerable	able to be tolerated, endurable; fairly good
transnational	transcending the interests of a single nation, concerning many nations
typifying	symbolizing, exemplifying
underpin	to support or strengthen
uniqueness	unusualness
upgrading	promoting to a more skilled job, raising in importance

Vocabulary

Without referring to the article, fill in the blanks in the following sentences with the correct words from this list. You may change the tense, number, or form of the words to fit the context. Use each word only once; not all of the words on the list will be used.

| mentor | alien | multinational | expatriate | relinquish | requisite | prolong |
| subtlety | acquisition | acutely | | insularity | plague | customize | jeopardize |

1. The Japanese are successful as a global power because their overseas employees are skilled

   at doing business in _____ countries.

2. _____ personnel need extensive training and thorough preparation for the _____

   _____ involved in adapting to foreign cultures while working outside their native

   countries.

3. Surveys show that a large percentage of overseas personnel of U.S. _____ corporations had to be recalled or fired because of their unsatisfactory performance.

4. Assigning a(n) _____ to a new manager to help with any problems is one technique used by Japanese companies to ensure that their overseas employees become acclimated to the foreign country.

5. There are three _____ for achieving success in working overseas: (1) managerial competence, (2) effectiveness skills, and (3) coping skills.

6. Overseas training should emphasize the _____ and practice of the particular skills needed for working and living in a foreign culture.

7. Unless U.S. companies are willing to _____ the global market to Japan and other competitors, they must improve the effectiveness of their overseas managers and technicians.

8. Expatriates need guidance from people experienced in intercultural affairs and familiar with the common problems that _____ overseas personnel.

9. Japanese companies offer their overseas employees _____ training and long-term support; however, most American companies provide brief general training and limited support.

10. American expatriates often worry that lengthy assignments overseas will _____ their future careers, so they are unwilling to _____ their stay.

Idioms and Expressions

Read the paragraphs in which the following italicized idioms and expressions are found. Then circle the letter next to the answer that best describes the meaning of the idiom as used in the context of the article.

1. "... U.S. overseas managers, who have learned the *ins and outs* of doing business in a world of unfamiliar customs and markets." (Paragraph 3)
   a. government regulations
   b. daily schedule
   c. details and complexities

2. "... we find that American managers and technicians assigned overseas *run a poor second*." (Paragraph 3)
   a. are much worse than [someone else]
   b. are not improving
   c. are very slow in adjusting

3. "... the same factors causing failures also *act as a drag on* the performance of those who manage to complete overseas assignments." (Paragraph 6)
   a. influence
   b. weaken
   c. strengthen

4. "A look at what Japanese multinationals do to keep their failure rate so low provides *food for thought*." (Paragraph 7)
   a. answers
   b. worthwhile ideas
   c. arguments

5. ". . . skills that get the job done in one country *lose something* when transplanted to a country with different values. . . ." (Paragraph 15)
   a. become less effective
   b. disappear entirely
   c. are unnecessary

6. ". . . 'culture fatigue' *plays havoc with* personal and family life. . . ." (Paragraph 16)
   a. causes disagreements in
   b. causes anxiety in
   c. causes disruption in

7. "Informational briefings don't *come to grips with* the principal causes of failure." (Paragraph 19)
   a. properly deal with
   b. briefly talk about
   c. accidentally overlook

8. "More is *at stake* than reducing the number of failures." (Paragraph 21)
   a. to be gained or lost
   b. to be analyzed
   c. to be considered

9. ". . . if, *over the long run,* they are going to avoid succumbing to culture fatigue . . ." (Paragraph 22)
   a. in general
   b. for the entire time
   c. in the future

10. "This active participation in diagnosing one's own needs starts the training *on the right foot*." (Paragraph 26)
    a. efficiently
    b. correctly
    c. quickly

11. "To *fit in with* Saudis and do business with them a person doesn't act as with the Japanese." (Paragraph 27)
    a. adapt to
    b. imitate
    c. accept

12. "Usually about six months to a year after arrival in an unfamiliar country, the newness of an assignment *has worn thin*." (Paragraph 31)
   a. has become more interesting
   b. has decreased
   c. has changed

13. ". . . they *get a new lease on life* overseas." (Paragraph 32)
   a. become full of energy again
   b. gain more knowledge of life
   c. get a different perspective on life

Paraphrasing

Read the following sentences carefully, and then rewrite them using your own words. Change the vocabulary and sentence structure, but do not change the authors' intended meaning or paraphrase any technical terms. There are several ways of paraphrasing each sentence.

Original: "Not by chance do they have this understanding."
Paraphrase: That they have such an understanding is not accidental.

1. "They've acquired it through a concerted effort to develop a corps of international managers and technicians adept at doing business in alien countries and cultures." (Paragraph 1)

   _____

   _____

2. "Japanese managers and technicians, despite their insularity and strong attachment to their homeland, perform well on overseas assignments." (Paragraph 13)

   _____

   _____

3. "But apparently it is the skepticism of many companies regarding the value of training for overseas that principally explains their neglect of it." (Paragraph 18)

   _____

   _____

4. "Unless the training of expatriates is upgraded, American companies may soon discover that their life expectancies as global businesses are limited." (Paragraph 34)

   _____

   _____

Comprehension

Answer the following questions by finding the relevant information in the article. Give the numbers of the paragraphs that contain the answers.

1. What is the main idea of this article?

2. What are the costs of the high American failure rate in overseas personnel?

3. What have Japanese companies done to equip their expatriate personnel to perform well on foreign assignments?

4. What are effectiveness skills?

5. What are coping skills?

6. Why don't American companies invest more heavily in preparing expatriates and their families for overseas assignments?

7. What are the principal causes of failure of American overseas personnel?

8. What is the difference between the types of skills needed by short-term expatriates and those needed by long-term expatriates?

9. What methods can be used to analyze the individual needs of overseas personnel before they are given the appropriate training?

10. Why is continued support of overseas personnel necessary and effective?

11. What would be the benefits of giving American expatriates better training?

Inference/Interpretation

Circle the letter next to the best answer. Choose your answer according to the meaning the authors suggest but do not state explicitly.

1. It can be inferred from the article that success in an overseas assignment (Paragraphs 14–16)
    a. depends equally on technical job competence, effectiveness skills, and coping skills.
    b. depends mostly on effectiveness skills.
    c. depends mostly on technical job competence, but effectiveness skills and coping skills are necessary.
    d. depends mostly on effectiveness and coping skills.

2. We can infer from the article that the phrase "culture fatigue" means (Paragraph 16)
    a. exhaustion resulting from working hard in a foreign environment.
    b. exhaustion resulting from facing family problems in a foreign environment.
    c. exhaustion resulting from failing to adapt to a foreign environment.
    d. exhaustion resulting from successfully adapting to a foreign environment.

3. It can be inferred from the article that the entire family's adjustment to a foreign environment is (Paragraph 19)
   a. less important than the employee's adjustment.
   b. just as important as the employee's adjustment.
   c. more important than the employee's adjustment.
   d. more difficult to achieve than the employee's adjustment.

4. We can infer from the article that "Perhaps it is later than we think" means (Paragraph 34)
   a. American companies may have already been beaten by Japan in the global business market.
   b. American companies should reconsider sending personnel overseas.
   c. American companies should send more personnel overseas.
   d. American companies should implement comprehensive training programs for expatriate personnel immediately.

Structure

Circle the letter next to the correct answer(s). More than one answer may be correct. Be prepared to explain and justify your choices.

1. In which paragraph(s) is the main idea stated?
   a. Paragraph 2
   b. Paragraph 3
   c. Paragraph 14
   d. Paragraph 33
   e. Paragraph 34
   Write a paraphrase of the main idea in *one* sentence, using your own words as much as possible.

   _____

2. In paragraph 6, what is the purpose of the quotation from an American engineer ("Here I'm only able to work at 30 percent of my effectiveness in the U.S.")?
   a. To show how difficult it is to work in an alien culture
   b. To show how few employees complete overseas assignments
   c. To show how failures occur in overseas assignments
   d. To show the negative attitude of American expatriates
   e. To show the weak performance of American expatriates

3. List the four sets of causes and effects discussed in paragraph 18.

Causes	Effects
a. _____	_____
b. _____	_____
c. _____	_____
d. _____	_____

4. What overall method of development is used in this article?
   a. Chronologically describing a process
   b. Defining a technical system
   c. Analyzing a new technique
   d. Justifying an argument by contrasting two approaches
   e. Refuting the assumptions of an argument

Style

Circle the letter next to the correct answer(s). More than one answer may be correct. Be prepared to justify your choices by giving specific examples from the article.

1. How would you describe the writing style of the authors?
   a. Technical
   b. Businesslike
   c. Poetic
   d. Journalistic
   e. Formal
   f. Impersonal

2. How would you describe the tone of the article?
   a. Ambiguous
   b. Sarcastic
   c. Critical
   d. Analytical
   e. Emotional
   f. Witty

3. The authors' attitude toward Japanese success in becoming a global economic power can be described as
   a. admiring.
   b. envious.
   c. indifferent.
   d. angry.
   e. concerned.
   f. surprised.

4. The authors use a complex structure in the following sentence: "In addition, if, over the long run, they [long-term expatriates] are going to avoid succumbing to culture fatigue, they will have to acquire the ability not only to respect and appreciate the 'differentness' of another culture, but also recognize its value and enjoy it" (Paragraph 22). What is the cause and what is the effect in this sentence?

Discussion

1. How essential are comprehensive and extensive training programs for preparing employees for foreign assignments?

2. How important is it to know the language of the country you are assigned to in order to succeed in your assignment?

3. Can a person in a foreign country really learn to "accept, respect, and eventually even enjoy unfamiliar and inconvenient customs and procedures"? How can this be accomplished?

4. Why is it difficult to do business in a country whose culture is different from yours? Give specific examples of problems that could occur.

5. What other reasons besides better training programs could explain the difference in failure rates between Japanese and American overseas personnel?

6. Have you ever experienced "culture fatigue"? How does it affect an individual?

Research Assignment

Look up several of these articles in the library. Choose one article to read and take notes on.

Barnum, Cynthia F. "The Making of a Global Business Diplomat." *Management Review* 78 (November 1989): 59–60.

"Breaking the Sushi Barrier." *Business Month* 135 (April 1990): 56–60.

Carey, Patricia M. "The Making of a Global Manager." *North American International Business* 3 (June 1990): 36–41.

Fadiman, Jeffrey A. "A Traveler's Guide to Gifts and Bribes." *Harvard Business Review* 64 (July-August 1986): 122–36.

Fallows, J. M. "So You'll Be Moving to Asia." *Fortune* 120 (Fall 1989): 91ff.

Guterl, Fred V. "Europe's Secret Weapon." *Business Month* 134 (October 1989): 63–66.

Hall, Edward T. "The Silent Language in Overseas Business." *Harvard Business Review* 38 (May-June 1960): 87–96.

Knotts, Rose. "Cross-Cultural Management: Transformations and Adaptations." *Business Horizons* 32 (January-February 1989): 29–33.

Ohmae, Kenichi. "Managing in a Borderless World." *Harvard Business Review* 67 (May-June 1989): 152–61.

Otsubo, Mayumi. "A Guide to Japanese Business Practices." *California Management Review* 28 (Spring 1986): 28–42.

Powell, Bill. "Serving Mother Yen." *Business Month* 135 (April 1990): 61.

Rau, Pradeep A., and John K. Ryans, Jr. "An Executive's Guide to E. C.—1992: A Glossary of Terms." *Business* 39 (July-August-September 1989): 48–50.

Reich, Robert B. "Who Is Them?" *Harvard Business Review* 69 (March-April 1991): 77–88.

Seward, J. "Speaking the Japanese Business Language." *European Business* (Winter 1975): 40ff.

Stewart, Thomas A. "How to Manage in the New Era." *Fortune* 121 (January 15, 1990): 59–72.

Tully, S. "The Hunt for the Global Manager." *Fortune* 121 (May 21, 1990): 140–44.

Whitehill, A. M. "American Executives through Foreign Eyes." *Business Horizons* 32 (May-June 1989): 42–48.

Work, Clemens P. "If This Is Belgium, It Must Be Tuesday." *U.S. News & World Report* 109 (July 16, 1990): 31–32.

Wright, P. "Doing Business in Islamic Markets." *Harvard Business Review* 59 (January-February 1981): 34–40.

Oral Presentation

Working with a small group, give a fifteen-minute oral presentation to the class on the articles that you chose in the research assignment. Include the author's main idea, major points, and some supporting data. Be prepared to answer questions on your topic. (See Appendix B: Giving an Oral Presentation.)

Writing Assignments

1. Write a short report in which you analyze and evaluate the factors that determine the success or failure of expatriate managerial employees. Based on your analysis, recommend the kind of training program a global company should implement for its global managers. Use the additional reading in this chapter and the articles listed in the research assignment. In the report, describe the type of person who is well suited for being an expatriate manager. Include a 100-word abstract (very short summary) as the first section of the report.

    Use parenthetical references in the author-date system for each of the sources you cite: (Otsubo 1986). You may also choose to give the page number: (Otsubo 1986, 29). List all sources at the end of your report as References. Entries should be alphabetized according to the last name of the author: Otsubo, Mayumi. 1986. "A Guide to Japanese Business Practices." *California Management Review* 28: 28–42.

    Purpose Statement: The purpose of this report is to analyze and evaluate the major factors that determine the success of a global manager.

    Thesis: It is recommended that . . .

Format:
    I. Abstract (Purpose, Conclusions, Recommendation)
    II. Introduction (Background, Purpose, Thesis)
    III. Discussion (Success Factors)
    IV. Discussion (Failure Factors)
    V. Conclusion (Recommendation)

2. Discuss the problems that could prevent an American company from doing business successfully in your country. What cultural, religious, political, regulatory, or economic conditions could prove difficult for American personnel? Use cause-effect organization.

3. If you could live and work in any country in the world, which country would you choose and why?

Peer Critique

Choose a person to work with. After you have completed your writing assignment, let your partner read and critique your writing. Then you will read and critique his or her writing. Use the Writing Evaluation Form in Appendix F.

Case Study: A Problem in Being a Global Manager

Working in groups, read the following case study. Discuss the problem, answer the questions, and write a brief report on how your group would solve the problem. (Choose one member of the group to do the writing.) Follow the format in Appendix E (Case Study Report) in writing your report.

Ted Jordon works for Global Manufacturing Corporation. For the past six months he has been on an overseas assignment in Tokyo as the Manager of Business Development. His family (wife Dorothy, teenage children Sam and Laurie) are with him in Tokyo. They are living in a quiet suburb of the city in a small but comfortable home.

When offered this overseas assignment, Ted discussed the pros and cons with Dorothy. They both decided that this was a good opportunity and that Ted should accept the offer; even the children agreed. Because Ted (and his family) had never lived abroad, they were a little anxious about the relocation, but they felt better after Global's two-day informational briefing on working overseas. During their first few months in Tokyo, Ted and the whole family were very happy and excited about their new environment. Ted plunged into his challenging job enthusiastically, Dorothy began flower-arranging and painting classes, and the children entered the American junior high school.

Now, however, it is December, and the family's spirits are quite low. Ted's job has proven much more difficult than he envisioned. Production is not on schedule, budgets have been overrun, and several key personnel (Japanese) are not performing well. Dorothy, who took a leave of absence from her high school teaching job to come to Japan, is missing her work. The children haven't been able to make any good friends, American or Japanese. Furthermore, no one in the family speaks Japanese. Despite their weekly lessons, they can't seem to catch on to the language.

With Christmas fast approaching, Ted has decided to ask for a month's leave to take his family home for the holidays. In fact, he is thinking of resigning his position and not returning to Japan.

He knows he has failed to adjust to the Japanese business environment and to the customs of the country, but he doesn't understand why his usually excellent job performance has undergone such a negative change. If only he knew more about Japan and Japanese cultural values.

Ted's boss in the United States, Richard Connolly, is also displeased with Ted's performance. He is wondering whether to recall Ted to the states, but he is somewhat reluctant to do so, considering the costs expended in relocating his entire family to Tokyo. He has often thought back to how much Ted and his family enjoyed the company's two-day informational briefing last summer and what an outstanding manager Ted had been in the United States. Richard would never have predicted this situation. Of course, Ted is not the first Global employee to fail in an overseas assignment. Richard is aware that Global has a major problem in regard to expatriate personnel.

Questions

1. What should Richard Connolly do to solve this problem?

2. Should Ted Jordon resign from Global?

3. What alternatives does Ted Jordon have?

4. What type of training should Ted and his family have had? Is it too late?

5. What methods of support could Global give to Ted and his family?

Solution: Case Study Report

I. Define and analyze the problem.
II. Suggest possible solutions.
III. Evaluate possible solutions.
IV. Select a solution.

Case Study Business Writing Assignment: Memorandum

Write a memo from Ted Jordon to his supervisor, Richard Connolly, giving a status report on his job in Japan. The memo should list the major problems Ted has encountered and offer his analysis of the causes of these problems. It should also contain a tentative and unofficial request for a new assignment in the United States.

Format:
I. Introduction (Background and Main Idea)
II. Discussion (Problems and Analysis)
III. Closing (Request for Reassignment)

Style: Formal
Tone: Objective and analytical

Case Study Business Writing Assignment: Memorandum

Write a memo from Richard Connolly to Ted Jordon in response to Ted's memo. (See preceding writing assignment.) Discuss Ted's problems, offer solutions, and answer his request for reassignment.

Format:
    I. Introduction (Background and Main Idea)
    II. Discussion (Problems and Solutions)
    III. Closing (Response to Request)

Style: Informal
Tone: Subjective and friendly

Additional Reading

"Sorry, Wrong Number"
Peter G. W. Keen
Business Month 135 (January 1990): 62–67

HERCULES MOTORS OF Detroit and Prometheus PLC of London are collaborating on a high-stakes global venture. The goal: to produce a $35,000 sports car that would attract huge numbers of buyers in the U.S. and Europe. The project, which involves technical and administrative managers in 10 countries, is well past the design stage. Just as the enthusiasm of the companies' top executives has heightened, the venture has reached a stalemate. U.S. engineers, who assumed the Europeans would follow their lead, are frustrated by a lack of progress. Across the Atlantic, their colleagues say they are tired of catering to Americans who won't even listen to their ideas, let alone accept one of them. "Work here is at a stand-

still," says an American manager. "We have no idea how we can get these people working together." Will the big auto companies ever solve their problem?

They'd better. There's far more than one joint venture at risk. Every big American company today is part of a global market—whether it wants to be or not—and will have to learn to deal across national and cultural borders. The notion of a company doing $500 million a year in sales and confining itself to the U.S. is increasingly obsolete. More likely than not, that kind of company will soon be swallowed up by a foreign competitor with an international bent. Today, if a U.S. company is in a business where the Japanese are not a problem, it is undoubtedly in the wrong business. The more astute American companies do

not fear a Fortress Europe after the Common Market becomes more unified in 1992; they have already established themselves there.

Today's successful managers, like the ones at the mythical Hercules Motors, must manufacture and sell in many other nations. But first they must learn how to deal with managers from other cultures—and then use the expanding array of technology at their disposal to communicate with them. A recent *Financial Times* survey concluded, "Suffice it to say that from now on individual careers will be hampered, and employing organizations' resources be wasted, by ignorance of how the rest of the world works." Unfortunately for them, many American executives are woefully unaware of how to survive in the global markets. When it comes to communicating across cultures, their European counterparts say Americans are at best naive and at worst ignorant and incompetent.

Part of the problem is upbringing. A generation of American managers has been indoctrinated in the Peter Drucker school, which teaches that "manager knows most, therefore manager knows best." The attitude is hardened at business schools, where every student thinks he or she is a CEO, skilled in all facets of every trade. Americans so trained aren't ready to form teams whose members speak several different languages and view markets in different ways. Many Americans think they know Europe because they know where the good hotels are. But knowing the desk clerk at the Paris Hilton is not knowing how a French executive thinks and operates. Critics say American parochialism is reminiscent of the British attitude after World War II—a posture that helped push Britain into a long-term economic decline.

The list of American demerits is long. U.S. managers have a minimal understanding of what 1992 entails, Europeans say. Furthermore, Americans assume that U.S. trends in matters such as regulation will automatically be followed abroad. Often, Americans are said simply to misread

SORRY, WRONG NUMBER

When it comes to cross-cultural communications, why can't American companies connect?

BY PETER G.W. KEEN

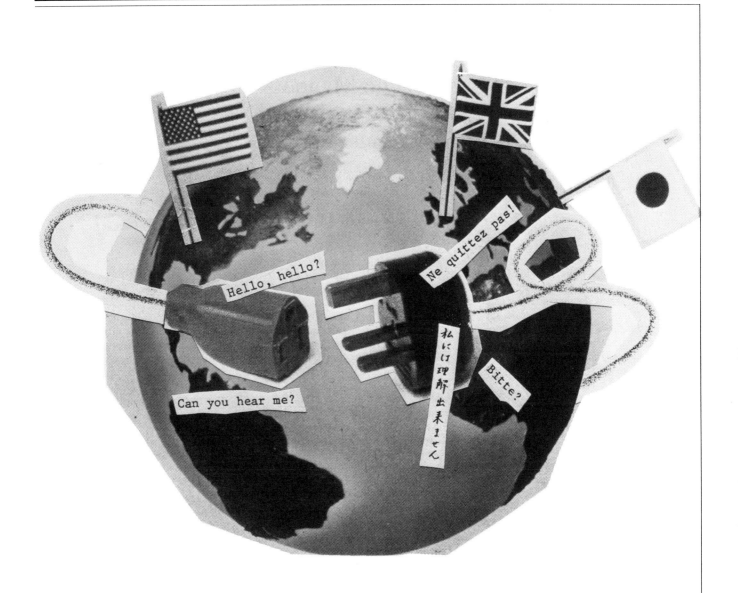

events. Many, for instance, think that British Telecom is no longer a regulated company because the British government sold it to the public. Americans can't, or won't, understand that in many business areas, Europeans are more advanced. Europe's companies, for example, can respond faster to changing market conditions because they are far better at using electronic technology to link themselves with their customers and suppliers.

Often Americans don't know what they don't know. U.S. managers feel at home with British executives simply because they speak the same language. What they don't realize is that at times they ought to look at the Brit-

ish as English-speaking Japanese. They would then realize that when the Brits seem to be dawdling, they are really saying no. When Americans push for a yes anyway, they reinforce the British image of pushy Americans who think talking louder will improve communications.

Americans are the worst offenders, but other nationalities fail cross-cultural tests, too. Europeans often suspect that American companies won't assign their top executives to international projects and that they are dealing with falling stars rather than rising ones. (This suspicion may have been justified years ago but is no longer valid.) The French may be formal to a

fault and, like Americans, think that top managers are supposed to lead, not listen. Impeccably dressed Italian executives are bewildered when a U.S. manager comes to a meeting in a blue blazer, no matter how well cut or expensive the jacket might be. British mangers often use humor to indicate that they are extremely serious or even antagonistic. But humor falls dead with the always-serious Germans and Swiss (there may be no such thing as a Swiss joke). Deciphering the actions of the Japanese, of course, has long been the biggest problem in transnational communication. Troubles between Japanese companies and Americans who run their U.S. subsidiaries have been legion, running from suspicion to downright deceit.

Retraining Americans to be truly international executives is no small chore. It can't be done by dragging them to a few seminars or showing them a video on how to bow when greeting a Japanese colleague. Global-minded companies send their best young executives to assignments around the world. Up-and-coming cosmopolitan managers read the *Financial Times* and *The World Press Review*, not just *The Wall Street Journal*. They travel to Liverpool as well as to London—having discovered that they learn far more in the industrial heartland than at company headquarters. Wherever they go, they listen. It may not be necessary to learn another language or two, but it might help. Institut Européen d'Administration des Affaires (INSEAD), Europe's leading business school, tries to attract students who have lived in two cultures and who speak a second language. The atmosphere at INSEAD forces students to see how different cultures approach the same business problems.

Companies that listen might end up making major changes in the way they do business. Most European companies, for instance, attack the global market with a federation of largely autonomous national units. Harvard professor Christopher Bartlett explains the system in his recent book, *Managing Across Borders*. The businesses in any one country have the advantage of being close to their customers and to the local political scene. The units are coordinated by headquarters, but not so much as to stifle innovation. Nestlé, Shell, and IBM Europe all operate this way. American and Japanese companies may set up what look like autonomous national units, but they often fail to give them full rein.

U.S. managers might do well to put themselves behind the desk of a Dutch or Swedish executive. As small nations, the Netherlands and Sweden have been forced to trade internationally and communicate across cultural lines. It is not surprising that in the past year, Swedish businesses have ac-

Techno-Manners For the Millennium

We recently interrupted a book tour by Miss Manners (aka Judith Martin), the doyenne of etiquette, to get her advice on how to use the latest technologies without alienating colleagues or customers. It is a topic she covers extensively in her fifth book of advice, *Miss Manners' Guide for the Turn-of-the-Millennium* (Pharos Books, $24.95). Over salad at the Ritz in Dearborn, Michigan, she set BUSINESS MONTH staff writer Alex Prud'homme straight on how to deal with "stuff that flashes tiny red lights at you." Some snippets of their (very polite) conversation:

AP: *People get surprisingly emotional about their widgets. Take answering machines: The legitimacy of call screening seems to polarize people almost as much as religion or politics.*

MM: For all these decades, people have accepted the notion that if the phone rings, you must interrupt whatever you're doing—having a nap or eating a meal or making love—to answer it. I never accepted this. Now, there are rude and polite ways to discriminate, but if you don't discriminate at all, your life is not your own. You're like the girl who can't say no—then you have to do it with everybody!

AP: *But there are those who believe that screening calls is like playing God.*

MM: Do they screen their mail, or do they give it all equal attention? Do they have front doors on their houses? Or do they say, It is playing God to decide who can come into my house and who can't, so I will leave the door open all the time, any hour, day or night? There is nothing wrong with setting up hierarchies.

AP: *If that is the case, what's so horrible about call waiting?*

MM: The principle there is last come, first served. You drop the person you are with because the next one might be better. You are saying, I am important and have to attend to a lot of things, but you can stay in limbo. That is rude and unfair. If your life is that urgent, perhaps you should hire some deputies.

AP: *Sure, but we don't always have time to play telephone tag. What do you do if you're unavoidably stuck on power hold?*

MM: It's obvious the people you are trying to talk to are not equipped to handle the business they have. You don't have to stay on hold. If you do get stuck there, the person handling calls should check back periodically. In turn, you should be gracious about providing minimal information, including, What is the call about?—a question that offends a lot of people. Never mind that Mr. Bigwig knows all about you and has your number.

AP: *You really feel ambivalent about the telephone, don't you?*

MM: The telephone has a false sense of urgency that leads people to deal with it immediately. Time and time again, I've seen businesspeople abandon live customers with money in hand for someone on the phone, which always seemed puzzling. It's not only a violation of etiquette; it's also bad business.

AP: *Don't you find such toys as porta-*

ble phones and beepers obnoxious?

MM: If I drive into your car while I'm on the car phone, then you may have a legitimate complaint, but I don't object to using the tool as long as you are within the etiquette of the situation. Talking on a phone on a public bus is no different from having a conversation, really. As for beepers, well, if you are so essential to the continuation of civilization that not a moment can go by when you can't be reached, use the beeper that vibrates instead of beeping. If your pocket starts quivering during a symphony concert and you wish quietly to excuse yourself, fine.

AP: *Surely, then, you must despise faxes.*

MM: I love my fax! It makes one quiet little beep and then sits there patiently waiting for me to attend to it. I think that's very civilized. But junk fax, where I am paying for the paper and my machine is tied up, is awful.

AP: *Some people use the office computer almost as much as the phone to communicate. Is it acceptable to send personal notes by electronic mail?*

MM: No! You are working on office time and on office equipment. Besides, it carries it's own punishment: The minute you write 'It was heaven last night, darling' to a coworker, or put your diary in your private file, there will be an accident and it will show up on your boss's screen.

AP: *With all the hoo-ha surrounding these new gizmos, are there underlying rules of etiquette that apply to things we haven't even seen yet?*

MM: You can invent 10 million different noisemakers, and the principles of communication stay the same: it's acceptable to discriminate when and where you will receive people; on the other hand, it is rude to be engaged with one person and drop that person to attend to another. Those principles are eternal, because they are based on human nature and the requirements of community living.

AP: *Thank you very much.*

MM: You are very welcome.

quired more companies overseas than Japan, or that for decades, the Dutch have been among the top three nations investing in the U.S.

Shell, the huge Anglo-Dutch oil company, has long been a model of cultural cooperation. There's a joke that even when you go to the rest room at Shell, you find that 60 percent of your companions are Dutch and 40 percent are English (ownership of the giant company is split 60-40 between the Dutch and the British). A major international petroleum company recently spent a full year searching for a consultant who could install a new communications system for its research laboratories without offending any of the nationalities he had to work with.

Once senior American managers realize they must communicate better, they will discover a new world of electronic tools to help them. Used properly, electronic mail, videoconferencing, fax machines, and telephones all break down the barriers. Technology lets managers communicate "in person" without jet lag or interminable waits at airports. Most important, it gets the work done faster. No company today can have an effective strategy without a global telecommunications and computer network to support it. In many companies, the communications system dictates the organizational structure; it's the way things get done.

The new technology helps in innumerable ways. Ford of Europe uses its videoconferencing setup to solve quickly quality problems that might otherwise hold up assembly lines for days. If a part fails and a line goes down, engineers in Britain and West Germany can get together via a television screen; they talk over the problem and consult each other's engineering diagrams. They may be able to spot the solution and get the factory moving again in a matter of hours or even minutes. Motorola and Citicorp tap engineering and programming talent in Israel and India, respectively, without having to bring people to America. The employees work in their home nation, linked by satellite to computers in the U.S.

Exxon reduces its cash costs by feeding many of its financial transactions into the same computer in the U.S. Thus, the computer knows if one Exxon unit has an excess of British pounds that can be shifted to a division needing currency—a transaction that saves the cost of buying the pounds on the foreign-exchange market. When Digital Equipment Corp.

> **If a part fails and a Ford line goes down, engineers in Britain and West Germany can get together via television screen.**

has a tough engineering problem, it broadcasts it to all its worldwide units simultaneously using electronic mail. Without E-mail, DEC engineers would have to contact each of its global units by telephone. The World Bank does economic analysis around the clock by linking economists in Washington, Paris, and Djakarta by computer. When analysts in Washington go home for the day, the work is picked up by colleagues in Djakarta; bank officials refer to Djakarta as "Washington's night shift."

To compete in the 1990s, companies must master the new technology. But high-tech tools are only as good as the mangers using them. American executives still have much to learn about dealing with the rest of the world. And they don't have a lot of time to catch up. ∎

Chapter 13

"Wagon Masters and Lesser Managers"

J. S. Ninomiya

Preview

Skimming. Skim the article quickly to find the following general information.

1. Read the author's name, the title, all headings, and illustrations.

2. Read the first and second paragraphs, looking for the author's purpose and main idea.

3. Read the last paragraph, looking for a summary or conclusion.

Questioning. Answer the following questions and discuss your answers in class.

1. What are wagon masters? What do they do?

2. What are managers? What do they do?

3. What is the relationship between wagon masters and lesser managers?

Scanning. Scan the article quickly to find the following specific information.

1. Why is the effective manager difficult to describe?

2. What do all good managers seem to have in common?

3. What is perhaps the most important trait of an effective manager?

4. Who is the best judge of a supervisor's character?

Vocabulary in Context. Read the following sentences and try to guess the meaning of the italicized words by using the context. Then replace the italicized words with synonyms (words or phrases that have nearly the same or similar meanings).

Harvard Business Review 66, no. 2 (March-April 1988)

1. "Many of these newly promoted managers perform in the managerial styles of a past era, characterized by *self-serving* attitudes, empire building, and *autocratic* methods."

2. "The fact is progress cannot be achieved without conflict, and a preference for the *status quo stifles* growth and can weaken morale."

3. "He also had to maintain *harmony* and a spirit of teamwork among the members of his party and to resolve daily problems before they became *divisive*."

4. "Indeed, good managers all seem to have one thing in common: they *delegate* well, and trusting people to do the right thing, give *minimal* direction."

5. "Teamwork decisions can *minimize* mistakes in such situations and *ward off* much dissatisfaction among employees whose voices would not otherwise be heard."

6. "But what matters is to broaden the *perspectives* of the organization and to find executives who can manage people. Inside or outside [the organization] is *irrelevant*."

The wagon trains demanded leadership. Ward Bond was a great manager.

Wagon Masters and
Lesser Managers by J.S. NINOMIYA

1 Over the past several years, I've seen more and more books and articles about managerial effectiveness and how it can increase productivity. I've also seen more and more companies try to improve executive skills through education programs, sensitivity training, and participatory management. Yet at the same time I see businesses continuing to promote people into administrative ranks with apparently little consideration for their ability to manage others, their willingness to include subordinates in decision making, or their suitability as teachers and role models for a coming generation of supervisors. Many of these newly promoted managers perform in the managerial styles of a past era, characterized by self-serving attitudes, empire building, and autocratic methods. Eventually they too need sensitivity training and remedial seminars to try to correct their ineffective behavior.

HARVARD BUSINESS REVIEW March-April 1988

2   In short, too many companies are making the same mistake with managers that the auto industry used to make with quality: build it now, fix it later. We've finally started building automobiles right in the first place. Now we need to do the same with managers: hire and promote the right men and women to begin with instead of trying to "fix" them years later after they've done their damage.

3   am neither a social scientist nor a management consultant. For the last 20 years, I've worked at middle management jobs in the auto industry, where I have supervised many people and worked for many supervisors. In addition, I worked on a research team in the 1970s that took me into the offices of colleagues in the oil and auto industries, and there, for weeks at a time, I was able to watch managerial behavior in other companies from a fly-on-the-wall perspective. In my experience, it is rare that managers are selected for their supervisory ability. Indeed, most of those I've known lacked what I consider the most basic requirements for effective management—an understanding of the human condition and an appreciation of people. Most managers today are still selected solely on the basis of business expertise or success in nonsupervisory positions, and the styles they develop are inadequate, to say the least.

4   It may help to describe some of these styles. Here are seven I meet regularly:

5   **The Godfather.** Despite the current emphasis on teamwork and participatory management, the Godfather style still prevails. Godfathers typically demand complete control of their organizations and total loyalty from their employees. Subordinates are given freedom in their routine duties, but their goals

In his 27 years at Ford, J.S. Ninomiya has held a variety of line, research, and management positions. He is currently safety planning manager for the company's environmental and safety engineering staff.

are dictated from above. A Godfather's image and ego require frequent nurturing, usually in the form of successful confrontations with outsiders. To be recognized as good employees, subordinates need only stand at ringside and root for the boss.

6   People who have been subjected to this style for many years rarely become good managers themselves. Most often they become new Godfathers. At the opposite extreme, they become submissive and ineffectual.

7   Groups led by Godfathers are normally goal oriented and known for getting things done. Outsiders see them as well-oiled machines. Superiors depend on them. Because they rely on one person for nearly all decisions, however, the goals of Godfather groups are often self-serving and not always in the best interests of the organization as a whole.

8   **The Ostrich.** Ostriches love the status quo and fear discord. They always hope problems will simply go away and would rather stick their heads in the sand than face unpleasantness of any kind.

9   Ostriches believe firmly in nonconfrontational approaches to problem solving, and they avoid issues and debate. They are often capable and knowledgeable in their own areas of expertise, but they are usually better suited to serve as assistants than as managers. The fact is, progress cannot be achieved without conflict, and a preference for the status quo stifles growth and can weaken morale. Ostriches are more concerned with a superior's opinion of their job performance than with the morale of their subordinates, who often lack initiative, imagination, and productivity, especially if they've had their Ostrich managers for a long time.

10   **The Do-It-Yourselfer.** Do-It-Yourselfers want to handle everything themselves, especially the more challenging assignments. The only tasks they ordinarily delegate are the ones that they find trivial or that require special skills. They are often capable

individuals; many are workaholics. All live by the motto: "If you want a job done well, do it yourself!" They spend long hours at their jobs and are seen by upper management as candidates for promotion.

11 Unfortunately, they often make themselves indispensable. In several cases I know, a Do-It-Yourselfer's sudden illness has brought an entire department to a standstill. In addition, people who work for them often react like the people who work for Ostriches. Unable to get recognition and challenging assignments, they turn into mere hired hands. If the goals of an organization include productivity improvement and personnel development, then Godfathers, Ostriches, and Do-It-Yourselfers make poor managers.

12 **The Detailer.** Detailers want to know everything their subordinates do "in detail." In larger organizations, Detailers are so busy trying to keep up with their employees that they are virtually incapable of managing groups of any size. As they see it, their task is to be wiser and know more than their subordinates, so that they can make correct decisions by themselves. Detailers don't like group decisions and find delegating difficult. When they do delegate, they stay constantly in touch to make sure that subordinates do not arrive at independent decisions. Detailers generally lack confidence in others and make subordinates redo assignments again and again.

13 The decisions made by Detailers are often good ones, but they are rarely prompt. Since the usefulness of a decision is seldom a function of the time it takes

to make it, a good but leisurely decision is often too late to be useful. Detailers are best suited for supervising small groups that can afford to work slowly.

14 **The Politician.** Many of us like to work for Politicians because they tell us what we want to hear. Their superiors like having them around for the same reason. One of the drawbacks to this style is that Politicians tend to overdo it. A colleague of mine received 37 notes of commendation in one year, though the boss who sent them rated his overall performance average. Praise of this kind produces nothing but frustration and resentment. No one looks forward to the 38th insincere note from the boss.

15 Another drawback is that Politicians tend to stratify employees and management. On hearing objections from his or her own boss, for example, the Politician may abruptly overturn a decision previously approved by subordinates. What passes for managerial skill is nothing more than a talent for dodging bullets. Politicians with fast reflexes may succeed for a while, but few manage to dodge forever.

16 **The Arbitrator.** Arbitrators are often very successful at dealing with large groups because they possess a deep understanding of people and human conflict. They believe in teamwork and team decisions. If an organization's goal is to promote harmony and increase productivity, then this style is effective, especially in mid-management ranks. On the other hand, if what the organization needs is a vocal spokesperson and a competitive leader, then the Arbitrator may not meet the need. Arbitrators are usually personable and well liked, but they do have a weakness for compromise at the wrong moment, and they tend to be so friendly with subordinates that they find it hard to crack down when the going gets tough.

17 **The Eager Beaver.** In the same way that beavers build ever larger dams to interrupt the flow of water, so Eager Beavers create ever greater workloads and eventually interrupt the smooth functioning of their organizations. These managers measure their worth by the number of letters and reports they generate and by how hard their subordinates work. They are seldom content unless their subordinates put in overtime and work weekends at least occasionally. In many cases, even those who don't need to put in overtime are pressured into it. In my experience, unnecessary work

The Godfather's heavyweight ego puts him in the center of the ring.

The Ostrich's fear of discord leaves conflict unresolved.

demoralizes employees, and constant work pressure wears them down.

18 Many managers of the past were Eager Beavers and Godfathers who rationalized hiring more and more employees on the grounds of minimizing overtime expenditures. But the fact is, these empire builders don't change their habits even when their departments double in size. Eager Beavers and Godfathers did so much empire building at Ford between 1979 and 1982 that new management was able to cut back the number of employees by more than one-third without affecting productivity.

19 On the positive side, Eager Beavers are thorough. On the negative side, they produce a mass of useless information that often gets filed in wastebaskets.

20 A catalog of management styles could go on and on, but these seven styles, singly or in combination, describe more than three-quarters of all the managers I've known and many I have worked for. Every one of them meets some of the needs of an organization some of the time, but not one of them is what I would call an effective manager. Six of the seven types have more weaknesses than strengths, and they all train subordinates in their own inadequate image.

21 The effective manager is more difficult to describe, for the very reason that he or she refuses to be type-cast. The trouble with most of us is not that we sometimes act like, say, Godfathers, but that we act like Godfathers all the time. An effective manager is sometimes a Godfather and sometimes a Do-It-Yourselfer, often an Arbitrator and occasionally even an Ostrich. After 27 years, I think I know good managers when I see them, and I think I know what it is they do. I even think I know how to find them. Let me illustrate with one of my favorite examples.

22 Some of the most effective managers this country has ever seen were the wagon masters of the west-ward movement in the last century. A wagon master had two jobs. He had to keep the wagons moving toward their destination day after day despite all obstacles. He also had to maintain harmony and a spirit of teamwork among the members of his party and to resolve daily problems before they became divisive. A wagon master's worth was measured by his ability to reach the destination safely and to keep spirits high along the way. He had to do both in order to do either. I see the skills of effective managers as essentially the same, and I can sum them up in the roles they play:

23 *Decision Maker.* To begin with, effective managers are decisive. Despite all our newfound emphasis on teamwork and consensus, decision-making ability is by far the most important tool a manager needs on a daily basis. Teamwork is right for many decisions. Managers alone must make many others, including most of those involving job assignments, people, and interorganizational disputes. But here as elsewhere, an executive's responsibility is twofold – to make the right decision but also to encourage subordinate participation. In my experience the best policy is to involve as many employees as practical, to present them with the whole issue to be resolved (not just pieces of it), to sincerely seek and appreciate their suggestions, and throughout the process, to display the kind of decisiveness it would take to act alone.

24 *Listener and Communicator.* Many managers hear their subordinates but do not "listen." It takes enormous effort to get to know employees individually and to learn how to sense the group dynamics in an organization. A supervisor, like the leader of a wagon train, must be sensitive to moods and attitudes. By listening and communicating well, managers can fulfill the basic human need employees have to be recognized and appreciated. Good listening is also

part of an effective style in meetings. The successful managers I've known never dominate the table but let everyone express his or her views.

25   *Teacher.* One of the responsibilities of a good manager is to train subordinates to become managers. This does not mean having one or two favorites who are seen as anointed successors. It means training everyone who has potential. There are many ways to help people learn to make decisions: delegate responsibility, even to the lowest ranks; include subordinates where feasible in every project; hold regular discussion sessions; let employees represent the company with outside contacts. The effective managers I've known use all these ways of building positive self-images in their employees.

26   Indeed, good managers all seem to have one thing in common: they delegate well, and trusting people to do the right thing, give minimal direction. They don't reprimand subordinates who fail but encourage them to try again and to seek the help of coworkers and their own subordinates whenever possible. Good supervisors rarely find themselves burdened with unimaginative staff work because they constantly challenge the limits of their subordinates' creativity.

27   *Peacemaker.* Effective managers know how to minimize conflict. Some supervisors simply ignore its existence or become abusive and threaten to dismiss everyone involved. But managers who want their organizations to function productively face day-to-day problems directly. One way is to confront employees in order to determine the causes of conflict. Another is to encourage work groups like quality circles; a third is to rotate jobs and reassign people. Every workplace has conflicts. Effective managers sense them early and deal with them head-on.

28   *Visionary.* Wagon masters pushed their wagons toward specific destinations—Oregon, the California gold fields. Effective managers set goals that are just as firm and meaningful. Identifying goals is no less important than creating the means to achieve them. We have all looked for a car in a crowded parking lot. We trudge up one aisle and down the next, growing increasingly frustrated and embarrassed. Any clear sense of where we had left the car would have saved us enormous time and energy. In an effective organization, collective as well as individual goals are well defined and understood. Good managers never let themselves or their subordinates lose sight of them.

29   *Self-Critic.* How many times have you heard the expression "The boss is always right" or "The boss is the boss"? Not many managers are self-confident enough to admit their mistakes. Most believe that making mistakes is the worst corporate offense, and they don't allow the notion of human error to enter their philosophies. In fact, some insist on having their way even when they know they're wrong. Worse yet, subordinates who recognize the boss's mistakes can't correct them for fear of reprisal. Employees lose respect for their supervisors, and blunders achieve the status of doctrine. Effective manag-

The Politician's relentless insincerity wears subordinates down.

ers are quick to admit their own mistakes and don't dwell on the mistakes of others. They want to learn from mistakes so as not to repeat them. They know that while assessing damage and causes is often important, assigning blame is not.

30 *Team Captain.* Consensus decision making is one of the most powerful tools at a manager's disposal. Working alone, executives may find it difficult to make decisions affecting the whole organization—retooling a plant, reorganizing departments, even remodeling office space—because they are so often limited by the self-serving and conflicting information arriving from different departments. Teamwork decisions can minimize mistakes in such situations and ward off much dissatisfaction among employees whose voices would not otherwise be heard.

31 *Leader.* An executive's attitude toward subordinates is perhaps the most important trait of all. Effective managers have drive and determination, but they also have qualities like trust, modesty, politeness, patience, and sensitivity. Good managers genuinely like and appreciate people. They don't just manipulate or command; they lead. And they understand their dual function. Getting the wagons to Oregon without the passengers is no achievement. Keeping everyone in high spirits right up to the moment they perish in the desert is not success.

32 The need for good managers is growing. Many companies are downsizing in an effort to operate more efficiently. They are combining departments and cutting the work force but creating larger groups to be supervised. If we have fewer managers, we need them to be even more effective, which means that the ability to manage people is becoming more and more important. Yet the way we select managers hasn't changed much, and the managers we find are not much better than they ever were.

33 One short-term approach to the problem is to retrain today's executives. I've seen numerous efforts to introduce participatory management, promote teamwork, alter managerial attitudes, even change the so-called corporate culture. These are all moves in the right direction, but the results are often disappointing. Many people simply cannot see their own shortcomings. Others pay only lip service to such programs. Most disappointing of all, many seem to overestimate how much they've learned and changed in the course of retraining. After some recent participatory management workshops at Ford, for example, managers and their employees were asked to rate the benefits: nearly two-thirds of the executives felt they had become better supervisors, but

only a quarter of the subordinates shared that view. We must be careful not to fool ourselves with rosy self-assessments, or to believe we have solved a problem when we have really only talked about it.

34 For the long term, we need to make changes in the way we hire, reward, and evaluate managers. We need to improve the methods we already use—better personality profiles, better interviewing techniques, a better environment for people to work in once they've been hired. In addition, I have three unconventional suggestions:

35 **First, abandon excessive perks.** I believe effective managers always treat subordinates as people first and employees second. I know one such manager who left thank-you notes on his desk for the evening cleaning crew (who, as you might guess, kept his office immaculate). I know executives who take turns with their subordinates cleaning the office coffee maker and others who automatically pick up trash on their plants' floors instead of stepping over it. The people who work for such managers can be vehement in their unwillingness to work for anyone else.

36 On the other hand, I've met managers who think they are cast in a different mold from their employees—even when they all come from similar backgrounds. These executives consider themselves members of an elite and take pride in the symbols of their status, which they believe will increase their authority and make them more effective.

37 In fact, perks and status symbols often act as obstacles to good management. After many years of enjoying these rewards, some managers develop such a sense of privilege that they begin to look on employee concerns and complaints as encroachments on their prerogatives.

38 Demonstrations of rank have nothing to do with good management; yet in the United States the practice of granting special privileges is almost universal.

39 I recently discussed this subject with a vice president of one of the country's largest companies. He maintained that management perks were needed to inspire people to achieve corporate goals. Without them, he felt, people would have no incentive to work harder. I agreed that perks can be useful in some cases to reward achievements. But what about the rewards of approval and self-satisfaction? He was puzzled. Who would work harder for nothing but self-satisfaction? I asked then how he justified rewarding his executives but not his workers since, in his own view, people will not perform without the prospect of rewards. He said he could not reward everyone or his company would face bankruptcy.

40 I suspect that this man's view—the carrot for executives, the stick, presumably, for others—is shared by

many in top management. There are other industrial countries, however, where such privilege is rare, yet productivity remains high.

41   Several years ago, a friend of mine—an American executive at a large U.S. corporation—went to work for a Japanese company in the United States. Previously, he had been a profit-oriented manager with short-term goals and had enjoyed a wide range of perks and privileges. The last time I saw him I was astonished at the change in his outlook. He had become a respected manager of people, with long-term goals and a vision for his company's future. He no longer had all the accustomed perks. He was no longer isolated in his executive suite but spent much of his time on the factory floor.

42   I am not suggesting that all managers adopt the Japanese style and abandon traditional American values. I cannot say that all perks are bad business practice. Many successful companies use them, some as a means of projecting company images to outsiders.

The Eager Beaver's gnawing ambition dams up the company works.

Still, the thought of doing without them is attractive. Managers need to mix with subordinates to promote a spirit of teamwork, to nurture commitment to the job, to monitor the heartbeat of the company, and to remind themselves how well and how quickly many of their subordinates could fill their shoes.

43   **Second, ignore narrow expertise.** Common sense tells us to hire supervisors with expertise in the field they're expected to manage, but there are several drawbacks to this practice. To begin with, one of the most frequent complaints of managers themselves is that they become typecast in their particular expertise and have little opportunity to grow into other areas of business. Their promotional paths are similarly limited. But the man or woman who feels stifled by typecasting is not likely to be a truly effective manager, stimulated by new challenges, open to new ideas, creative, enthusiastic, optimistic. Moreover, expertise tends to become outdated, and in my experience this phenomenon presents two very real dangers. One is that entrenched managers will suppress innovation. Another, more dangerous possibility is that a manager with fossilized expertise may give subordinates too little room to grow.

44   Managers whose technical expertise is in another area will take a broader view of organizational goals, will depend more on subordinates, and will insist on teamwork, thus freeing themselves to manage people—the task for which they were hired.

45   In my view, the same considerations ought to apply to the old question of whether to promote from within or hire from without. Most people dislike the idea of bringing in outsiders from other companies or even transferring them from other departments. This is probably because most people fear for their own chances of promotion. But what matters is to broaden the perspectives of the organization and to find executives who can manage people. Inside or outside is irrelevant.

46   **Third, get references from a candidate's old subordinates.** This may sound radical. It is certainly unorthodox. I know of only one organization that contacted the candidate's former subordinates. Why should the references of past subordinates be less important than the references of past employers? When we hire someone to manage people, we need to know what previous employees thought. Unlike old bosses, who often write complimentary letters in behalf of people they were happy to see go, old subordinates are likely to say what they mean. There is no better judge of a supervisor's character than the people who depend on him or her to hear their complaints, arbitrate their differences, sharpen their skills, and lead them to the fulfillment of their goals.

47   I am convinced that the key to all our business goals—better quality, bigger sales, increased profits—is this emphasis on people. Like wagon masters, effective managers understand that their own success is inseparable from the success of their fellow travelers. Good managers get things done by caring about the people who do them.   ▽

Reprint 88209

Glossary

abusive	harshly scolding; coarse and insulting in language
anointed	chosen specially
arbitrate	to decide or judge a dispute
arbitrator	person authorized to judge or decide a dispute
autocratic	domineering, dictatorial, having unlimited power over others
blunders	errors, foolish or stupid mistakes
commendation	praise
delegate	to entrust authority to a person acting as one's representative
demoralizes	lowers the morale of, weakens the spirit
divisive	causing disagreement or dissension
doctrine	rules, theories, principles, teachings, official statements
downsizing	becoming smaller
drive	power or energy to get things done; enthusiastic vigor
dwell	to think about or discuss at length
ego	a person's sense of self or self-worth; the self as contrasted with another person or the world
elite	the group regarded as the finest, best, most powerful
empire building	building up an organization under the control of one person; increasing power
encroachments	intrusions; trespasses on the rights of others
entrenched	securely established
era	period, age, epoch
feasible	possible, practicable, within reason
fool	trick, deceive
fossilized	out of date; rigid, incapable of change
generate	to produce, bring into being, originate
Godfather	a male godparent (slang—mafia [organized crime] leader with complete power and control over the members of his organization)
harmony	agreement in feeling, action, ideas, interests
immaculate	perfectly clean, perfectly correct
ineffectual	not able to produce the desired effect, ineffective
irrelevant	not relevant, not relating to the subject
manipulate	to manage or control by shrewd use of influence, often unfairly
minimal	smallest, least possible
minimize	to reduce to a minimum
morale	mental condition within a group with respect to confidence, enthusiasm, courage
overdo	to do too much; to overwork
perish	to die
perks	privileges; benefits in addition to regular pay, resulting from one's position
personable	having a pleasing appearance and personality; attractive
perspectives	specific points of view
prerogatives	exclusive rights or privileges peculiar to a rank or class
projecting	getting something across to others effectively

prospect	expectation, anticipated outcome
rationalized	devised excuses or explanations for their actions (without being aware that these are not the real motives)
reflexes	quick, automatic, habitual responses
remedial	providing a remedy, helping overcome deficiencies
reprimand	to rebuke severely or formally
reprisal	retaliation, injury given in return for injury received
rosy	optimistic, cheerful, bright
self-serving	serving one's own selfish interests, at the expense of others
shortcomings	defects, deficiencies
singly	alone
so-called	inaccurately designated as such
standstill	stop, halt
status quo	the existing state of affairs
stifles	stops, holds back, represses
stratify	to classify or separate into groups graded according to status
submissive	yielding, having a tendency to submit without resistance
suppress	to keep from appearing, restrain, stop
thorough	complete, very exact, accurate
trivial	unimportant, insignificant
trudge	to walk wearily
twofold	having two parts, dual
typecast	to cast repeatedly in the same type of role or part
unconventional	not conforming to customary or accepted practices, standards
unorthodox	not conforming to usual beliefs or established practices, unconventional
vehement	characterized by intense feeling or passion, impassioned
virtually	for all practical purposes
ward off	to turn aside, keep away

Vocabulary

Without referring to the article, fill in the blanks in the following sentences with the correct words from this list. You may change the tense, number, or form of the words to fit the context. Use each word only once; not all of the words on the list will be used.

arbitrator	ineffectual	stratify	autocratic	divisive	demoralize
reprisal	manipulate	downsizing	morale	prerogative	irrelevant
status quo	elite				

1. Many managers of the past were dictatorial; consequently, they used _____ tech-niques of management, which have generally been replaced today by teamwork and partic-ipatory management.

2. In reaction to dictatorial managers, some employees become weak and submissive managers

   who are _____ in accomplishing their goals and objectives.

3. Certain types of managers fear conflict and lack initiative; as a result, they prefer the _____ , which prevents growth and weakens employee _____ .

4. Another unsuccessful management technique is that of the politician-style manager, who tends to _____ employees and management by not encouraging communication between them.

5. When employees are given unnecessary and excessive work just to make their managers look important, they may feel angry or become _____ by the pressure.

6. A central characteristic of an effective manager is the ability to promote teamwork by preventing problems from becoming _____.

7. Subordinates who can correct the boss's mistakes without fear of _____ are likely to be working for a self-confident and effective manager.

8. An executive who is a true leader tends to be appreciative of people rather than attempting to _____ their behavior or command them.

9. Unfortunately, managers often believe they are a(n) _____ group that has a right to special status symbols and _____ .

10. Whether a manager is promoted from within or hired from without is _____ ; what matters is whether the manager honestly cares about the employees.

Idioms and Expressions

Read the paragraphs in which the following italicized idioms and expressions are found. Then circle the letter next to the answer that best describes the meaning of the idiom as used in the context of the article.

1. "I was able to watch managerial behavior in other companies from a *fly-on-the-wall perspective*." (Paragraph 3)
   a. global point of view
   b. hidden point of view
   c. realistic point of view

2. "To be recognized as good employees, subordinates need only *stand at ringside and root for the boss*." (Paragraph 5)
   a. be very loyal to the boss
   b. listen carefully to what the boss says
   c. stand next to the boss at meetings

3. "They . . . would rather *stick their heads in the sand* than face unpleasantness of any kind." (Paragraph 8)

   a. look at problems from a different perspective

   b. get a headache

   c. ignore problems

4. "What passes for managerial skill is nothing more than a talent for *dodging bullets*." (Paragraph 15)

   a. achieving compromise

   b. solving problems

   c. avoiding trouble

5. ". . . they tend to be so friendly with subordinates that they find it hard *to crack down.* . . ." (Paragraph 16)

   a. apply discipline

   b. give criticism

   c. get upset

6. ". . . *when the going gets tough.*" (Paragraph 16)

   a. when employees are quitting

   b. when there are many difficulties

   c. when productivity decreases

7. "In my experience, unnecessary work demoralizes employees, and constant work pressure *wears them down*." (Paragraph 17)

   a. tires them out

   b. makes them hostile

   c. demotes them to a lower job

8. ". . . they produce a mass of useless information that often gets *filed in wastebaskets*." (Paragraph 19)

   a. misinterpreted

   b. organized carelessly

   c. thrown away

9. "Every workplace has conflicts. Effective managers sense them early and deal with them *head-on*." (Paragraph 27)

   a. directly

   b. face to face

   c. logically

10. "Many people simply cannot see their own shortcomings. Others *pay only lip service to* such programs." (Paragraph 33)

   a. attempt to discuss

   b. pretend to believe in

   c. refuse to accept

11. "I suspect that this man's view—*the carrot for executives, the stick, presumably, for others*—is shared by many in top management." (Paragraph 40)
   a. a raise for executives, but not for others
   b. privileges only for executives
   c. rewards for executives, punishments for others

12. ". . . to remind themselves how well and how quickly many of their subordinates could *fill their shoes*." (Paragraph 42)
   a. take their place
   b. steal their belongings
   c. rise above them

Paraphrasing

Read the following sentences carefully, and then rewrite them using your own words. Change the vocabulary and sentence structure, but do not change the author's intended meaning or paraphrase any technical terms. There are several ways of paraphrasing each sentence.

Original: "In my experience, it is rare that managers are chosen for their supervisory ability."

Paraphrase: According to what I have seen, managers are rarely chosen because of their skill in management.

1. "Subordinates are given freedom in their routine duties, but their goals are dictated from above." (Paragraph 5)

   _____

   _____

2. "These managers measure their worth by the number of letters and reports they generate and by how hard their subordinates work." (Paragraph 17)

   _____

   _____

3. "By listening and communicating well, managers can fulfill the basic human need employees have to be recognized and appreciated." (Paragraph 24)

   _____

   _____

4. "Identifying goals is no less important than creating the means to achieve them." (Paragraph 28)

_____

_____

5. "Teamwork decisions can minimize mistakes in such situations and ward off much dissatisfaction among employees whose voices would not otherwise be heard." (Paragraph 30)

_____

_____

6. "Common sense tells us to hire supervisors with expertise in the field they're expected to manage, but there are several drawbacks to this practice." (Paragraph 43)

_____

_____

Comprehension

Answer the following questions by finding the relevant information in the article. Give the numbers of the paragraphs that contain the answers.

1. What is the main idea of this article?

2. What types of people are continuing to be promoted into administrative ranks?

3. Why are the wagon masters of the westward movement in the last century good models for effective managers?

4. What is the best policy for managers to adopt in regard to decision making?

5. How can effective managers build positive self-images in their employees?

6. What makes a manager a leader?

7. Why is the ability to manage people becoming more and more important?

8. Why are the results of retraining today's executives often disappointing?

9. What are the advantages of hiring managers whose technical expertise is in another area?

10. Why is it beneficial to get references from past subordinates?

Inference/Interpretation

Circle the letter next to the best answer. Choose your answer according to the meaning the author suggests but does not state explicitly.

1. It can be inferred from the article that the one management style that has more strengths than weaknesses is the (Paragraphs 20–21)
   a. Godfather.
   b. Ostrich.
   c. Politician.
   d. Arbitrator.

2. We can infer from the article that excessive perks and status symbols for managers (Paragraphs 36–37)
   a. tend to motivate subordinates to work harder.
   b. have a negative effect on teamwork.
   c. cause envy in subordinates.
   d. encourage managers to mix with subordinates.

3. What can be inferred about Japanese management style? (Paragraphs 41–42)
   a. It offers few perks and privileges to managers.
   b. It expects managers to spend much time with subordinates.
   c. It is more people-centered and democratic than the American style.
   d. It is more autocratic than the American style.

4. What is the meaning of the following statement: "Good managers get things done by caring about the people who do them"? (Paragraph 47)
   a. Understanding people is necessary in order to achieve goals.
   b. Understanding people is more important that achieving goals.
   c. Understanding people and achieving goals are equally important.
   d. Good managers are people who get things done.

Structure

Circle the letter next to the correct answer(s). More than one answer may be correct. Be prepared to explain and justify your choices.

1. In which paragraph(s) is the main idea stated?
   a. Paragraph 2
   b. Paragraph 3
   c. Paragraph 20
   d. Paragraph 21
   e. Paragraph 47

   Write a paraphrase of the main idea in *one* sentence, using your own words as much as possible.

2. What techniques does the author use to support his main idea?
   a. Comparison
   b. Definition
   c. Process
   d. Chronology
   e. Classification

3. In which paragraphs does the author explicitly use analogy?
   a. Paragraph 22
   b. Paragraph 28
   c. Paragraph 31
   d. Paragraph 41
   e. Paragraph 47
   Explain the analogy by completing the following sentence:

   _____ _____ are like

   _____ _____ because they

   _____.

4. What overall method of development is used in this article?
   a. Describing a controversial technique
   b. Analyzing a policy and criticizing its weaknesses
   c. Identifying the effects of a future course of action
   d. Arguing against an accepted theory
   e. Justifying a proposal through enumeration of specific skills

Style

Circle the letter next to the correct answer(s). More than one answer may be correct. Be prepared to justify your choices by giving specific examples from the article.

1. How would you describe the writing style of the author?
   a. Impersonal
   b. Technical
   c. Personal
   d. Nontechnical
   e. Literary
   f. Academic

2. The tone of the article can best be described as
   a. analytical.
   b. balanced.
   c. ironic.
   d. argumentative.
   e. negative.
   f. dramatic.

3. The author's attitude toward the current hiring and promotion policies in many companies can be described as
   a. disapproving.
   b. disinterested.
   c. hostile.
   d. admiring.
   e. positive.
   f. concerned.

4. A rhetorical question is a question for which no answer is expected. The author asks a rhetorical question in the following sentence to emphasize a point: "Why should the references of past subordinates be less important than the references of past employers?" (Paragraph 46) What point is the author emphasizing? What is the answer to this question?

Discussion

1. What is more essential for a manager—understanding and appreciation of people or technical expertise and experience? Why?

2. Do you agree with the author that the skills of the wagon master are essentially the same skills an effective manager needs ("to reach the destination safely and to keep spirits high along the way")?

3. How important is it to grant special privileges and status symbols to managers in order to motivate them to achieve corporate goals?

4. Would you work hard if the only rewards were approval and self-satisfaction, rather than special perks?

5. How important is a spirit of teamwork in accomplishing corporate goals and making business decisions?

6. Which management style best fits your concept of management?

Research Assignment

Look up several of these articles in the library. Choose one article to read and take notes on.

Ames, Charles B. "Straight Talk from the New CEO." *Harvard Business Review* 67 (November-December 1989): 132–38.

Bartolomé, Fernando, and André Laurent. "The Manager: Master and Servant of Power." *Harvard Business Review* 64 (November-December 1986): 77–81.

Bonoma, Thomas V., and Joseph C. Lawler. "Chutes and Ladders: Growing the General Manager." *Sloan Management Review* 30 (Spring 1989): 27–37.

Drucker, Peter F. "How to Make People Decisions." *Harvard Business Review* 63 (July-August 1985): 22–26.

Etzioni, Amitai. "Humble Decision Making." *Harvard Business Review* 67 (July-August 1989): 122–26.

Hax, Arnoldo C. "Building the Firm of the Future." *Sloan Management Review* 30 (Spring 1989): 75–82.

Jacques, Elliot. "In Praise of Hierarchy." *Harvard Business Review* 68 (January-February 1990): 127–33.

Jaffe, Charles A. "Management by Fun." *Nation's Business* 78 (January 1990): 58–60.

Kanter, Donald L., and Philip R. Mervis. "Winning the Hearts and Minds of Cynical Employees." *Business Month* 134 (September 1989): 81–82.

Kanter, Rosabeth Moss. "The New Managerial Work." *Harvard Business Review* 67 (November-December 1989): 85–92.

Kotter, John P. "What Leaders Really Do." *Harvard Business Review* 68 (May-June 1990): 103–11.

Mintzberg, Henry. "The Manager's Job: Folklore and Fact." *Harvard Business Review* 68 (March-April 1990): 163–76.

Rosener, Judy B. "Ways Women Lead." *Harvard Business Review* 68 (November-December 1990): 119–25.

Samuelson, Robert J. "What Good Are B-Schools?" *Washington Post* (May 9, 1990): A27.

Schaffer, Robert H. "Demand Better Results—And Get Them." *Harvard Business Review* 69 (March-April 1991): 142–49.

Schein, Edgar H. "Does Japanese Management Style Have a Message for American Managers?" *Sloan Management Review* 23 (Fall 1981): 55–68.

Schein, Edgar H. "Improving Face-to-Face Relationships." *Sloan Management Review* 23 (Winter 1981): 43–52.

Semler, Ricardo. "Managing without Managers." *Harvard Business Review* 67 (September-October 1989): 76–84.

Wriston, Walter B. "The State of American Management." *Harvard Business Review* 68 (January-February 1990): 78–83.

Zaleznik, Abraham. "Managers and Leaders: Are They Different?" *Harvard Business Review* 64 (May-June 1986): 48.

Oral Presentation

Working with a small group, give a fifteen-minute oral presentation to the class on the additional reading in this chapter and the articles that you chose in the research assignment. Include the author's main idea, major points, and some supporting data. Be prepared to answer questions on your topic. (See Appendix B: Giving an Oral Presentation.)

Writing Assignments

1. Write a five- to ten-page research paper on how to achieve state-of-the-art management. Use the additional reading in this chapter and the articles listed in the research assignment. After reading the articles, develop a thesis about the type of manager or system of management needed in today's global business environment. Support your thesis with specific references to the information in the articles. Include a 100- to 150-word abstract (very short summary) as the first section of the research paper.

   Use parenthetical references in the author-date system for each of the sources you cite: (Schein 1981). You may also choose to give the page number: (Schein 1981, 50). List all sources at the end of your research paper as References. Entries should be alphabetized according to the last name of the author: Schein, Edgar H. 1981. "Improving Face-to-Face Relationships." *Sloan Management Review* 23:43–52.

2. Working with a partner, develop an annual performance appraisal system for managers. Describe the criteria by which a manager would be evaluated (no more than five) and how much weight each criterion would have. Explain this system in an in-house memo to all company managers from the CEO.

3. Describe the type of boss you would like to work for: male or female, old or young, strong in technical expertise or interpersonal skills, a conservative "number-cruncher" or a creative entrepreneur.

Case Study: A Problem in Management Style

Working in groups, read the following case study. Discuss the problem, answer the questions, and write a brief report on how your group would solve the problem. (Choose one member of the group to do the writing.) Follow the format in Appendix E (Case Study Report) in writing your report.

Morris Schmidt is the director of the Management Information Systems Division (MISD) at Atlas Engineering Corporation. Mr. Schmidt has doubled the size of his division since he took over in 1988. He is a technically competent, overly ambitious manager, but in spite of the increase in number of employees in his division, the productivity rate has remained the same during the years he has been the director. (Lately, in fact, the productivity rate in MISD has shown a definite decrease.)

Mr. Schmidt believes in making his employees work very hard, and he expects them to work overtime and weekends. He also demands that each employee generate many letters, memos, and at least three reports per week, including a weekly progress report. In Schmidt's opinion, the work actually accomplished cannot be measured unless there are lengthy written records documenting what has been or will be done. Although the unusually large flow of redundant paperwork is often an obstacle to efficient and timely completion of tasks, Schmidt remains convinced that it is necessary. Indeed, he has just had a complete new system of automated office equipment installed to provide every employee with a personal computer.

During the past few months, several of Schmidt's employees have been comparing notes and complaining about how demoralized they are; the constant work pressure is really getting them down. Now that productivity rates are decreasing, the pressure from Schmidt has been even heavier. Don Dawkins, manager of the Business Applications Systems Department and a long-time employee, is thinking of quitting. He can see the effects of the difference between the management style of Schmidt's predecessor and Schmidt's "eager-beaver" style. Before Schmidt came, morale was high and so was productivity. Today, the log-jam in the Management Information Systems Division is disrupting the smooth functioning of the entire company.

Dawkins would like to call a meeting of all the MISD employees to discuss the crisis in morale, but he is unsure if he should do so. Morris Schmidt is the son-in-law of the President of Atlas Engineering Corporation and an extremely powerful person in the organization. Moreover, he is known to be intolerant of anyone's suggestions for change and extremely sensitive to criticism. On the other hand, the mounds of useless paperwork covering every inch of space in the MISD testify to the enormous waste and inefficiency Schmidt has created just to inflate his reputation as a hard-working manager.

Questions

1. Should Dawkins call a meeting of all MISD employees to discuss the low morale and productivity?

2. Should Dawkins ask for a meeting with Schmidt?

3. Should Dawkins ask for a meeting with the President of Atlas?

4. What could Schmidt do to improve morale and productivity?

Solution: Case Study Report

I. Define and analyze the problem.
II. Suggest possible solutions.
III. Evaluate possible solutions.
IV. Select a solution.

Case Study Business Writing Assignment: Letter

Write a letter from Don Dawkins, manager of the Business Applications Systems Department, to the employees in the Management Information Systems Division of Atlas Engineering. The letter should outline the deteriorating work environment in the division and ask for a meeting of all employees to discuss the productivity and morale problems that have resulted from Morris Schmidt's questionable management methods.

Format:
    I. Introduction (Background and Main Idea)
   II. Discussion (Productivity and Morale Problems)
  III. Closing (Request for Meeting)

Style: Informal
Tone: Informative and persuasive

Case Study Business Writing Assignment: Memorandum

Write a memo from Morris Schmidt, director of the Management Information Systems Division, to all MISD emplyees. The memo should outline Schmidt's policy of maintaining extensive written records of every action taken in MISD. It should convey Schmidt's insistence that all MISD employees carefully adhere to this policy and state the results of not complying with it. The memo should also discuss the decrease in productivity.

Format:
    I. Introduction (Background and Main Idea)
   II. Discussion (Statement of Policy)
  III. Closing (Results of Noncompliance)

Style: Formal
Tone: Dictatorial and harsh

Additional Reading

"American Management as Viewed by International Professionals"
Ashok Nimgade
Business Horizons 32 (November-December 1989): 98–105

Business Horizons / November-December 1989

American Management as Viewed by International Professionals

Ashok Nimgade

Ashok Nimgade is vice president of Genesis Technology Group, Cambridge, Mass., and a research associate at Harvard Business School, Boston. The author wishes to thank N. Venkatraman, Sloan School of Management, MIT, Cambridge, Mass., for his advice and guidance.

The American style of management is like any other—it may have its weaknesses, but it also has strengths that need to be emphasized.

About the time of the American Revolution, Robert Burns wrote stingingly of a beautiful but vain lady unaware of a louse crawling up her bonnet: "O wad some Pow'r the giftie gie us / To see oursels as others see us!" Two centuries later the Scotsman's words still apply—this time to the U.S. economic system that, coasting from a post-World War high, paid hardly any attention to the gradual encroachment of Japan and other rising nations on her world markets.

Perhaps international managers are better able to diagnose the malaise besetting the United States. After all, in the eighteenth and nineteenth centuries the most insightful observations of American character came from the pens of peripatetic European writers such as St. Jean de Crèvecoeur, Alexis de Tocqueville, Jules Verne, Charles Dickens, Oscar Wilde, and Herbert Spencer. With this in mind, I interviewed 40 international managers about the character of American management today.

Numerous studies show that for a tantalizingly wide variety of problem-solving situations—IQ tests, verifiable forecasting problems, "almanac" problems, and so on—the mean opinion of a group of experts is usually far more accurate than that of any one individual in the group. Although the interview questions were generally open-ended, the use of several "yes-no" questions helped gauge consensus on vital issues.

For my own group of de Crèvecoeurs, Vernes, de Tocquevilles, Wildes, Dickens, and Spencers, I chose managers with considerable work experience in more than one country, including, of course, the U.S. (The three American interviewees included a Puerto Rican and a Hawaiian). Because the American style of management cannot easily be compared with styles of management from nonmarket economies, the largest number of interviewees came from the heavily industrialized regions of the globe; 15 were from the Western-industrialized regions and nine from the NIC-Pacific Rim area. The rest came from developing nations in Asia, Africa, and Latin America, communist nations, and nations such as Israel, Lebanon, and South Africa. Throughout the discussion that follows, insightful responses will be linked to the interviewees' nationalities.

The interviews were conducted in the spring of 1988, when most of these international managers were in the Boston area or on the East Coast. About three-fourths had attended or were currently attending business school at either MIT or Harvard. The average foreign interviewee had worked 4.5 years at home, 2.5 years in the U.S. (not including time spent obtaining an American MBA or working in an American multinational firm overseas), and almost one year in one other country. Only six of the 40 subjects were more than 35 years old. This group's relative youthfulness may have ensured a heightened trenchancy, and presumably its relative demographic homogeneity helped accentuate its geographical diversity. (Throughout the discussion, please note that not all subjects answered each interview question.)

Fortunately, all 40 respondents felt that even today there is something that can be considered an American style. Several respondents stated that a common denominator had evolved in the U.S. because all immigrants had ended up adopting "American ways." A Colombian interviewee, for instance, found that several years in the U.S. had made him more direct, aggressive, and impatient. An Argentinean noted that his own nation was as much a land of immigrants as the U.S., but it was not a melting pot.

In a strictly managerial context, a respondent from Hawaii felt that the recruiting companies she had observed at the Wharton School presented a tiringly similar front: being "committed to risk-taking, innovative, dynamic, and seeing people as their most valuable resource." Nonetheless, in examining the remainder of the findings, one must keep in mind that many respondents discerned a variation within the American style of management stemming from differences in firm size, CEOs, industry age, firm reputations, and geography.

WHAT MAKES AMERICA AMERICAN?

The 40 international interviewees pointed out three major characteristics that separate the United States from other nations (see **Figure 1**). The first is the often-overlooked sound infrastructure for conducting business. Several interviewees marveled at the efficient telephone

Figure 1
Economic Characteristics of American Business

Frequently mentioned features that distinguish the U.S. from other nations
(+) indicates a positive feature, (-) indicates a negative feature

+ Sound infrastructure for business (telephone, mail, utilities).
+/- Strong commitment to meritocracy and laissez faire.
  Results: a two-tiered workforce (and society) leading to top-down management; dominant private sector that often supplants national good or social consciousness; insufficiently regulated business; high mobility caused by easy hiring and firing; litigious corporate environment.
+/- Largeness of economy. A large domestic market.
  But largeness fosters inertia and parochialism.

Figure 2
National Problems the U.S. Must Address to Improve its Business Climate

In order of decreasing frequency of mention by interviewees

- Low pre-college educational level. Parochialism.
- Stifling legal system and litigiousness.
- Inappropriate regulations: over-regulation such as with outdated antitrust laws, yet insufficient government monitoring of business fraud.
- Insufficient stress on manufacturing compared to, say, finance.
- Budget deficit; insufficient savings; unfair practices of trading partners.
- Short-run outlook in industry.
- Wide income disparity.

system, postal system, and other basic utilities Americans often take for granted or deride. If the business of America, as Calvin Coolidge claimed, is business, then all the fundamental building blocks are in place for a sound economy.

The next distinctively American societal characteristic, one corroborated by 36 of the 40 interviewees, is a strong commitment to the philosophy of meritocracy. Indeed, because of the opportunity to take on significant responsibility and do well at a young age in the U.S., many respondents planned to stay in the U.S. for a few years after completing business school.

But there is a stygian side to meritocracy. A Japanese banker felt meritocracy threatened the stability of an organization by overturning a seniority system. Other respondents hinted that meritocracy, "the spirit of laissez-faire capitalism," and a consequent lack of social consciousness might directly or indirectly increase inequality within a firm.

For a land that is supposedly egalitarian and democratic, it is striking that roughly one-fourth of the respondents, mostly from heavily industrialized regions, noted a deep rift between American white-collar and blue-collar workers. All three Japanese respondents perceived this rift as one of control, with top managers dictating policy and with "mutual suspicion" prevailing. A Canadian subject used the term "two-tiered society" to encapsulate his perception of how an elite core group of about 1 percent of the U.S. led the rest of the population.

Several Europeans and Asians perceived the rift as a gross inequality, closely associated with a wide educational disparity. Not unexpectedly, the interviewees listed precollege education (particularly in math, science, and foreign languages) most frequently among problems the U.S. must address at a national level (see **Figure 2**) to improve its business climate. For instance, a Soviet émigré called receiving a lower-level engineer's resumé that mentioned among his job skills the capability to convert milliliters to liters! A French-American felt that one of the forces driving automation in certain industries was the lack of capable workers or professionals. In the final analysis,

Figure 3
Corporate Level Characteristics

Frequently mentioned features that distinguish the U.S. from other nations.
(+) indicates a positive feature, (-) indicates a negative feature

+ Performance-oriented, efficient. Less red tape.
+/- Make and implement quick decisions; flexible.
    Short-term orientation; constant change prevents standard procedures.
+/- Emphasis on rational strategic planning.
    But simplistic strategies overlook true complexity. Too much paperwork and
    control from top.
+/- Smoother relations among different corporate levels than within a level.
- Faddism, superficiality. Emphasis on image; style over substance.
- Emphasis on charismatic leadership.

many respondents warned that an educationally declining bottom tier would effectively result in the bureaucratization of private industries, with workers or lower-level managers ploddingly implementing the dictates of upper-level management.

Interviewees from all regions also denounced the brutality of the laissez-faire philosophy that condoned easy hirings and firings. Several Europeans stated that the ugly massive layoffs on Wall Street following the Black Monday of 1987 would have been inconceivable in their homelands. Apart from just aggravating job insecurity, a Chinese interviewee pointed out that a pattern of quick layoffs decreases each worker's sense of control in the world by separating job termination from job performance.

Yet another danger to overemphasizing the bottom line, a Persian émigré pointed out, is that managers are pressured into overlooking social responsibilities to debtors or to less fortunate members of society. Occasionally this may boomerang. Thus, a Mexican noted how American suppliers actually sued his prospering family business for payment during the 1982 Mexican crisis rather than pursuing a policy of leniency that would have continued a long-term relationship capable of withstanding temporary downturns.

A number of respondents perceived an overemphasis on laissez-faire as shifting the onus of proof upon victims of wrongdoing. This, a French-German claimed, accounts for the relatively high level of sham operations he observed in the course of his entrepreneurial activities in the U.S. Such a climate has also

exacerbated the litigious tendencies of an individualistic society. A German lawyer-businessman stated that the U.S. has slipped into a vicious cycle, with Say's law applying: A large supply of lawyers creates its own demand as protagonists on both sides of a dispute are driven to arm themselves with legal counsel. Not surprisingly, the interviewees listed litigiousness second most frequently among problems the U.S. must address to improve its business environment.

The third important national-level characteristic mentioned was the gargantuan size of the American economy. This trait, apparently, helps kindle the spirit of meritocracy and laissez-faire by affording suppliers, distributors, and other players a certain anonymity vis-à-vis each other. In contrast, a respondent from Puerto Rico felt the small business community of his homeland forced a reliance on the same set of suppliers or customers, regardless of their imperfections. Apparently, according to a Canadian, even the U.S.'s large northern neighbor lacks sufficient critical mass for perfect competition: The professional business class is still a relatively small club with players often knowing each other's families.

Size comes with its disadvantages, however. Many interviewees, especially Europeans, felt the U.S. market's self-sufficient size tempts American business people to turn their backs on foreign markets. Such hubris is in stark contrast with the resource-poor island mentality of Japan that makes it fiercely dependent on exports.

Many respondents were surprised by the general cultural and linguistic

ignorance of American managers. The French-German respondent claimed he had grown up admiring the American way of doing things, until he worked in an American multinational corporation and discovered that French professionals were educationally more well-rounded. A South African noted that many of his American colleagues envisioned his homeland as an Edgar Rice Burroughs wilderness complete with giraffes grazing by a small dirt landing strip that serves as the airport's main runway. Such views are hardly conducive to international business tête-à-têtes. Ironically, the source of the U.S.'s strength—its vast internal resources—is turning out to be its Achilles' heel in an increasingly globalized economy.

WHAT MAKES AMERICAN FIRMS AMERICAN?

Most interviewees felt that American firms possessed the requisite qualities for high performance: efficiency, an orientation toward performance, dislike for red tape, and a rational outlook on strategic planning (see **Figure 3**). Several problems, however, blot an otherwise verdant landscape, and these will be discussed below.

An Overemphasis on Scientific/ Rational Strategic Planning

Out of 33 interviewees, 17 agreed with the contention that American managers may rely too much on scientific strategic planning by overemphasizing reductionism and quantitative models and overlooking the artistic, diplomatic, and humanistic aspect of business (four disagreed and 12 were unsure). To rub salt in the wound, 25 respondents felt that American managers held simple-minded views or strategies (six disagreed). The interviewees interpreted "simple-mindedness" in many ways: brashness, aggressiveness, impatience, provincialism, technical illiteracy, "management by numbers," "hands-off" management, lack of diplomacy, and viewing issues in black and white.

Several respondents knocked the technical ignorance and inordinate faith

295

"Some interviewees felt American managers adopt business concepts in a faddish manner—for example, engineering corporate culture overnight instead of through a serious commitment over many years."

in quantification and computerized output that they felt leads Americans to computerize facilities without taking the human element into account. An Israeli MIS systems analyst at a Boston bank complained about the eagerness of American managers to rely too heavily on information and the use of computers to standardize procedures. The net result at his bank, he feels (as do many economists), has been a bloating of the white-collar force and the use of information to the point of marginal or even negative returns.

An Indonesian pointed out how blind reliance on quantitative analysis led his American multinational corporation to neglect cutting costs as long as it made a benchmark level of profit. Using the American dollar instead of the weaker local currency for accounting purposes, he felt, ended up masking gross inefficiencies. In a related vein, an MIT business scholar warned that in trying to use optimizing models, Americans often forget that maximizing locally does not always maximize globally.

Some managers attributed the rationalistic trend to consultants who rely blindly on consulting tools or "laundry lists" for reshuffling a firm's divisions—or to "young, whippersnapper MBAs" from business schools that teach one can manage anything. A Japanese interviewee noted, in contrast, that his compatriots have a harder time using consultants because they often separate the planning and implementation processes.

Some respondents noted that the simple-mindedness of certain American views existed merely in the way arguments were couched. For example, two Americans felt that simple slogans like General Electric chairman Jack Welch's mission statement, "Be number one in every business we enter," are actually quite complex in execution. Furthermore, they added, sometimes chairmen must resort to simple messages to create a common denominator of understanding in large companies. A West German, however, dismissed unrealistic goal setting as propagandistic raillery.

Perhaps the American business world is starting to reassess its strategy, since firms such as General Electric have de-emphasized rational planning in favor of individual risk taking and entrepreneurship. In any case, however, it seems likely American businesses will never quite approach the artfulness of Latin Americans who, according to a Mexican respondent, often write business letters that are judged and sometimes saved for their literary merit alone.

A Short-Term Orientation

An overwhelming 38 respondents noted what is almost axiomatic today: the short-term orientation of American managers, with money (in the form of stock market valuation, quarterly profits, or even personal advancement) as a prime motivator. Faulted here were mobility, individualism, and impatience that often leads Americans to switch jobs and connive to retire by age 50, before a manager's peak business years. Although American firms such as Squibb, which updates a five-year plan every year, are starting to combat this short-term orientation, the dead horse still needs beating.

Some interviewees felt American managers adopt business concepts in a faddish manner—for example, engineering corporate culture overnight instead of through a serious commitment over many years. Two Indian interviewees also stated that a short-term orientation leads managers to avoid giving ideas a "fair shake." This decreases the sense of permanence necessary to ensure corporate continuity and the development of standard operating procedures.

Two Japanese bankers noted that a short-term orientation has led bright American managers away from manufacturing and into high-paying, glamorous jobs that are often less personally fulfilling. Other interviewees excoriated the robbing of long-term R&D piggy banks or discounting R&D personnel. A Soviet émigré, for instance, decried her former firm's policy of issuing 30 percent bonuses for the company's performance to salespeople but only 5 percent bonuses to engineers, who drove the firm's long-run competitiveness. Among other problems, she noted, this policy often led salespeople to sell items that were still in production or to ship products that had yet to be tested.

The international respondents were also critical of American human relations management. They noted, for instance, how Americans hire to fill particular job positions while Pacific Rim or European businesses generally train or "grow" existing employees to fill constantly arising needs. Along with quick hirings, of course, come quick firings. Thus, an American mentioned how his Chicago office of a prominent management consulting firm—a supposed purveyor of fine management techniques—once cut staff merely to meet the quarter's earning goals.

Relating to this grow-versus-graft issue, a Taiwanese engineer-manager expressed his strong preference for the East Asian system of providing continuous, informal feedback instead of the yearly formal job evaluations at the American multinational corporation for which he had worked. This is because he felt that neither an hour's worth of evaluation nor a year's worth of performance was sufficient to truly assess one's long-term contribution to a firm.

A bright side to Americans' short-term orientation that several interviewees mentioned is the willingness to make and implement quick decisions. Many Europeans (French, Swedish, and Swiss) felt their compatriots, in contrast to Americans, complicated and muddled matters and often ended up temporizing.

To epitomize this difference, a Swiss business scholar related the story of Southern Bell's installation of nine computer systems. With the ink barely dry on the plans, the firm rushed into the field. Problems plagued the first one or two sites, but Southern Bell persevered and kept adjusting its plans so within six months the last few sites were installed without a hitch. The interviewee noted, had this been a typical Swiss corporation, it would have stuck to the drawing board for a year longer and, like an oil tanker at sea, would barely have modified its course.

Regimentation and Style over Substance

Several respondents understood the need for a company to put up a polished front for the sake of its customers,

Figure 4
Personal Characteristics of the American Managers
Frequently mentioned features that distinguish the U.S. from other nations.
(+) indicates a positive feature, (-) indicates a negative feature

+   Informal, frank, trustworthy.
+   Innovative, open-minded, objective, pragmatic, flexible.
+/- Work harder than Europeans.
       But less than many Asian nations. Often "spinning wheels."
+/- Impatient; get things done; hands-on mentality.
       But short-term orientation.
+/- Materialistic, profit-oriented. Business is a valid, worthy profession.
       Judge persons' worth by their wealth. Shun low-pay manufacturing jobs.
+/- Individualistic, entrepreneurial.
       Loyal to division, not firm.
+/- Aggressive, hard-nosed, pragmatic.
       Overlook simpler, diplomatic means.
-     Not well-rounded educationally. Parochial.

but many—25 out of 35—felt American firms in general overemphasized corporate image. The international respondents' general distaste for superficiality encompassed not only corporate dress, but also documentation formats and office decor.

Many European and Latin American interviewees likened dress in the American corporate world to a "masquerade" or an "image hang-up" and decried injunctions against light-colored suits, women wearing slacks, or even rolled-up shirt sleeves in the summer. Because corporate dress was generally viewed as being more relaxed and fashionable in Europe and Latin America, some even likened the American code—white shirts, dark suits, silk ties—to militaristic uniforms. An American went so far as to interpret this penchant for conformity, team spirit, and charismatic leadership in American business society as a mildly fascist phenomenon.

On non-dress issues of corporate image, the interviewees complained about American corporate standards for documents such as letters and resumés and for office decor. For instance, one respondent noted that his consulting firm's Chicago branch (of which we have heard before) employed 70 full-time workers in its graphics department (representing about 20 percent of corporate expenses). He claimed that half his time was spent drawing graphs, the end-product of his work, for customers. Similarly, an Israeli MIS

systems analyst at a Boston bank felt the advent of word processing and document formatting correlated with a decline of substance. A Japanese respondent complained that in his country, but not in the U.S., he could handwrite addresses even on business envelopes. In all fairness, however, this is partly due to the unwieldy Japanese script.

Europeans and Latin Americans expressed a dislike of the regimented American corporate environment; Asian and communist bloc interviewees focused more on the cost issues of buying extravagant interview suits or otherwise maintaining a plush corporate image. A South Korean noted with irony, American "innovativeness" in office decor merely deepened the rift between American managers and workers. In contrast, junior and senior staff members at his Korean office often sit together in the same room. One multicultural interviewee from Kenya and Hong Kong went so far as to decry firm psychologists and human resource departments as yet another form of corporate fluff.

WHAT MAKES AMERICAN MANAGERS AMERICAN?

The hair of Americans turns gray ten years earlier than in England," complained Herbert Spencer a century ago. Similarly, de Tocqueville asserted, "No men are less addicted to reverie than the citizens of a democracy." Not surprisingly, therefore, the personal traits of American managers mentioned most often by the international managers were industriousness, entrepreneurship, impatience, pragmatism, aggressiveness, materialism, informality, and parochialism.

These traits fit well with the smoothly functioning business system of a land that enshrines the gambling game of laissez-faire; most likely they have led to a corporate style characterized by directness, speed, professionalism, and a mentality geared toward matching customers' needs. Yet a gloomier way to view these traits is as increasingly irrelevant attributes of a bygone frontier society. Some of the negatives mentioned here can never be expurgated because they form the woof and warp of the American cultural fabric. Let us examine some of these traits (see **Figure 4**) more closely.

Informality and Frankness

At the casual, short-term level, 26 of 35 respondents agreed that American managers are relatively informal and easy to get along with (only one disagreed while eight were unsure), making it relatively easy for a stranger to enter the social network of an American firm. The majority of interviewees—19 out of 26—agreed that American managers are more frank and felt this to be a positive trait (one disagreed and six were unsure). Many interviewees warned, however, that corporate politics still limit the amount of frankness in American corporations.

Several respondents noted that American informality and frankness greatly facilitated communications within the firm by eliminating the need to make an appointment days or even weeks in advance with one's boss. A Taiwanese, marveling at the ability of Americans to disagree openly with their superiors, confessed that the only reason he chose MIT over Stanford for graduate education was because doing otherwise would have meant disregarding his boss's advice.

The extreme characteristics of informality, however, contain considerable drawbacks. A married French-American professional couple felt that

American informality blurred the distinction between individuals' professional and social lives, which often meant that employees and bosses were occasionally supposed to socialize together outside of work. They much preferred the French separation of the "work me" from the "social me." The husband hypothesized that the mingling of the social and work domains in the United States may be linked to the American educational concept of students living on university campuses.

However, several Pacific Rim respondents, and even some Europeans, felt American informality was superficial; they never feel as much at home in a U.S. firm as in their own corporations, where personal lives of coworkers (who might even live together in company apartments) are tightly interwoven. One interviewee noted that his Chinese bosses not only attended employee weddings, but would sometimes even play matchmaker. It seems that, overall, relationships between different hierarchical levels may generally be better in the U.S.; relationships within levels may be better in the older world.

Directness and Aggressiveness

The respondents viewed aggressiveness negatively, or at best as a double-edged sword. On the one hand, many could marvel at the hustle of firms such as Southern Bell, which bring to mind Gustave Flaubert's observation that "nothing is more humiliating than to see idiots succeed in enterprises we have failed in." Others, such as one Chinese respondent, saw American frankness and directness as an alternative to the Japanese temporizing during negotiations. Yet most interviewees—26 out of 39—felt American managers emphasized pushiness and competitiveness over intelligence (9 disagreed while 4 were uncertain).

Aggressiveness was viewed in various negative ways by respondents. A Japanese viewed it as rudeness, as in the case of an American cashier commanding the customer to replace an item on the shelf. A Bangladeshi real estate developer perceived aggressiveness as a wrongly used motivational tool, as in the case of construction

managers coaxing workers with curses. An American saw the large number of lawsuits as an extension of the "firm handshake" mentality. A French-Lebanese, viewing aggressiveness merely as a face-saving device to camouflage incompetence, commented, "Sometimes I wonder if the word 'subtlety' exists in the American dictionary."

Sometimes, however, there may be more bark than bite to American aggressiveness. A British respondent, while job hunting in Boston, confessed that he was quickly dissuaded by the number of classified ads seeking "aggressive candidates." Fortunately, he soon learned these firms merely wanted what the British called "self-starters."

Materialism

A materialistic outlook has helped business in the U.S. become a valid and worthy profession, but many respondents shunned the American use of money as a gauge of social worth. A South African complained that people in the U.S. "write their salaries on their foreheads." A French Catholic, noting that her cultural background made open talk of money or sex dirty, felt it was no wonder the term "nouveau riche" had to be imported into American English. Noting the tremendous psychological costs of materialistic pursuits, one interviewee observed that almost three-fourths of the partners of his American consulting firm were divorced.

The materialistic, utilitarian bent of the United States, however, was perhaps best captured in Oscar Wilde's comments on the American Man: "He thinks that civilization began with the introduction of steam and looks with contempt upon all the centuries that had no hot-water apparatuses in their houses. The ruin and decay of time has no pathos in his eyes. . . . His one desire is to get the whole of Europe into thorough repair . . . ."

Willingness to Change

According to 19 out of 22 interviewees, American managers, especially at upper levels, are relatively willing to improve themselves. A Japanese entrepreneur, impatient with the Japanese ideal of familial, seniority-based management, interpreted mobility as a symptom of American managers' desire for self-improvement. Seven out of the 11 who responded to this question, however, felt Americans were no more self-critical than people elsewhere.

A Taiwanese, however, felt the American willingness to change often led Americans down short paths in search of instantaneous improvement. Similarly, two Indian respondents noted that a penchant for constant change sometimes led Americans to lose perspective.

Impatience, Mobility and Disloyalty

Impatience, disloyalty, and a lack of pride in work were seen as contributing factors to what several East Asian respondents perceived as a low quality of labor and lower-level management. Not surprisingly, many interviewees from other parts of the globe attacked excess mobility because it wastes a firm's training resources and hampers development of a long-term perspective. One interviewee mentioned the extreme case of a New Hampshire firm where, despite good salaries, only two out of 12 original employees remained after two years.

An American hallmark, several respondents observed, is loyalty to the lowest common denominator: the individual or the division. An Indonesian engineer noted how the drafters in his American multinational firm had to be cajoled, even bribed, to get their priorities to better match those of the firm.

The observations here eerily echo those of de Tocqueville a century and a half ago: "Among democratic nations new families are constantly springing up, others are constantly falling away, and all that remain change their condition; the woof of time is every instant broken and the track of generations effaced . . . the interest of man is confined to those in close propinquity to himself."

PEARLS IN THE EBBING TIDE

For all its faults and weaknesses mentioned above, American business still forms a key model for much of the world. Although Japanese conquests of world markets may have galvanized other nations into bolstering their performances, the individualistic American style may be more palatable than any style involving tremendous self-sacrifice.

An important force in disseminating the American style of management is the role of the U.S. as the world's largest manufacturer of contemporary culture. Golden arches, muted but still obvious, form popular waiting spots in the sanctified altstadts and vieille villes of the Old World. Also to be blamed or credited is the establishment of MBA programs and multinational corporations overseas. A significant proportion of interviewees (13 out of 15, with two "unsures") explicitly asserted that business schools have helped propagate the U.S. style through emphasizing rational management techniques. Indeed, the very idea of business schools is American: many interviewees came to the U.S. because their own countries did not offer MBA programs of comparable quality.

Partly because of the pervasiveness of American culture, managerial education, and multinational corporations, the younger business people in Japan and the Pacific Rim—according to several interviewees—are relaxing more, while Europeans and members of other industrialized or industrializing nations are working harder. Almost everywhere, respondents noted an increasing convergence, however slow, to a style marked by increased rationalization (through computerization, strategic planning, or pursuit of management by objectives), impatience and mobility, and informality. Slowing this drift toward Americanism, an Israeli interviewee ruefully admits, is the tenacious grip of bureaucracy that allows for "the carrot but not the stick."

Managers the world over must carefully scrutinize the American problems mentioned earlier at the national, organizational, and individual levels. Some uniquely American "problems" in an international context are not problems so much as misunderstandings stemming from cultural differences. A Swiss, for instance, noted that communication classes here teach students to write direct memos, which are often insultingly direct for foreign business people. Similarly, as a handful of interviewees pointed out, the American style of settling down directly to business bodes poorly in nations such as Mexico or France, where artistic discussions often open after-dinner business talks. A Taiwanese noted that many of his compatriots would resign in shame at receiving the abrupt negative feedback that is commonplace in the United States.

Culture may limit a nation's potential for change and accommodation, because it ultimately limits the extent to which individual change can contribute to organizational or national reform. If this is true, the Trojan Horse of change may already be storming American management in the form of bright, new immigrants. Unfortunately, perhaps, these groups are frequently Americanized before they can make their own cultural impact on the business system.

A more reliable engine for breaking the vicious cycles that entrench existing practices may be American business schools. Managerial programs, however, came under attack by interviewees, who characterized a fair proportion of MBAs as arrogant, money-hungry mercenaries and who chided the faculty for generally remaining ivory-tower scholars. One interviewee, a Ph.D. student in management who was advised by his professor that his dissertation might be too readable to be perceived as "scholarly," remarked that while ivory-tower business scholars are dismantling the walls between them and the rest of academia, they are erecting a wall between business schools and industry. Since the mid-1980s, however, top business schools have been consciously admitting older, more mature, more diverse applicants, and are increasingly reevaluating their curricula.

Today, the U.S. is caught in a vise between the European ideal of "qualité de vie" and East Asian industriousness. To many European and Third World respondents, the American managers are, in the words of a British interviewee, "slogged to death" in a climate of job insecurity. A French-German interviewee said it was no wonder many Europeans ungrudgingly give half their wages in taxes in return for almost total security from the state. What the Americans are to the Europeans, however, the Japanese are to Americans.

As the U.S. faces greater overseas competition, it will become important to consider whether an economic engine is to be the slave or master of a people. Perhaps the relative slowdown of the American economy should lead to new frontiers for growth. If the rapid rate of constant change in the past has often made Americans lose perspective, perhaps the coming years of economic challenge should be a time for active self-assessment—a time to regain poise for future growth.

For example, the Japanese and other Pacific Rim respondents admonish "American laziness," but an increased work load might extinguish the entrepreneurial and creative fire of the American environment. A satisfactory solution here would be to focus on working smarter, not harder. This means relegating matters of corporate fluff and image in favor of more substantive issues. Or, for instance, would a company be better served by hiring more professionals at slightly lower wages than by hiring fewer at higher salaries in a pressure-cooker atmosphere? Would the individualism and meritocracy of the American management culture permit such a shift? Would a lower-paid, less-pressured worker willingly choose the pressure-cooker atmosphere of a firm mainly for the status and glamour of money? These are problems for which each firm must tailor its own solutions.

The key to dealing with this dilemma is to realize that often what separates a negative from a positive is merely a matter of degree. Thus, although Americans may always, on average, be more impatient, parochial, and aggressive than their counterparts, they should focus on retaining their direct, can-do attitude. In a similar vein, while many Asian interviewees felt American schools need to inculcate a greater sense of discipline, a French businessman warned against extremes. He stated that the U.S. should not repeat France's mistake of overemphasizing education to the point of impairing people's entrepreneurial spirit or ability to think concretely. Similarly, a Chinese scholar who had spent the Cultural Revolution as a grain porter warned that the American educational system must never, through overemphasizing discipline, slay the gold-egg-laying goose of American creativity.

In the final analysis, the 40 international managers show that cultural and educational orientation toward work and money count heavily. As the New World approaches economic middle age—a stage where success breeds complacency and failure—American managers must try to weed out personal and organizational negative traits while simultaneously building on the strengths mentioned above. Of necessity, each firm must tailor its own milieu to best suit its needs. The Japanese have a saying that when the water drains out, the rocks are revealed. The ebbing of American competitiveness is starting to show up the pearls as well as the rocks in the American style of management. ❑

Appendixes

Appendix A

Definitions of Writing Terms and Examples of Writing Styles

Definitions of Writing Terms

Abstract: A very short summary of the main ideas and topics of a report, research paper, journal article, or technical document, which appears ahead of the document and is usually 150 words or less.

Analogy: Similarity in some respects between things otherwise unlike.

Analysis: Breaking up a whole into its parts and examining these parts in order to solve a problem or reach a conclusion.

Argument: An essay in which the writer presents a point of view and attempts to persuade others of the validity of his or her opinion.

Author-Date System: Reference citation system for documenting sources in a report, research paper, journal article, or technical document; it places the author's name and the work's year of publication in the text.

Business Letter: Common form of external business correspondence, usually sent from a representative of an organization to people outside the organization.

Case Study: Method of instruction that is used in American business schools and involves the analysis of actual business situations in order to teach problem solving.

Critique: An essay based on critical reading of a text in which the writer summarizes, reacts to, and evaluates an author's ideas.

Deductive Organization: Placement of the main idea of a text at the beginning; the writer gives the conclusion first and then presents supporting evidence.

Essay: An analytical or interpretative composition that deals with its subject in a limited way.

Figure of Speech: An expression (metaphor or simile) using words in a nonliteral or unusual sense to add vividness to what is said.

Format: The general arrangement or plan of a document; the physical presentation of a document on the page.

Idiom: An accepted phrase or expression that is contrary to the usual patterns of the language or that has a meaning different from the literal meaning of the words.

Inductive Organization: Placement of the main idea of a text at the end; the writer gives supporting evidence and leads the reader to a conclusion.

Irony: A method of humorous or sarcastic expression in which the intended meaning of the words used is the direct opposite of their usual sense.

Main Idea: The most important idea or unifying theme of a paragraph or longer text.

Memorandum: An informal written business communication, usually from one person or department to another within an organization.

Methods of Development: Organizational patterns used to structure the content; these include analysis, argument, cause-effect, chronology, classification, comparison-contrast, definition, description, enumeration, exemplification, problem-solution, process, and spatial order.

Parallelism: The use of the same or similar grammatical forms to express the same or similar ideas.

Paraphrase: A rewording or restatement of an author's meaning.

Purpose Statement: A statement of intention found in the abstract and introduction of a report; it announces the topic and tells readers why the report is being written.

Report: A written document that contains an objective presentation of the facts of an investigation; an organized presentation of data, serving a practical purpose by supplying needed information.

Research Paper: A lengthy paper based on research and using numerous sources in order to answer a specific question, support a thesis, or prove a hypothesis.

Rhetorical Question: A question asked only for effect, or to emphasize a point, and for which no answer is expected.

Style: The writer's manner of expression in language; the way of using words to express thoughts.

Summary: A brief restatement of the main ideas and major points of a longer written document, usually paraphrased.

Synthesis: An essay that is developed from two or more sources from which the writer selects information to support a thesis.

Thesis: The main idea of a text, expressed as a sentence; a statement assumed as a premise in a research paper, argument, critique, or synthesis.

Tone: A manner of writing that shows the attitude of the writer toward the subject and the audience and results from word choice, sentence structure, and phrasing.

Topic Sentence: A sentence that contains the main idea of a paragraph and often is the first or last sentence of the paragraph.

Examples of Writing Styles

Informal: Let's try to get together to talk about this right away, or else we won't be able to change the policy.

Formal: I suggest that we meet to discuss this issue at a mutually convenient time in the near future; otherwise, we will not be able to effect a change in the policy.

Impersonal: There have been reports that some managers are not complying with the smoking guidelines. This is having a negative impact on the company, and these guidelines must be followed by all employees.

Personal: I have heard that some managers are not complying with the smoking guidelines. This displeases me greatly, and I expect all employees to follow these guidelines.

Bureaucratic: Since first inventorying Agency activities subject to OMB Circular A-76, we have reviewed those activities for adequacy under revised guidelines from OMB. After recent discussions with the Productivity Clearinghouse, it has been determined that one Productivity Improvement Program (PIP) review category, "Accounts Management," is not an appropriate review activity for this Agency. That activity, therefore, is being deleted from the PIP review list for this Agency.

Technical: CDC Systems, Inc., is a globally recognized custom designer, fabricator, manufacturer, and provider of turnkey antenna systems; earth stations; radio and optical telescopes for communications, telemetry, tracking control and monitoring; and special purpose antenna systems. Our complete antenna designs include Ku-band, C-band, E-band, and/or L-band performance capabilities. Included with our designs are antenna servo control and tracking system products specializing in microprocessor-based controls and monopulse tracking.

Nontechnical: CDC Systems, Inc., is known worldwide for our custom design and production of antenna systems. We provide a large variety of communications equipment, including earth stations, radio and optical telescopes, and tracking systems.

Scientific: The Hemostasis and Thrombosis Group consists of five senior investigators and two junior investigators. The program trains predoctoral and postdoctoral fellows in biochemical, immunologic, physiologic, and pharmacologic approaches to problems in hemostasis and thrombosis.

Business (Informal): ABC Corporation is pursuing a program to purchase minority interests in small business companies that indicate potential growth opportunities in the future. We would like to discuss this aspect of our interest in small business at your convenience.

Business (Formal): This letter is to certify that a money market account in the name of Sarah Hoffman was established today. Please be advised that this letter is issued at the aforementioned customer's request for whatever legal pupose it may serve her.

Legal: Before this Court is Defendant's motion for summary judgment pursuant to Fed. R. Civ. P. 50. The foundation for Defendant's request is Plaintiff's failure to establish any factual basis upon which liability may rest, thereby making appropriate disposition as a matter of law.

Conversational: "My first real job was junior salesman for the Quality Park Envelope Company. When it came to training salespeople, Quality Park believed in the basics. They gave you a desk, a phone, and the key to success, a 500-page sales manual" (Harvey B. Mackay, "The CEO Hits the Road (and Other Sales Tales)," *Harvard Business Review* 68 [March-April 1990]: 32).

Journalistic: "Environmental companies in Europe are looking attractive, as a result of dirty water, dirty air, acid rain, hazardous waste, sewage and little room for landfills.

"One of the pluses, analysts and executives say, is the growing pressure for central regulation of the environment in a united Europe, which is likely to mean stricter and more uniform standards in different countries so that, for example, a business in France does not have an advantage over a company in Germany" (Jonathan Fuerbringer, "Market Place: Cleaning Up Europe," *Wall Street Journal* [June 1, 1990]: D4).

Academic: "Power is a most basic facet of organization life, yet inevitably it generates conflict because it constricts the autonomy of those who respond to it. Anticipating precisely how the use of power will create a conflict relationship provides an enormous advantage in the ability to achieve the desired levels of control with minimal dysfunctional side effects" (Leonard Greenhalgh, "SMR Forum: Managing Conflict," *Sloan Management Review* 27 [Summer 1986]: 51).

Colorful: "The word 'uniform' commonly evokes images of soldiers, police officers, doctors, nurses, sports figures, even Boy Scouts, Girl Scouts, and parochial school students—a kaleidoscope of olive drab, blue, white, gray, stripes, logos, and plaids. But uniforms have also played an important role in commercial image making. Like great billboards, the best commercial uniforms proclaim an organization's identity in a striking and unforgettable way" (Julia M. Collins, "Off to Work," *Harvard Business Review* 67 [September-October 1989]: 105).

Pictorial: "Effortlessly we rose; we were off; a long curve upward. The squat ferryboats below plowed across our wake, and great flat barges carrying rectangular mounds of different colored earth like spools of gold and tawny silk" (Anne Morrow Lindbergh, "Take-Off," in *North to the Orient* [New York: Harcourt, Brace and Company, Inc., 1935]).

Literary: "Three passions, simple but overwhelmingly strong, have governed my life: the longing for love, the search for knowledge, and unbearable pity for the suffering of mankind. These passions, like great winds, have blown me hither and thither, in a wayward course, over a deep ocean of anguish, reaching to the very verge of despair" (Bertrand Russell, "What I Have Lived For," in *The Autobiography of Bertrand Russell* [Boston: Atlantic-Little, Brown and Company, 1967]).

Poetic: "A soft liquid joy like the noise of many waters flowed over his memory and he felt in his heart the soft peace of silent spaces of fading tenuous sky above the waters, of oceanic silence, of swallows flying through the seadusk over the flowing waters" (James Joyce, *A Portrait of the Artist* [New York: The Viking Press, Inc., 1964]).

Appendix B

Giving an Oral Presentation

To be successful in giving an oral presentation, speakers should use a simple, direct, natural, and relaxed style. They must know their subject very well and present the information in logical order. Planning, preparation, and practice are the keys to effective oral presentations.

The following are seven suggestions for making a successful oral presentation.

1. Know your subject well by planning, preparing, and practicing in advance.

2. Organize your material logically so that one idea leads to the next.

3. State the main idea at the beginning of your presentation, and restate it at the end.

4. Speak in a loud, clear voice, and do not speak too quickly.

5. Maintain eye contact with every member of the audience.

6. Stand up straight and use natural gestures.

7. Use concrete language and words that create mental images.

The following are seven suggestions for organizing an oral presentation.

1. Organize your material into a main idea, major points, and supporting details or examples.

2. Divide your talk into three parts: introduction, body, and conclusion.

3. State your purpose and the main idea in the introduction and give necessary background information.

4. Organize the major points logically and explain them clearly in the body.

5. Restate your main idea in the conclusion.

6. Use visual aids (pictures, charts, or graphs) to support your major points.

7. Put your information in outline form on 3" x 5" or 4" x 6" index cards that you can refer to whenever necessary. Do not read your entire oral presentation from the index cards or memorize it.

Example of a Purpose Statement: The purpose of this presentation is to explain Peter Drucker's article: "What Business Can Learn from Nonprofits." This article appeared in the July-August 1989 issue of the *Harvard Business Review*.

Example of a Main Idea Statement: Drucker believes that nonprofit organizations are becoming America's management leaders because they are implementing policies and practices that business will have to learn in regard to motivation and productivity of knowledge workers.

Appendix C

Writing a Summary

A summary is a brief restatement of a longer written document. Its purpose is to convey knowledge in a clear and concise form. The summarizer must extract only the most important information from the entire document. Writing effective summaries is challenging because it depends on the skills of reading comprehension, critical analysis, and paraphrasing.

In the business world, summary writing is a skill that is in great demand. Learning to present only the essential information takes time and effort, but it can be done by thinking logically and using a systematic approach.

When summarizing a text, follow these four steps:

1. Read

2. Write

3. Edit

4. Rewrite

I. Read
   A. Read the text quickly, looking for major points.
   B. Reread the text carefully. Underline or highlight the author's main idea, major points, and key supporting data.
   C. Reread your underlined or highlighted statements and delete any that are not relevant.

II. Write
   A. Write a rough draft using the underlined statements.
   B. Give the author, title, and source and the main idea of the text in the first paragraph.
   C. Paraphrase the author's words; do not copy directly from the text.
   D. Write in a clear, concise, and objective style.
   E. Do not add any extraneous information or give your opinions.

III. Edit
    A. Be certain that the content is accurate and coherent.
    B. Delete any unnecessary information.
    C. Add information if the meaning is not clear and complete.
    D. Rearrange the information if the organization is not logical.

IV. Rewrite
    A. Write the summary again with the editorial changes.
    B. Proofread the summary for errors in grammar, punctuation, or spelling.
    C. Make all necessary corrections for the final copy.

Example of Summary (220 words)

In "Making Time to Manage" (*Harvard Business Review* 66 [January-February 1988]: 38–40), Robert Dorney stresses the importance of effective time management for executives. He says that although managers may think that they know how they ought to spend their time, few know how they actually spend it. Managing time effectively is discussed often but seldom practiced. Dorney advocates doing a quantitative evaluation of how time is spent in order to determine the value of executive time.

Dorney believes that time management is more about management than about time, and he says balancing various activities and responsibilities is the hardest part of time management. The key is to separate tasks according to their value as they affect the future of your organization. The matters that most directly influence the success of the organization are those you should focus on. Less vital matters should be delegated. Delegating is, according to Dorney, "The executive's greatest need as well as greatest privilege" (40). The question to ask is: Can someone do the job better than I can?

In addition, Dorney suggests having a loyal employee monitor the executive's allocation of time to see how well his or her objectives are being met. Executives who ask "Did I earn my salary today?" and have a quantitative method to answer that question will be motivated to manage their time effectively.

Appendix D

Writing an Essay

An essay is an analytical or interpretative composition that deals with its subject in a limited way. It may be completely objective or contain the writer's opinion. Writing an essay can be done efficiently if the writer takes a systematic approach to the writing process by using the POWER Method. The following are the five steps in the POWER Method.

1. Plan

2. Outline

3. Write

4. Edit

5. Rewrite

I. Plan
   A. Determine the purpose of the essay, the audience, and the type of information to be included.
   B. Collect and evaluate the information needed.
   C. Develop a tentative thesis (main idea).
   D. Choose a method of organization.

II. Outline
   A. Write a one-sentence thesis or main idea for the essay.
   B. Write an outline of three or four major points, minor points, and supporting data.
   C. Arrange the major points and minor points in logical order.
   D. Write a topic sentence for each major point.

III. Write
   A. Write the introduction to the essay, including the thesis (main idea).
   B. Write the body of the essay, following your outline and making each major point a separate paragraph.
   C. Write the conclusion to the essay by restating or paraphrasing your thesis.

IV. Edit
    A. Check for accurate and coherent content.
    B. Check for logical and clear organization.
    C. Be certain that the style is appropriate to the content.
    D. Delete any unnecessary information or add missing information.

V. Rewrite
    A. Write the essay again with the editorial changes.
    B. Proofread the essay for errors in grammar, punctuation, or spelling.
    C. Check the format for correct title, headings, spacing, and margins.
    D. Make all necessary corrections for the final copy.

Examples of Essays

Women in the Workforce

In many countries throughout the world, working women face problems because of their inability to achieve equality in the workforce. Rather than superficial remedies that don't really end discrimination against women, creative solutions that truly allow women to enter and advance to the highest levels in the workforce are necessary. Furthermore, there must be a realization that the workforce is a different place today since most women work and women bear children.

It is time for governments and companies to implement policies that address the needs of working women. These policies should not merely break down superficial barriers, but should work at eliminating the root of discrimination. They should also take advantage of what this segment of society can uniquely offer the workforce. But first, everyone must recognize the fact that most working women will have children, will want time out to do so, and will need child care for them after they are born.

If women are not given an answer to their child-care needs, not only the children but the entire society will suffer. One question to be answered is how women can be given equal opportunity and advancement within a company and still be able to take time out to have children. This is a complex issue, considering the high cost to companies, especially small companies, when a woman leaves to have children after years of training. However, solutions can be found, such as allowing employees to work at home.

My view is that equality in the workplace comes not from treating women like "men in skirts." Rather, women's differences and the changed workplace that has resulted from women entering the workforce must be considered in establishing true equality. Family leaves, child care, and flexible working hours are benefits that should be offered to all working women to enable them to realize their fullest potential as valuable resources in the modern workforce.

Vera Mezvinsky

Jacques-Yves Cousteau

The person who is an important role model for me is Jacques-Yves Cousteau. He is a sailor, a scientist, an inventor, and an adventurer. Fascinated by the sea, he became a naval officer, and later to have a better understanding of it, he studied the sea. He started to explore it, not for economic purposes, glory, or conquest, as were many earlier explorations, but only for the joy of the discovery and the expansion of the limits of knowledge.

Jacques-Yves Cousteau has played many roles during his life. To solve the problems encountered in his underwater exploration, he became an inventor. His first and perhaps least known invention was the modern scuba device. He is also an adventurer because he has risked his life by going where nobody has gone before and opening the way for many other scientists. Furthermore, he was one of the first to understand the danger our environment is in. Using his knowledge and the audience that results from his celebrity, he is trying to make the world aware of this problem before it is too late. To the contrary of many others, there is no political objective or desire for publicity in his fight, only the fear of the destruction of our environment.

I have learned many different lessons from Jacques-Yves Cousteau. First, I learned that science may be a kind of adventure and not just work in a laboratory or in books. Second, I learned that having imagination and knowledge in other areas is sometimes a better way to solve a problem than being highly specialized in one domain. Finally, I also learned that the search for knowledge must be not only for money or glory but also for the joy of the discovery and of going ahead.

Stephan Ginion

Nelson Mandela

Nelson Mandela is highly respected all over the world. He is the president of the African National Congress, and he is widely regarded as the leader of the anti-apartheid struggle. Nelson Mandela is a role model for me because of the way he approached the problem of apartheid and because of his commitment to his people.

Nelson Mandela has always wanted a South Africa for both black and white. He understood that the whites were afraid that they would be forced out of the country if the blacks took charge of the government. Thus, his goal is to eliminate the inequality between black and white, not to reverse it. Recently, at the first meeting between the African National Congress and the government of F. W. de Klerk, he addressed the government leaders in their language, Afrikaans; he was showing them respect. Although he and his people have been discriminated against, he has always stood for an equal society.

Another reason why Mandela is a role model is that he sacrificed his freedom for his people. He was in jail for 27 years and refused to be released until the government accepted his demands. Several times he was given the chance to get out on the condition that he would not engage in political activity, but he refused the offers. Instead he chose to remain in jail and fight for the freedom of his people.

Mandela is therefore a role model for me. He put the cause of freedom for his people above his own freedom.

Diawara Papa

Henry Kravis

There are many people whom I admire because of the attributes that they possess. One of the persons who comes to mind is Henry Kravis. Henry Kravis is much respected by his peers, who know him as an ambitious and motivated businessman. However, he does not exist just for business, but is also interested in the arts and is a well-read and culturally aware person. Therefore, he serves as a role model for me.

Henry Kravis of KKR (Kohlberg Kravis Roberts), the well-known leverage buyout specialists, possesses the characteristics that I feel are important in a businessman or businesswoman. Kravis is known to be very aggressive in acquiring what he wants, and he usually succeeds in getting what he goes after. A good example of this would be the huge LBO (leveraged buyout) of RJR Nabisco. Before KKR became known as LBO specialists, it would mostly help finance small, friendly takeovers. Kravis, disregarding the opposition of a partner, decided to act on his belief that leveraged buyouts of large companies, whether they be friendly or not, were the wave of the future. Thanks to Kravis's foresight, KKR is one of the largest, if not the most recognizable, financial specialists of takeovers or buyouts. Kravis realized that KKR had to grow to compete, and he acted on his belief in the face of opposition.

The attributes that I admire in Henry Kravis are his astute business knowledge, ambition, aggressiveness, motivation, and intelligence. In addition, he recognizes that a person should not stagnate, that growth is important no matter how successful you are, and he is willing to act on his beliefs despite opposition. On the personal side, I admire the fact that business is not his whole existence. Kravis is known for endowing many art institutions, and he has knowledge of the arts in many forms. For all these reasons, Henry Kravis has become a role model for me.

Yeong-Su Seo

Example of Synthesis (cause-effect organization)

In the articles "New Coke's Fizzle—Lessons for the Rest of Us," published in *Sloan Management Review*, and "Coke's Brand-Loyalty Lesson," published in *Fortune*, Betsy D. Gelb, Gabriel M. Gelb, and Anne B. Fisher demonstrate that the consumer's emotional tie to a product is often greater than expected. As a result, brand loyalty may be the origin of a commercial disaster, as seen in the New Coke fiasco. In order to prevent such mistakes, companies planning to introduce "improved" products should first do extensive and sophisticated market research, including qualitative studies.

In 1985, the Coca-Cola company made the decision to modify the formula of its leading soft drink. The change was based on the findings of many market studies (Gelb and Gelb 1986, 71). These studies had shown that the consumer's response to the new product was positive. However, the replacement of the traditional Coca-Cola by New Coke was rejected by the majority of consumers. In fact, the company had to step back and resume production of the old formula of Coca-Cola (Fisher 1985, 44).

The most important factor that led to the rejection of New Coke was the emotional relationship that existed between consumers and the old soft drink formula. Drinking Coca-Cola had become a tradition for many people over its 99 years of existence. The change made by the company was not only in Coke's formula but also in the traditional values and memories that it represented to the consumer. "We had taken away more than the product Coca-Cola. We had taken away a little part of them and their past" (Fisher 1985, 45). The resistance of the consumer to this "improvement" was the result of the fact that "Coke drinkers believed that Coke stood for traditional values, . . . so they felt betrayed when the product changed radically overnight" (Gelb and Gelb 1986, 71).

Although a lot of research was done by the Coca-Cola company, it didn't reveal the depth of consumer attachment to the product. The studies took many forms, such as blind tests, questionnaires and taste comparisons, but none of the tests was able to measure the degree of personal and emotional reactions caused by the disappearance of the old, traditional Coca-Cola (Gelb and Gelb 1986, 71). The defect of the research was that it was essentially quantitative in form. The result was only numbers that could not show the profound meaning the product had for many people. A more extensive study focusing on the qualitative aspects of the change would perhaps have been able to demonstrate the close relationship existing between consumer and product (Gelb and Gelb 1986, 75).

Brand loyalty, which is a very powerful factor in consumer purchasing, "is an elusive quality" that is influenced by people's memories and emotions (Fisher 1985, 44). In fact, according to both the Gelbs and Fisher, a misunderstanding by the producer of the impact of its products on the consumer may lead to a commercial disaster, like the New Coke fiasco. Thus, research must be carefully planned and take into account not only pure numbers but also the psychological and emotional relationship between consumer and product.

References

Fisher, Anne B. l985. "Coke's Brand-Loyalty Lesson." *Fortune* 112:44–46.

Gelb, Betsy D., and Gabriel M. Gelb. 1986. "New Coke's Fizzle—Lessons for the Rest of Us." *Sloan Management Review* 28:71–76.

Stephan Ginion

Appendix E

Case Study Report

I. Statement of the Problem
   A. Definition
   B. Analysis

II. Suggestion of Possible Solutions
   A. Solution A
   B. Solution B
   C. Solution C

III. Evaluation of Possible Solutions
   A. Solution A
      1. Advantages
      2. Disadvantages
   B. Solution B
      1. Advantages
      2. Disadvantages
   C. Solution C
      1. Advantages
      2. Disadvantages

IV. Selection of a Solution
   A. Choice
   B. Justification

Appendix F

Writing Evaluation Form

Evaluate writing assignments as Excellent (E), Satisfactory (S), or Unsatisfactory (U) in each of the following categories:

1. Grammar   correct standard English   _____

2. Mechanics   correct and consistent punctuation, capitalization, and spelling   _____

3. Organization   logical and effective presentation of ideas   _____

4. Content   accurate, coherent, and relevant discussion of the subject   _____

5. Format   clear and readable presentation on the page   _____

Suggestions and Comments

_____

_____

_____

_____

_____

_____

_____

Examples of Memoranda and Business Letters

Delta Corp

Interoffice
Communication

Originator

Reference ___PAZ/91/057___ Page _1_ of _1_

Date ___1/15/91___

To: All Delta Headquarters Employees	From: Pamela A. Zimmernam Office Systems and Telecommunications Administrator *PAZ*

Subject and References ___Reducing Copier Costs___

The purpose of this IOC is to remind everyone to help reduce copier costs. The price of copier paper has risen this year, making the cost for each copy higher.

Remember that all copiers have reduction capabilities, and the two IBM machines offer double-sided copying. Try to use these features whenever possible in order to cut down on the amount of paper. Double-sided copies also take up less space in your files.

We have a new Canon NP-500 AF copier that has replaced the Canon NP-400 on the second floor in Personnel. The new Canon is a faster machine, while maintaining the reduction and enlargement features. Please use this copier when it is convenient, and give us your comments on its features and copy quality.

We appreciate your cooperation in this matter.

PAZ/acs

cc: Ron Oliphant

FORM 00-7001 (Rev. 6/87)

Memorandum

TO: All Executives, XYZ Corporation

FROM: Clayton E. Gray   *CEG*
       Chief Executive Officer

DATE: September 3, 1991

SUBJECT: Business Conferences via Global Television to Begin in December

For your information, Intercontinental Hotels Corporation and Comsat General Corporation announced an equally owned joint venture to provide the first international televised conference service available to the public.

The service, to begin in December, initially will link Intercontinental's hotels in New York and London. The link will enable small groups, such as business executives, to conference with two-way audio, video and document display, and print-out facilities.

Paul Sheeline, Chief Executive Officer of Intercontinental, said the system probably would be expanded later to include such cities as Houston, Paris, Frankfurt, Riyadh, and Tokyo. He added that the system could be adapted to handle large groups.

Richard Bodman, President of Comsat General, said that prices for use of the systems would vary, depending on which facilities a customer wanted to use. But he added that a typical meeting would cost between $1,500 and $2,000 an hour. The system will use satellites to beam signals.

As travel costs increase, analysts generally expect the concept of televised conferences to grow. "It makes more sense to get a half-dozen executives into our hotel in New York for a two-hour teleconference with London, rather than taking the time and going to the expense of flying them all there," Mr. Sheeline said.

Because of time differences, officials of Comsat General and Intercontinental said their system would be available practically around the clock.

I want all of you to consider using this system in communicating with your subsidiaries around the world when more than three individuals are involved. I believe we can save time and travel expenses by having conferences in this mode, as well as exceed our current productivity levels.

CEG/lrd

cc: Ruth Lerner

Business Letter (Modified Block Style)

```
                              4567 Waggamon Circle
                              McLean, VA  22101
                              June 27, 1991

Graduate School of Business Administration
Admissions Office
The University of Michigan
1235 Business Administration Building
Ann Arbor, MI  48109

Dear Sir or Madam:

I would like to apply for admission to the University of
Michigan Graduate School of Business Administration.  I have
just received my B.A. from the University of Virginia with a
G.P.A. of 3.3.  My major was international business, and I
hope to receive an M.B.A. with specialization in that field.

Would you please send me the following information:

          — Application forms for the graduate school,
          — University catalogue,
          — Housing information, and
          — Application for financial aid.

Thank you for your attention to this request.  I look forward
to hearing from you.

                              Sincerely,

                              Rebecca Williamson

                              Rebecca Williamson
```

Business Letter (Semiblock Style)

```
KELLY ASSOCIATES
════════════════════
INVESTIGATIVE CONSULTANTS
```

2125 Virginia Avenue, NW
Washington, DC 20037
(202) 555-7905
June 27, 1991

His Excellency Fernando Diaz Garcia
Ambassador of Salvadorica
Embassy of Salvadorica
3781 Massachusetts Avenue, NW
Suite 100
Washington, DC 20008

Dear Mr. Ambassador:

 I hope that you are enjoying the challenge of your tour in the United States of America. Perhaps my firm can be of service to you in meeting that challenge.

 Kelly Associates specializes in the prevention and detection of business frauds, which are a significant problem in the United States. The U.S. Department of Justice estimates that frauds cost U.S. businesses more than $40 billion per year. That is nearly 10 percent of the U.S. Gross National Product.

 Much of our experience involves frauds by unscrupulous U.S. businessmen against foreign firms and foreign governments. Regrettably, we have nearly always been engaged after the fact, that is, after the economic damage has been done and embarrassment is unavoidable. We will, of course, continue to conduct such inquiries, but we would prefer to prevent these frauds through earlier investigations.

 I am enclosing a brochure reflecting some of our qualifications. Whenever you feel you need to know more about companies or individuals with whom your government or compatriots are preparing to do business, please call on us. We assure you of our complete discretion.

                                    Sincerely yours,

                                    Gerald Graham

                                    Gerald Graham
                                    Operations Director

GG/ml

Enclosure

Business Letter (Full Block Style)

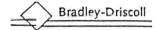 Bradley-Driscoll

Data Systems Group
Computer Sales Service Division
5645 Arlington Boulevard
Falls Church, VA 22046
(703) 555-6500

July 10, 1991

Mr. Paul Lowry
Bradley-Driscoll Corporation
Customer Service Organization
7001 Elkridge Landing Road
Baltimore, MD 21203

Dear Mr. Lowry:

Approximately four months ago, Strategic Data Corporation (SDC) contracted with Bradley-Driscoll for software maintenance. Recently, I received feedback from their employees indicating that they were dissatisfied with the level of service they had received. Enclosed is a copy of the letter from Strategic Data Corporation on this subject. As a member of the sales team responsible for technical support, I am concerned that their discontent with the software support might hinder future sales.

It is possible that the problem might lie in the expectations that Strategic Data has developed for the software maintenance process. It was SDC's intention to be able to call upon the Technical Assistance Center (TAC) if questions arose dealing with operational concerns or general information. According to Strategic Data, these types of questions elicit a snobbish response from the TAC staff. Apparently, the software analysts believe that customers should have thoroughly investigated the manuals before calling to obtain answers to questions that are documented.

Although this might be theoretically valid, it is not appropriate to criticize customers in a harsh manner about TAC policies. Instead, these procedures should be stated in a polite way with the hope that customers will not contact the TAC unless they have a valid reason.

At this point, I think it would be appropriate for you to send a letter to Strategic Data, apologizing for the misunderstanding and explaining the policies of the TAC. I hope that you will be understanding of the needs of our customers during their initial learning curve and compromise somewhat so they may obtain the support they need. Your understanding and professionalism will help to foster a positive and successful customer-vendor relationship.

If you wish to contact me to discuss the situation, please feel free to do so at (703) 555-6500.

Sincerely,

Frank Jansen

Frank Jansen
Systems Engineer

FJ/iab

Enclosure

cc: Anna Brauner
     Rick Halstead

Index